Green Business Practices FOR DUMMIES®

by Lisa Swallow, CPA, CMA, MS

WILEY

Wiley Publishing, Inc.

Green Business Practices For Dummies®

Published by
Wiley Publishing, Inc.
111 River St.
Hoboken, NJ 07030-5774
www.wiley.com

Copyright © 2009 by Wiley Publishing, Inc., Indianapolis, Indiana

Published simultaneously in Canada

For general information on our other products and services, please contact our Customer Care Department within the U.S. at 877-762-2974, outside the U.S. at 317-572-3993, or fax 317-572-4002.

For technical support, please visit www.wiley.com/techsupport.

Wiley also publishes its books in a variety of electronic formats. Some content that appears in print may not be available in electronic books.

Library of Congress Control Number: 2008943501

ISBN: 978-0-470-39339-0

Manufactured in the United States of America. This book is printed on recycled paper.

10 9 8 7 6 5 4 3 2 1

WILEY

About the Author

Lisa Swallow is a professor, CPA, CMA, community volunteer, and writer based in Missoula, Montana. She takes an active role in many aspects of her local green business community, including consulting with local businesses and serving as a board member on the Sustainable Business Council and Sustainable Campus Committee. Lisa is also a past board member and president of homeWORD, a nonprofit that develops affordable green housing and advocates for best-practice policies in housing.

She co-writes a column on the green global economy, which appears the first of each month in the "In Business" section of her local newspaper, *The Missoulian*. She has also written chapters on sustainable marketing and sustainable business for a leading Principles of Business textbook.

Lisa is at the forefront of promoting sustainability literacy curriculum at the University of Montana and teaches two classes adopted into UM's interdisciplinary Climate Change Studies minor. She is the Program Director for Accounting Technology at UM College of Technology and integrates sustainable business concepts into all the courses she teaches.

She has long been an advocate that the economy, the environment, and social justice can all be well-served by smart, strategic business thinking that focuses on long-term solutions rather than solely on short-term profits. In 2005, she discovered the exemplary Bainbridge Graduate Institute on Bainbridge Island, Washington — one of the first institutions of higher education in the U.S. to offer course work with an emphasis in sustainable development. Lisa received a graduate certificate in Sustainable Business from BGI in 2006. She also has a Master of Science in Accountancy from California State University, Chico.

Dedication

To my best friend and lifetime partner, Dann Swallow, for his unwavering support and belief in my ability to complete this project, and to my teenagers, Dylan and Dante, for all the times I had to say, "I'm writing — catch me later!" Also, to my Texas family members for their unequivocal enthusiasm for this project, even when mine had dwindled.

Author's Acknowledgments

"Education is not the filling of a pail, but the lighting of a fire."

— William Butler Yeats

Writing a book about something I feel so passionate about has been extremely rewarding — the incessant educator in me has found an outlet that many folks only get to image.

I'm blessed to work with hundreds of students every year. Their eager minds, desire to be a part of the solution to the challenges facing our world, and insightful and provocative questions drive me to be the best that I can be in order to inspire their generation toward creative and sustainable thinking.

This book would have been unthinkable five short years ago. My deepest gratitude goes out to Gifford and Libba Pinchot for their vision of a business school (Bainbridge Graduate Institute) that embraces environmental and social responsibility and to Jill Bamburg for inspiring me from the first day I landed there. I'd also like to thank Eric Ziegler, a fellow student at BGI, who got my foot in the door for my first writing gig on sustainability.

The research on sustainable business is exploding, and I can't begin to thank all the professionals and scholars whose work I relied on to guide, solidify, and inspire my work. I'm in awe of many of the creative entrepreneurs and managers who are positioning their companies to flourish in the face of significant global challenges. Without your success stories, there would be no case for a sustainable business model.

On a personal level, I want to thank my dear friend, Niki Robinson, for helping me redirect my career and research when I was floundering. Her insight helped me to think holistically about how to bring together my passion for the environment and social justice with my long-term profession as an accountant and businesswoman.

Lastly, this book would never have gotten off my computer and into print if it weren't for the ceaseless prodding, cajoling, and counseling of Kristin DeMint, my project editor. I'd also like to give a big shout out to Mike Baker at Wiley for being so receptive to my ideas for the book, as well as to Jen Tebbe for her editorial comments, corrections, and ideas. This book was a collaborative effort, to say the least, and would never have come together without true partnering.

Publisher's Acknowledgments

We're proud of this book; please send us your comments through our Dummies online registration form located at http://dummies.custhelp.com. For other comments, please contact our Customer Care Department within the U.S. at 877-762-2974, outside the U.S. at 317-572-3993, or fax 317-572-4002.

Some of the people who helped bring this book to market include the following:

Acquisitions, Editorial, and Media Development

Project Editor: Kristin DeMint

Acquisitions Editor: Mike Baker

Copy Editor: Jennifer Tebbe

Assistant Editor: Erin Calligan Mooney

Editorial Program Coordinator: Joe Niesen

Technical Editor: Timothy Koponen, PhD

Editorial Manager: Michelle Hacker

Editorial Assistant: Jennette ElNaggar

Art Coordinator: Alicia B. South

Cover Photo: © Botanica

Cartoons: Rich Tennant (www.the5thwave.com)

Composition Services

Project Coordinator: Katherine Key

Layout and Graphics: Samantha K. Allen, Stacie Brooks, Reuben W. Davis, Sarah Philippart, Christin Swinford, Christine Williams

Proofreader: Linda Seifert

Indexer: Sherry Massey

Publishing and Editorial for Consumer Dummies

    Diane Graves Steele, Vice President and Publisher, Consumer Dummies

    Kristin Ferguson-Wagstaffe, Product Development Director, Consumer Dummies

    Ensley Eikenburg, Associate Publisher, Travel

    Kelly Regan, Editorial Director, Travel

Publishing for Technology Dummies

    Andy Cummings, Vice President and Publisher, Dummies Technology/General User

Composition Services

    Gerry Fahey, Vice President of Production Services

    Debbie Stailey, Director of Composition Services

Contents at a Glance

Table of Contents

Introduction

· ·

Many entrepreneurs and managers are looking for ways to conduct business that are easy on the environment and have the capacity to increase community welfare while yielding commercial success. If you're interested in discovering how to maximize your organization's *triple bottom line* (considering all stakeholders — people, planet, and profit — rather than just shareholders), *Green Business Practices For Dummies* can be your how-to guide.

Converting a company to a sustainable business model is largely a matter of transformative thinking — looking at how to accomplish economic goals in a way that recognizes and respects the constraints of the planet. Some of the resulting action items are easy to implement; others aren't so easy. But the beauty of starting to think and act sustainably is that the ripple effect of both becomes apparent pretty quickly: Employees start offering creative, green ideas; external partners see your progress and hop on the green bandwagon; and customers query you about your new green ethos and how that will impact new products and processes.

If achieving sustainability is a journey (and it is!), then by virtue of buying this book, you're now on the green path. I commend you for taking the initiative to become informed on sustainable business and for all the small, yet significant, steps you'll take in the future as a result of this information. Although no one can predict how your unique business can take advantage of the opportunities inherent in sustainable development, I can promise you one thing: You'll never have felt so great about going to work in the morning as you will when you truly become a disciple of triple-bottom-line thinking!

About This Book

The purpose of this book is to give you guidance on how to think about business decisions, strategies, products/services, and policies within a wider, greener lens. Sound like a tall order while trying to generate profits to stay alive another day? There's no single guiding model as to what a green business should look like. But there *are* great stories of companies that have embraced sustainable development and flourished in ways they'd never imagined (think GE, Patagonia, Dow Chemical, IKEA, Volvo, and Herman Miller).

Green Business Practices For Dummies is not only going to convince you that greening your business is important but it's also going to show you exactly how to do that. This book provides examples, tangible action items, checklists, ideas, and frameworks that you can use to develop your own unique spin on greening your organization in a way that makes sense for you, your employees, and your operating environment. It offers you salient how-to advice on topics like

- ✔ Creating a sustainability plan
- ✔ Motivating employees through ecoefforts
- ✔ Strengthening your sustainable marketing endeavors
- ✔ Greening your daily office practices

I wrote this book primarily for all the small and mid-sized business owners and managers I know and work with who want to embrace green business practices but don't know where to start or what that really even means. *Green Business Practices For Dummies* contains tons of information about ways you can make your unique business greener — and gain a competitive advantage in the process.

Conventions Used in This Book

All *For Dummies* books employ similar conventions for a sense of continuity and familiarity. Here's what the following conventions alert you to:

- ✔ Web addresses appear in a typeface called monofont. If the URL wraps to a second line of text, type the address in exactly how it's presented. Hyphens are inserted only when they're included in the Web address.
- ✔ **Bold** text indicates key words, phrases, or concepts and makes critical pieces of info easy to find.
- ✔ When a new term is introduced, it appears in *italics* and is followed by an explanatory phrase or sentence.

Also, as you go through the book, you'll notice I use the phrases *green business practices* and *sustainable business practices* interchangeably in order to heighten your awareness that different people you encounter throughout your greening process will use different terminology. Don't worry that you're missing out on anything though. Both phrases mean the exact same thing.

What You're Not to Read

The main text is full of relevant, helpful tips, ideas, lists, and specifics for greening your small or mid-sized business, so don't miss one juicy word! On the other hand, the Technical Stuff icon indicates ecodata or other techie details that you can safely skip and still get the complete gist of the book. If, however, techie talk is your cup of green tea, be sure to check out the paragraphs marked with this icon.

The sidebars contain information that's supplementary and relevant, but not absolutely imperative to greening your business. You can skip these bits of info without missing an ecobeat and still have lots of practical suggestions in your grab bag.

Foolish Assumptions

Any businessperson knows to keep the client foremost in mind, and an author is no different. So as I wrote this book for you, I made the following assumptions about you and your organization:

- Your first priority is to stay in business and to do that you must remain solvent and profitable.
- You're concerned with your company's impact on the environment and want to do all you can to reduce that footprint.
- You value your stakeholders — employees, customers, communities, creditors, owners, and suppliers — and want to contribute to their overall well-being through your business's efforts.
- You believe that lots of small changes add up to big impact and are ready to take on the role of change agent in your organization.
- You understand that the media, as well as Wall Street, are on the ecobandwagon and want to know how to take advantage of the opportunities inherent in that.
- You find yourself wary of putting your works up on a pedestal and are heartily committed to self-reflection to ensure your ecosteps remain true to your company's mission and sustainability goals.
- You perceive sustainability to be a good business strategy, even though you may not be able to define it.

How This Book Is Organized

Green Business Practices For Dummies is organized into five parts and designed so that you can easily read any part by itself and feel fully informed on that topic without any other background. Take a gander at the following overview and then dive on in depending on your individual interests.

Part I: Sustainability: The Visionary Way to Grow a Business

Chapter 1 introduces you to the business case for sustainability and addresses *why* sustainability is not only a good business model but also one that'll prevail in years to come. It also explains how your company can get onboard. Chapter 2 gives you an overview of the most challenging issues facing businesses today, identifies how these situations were created, and guides you in navigating these new waters. Chapter 3 shows you what it means to think like an eco-minded businessperson and helps you identify other like-minded individuals in order to build a green team to lead your sustainability efforts. It also explains the key frameworks that guide green business strategies. Chapter 4 helps you develop a very important document — your company's sustainability plan! It walks you through the process of conducting a SWOT analysis to assess your business's current state of sustainability and then leads you through crafting long-term goals, initiatives to reach them, and indicators to measure them. Chapter 5 explains the regulatory pressures and policymakers that are influencing sustainable development in the commercial world and how you can make your voice heard.

Part II: Pushing Up Your Green Sleeves: Implementation

Part II gets you started with the nuts 'n' bolts of greening your organization. Although every company begins its sustainability efforts in the area that makes the most sense for that individual organization, many companies start by looking at their daily office practices, their product development and production processes, and the physical facilities that house their operations. There are many financial aspects and transactions in your business that offer green opportunity as well. The four chapters in this part offer you practical guidance on how to approach tangible action items for each of these areas.

Part III: Involving Stakeholders in Your Sustainability Efforts

This part takes your sustainability efforts out into the world and aids you in greening business relationships with your key stakeholders. Chapter 10 helps you identify which of your customers, distribution channels, and messaging methods are most appropriate to change. Marketing is a critical area to get right because of the inordinate amount of misleading green information out there. Educating your customers through your marketing initiatives is thus a core component of a sustainable business. Chapter 11 helps you see how to develop community relationships to enhance your sustainability efforts by encouraging other like-minded organizations to gather together and harvest the triple-bottom-line effects of the buy-local movement that's sweeping the U.S. Chapter 12 guides you through the process of finding, forming, and nurturing relationships with nonprofits in order to expand your scope of influence. Finally, Chapter 13 outlines how to develop your employees, as well as your human resource policies and procedures, in a sustainable manner. The info in this chapter is absolutely essential because the core of your sustainable development resides with your employees.

Part IV: Measuring and Reporting Results

Making huge green strides means little without a way to measure and communicate your results, so Part IV walks you through how to do just that. Chapter 14 introduces you to the standards that are being established for different aspects of greening your business, as well as some overarching ecocertifications you can apply for. Chapter 15 introduces you to ways of accumulating and conveying data in order to measure your sustainability progress. For companies that are pretty far down the green path, Chapter 16 leads you through how to design, write, and distribute a sustainability report that both informs and impresses your key stakeholders.

Part V: The Part of Tens

Every *For Dummies* book contains this part, which features a couple entertaining and informative lists of tens. Turn to Chapter 17 to gather inspiration from the success stories of (more than) ten truly green corporate visionaries. (I promise you, one look at this list to see how ordinary people have accomplished extraordinary sustainable business goals, and you'll be feeling inspired about where your business can go.) Chapter 18 highlights ten common myths people have about sustainable business practices; it also arms you with good ways of refuting these myths in a gentle and articulate manner.

Icons Used in This Book

If you peruse *Green Business Practices For Dummies,* you'll see little pictures, or icons, in the margins. These icons spotlight the following helpful info and key ideas:

This icon indicates the presence of time-, money-, and energy-saving advice and ideas.

The details highlighted by this icon are worth keeping in mind for future use.

Don't skip over this icon. It indicates that you're about to discover some pearls of wisdom designed to keep you from making costly mistakes.

Perhaps you're not in charge at your company. The tidbits marked with this icon are here especially for you so that you can help bring about positive green change in your company.

This information explains techie phrases, procedures, or ideas in a way that a layperson can understand. It also features data that explains, in quantitative terms, the background on information you're reading. Sound a bit drab? Never fear. You can skip these paragraphs and still get the entire gist of the chapter.

Where to Go from Here

Because greening your whole business may feel daunting, you can jump in wherever you perceive the easiest entry point to be. Use the Table of Contents in the front or the Index in the back to guide your plan of action.

If you're new to the world of sustainability, I advise you read the first two chapters so you can gather a solid foundation as to why you want to green your business practices. These chapters identify exactly *why* sustainable business development is so important at this juncture in history and outline the business case for pursuing this new model (by the way, it has never been stronger).

Ultimately, my hope is that you use this book to start somewhere, anywhere — whether that's looking at your product development process or daily office practices — and then scale up to include sustainable thinking in all of your company's operational areas. As you branch out in this ecoprocess, you'll gain confidence and creativity in ways you can't imagine right now. Keep coming back to this book for guidance because it'll spark different thoughts at the varying stages of your organization's sustainable development.

Part I
Sustainability: The Visionary Way to Grow a Business

The 5th Wave
By Rich Tennant

"I asked for software that would biodegrade after it was thrown out, not while it was running."

In this part . . .

A potent part of moving toward a sustainable world is the greening of the business model, a process that requires businesses to not only meet today's commercial goals but also consider how they'll flourish in the future in the face of many global challenges and changes. This type of consideration involves carefully crafting a plan that will guide your greening efforts from start to finish. It also requires you to keep abreast of the ever-evolving public policies related to sustainability.

In this part, I provide an overview of the most compelling issues facing commerce in the 21st century and examine why sustainable business makes so much sense. I also help you with the sustainability-planning process, from doing the background work necessary to create your plan to communicating your plan to key stakeholders. Finally, I show you how to navigate the sustainable public policy realm.

Chapter 1

What's in It for My Company; What's in It for My World?

In This Chapter

▶ Delving into what sustainable development really means

▶ Defining the environmental and social challenges shaping today's world

▶ Identifying how your company can benefit from green business practices

▶ Seeing how going green creates value and opportunity for your company

Major newspapers announce that "green is the new black," and advertisements encourage consumers to "get their green on." TV entices viewers to use their ecoimaginations, and bumper stickers implore drivers to "live locally, think globally." Phrases like *carbon neutral* and *global warming* are becoming everyday terms. Being bombarded with all this different media challenges people to look at their homes, cars, schools, food, and businesses with a new sense of how to live on this Earth a bit lighter.

Your business has probably experienced some shifts in the availability and pricing of natural resources of late. Perhaps you see that continued reliance on increasingly expensive fossil fuels puts your business at long-term risk. Combined with stakeholders, regulators, customers, and markets that are becoming more sophisticated about the green movement, the imperative to revisit your old business model has never been stronger. On the flip side, the opportunities for doing so have never been greater either.

You may have heard about various organizations "going green" in recent years, but the paradigm shift, as a whole, is still in its infancy. (Although some say the Green Revolution's impact on daily life will dwarf the changes caused by the Industrial and Information Revolutions combined.) Adapting to a new, green business model takes both radically fresh ways of thinking (in long-term, systems-based ways) and innovative methods for measuring success.

For companies that get it, so to speak, the rewards can be substantial — for people, the planet, and your organization's profitability. But before you can reap those rewards, it helps to know why taking the plunge into green business practices (also known as sustainable business practices) is worthwhile — and even necessary — and how exactly they can add to your company's overall value.

Looking at the Three Ps of Sustainability

Most business managers and owners have some ideas about what sustainability is, but often can't define it. Perhaps you yourself are hard-pressed to characterize what a sustainable business is, or to identify specific actions you can take to green your own company. You have a vague sense that you *should* be doing just that — you're just not sure how to add "go green" to your to-do list. Never fear! The time has come to demystify this process and start you down the path to increasing both your profits and your contributions to the planet and its people.

Sustainability is generally defined as meeting your current needs while allowing future generations the capacity to meet theirs. Painstakingly simply, right? *Sustainable development* acknowledges that your company's commercial achievement is intricately linked to ecological and social successes. The driving idea behind sustainability is that humans can't deplete the Earth's natural capital (water, minerals, soil, and the like) faster than its capacity to regenerate because eventually those natural resources are going to run out. Business not only needs to operate within natural capital's constraints but it also must acknowledge the potential it has to serve as a restorative force to mitigate the problems of the past.

Companies are realizing that three equally important and interrelated bottom lines each need to be maximized to achieve true long-term sustainability. This triumvirate is now recognized as the triple bottom line (also referred to in some circles as TBL, Triple E, or the Three Ps). Coined in 1994 by John Elkington, the *triple bottom line* captures the idea that a sustainable business considers the needs of *all* stakeholders (including other species) instead of solely maximizing profit for shareholders. Here's how all the various terminology relates:

Three Ps	Triple E	What is it?
People	Equity	Human capital
Planet	Environment	Natural capital
Profit	Economics	Financial capital

The triple bottom line is made up of the following:

- ✔ **People:** Business viability requires healthy communities, strong supplier connections, empowered employees, and sound customer relationships. Consequently, a business that wants to succeed sustainably must have a heightened commitment to providing products or services that comply with social norms and rules while contributing to an enhanced quality of life for all stakeholders.

- ✔ **Planet:** A company that strives to keep this category in mind offers products or services that contribute to the rejuvenation of the Earth's ecosystems. It includes sustainability as a core element of its business plan and adapts to the planet's new challenges. A planet-focused business also identifies ways to mitigate some of the problems caused by past actions (climate change, pollution, overflowing landfills, and so on). Steps some businesses are taking to lighten their impact on the planet include decreasing waste flows and reducing their use of energy and other nonrenewable resources.

- ✔ **Profit:** Of course, a company must generate profit and cash flow in order to remain solvent and continue its operations. Triple-bottom-line strategy shows the deep interconnectedness of long-term profitability, strong relationships with people, and a commitment to improving the planet. For example, conducting business in a green facility improves employee productivity and health and decreases energy and water bills, thereby improving your company's bottom line. Additionally, offering ecofriendly products and services as solutions to problems and authentic needs creates satisfied customers, which ultimately results in increased profitability from an expanded product or service line that operates within nature's constraints.

Figure 1-1 shows the intersection of the three elements of sustainability (people, planet, and profit). As you can see, a deep interrelationship exists between your organization's financial success and the health of the planet and its people.

Figure 1-1:
Long-term sustainability is the intersection of people, planet, and profit.

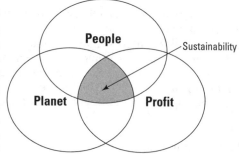

Considering the Need and Opportunity for Change from a Business Perspective

Because of the tremendous challenges facing the global village, your business may be looking toward sustainable development as a way to position itself for the future. Now is definitely the time to reduce future risk, increase your access to capital, realize opportunities inherent in green innovation, cut costs through ecoefficiencies, and show your stakeholders that you're positioned to be a player in the emerging green market. Why? Because all three kinds of capital necessary for commerce — natural, human, and financial (see the preceding section) — are changing in response to the new business paradigm.

Businesses need materials to operate, and many of these natural resources are either running out or becoming much more expensive to extract. Consumers are adjusting their decisions and habits in response to increased environmental concerns and energy worries, and businesses need to react quickly to these purchasing-pattern shifts in order to take advantage of this opportunity. Formal market mechanisms integral to capitalism — such as how insurance policies are rated and priced, how access to capital is granted, and what sorts of environmental and social issues are regulated — are shifting dramatically as well. That's why today's not too late to start the process of thinking and acting sustainably. Fortunately, you can do so with minimal effort by reviewing the factors I highlight in the following sections.

Crucial resources are dwindling

Almost all businesses rely on some sort of natural capital, so one of the biggest economic concerns for your business may be the nagging reminder that the natural resources and raw materials you need to operate are becoming more expensive and difficult to source. You probably don't need to look farther than your utility bills to see this truth in action!

One of the easiest ways to understand natural capital and its limits is to think of a trust fund. You have a chunk of change that's generating income. All's well — as long as you're living off of the interest that the fund is earning. The minute you start to spend down the principal, you're on a potentially slippery slope because the interest you'll receive next period will be less. Less interest means that next month you'll have to dip into more principal to continue your current level of consumption, thereby accelerating the depletion of your trust fund.

When it comes to the planet's natural capital, society has dipped pretty heavily into its trust fund. The various ecosystem services (such as pollination, water filtration, and flood control) that the Earth so generously provides for free are a result of natural capital. Although Mother Nature charitably produces minerals, groundwater, and fertile topsoil, she doesn't do it very quickly. Thanks to the pace of technological innovation, humanity's rate of consumption has increased much more rapidly than the planet's ability to support it.

Particularly in the United States, but in a growing number of other highly populated countries as well, people engage in a disposable-resource-intensive lifestyle. In fact, according to the ecological footprint model developed by Mathis Wackernagel and William Reese, mankind requires nearly one and a half planets to support its current level of activity, with some western nations living as if the Earth contained six or seven planets' worth of resources. Yikes!

For your business to flourish in the long term, you need to be prepared for the changes in access to natural capital. Thinking about reducing your company's reliance on fresh water, fossil fuels (particularly expensive foreign oil), and virgin raw materials today will help you prepare for the future. Companies that aren't actively acknowledging and planning for change in the global business model may find that they aren't positioned to take advantage of the various opportunities this model presents (like designing products that use recycled materials).

Key stakeholders are a-changin'

As access to affordable natural capital diminishes and education about environmental and social problems increases, key stakeholders in commerce are becoming much more astute, proactive, and demanding. I clue you in to these stakeholders from the larger entities on down to individuals in the following sections.

Government and regulators

You're probably already well aware, but policymakers at federal, state, and local levels are influencing how you conduct business.

- ✔ Tax incentives are being employed extensively to encourage the development of renewable energy, waste-reduction systems, green buildings, and water/energy conservation initiatives.

- ✔ Additional tax burdens are in the works for carbon emissions and waste-stream creation (and in fact, they already exist for pollution).

- ✔ Trade policies are being created to encourage local economic development, alternative fuel creation, and other sustainably oriented projects.

Companies that are pursuing sustainability are no longer satisfied with simple regulatory compliance. Instead, they're constantly being proactive with policy and taking a leadership role in developing new methods for reducing regulatory burden by greatly exceeding expectations.

Activist shareholders

They're passionate about the environment, they're educated, and they hold shares of stock in your business. In recent years, activist shareholders have driven many companies to go green and stop certain nonsustainable activities, so you can easily imagine how you might one day be affected by them, if you haven't been already.

Institutional shareholder activism in particular is on the rise, with big players demanding that companies disclose their carbon exposure, environmental records, and labor practices. Although this scenario may be far up the feeding chain from your organization, trickledown occurs quickly. Look for the trend to continue and filter down to the many small and mid-sized companies that provide products and services to the larger multinational corporations.

If you're part of a smaller organization that supplies the big guys, you may have a great chance to position your company as a sustainable vendor on their supply chain lists. You benefit from a steady stream of business, and your customers benefit from telling their shareholders that they're greening their supply chain. In short, everyone wins — people, planet, and profit.

Consumers

Decreasing thermostat temperature, turning off electronics when not in use, and flipping off lights when not in a room are the most common of American consumers' modest behavior changes, according to the Natural Marketing Institute, which tracks green behavior patterns. But these changes are affecting more than just household behaviors — they're increasing the demand for products with green attributes. Need proof? Fifty percent of Americans polled by Information Resources say that they consider at least one sustainability factor when making purchases.

People are simultaneously looking for ways to insulate their pocketbooks from escalating natural resource prices and align their purchasing behavior with their newly green values. Hence the resurgence in local commerce and green purchasing (and the downfall of *conspicuous consumption* — buying fancy objects to show off your wealth or status).

Consumer demographics can be stratified to the nth degree, but a good starting point is to look at the three major categories of green consumers:

✔ **Pine Greens:** These uber-informed consumers are astute and sophisticated about market niches such as ecotourism and whole foods. What's more, they're growing in number after stagnating for many years.

Pine Greens are also identified under a more formal market demographic known as *LOHAS,* or the Lifestyle of Health and Sustainability sector. An estimated 60 to 70 million Americans who actively support green and ethical businesses and products fall into this category. LOHAS consumers purchase products primarily because of their healthful and sustainable attributes, and they spend more than $200 billion annually on green goods and services, an amount that's expected to double in size by 2010 and quadruple in size by 2015. (LOHAS spending is still a spot on the wall compared to annual consumer spending of $10 trillion, but the speed at which it's growing is what's garnering attention.)

✔ **Jungle Greens:** Trendy and ecofriendly, the Jungle Greens will grow in number in the coming years. Why? Because they're professional, educated, have disposable income, and are hearing a *lot* about green these days in the popular media.

✔ **Moss Greens:** At the bottom of the green buying chain, Moss Greens (the environmentally apathetic consumers) are either unconcerned with social and ecological issues or unmotivated to change their behaviors or spend money on sustainable products and services. They typically only enter the green marketplace in search of ways to stretch their dollars, such as seeking out energy savings.

As for what consumers consider when deciding whether to purchase a particular good or service, the following three factors play a huge role:

✔ **The product/service itself:** How a product performs, the quality of a service, and the price of that product or service are still strong motivators in your customers' purchasing decisions. On the other hand, factors such as a product's amount of packaging, recyclability, and whether it came from virgin raw materials are important considerations for more and more consumers all the time.

✔ **The seller's and/or manufacturer's practices:** Four out of five Americans agree that companies need to be not only profitable but also mindful of their impact on the environment and society. More consumers are punishing companies they'd previously purchased their products from by switching brands after hearing about a business's sweatshop labor practices or its relocation of manufacturing facilities to a country with sparse environmental laws. The effect is often immediate when a company's poor corporate social responsibility (CSR) is publicly spotlighted. (*CSR* refers to pursuing commercial success while emphasizing your company's environmental and social contributions.)

In recent years, this negative publicity has been primarily due to the spate of media about abhorrent business ethics, sweatshop labor, out-of-control executive salaries, and excessive profits at the pump. In contrast, Whole Foods (a sustainable grocery chain that caps executive salaries at 19 times the lowest earner, features organic food, and sports a strong corporate citizenship profile) has experienced phenomenal growth over the last decade, whereas most grocery store sales have remained fairly flat.

✔ **The origin of the product:** Many consumers these days prefer to buy regional or local goods. The business model of days gone by relied on extremely cheap oil to transport items back and forth across the ocean for production in order to exploit inexpensive labor. Nowadays, consumer concerns about huge trade deficits, unsafe products from foreign countries, and the loss of many local businesses are creating the renaissance of farmers' markets, community finance, and local shops that provide building supplies, clothes, crafts, and household items. The U.S. Department of Agriculture tracks farmers' markets and shows an almost 19 percent increase nationally in the last decade, which illustrates the phenomenal growth of a distribution channel that's making locally grown food very accessible.

As you can see, the opportunities for taking advantage of this growing consumer shift are vast. Just check out Table 1-1, which shows the growing green presence in almost every industry sector, to see where your organization may be able to find its green niche.

Table 1-1	Greening of Existing Industries
Traditional Industry Sector	*Niche Market Riding the Green Tidal Wave*
Accounting, business consulting, & legal services	Sustainability reporting, environmental management systems, and green business design and support
Appliances	Energy Star certification
Automobiles	Hybrids, electrics, scooters
Clothing	Ecofashion (hemp and organic textiles, recycled clothing)
Financial products	Socially responsible investment, microfinance
Grocery	Organics and naturals
Housing	Green buildings
Lawn & garden	Nontoxic and biobased products
Medical care	Naturopathy, acupuncture
Travel & tourism	Ecotourism
Wood products	Sustainably harvested forestry, reclaimed wood products

Markets are moving

Traditionally, access to capital has been based on short-term profitability projections, usually presented on a quarterly basis. You present your cash flow projections to a lender, and the lender grants credit based on those forecasts. For investments to produce sustainable yields in the long term, however, you need to conduct a thorough internal review of all of your company's environmental and social impacts. This internal analysis may turn up potentially litigious areas and identify places to cut costs through ecoefficiencies, thus increasing your business's long-term solvency potential.

Sustainable business practices equate with proactive risk management in the eyes of investors, creditors, and financiers. In addition to understanding financial returns, these sources of capital increasingly want to know how your business is positioned to respond to environmental and social challenges. I delve into these subjects in more detail in the following sections.

Increasing access to capital

Four of the United States' biggest banks (Citigroup, Bank of America, JPMorgan Chase, and Wells Fargo) and 60 institutions worldwide have adopted the *Equator Principles*. These voluntary principles help financial institutions manage the environmental and social risks of their projects and give equal consideration to each aspect of the triple bottom line when making financing choices (see the "Looking at the Three Ps of Sustainability" section, earlier in this chapter, for more on the triple bottom line).

Capital sources are actively asking investees about how they're prepared for a carbon-constrained future. The next time you apply for a line of credit or a loan, or find an underwriter for your equity offering, be ready to answer questions regarding your renewable energy goals or energy-efficiency targets. Look for loan applications to ask about your environmental performance and benchmarks and internal lines of accountability for triple-bottom-line performance. Not considering these questions may make you less competitive for capital. If you run a nonprofit, you may have noticed that many grants are now including allocable points based on your sustainability efforts. Again, if these are issues you haven't even considered, you may find yourself losing funding from previously stable revenue streams.

Want to diverge from the traditional funding routes? Then you'll be glad to know that institutions are sprouting up specifically for the purpose of financing ecoentrepreneurs. New Resource Bank and ShoreBank Pacific are early examples of such lending institutions. If you're considering green product development or sustainable expansion, these are the capital sources for you.

Ensuring that you stay insured at a price you can afford

Controlling insurance costs is yet another benefit of sustainable business practices. Some of the items that the United Nations Environmental Programme Finance Initiative (UNEP FI, a global partnership between the UN and the financial sector) considers to be the most critical in terms of risk and protection in the 21st century include

- ✔ Climate change
- ✔ Environmental liability
- ✔ Man-made risks
- ✔ Recycling

The UNEP FI report details the challenges and opportunities inherent in a business's transition to sustainability from an insurer's perspective. One thread emerges clearly and is very pertinent to businesspeople: Insurability will increasingly be linked to internal evidence that a company understands its environmental and social risks and is developing ways to mitigate them. If you're not, you may face difficulties keeping your company insured down the road.

Recognizing the growing importance of socially responsible investing

Socially responsible investing (an investing model that takes environmental and social factors into account, in addition to traditional financial analysis) is becoming far more mainstream — resulting in an infusion of billions of new dollars into environmentally and socially just organizations. Investors now have a multitude of places to look if they're interested in greening their investment portfolios. Following are some of the main green investing opportunities to date to help you better understand this shift toward socially responsible investing:

- **Trading markets dedicated to sustainability:** The sophisticated needs of green investors are now being met by the Dow Jones Sustainability North America Index, which tracks the leading 20 percent of the 600 biggest North American companies in the World Index in terms of sustainability. In early 2009, the Green Exchange will offer trading capacity for environmental products designed to deal with pollution and alternative energy and offset climate change damage.

- **Green mutual funds:** At their investors' requests, almost all major mutual fund families are adding a green fund that offers investors opportunities to embrace the environment, help eradicate poverty, or contribute to climate change adaptation and mitigation. From small cap green sector funds to climate change funds based on global warming indices, the focus is on companies that can offer solutions to the major challenges facing today's world. Some of these funds focus on clean energy, some on the largest clean tech companies, and some on community participation and human rights.

- **Clean tech venture capital:** The nature of *clean tech* (or green tech) investing is that it requires highly specialized technology, lots and lots of start-up capital, and technically adept employees. Following are the five broad categories of clean tech investing:

  - Renewable energy production, storage, and distribution

  - Air quality monitoring and purification

  - Water quality monitoring and purification

  - Waste control, capture, and conversion to fuel

  - Sustainable products that reduce energy and manage resources

  Clean tech start-ups backed by venture capital have doubled in value between 2005 and 2007. If you want to take advantage of clean tech venture capital, plug that phrase into your web browser and see what pops up that's regionally appropriate. Then check out the venture capital source's Web site for business plan submission guidelines.

✔ **Green angel investors:** High-net-worth individuals who primarily invest in start-up companies are considered *angel investors.* They pool their money and invest in projects that are too small for traditional venture capital backing, and their number is growing. Money from green angel investors is finding its way into small social ventures and diverse areas such as media, healthcare, organic food, and renewable energy. Try doing an Internet search for "green angel capital" and your regional area to see what opportunities arise.

Understanding How Sustainable Practices Boost Your Business's Value

The argument for sustainable development as a path to success in the 21st century is widely documented. Companies with sound environmental management systems and corporate social responsibility policies and procedures outperform businesses that don't have either. Why? Because overall, the management of an organization that considers these issues is well-rounded, attuned to global challenges, and positioned to make ethical product design choices.

What challenges you may ask? Climate change, international strife, huge trade deficits, and growing income disparity are just a few of the developments that come to mind. Quite frankly, they're all bad for business prosperity in the long term. Fortunately, fresh ways of thinking and doing business are evolving, and I share these new ideas in the following sections.

Bettering your bottom line

The most common area for a business to see immediate and tangible results from its implementation of green business practices is in cost savings. Reducing expenses clearly and directly impacts your *bottom line,* or net profit figure. Because cutting costs is the easiest sell for top management (if the suggestions are coming from some other area of the company, that is), this step is often perceived as the best place to start.

The term *ecoefficient,* coined by the World Business Council for Sustainable Development, refers to a management philosophy geared toward producing goods and services that use fewer resources. Because fewer raw materials and energy go into the production process and less waste is produced, an ecoefficient company has a clear competitive advantage by cutting its costs.

Opportunities for ecoefficiency abound at all phases of your product and company life cycle. So how do you make the most of them? To embrace eco-efficiency, you need to look at three broad objectives and identify how each functional area within your business can achieve the following:

- ✔ **Doing more with less:** Looking at ways to decrease your business's use of energy, water, and land; improve product recyclability and durability; and close the loop on raw materials usage are all ways you can strive to do more with less.

- ✔ **Reducing waste:** Business waste is a cost that has no value-added capacity. Eliminating waste always contributes directly to an increased bottom line due to expense reductions.

- ✔ **Enhancing product functionality:** By focusing on selling your customers what they actually need, you can use fewer resources while maintaining the same (if not better) product value.

Identifying ways to make your company more ecoefficient isn't a take-it-or-leave-it mechanism, once-over, or series of rigid rules to comply with. It isn't even a framework, per se, but rather a way of thinking about how exactly you can deliver value to your customers while using fewer resources — or in other words, how you can strive for continuous improvement by using less.

Skyrocketing the top-line trajectory

Sustainability has the potential to greatly enhance your company's top line. In other words, green business practices can impact your revenue (and corresponding business value) in a number of important and tangible ways, such as

- ✔ **Enhancing your market share through innovation:** Applying sustainable principles to the product design process often leads to identifying entirely new product lines to bring to market. For example, thinking deeply about environmental and social principles while engaging in product research and development (R&D) may lead your office furniture company to consider using organic, hemp, or other plant-based textiles. This entirely new product line may open up new markets and expand your thoughts to even more fresh and creative potential.

    Innovating to solve problems is also a key component of sustainable product design. For example, when a textile firm's foreign supplier could no longer produce dyes because of European Union environmental regulations, the firm developed an alternative, nontoxic color palette that's now one of its strongest product lines.

- ✔ **Bringing the look and feel of nature into your product:** The idea that merging biological principles with product design is a visionary way to incorporate the lessons nature has already learned in nearly four billion years of evolution and adaptation is receiving more and more recognition these days. That's why you can now find adhesives that are as strong as mollusk shells, binding agents as tough as a spider's web, and buildings with underground chambers like termite mounds for natural cooling. For more on sustainable product design, see Chapter 7.

✔ **Identifying massive markets in the developing world:** Still another opportunity for green product development resides in meeting the basic needs of much of the developing world. The market for water purification, environmentally benign household products, efficient fuels, and high-yield foods is astronomical in the Third World.

✔ **Creating a competitive advantage by differentiating yourself:** Although the proliferation of companies that are self-identifying as green has grown by leaps and bounds recently, you still have tremendous opportunity to separate yourself from the pack through your green business practices and sustainable product offerings. Being completely truthful about your effort with product R&D, operational changes, and corporate value shift makes you credible to your customers. As consumers become more green-savvy, they'll continue to ferret out companies that *greenwash* (state that they're green without taking the actions necessary to back up that statement) — and make those companies pay the price for it through lost revenue.

✔ **Facilitating closed-loop customer relationships:** Today's consumers are increasingly interested in developing and maintaining relationships with companies that show a commitment to corporate social responsibility. Early sustainability advocates, such as Patagonia and The Body Shop, have built fanatically loyal customer bases. Survey after survey continues to indicate that Americans take corporate citizenship and sustainable product attributes into account when making purchasing decisions.

Fostering a desirable workplace for top-notch employees

Recruiting and retaining high-performing employees is obviously a key component of building a profitable and sustainable business. But did you know that more and more forward-thinking employees are interested in working alongside colleagues with similar values at a company that clearly promotes social and environmental responsibility?

As your lighting fixture company offers sustainable and efficient lighting education to old-timer electricians, or your small medical clinic offers naturopathic and homeopathic services in addition to traditional western medicine, you'll find like-minded employees clamoring to be a part of your progressive team. Why? Because top-notch green recruits want to work for companies that are reducing their carbon footprints and looking for nontoxic alternatives through green chemistry research. And here's how you can benefit as a result:

✔ **Linking sustainability with pride:** Because your company showcases its sustainability initiatives, employees become more invested in the company and stretch themselves and their co-workers to discover more creative ways to implement sustainable practices.

✔ **Enhancing employee productivity:** Research shows that employees who work in LEED-accredited buildings (see Chapter 8 for the scoop on this certification) or at companies with a high level of emphasis on corporate social responsibility are more likely to enjoy their jobs, have reduced rates of absenteeism, and indicate a much higher level of commitment to their employers' organizational missions.

✔ **Encouraging innovation:** After you start asking questions about how your business can operate in the most environmentally benign and socially just manner, creativity will be unleashed from within and outside of your firm. Just ask almost any business owner or manager who has taken this step.

✔ **Providing passion in the workplace:** You want your employees to be passionate about what you do, right? If your mid-sized company sells commercial real estate, you want your producers and support staff to believe in the product, your company, and its values. So why not hook up with a company that offers green mortgages and give a gift basket at closings that includes a smart power strip and a pack of compact fluorescent light bulbs? I can guarantee you that with a simple jump-start, your employees will be offering up ideas on how your business can push the green envelope even further.

Finding the Best Focal Points for Your Business: A Preliminary Assessment

This book isn't about instituting practices and procedures to lessen your unsustainable behavior; it's about encouraging you to actively engage in redefining what the world will look like tomorrow. After all, being less bad isn't the same as being good.

Clearly all the challenges and trends the global village faces today are interrelated; fixing one stand-alone problem may easily come at the expense of exacerbating another. For example, farmland is being diverted to create biofuels in response to fossil fuel prices. In turn, grain prices are increasing, leading to more global food insecurity.

For business, developing sustainably requires looking at the whole picture and understanding the symptoms of a flawed system. When looking at your business, you need to devote some systems-based thinking toward addressing problems such as excessive waste output and over-reliance on rapidly depleting natural resources. For example, if your manufacturing process is reliant on hazardous materials, the impact of this dependence will ripple through all aspects of the triple bottom line.

To maximize effects on people, planet, and profit, you may want to consider the following types of questions to stimulate preliminary conversation about where your business has the most opportunity for change:

- ✔ **How can your company help people and the planet to flourish in the future?** Instead of focusing on changing negative behaviors, this question helps you identify new market possibilities.

- ✔ **Do your products and services fill authentic needs?** As new raw materials become harder to source and waste streams become more difficult to handle, consumption is going to steer toward items that truly meet human needs and away from purely materialistic items. Quit trying to create new products for the already oversaturated and indulged consumer and focus on determining whether your product or service can meet real *needs*.

- ✔ **Can you measure your business success by broader terms than profitability and increased sales?** Positive impact on the planet and its people is just as important as positive financial statements for a truly sustainable business.

- ✔ **Is your company making meaningful efforts to decrease its energy use through efficiency and conservation efforts?** Essentially, how dependable is your energy supply? Identifying where you can access alternative energy will position you ahead of the curve in the coming decades.

- ✔ **How reliable is your water supply?** How dependent are your production processes or facility operations on cheap and available water? What sort of efficiency mechanisms and processes do you have in place to regulate your use of water? Identifying long-term options to access water and reducing your need for freshwater is an important systems-wide concern. Particularly in arid locales, requiring tremendous amounts of water for operations is a big area of exposure.

- ✔ **What concern might your customers have about toxicity in your facilities, products, or services?** Your potential for litigation from communities, shareholders, employees, and customers is increased if your company uses hazardous materials. Systems-based thinking may compel you to explore plant-based alternatives to the toxins currently used in your business.

- ✔ **How much greenhouse gas does your company emit annually?** What are you doing to reduce these emissions, and how will your business absorb the increased cost associated with emitting carbon in the future?

✔ **Are your products, services, and facilities poised competitively for a carbon-constrained future?** Consider whether you offer products and services that can help consumers mitigate and adapt to global warming. You just may wind up opening the door to innovative new products and services.

✔ **How dependent is your business on forests, farmland, and fish?** Look at ways you can cut back your dependence on natural capital in order to preserve these precious resources.

Chapter 2

How Nature's Laws Are Dictating Change

In This Chapter

▶ Understanding mankind's impact on the environment and how you can help mitigate it

▶ Gauging the Earth's response and what you can do to improve the current trend

*I*n order to craft a vision of how your business can benefit from the opportunities inherent in combating global challenges, it's important to honestly examine the state of today's world. Certain undeniable biological and physical laws are dictating the changes you're seeing in governmental policies, intercontinental commerce, individual behaviors, and grassroots movements everywhere. The law of diminishing returns, Newton's third law of motion (for every action there's an equal and opposite reaction), and the laws of thermodynamics (on energy creation and waste) are magnifying humanity's wasteful ways. This imperiled planet is suffering from overexploitation and downright carelessness. It seems almost impossible that humans could have such a negative impact on so very many complex planetary functions. The bright side to the story, however, is that mankind also possesses the capacity to have a positive impact and reverse negative trends while contributing to solving the world's problems.

The Deeds: Human Forces behind the Green Movement

No one wants to look in the mirror and see the cause of many of the world's environmental and social ills staring back. Yet although human behavior has driven and accelerated many of the perilous situations facing the world today, the capacity for solutions lies in those same hands. Global poverty, natural resource depletion, and toxic waste streams are all human-propelled problems that businesses can play a significant role in fixing. The following sections guide you through the most pressing problems facing businesses in the 21st century — and what you can do about them.

A snapshot of the world at large

More than 6.5 billion people currently occupy the Earth, according to the World Clock found at `www.peterrussell.com/Odds/WorldClock.php`. In addition to showing the world's approximate population, the World Clock provides an ongoing picture of the amount of oil extracted from the Earth, carbon dioxide emissions, the Earth's temperature, the rate of forest depletion, money spent on military items, and other rough snapshots of mankind's impact on the planet on a moment-by-moment basis.

Grasping globalization

The rise of the global business model, although touted as a way to boost economic growth for many of the world's poor, has actually increased income disparity both internationally and within individual countries' boundaries. Many large, polluting companies have resettled in countries with few or no environmental laws as part of the *race to the bottom,* the business tactic of moving manufacturing facilities offshore in order to get around environmental and workers' rights laws found in the developed world. These companies' polluting activities intensify as a result — as do their odds of creating *ecorefugees* (people driven from their homes due to serious environmental disruptions) and stripping native citizens of their ability to fish or practice subsistence farming.

The other side of the globalization problem is that the Earth's population isn't declining. In fact, population projections show that anywhere from 9 to 10 billion people worldwide will be relying on increasingly scarce water, forests, fuel, food, and fertile land by 2050, according to current growth rates. Add to this projection the fact that currently 800 million people are chronically hungry; 2 billion people live on less than a dollar per day; and 30,000 people die every day because they're too poor to stay alive.

These aren't shock-and-awe statistics. Rather, they reflect the reality of today's world. With such factors in play, it's not surprising that most people look at conserving the environment as a very distant second to scraping together enough calories to get through the day.

Working toward meaningful policies for poverty reduction is critical to the long-term sustainability of the Earth and its people. Yet the nagging questions remain: If this unchecked growth continues, people can't prosper economically, right? Environmentalists, free-market capitalists and social welfare folks can't all work toward common goals, can they? The unbelievable simplicity and solidity of sustainable development is the unequivocal response. Mankind can have it all. Maybe, just maybe, however, "all" looks a little different from what everyone thinks! Maybe the focus isn't on growing consumption but on developing community-based commerce, technology that lets people live lighter, and products that serve the world's poorest people. Perhaps your company can play a part in using its resources and innovative capabilities to reduce waste, increase the productivity of precious raw materials, and improve the lives of billions of people at the same time.

Many products, such as hand-held, solar-powered water purifiers and insecticide-treated malaria nets, are enhancing the triple bottom line for companies that are targeting improving the quality of life for the world's poorest (see Chapter 1 for the basics on the triple bottom line). Growing service-oriented sectors, like microfinance and microinsurance, are reshaping funding models in meaningful ways in the developing world. If your business is part of the supply chain for any of the big corporations, or if you have a vision for how to solve more localized problems, you too can be a part of the bigger solution to the challenges caused by globalization.

Focusing on the fate of fossil fuels

Fossil fuels, including crude oil (petroleum), coal, and natural gas, are a finite natural resource created under the Earth's surface during the last 200 million years by plant matter and great pressure. Since the discovery of coal a short 250 years ago, most of the planet's easily extractable petroleum has been removed.

Petroleum is a finite resource, and many people believe that the height of global oil production — what's called the *peak oil* period — is past and that petroleum extraction has entered a period of gradual but constant decline. Although oil still exists, it continues to be more difficult to extract and of lower quality. As oil exploration and extraction becomes more expensive and demand continues to grow, price will only be pushed higher and higher. In fact, many believe that the days of cheap energy sources are gone, replaced by permanent energy woes.

The crucial consideration for business is that much of commerce relies on stable and cheap fossil fuels. If your organization uses coal or petroleum as a raw material or relies heavily on it to power facilities and transport raw materials and/or products, now may be the time to look at how your company will be positioned in the future. Relying on a tenuous fossil fuel future may expose you to risk.

Start looking at ways to shift your energy consumption from fossil fuels to *renewable,* or alternative, energy. Also, consider making other changes to lessen your business's dependency on fossil fuels. For example, establish production and distribution centers that are close by each other.

Renewable energy relies on the Earth's ecosystems. The most common forms of it are

- ✔ Biofuels (ethanol and cellulosic)
- ✔ Biomass (including algae and waste products)
- ✔ Geothermal power
- ✔ Hydrogen and fuel cells
- ✔ Hydropower (including wave and tidal power)
- ✔ Solar power
- ✔ Wind power

Keep in mind that each of these renewable energy sources has pros and cons, and that the applicability, cost, and benefits of each are dependent on your situation. Part II covers the reduction of fossil-fuel reliance in your facilities; product research, development, and design; and transportation, delivery, and office practices.

Wading through waste

When the trash company comes and removes the unsightly garbage from your front curb, it's either taking that trash to a landfill or an incineration plant. Neither of these options is sustainable in the long term. Landfill space itself is decreasing; *methane* (a powerful greenhouse gas that contributes to climate change) is released from existing landfills; and toxins are emitted into the air when trash is incinerated.

The second law of thermodynamics states that matter and energy tend to disperse. Eventually, all matter introduced into society will be reprocessed by natural systems. That means everything that doesn't naturally *biodegrade* (reabsorb into the biosphere quickly and organically) will be around, sometimes for thousands of years, including materials like polystyrene and many of the 75,000 synthetic chemicals used in North America (legally!) today.

Some researchers estimate that an astounding 70 percent of garbage consists of recyclable items. Yet less than one-third of all businesses in the U.S. have formal recycling programs. The cost of all that waste to the environment *and* the businesses is astronomical.

There is, however, a way to break this cycle of depletion and waste, and commerce (that's you!) will be a driving force in this transition. As a business owner, you probably already know that waste costs money. So why not rethink your business model to focus on both gaining profit and protecting the planet and its people? By eliminating as much of your solid waste as possible, you can achieve positive triple-bottom-line results. By engaging in such sustainable business practices, you also have tremendous opportunities to design new kinds of products — ones that aren't wasteful or degenerative, and will meet your customers' needs without hurting the environment.

Pondering pollution and the Tragedy of the Commons

Sheltering, feeding, transporting, and producing products for the global village releases tons of chemicals and greenhouse gases into the air. Large-scale corporate agriculture relies on pesticides to protect crops — pesticides that leach into groundwater or run off into waterways — and overfertilizes in coastal regions, resulting in dead zones and algae plumes. Approximately 2.2 billion huge cargo ships shuttle goods back and forth overseas, spreading garbage, leaking pollutants, and occasionally wrecking and dispersing whatever contaminants and products they're carrying onboard in the process.

What's worse is that atmospheric, soil, and oceanic pollution prove difficult to control because no one owns the air, land, and seas. Consequently, no one country or entity is accountable for keeping them clean. Instead, these areas simply become dumping grounds for human waste, resulting in a phenomenon known as the *Tragedy of the Commons.*

As international companies develop green business practices on a large scale, the result will be a significant reduction in worldwide pollution levels. Corporate greenhouse gas reduction policies will help curb the air pollution that leads to global warming; the development of strategies to replace toxic materials and chemicals with more plant-based alternatives will reduce the pollution of both land and sea. Additionally, the technological innovations originating primarily from the business world will continue to offer exciting ways to convert landfill and animal waste into fuels.

Tackling toxins in everyday products and food sources

In the U.S. alone, 110,000 toxic chemicals are legally cleared for use, but only 5 percent of them have been tested by the Environmental Protection Agency (EPA) for their effect on human health. These toxins are present in such items as carpets, electronics, furniture, bedding, paints, toys, household plastics, cosmetics, and cleaning supplies — just to name a few.

Increasing press on these hazardous materials in daily life has contributed to the explosion of green products in homes, businesses, yards, cars, offices, nurseries, hotels, restaurants, and even cemeteries. So what can you do to contribute? The leaders of companies that are moving toward sustainability use *gray and black lists* to screen undesirable chemicals. Gray is for chemicals they want to phase out; black is for chemicals they refuse to allow in their products to begin with. Chemicals finding their way onto this list include cancer-causing agents, toxins that mimic hormones, and susbstances that can increase the frequency of mutations in future generations.

On the food side of the equation, factory farming, which involves the widespread use of synthetic hormones and other chemical additives to create low costs and high growth yields, has become the norm for the large-scale raising of farm animals in many parts of the world. These unnatural diets turn cows and chickens into petroleum products because the animals are now receiving their sustenance from food that has been sprayed with fertilizers and pesticides and not allowed to grow naturally. They also cause digestive-system damage that weakens the animals' immune systems and creates deadly gas bloating. Because factory-farm animals are raised so closely together, they also receive antibiotics for disease prevention.

If your business is involved in any way with food products, look at how you can capitalize on the growing movement toward slow food, organic products, and locally produced foodstuffs. Media discussions surrounding tainted food are alarming for many people, leading to a renewed interest in knowing who's producing your food and how they're doing it. For example, many grocery stores now have store brands that are oriented toward organic products. Chapter 11 delves into the growing consumer movement away from corporate food and toward local production and processing.

Interesting odds 'n' ends

To get a feel for the environmental impact of the average American consumer, check out these statistics:

- On average, individual Americans emit 22 tons of carbon dioxide per year. (The International Panel on Climate Change states that carbon dioxide must be reduced 80 percent by 2050 to stabilize the climate.)

- If Americans drove autos that got a meager three miles per gallon more, the U.S. would save one million barrels of oil per day. (That's more than what the Arctic National Wildlife Refuge is projected to produce in totality.)

- If every American household bought *one roll* of post-consumer-waste toilet paper per year, 155,000 virgin trees would be saved.

- If each human being used his or her "'fair Earth share" of resources, it would come to about 4.6 acres. (Americans typically use about 23.7 acres each.)

- Americans constitute about 4 percent of the world's population and emit about 25 percent of its carbon dioxide.

- Americans throw away about 4.6 pounds of garbage *per day*.

The Damage: How Mother Nature Propels the Green Movement

The Industrial Revolution enhanced the quality of life for many people throughout the past 250 years. Unfortunately, the rate at which humans have extracted oil, water, and natural resources in response to newfound technologies is causing Mother Earth to rebel at an alarming rate. In the next several sections, I highlight the major reactions affecting life on the planet today.

Warming up the globe

The most talked about international crisis of the times is *global warming,* a slight but continuing increase in the temperature of the Earth's atmosphere. In 2007, the Intergovernmental Panel on Climate Change (IPCC; a panel of 160 scientists from 130 countries, appointed by their respective governments) released its fourth in a series of reports spanning 20 years. The group's most worrisome finding about climate change was how incredibly far-reaching it is. Every single living being is interconnected, and when one ecosystem is thrown off the slightest bit, the whole system starts falling apart at the seams, escalating in speed. The IPCC concluded that there's a 90-percent chance the acceleration of global warming is due in large part to mankind's release of greenhouse gases (mainly carbon dioxide) into the atmosphere.

Six primary greenhouse gasses form a shield in the atmosphere and trap the solar heat that reflects from the Earth's surface, much like a greenhouse. They're emitted when people and businesses burn fossil fuels, primarily coal.

Off the cuff, most people think that cars are the heaviest contributors to greenhouse gas emissions. But oh, how wrong they are. In fact, building, operating, deconstructing, and renovating structures account for 47 percent of the greenhouse gas emissions in North America, which is 7 percent more than the transportation and agriculture industries combined. The primary contributors to greenhouse gas emissions are the buildings people live and work in (about 47 percent) and transportation (about 27 percent). Other big contributors include large-scale agricultural practices, deforestation, and industrial production.

If carbon dioxide emissions aren't cut drastically (some say 80 percent by 2050), all sorts of global instability may occur, including escalating drought (think more intense wildfire seasons, less arable land, and an alarming global food insecurity), increased flooding, and oceanic warming. For more on the effects of global warming, see the nearby "Climate surprises" sidebar.

Climate surprises

Global warming models show many predictable trends, such as oceanic temperature change and biodiversity migration northward. However, the truly scary things are the unknowns, called *climate surprises* — climate events that scientists can't accurately predict and that even the most sophisticated computer models can't forecast. The two big unknowns are

- How the warming of the oceans will affect the *oceanic conveyor belts* — those mass figure-eight currents that swirl around the globe — and the impact that permanently altering these natural currents will have on marine life, storms, and global weather patterns.

- What impact the melting of the West Antarctic Ice Sheet (WAIS) will have on global sea levels. Although modeling can show what happens when the ocean levels rise 1 meter, 2 meters, or 6 meters, the actual impact of losing the WAIS is impossible to predict.

Almost every proactive step you take (including greening your daily office practices, analyzing your product line for ways to ecoimprove, and developing sustainable employment policies) will help decrease your organization's carbon dioxide emissions. For example, lessening raw material input reduces the amount of fossil fuels embedded in transporting products. Increasing energy efficiency cuts down on emissions. Lessening water saves emissions because most industrial pumps are powered by electricity. Implementing virtually any suggestion you find in this book will lighten your business's carbon footprint.

Shrinking the Earth's usable water supply

The amount of usable water sources worldwide is dwindling, largely due to a global demand that's rising at roughly two times the rate of the Earth's population growth. Many scientists predict that groundwater depletion and freshwater *salinization* (the contamination of freshwater with salt) pose a growing threat. They see the wars of the future being fought over water rather than oil. Due to shrinking glaciers attributable to global warming, the IPCC's most recent report shows that water systems that rely on capturing snowmelt will be particularly at risk in the future.

Closer to home, some scientists expect the water-starved American Southwest (where population growth is outpacing the availability of resources to support it) will vie for dwindling supplies from its lakes and reservoirs. The Great Lakes are already experiencing algae blooms due to phosphate runoff from sewage and detergents. The demand for groundwater, like the giant Ogallala Aquifer that runs from Texas to South Dakota, pits agricultural interests against tourism, hydropower, industrial concerns, and the needs of urban areas.

Businesses have tremendous impact on water quality and supply. For example, giant agricultural interests threaten whole aquifers, and groundwater pollution attributable to runoff from toxic chemicals is a threat in many parts of the world. Consequently, analyzing your business's reliance on freshwater access is an important first step to helping improve the Earth's usable water supply.

If your production process is reliant on an uninterrupted supply of water, you may want to look at alternative processes or new materials that don't require such intensive reliance on water. Additionally, small daily changes in your office, such as installing low-flow plumbing fixtures and native landscaping (rather than water-intensive sod) can add up to big water reductions.

Accelerating the loss of biodiversity

Much of the world's *natural capital* (water, minerals, soil, and the like) has been overharvested to increase companies' short-term profits and meet a more demanding global population. This situation is disturbing because so many products — from medicines and building materials to food and clothing — partially come from the Earth's rich tapestry of biodiversity. I touch on three distinct ways biodiversity is fading in the following sections.

The dilemma of deforestation

Trees are arguably the world's most perfect creation. They feed on renewable solar energy, are aesthetically beautiful, and help control erosion and the hydrology cycle. They also *sequester,* or capture, carbon dioxide from the air. As the intensity of carbon dioxide in the atmosphere increases, the role of trees becomes more and more vital in controlling greenhouse gas concentration.

Unfortunately, deforestation is occurring at a truly alarming rate, particularly in richly biodiverse areas such as the Amazon. Forestry experts predict that by the middle of the 21st century, 95 percent of the wet tropics will be lost forever (which is extremely unfortunate because we need *more* trees to sequester carbon, not *less*). Add to that the effects of natural disasters such as Hurricane Katrina, which destroyed approximately 320 million trees in 2005 and released as much carbon dioxide into the atmosphere as all U.S. forests sequester in an entire year.

But there's hope! Because of the increased interest in assigning monetary value to carbon in the form of *carbon markets* (financial venues for the trading of carbon dioxide emissions), old-growth forests that have tons of sequestered carbon may be worth more for their carbon value than their timber, so deforestation might be greatly slowed!

The lack of fresh farmland

In much of North America, dirt doesn't seem to be a precious commodity. However, in some regions, it can take thousands of years for one inch of fertile topsoil to be produced. Worldwide demand for food, coupled with the transition to a heavier, meat-based diet in the developed world, has degraded much of the Earth's agricultural and grazing land. Consequently, precious little potential remains for expanding cultivation.

In fact, arable land has been lost to sprawl, erosion, monocultures (particularly cotton), and salinization at a pace that's much more rapid than the Earth's capacity to reproduce it. Today, 6.5 billion people are fed on 80 percent of the land that was available in 1950, when the world supported 2.5 billion people.

Sustainable agriculture, aquaculture, and organic fibers (like hemp) are showing promise for decreasing the impact on farmland. Additionally, businesses that are introducing organic and natural foods and products are helping to create demand for items that are more environmentally benign.

The case of the disappearing marine life

Birds, turtles, sharks, mammals, and many inedible fish are captured on the miles and miles of baited hooks found at long-line fisheries. By vacuuming the ocean of its contents, this practice is accelerating the extinction potential of many marine species.

If fishing practices continue at the current pace (with about 60 percent of the world's fisheries practicing unsustainable operations), biologists and oceanographers estimate that global fishing stocks will completely collapse by the mid-21st century. What was once thought of as the great protein source to feed a hungry world may utterly cease to exist.

Fortunately, big distributors and retailers are now demanding Marine Stewardship Council (MSC)–certified seafood products, which is helping advance the movement toward sustainable fisheries — a huge step in the right direction.

Chapter 3

Preparing to Create Your Sustainability Plan

In This Chapter

▶ Immersing yourself in the sustainability mindset

▶ Understanding well-known frameworks for green change

▶ Forming a team of people to blaze an ecoplanning trail for others to follow

▶ Addressing budgetary planning concerns

*J*umping into any new endeavor (like, say, greening your business) requires a good deal of foresight and planning — especially in regards to creating your plan. To have a shot at ecosuccess, you first need to establish a sustainable mindset and a solid framework for your actions. The sustainability frameworks I present in this chapter have helped some of the most visionary companies around stimulate creativity, add significant business value, and operate with new overall social and environmental goals in mind.

Of course, greening your business isn't a solo effort. Every company needs change agents to drive the ecoshift — this chapter helps you identify those folks and bring them together to form your *green team*.

Becoming a Sustainable Thinker

In order to successfully plan and implement sustainable business practices, you have to be an organized and action-oriented manager. In order to innovate, develop, create, and lead your business in its ecotransition, you must dial into where the actions originate: your mind. Yes, technically you can flip to any chapter in this book and start executing the changes I recommend without giving them much deep thought, but your efforts won't be as effective as they could be.

Most sustainability champions possess at least some of the traits described in the following sections. I've grouped them into personality traits and leadership and business-related skills to help you navigate through them.

Personality traits

Sustainable thinkers usually have some common characteristics pertaining to their interests, motivations, and convictions. By and large, these characteristics center on the idea of selflessness — or at least a pursuit of the greater good for the greatest number of beneficiaries. Some of the most common sustainability-related personality traits include the following:

- **A desire for information:** The world of sustainability is constantly evolving, so being committed to staying in the loop on all things green is invaluable. On average, ecothinkers have been exposed to at least one pivotal piece of sustainability literature, such as Hawken's *The Ecology of Commerce,* McDonough and Braungart's *Cradle to Cradle,* Banyus's *Biomimicry,* Ellkington's *Cannibals with Forks,* or Hart's *Capitalism at the Crossroads.* And usually one such work isn't enough — these folks keep on devouring whatever information they can get their hands on. They also stay up to speed on the latest trends in sustainability, which gives them not only the necessary foundational knowledge in environmental and social issues but also an awareness of the larger, evolving green picture and a strong business base.

- **A strong sense of empathy and justice:** One of the overarching premises of triple-bottom-line thinking is that each element — the people affected by your commercial transactions, the environment, and your business's profitability — has equal and viable importance. Sustainable thinkers have a strong sense of identification with stakeholders and communities that may share little in common with their personal or cultural norms. Because empathy conveys the ability to imagine oneself in another person's situation, it's a highly desirable trait when dealing with employees, impacted communities, and foreign suppliers and subcontractors, for example.

- **Patience:** If you've ever gotten exasperated when trying to convince someone to donate to your favorite charity or support the company's volunteering program, chances are you've seen firsthand why patience and consistency are essential for building support for your cause. And because green thinking doesn't come naturally to everyone — and in fact has been polarized as the enemy of traditional free market capitalism — patience is even more essential when building support for sustainable business practices.

- **A willingness to stick to principles:** Initiating true change and garnering others' buy-in is only possible if you have an unwavering dedication to your core values — in this case, the idea that people, planet, and profit can only be sustained through concerted and innovative business efforts.

- **An extraordinarily strong work ethic:** Although their work is tremendously important and at times arduous, green leaders don't quit advocating for sustainability — even when faced with negative reactions from senior management, peers, or external stakeholders. Such perseverance is essential when promoting ecochange. Without it, there'd be no hope of ever getting a project off the ground or effecting widespread cultural shifts.

✔ **A passion for spearheading outcomes that maximize the *triple bottom line* (benefits to people, planet, and profit):** Much of a sustainability champion's success is based on the fact that you'll usually find her following her passion, diligently trying to "bring along" those around her. Another characteristic is the knowledge that passion must be married to high-impact solutions.

✔ **A willingness to share success:** The sustainability champion recognizes that multiple people play a part in greening a company and that everyone should share in the kudos for efforts expended. Green advocates acknowledge everyone who contributes to a particular green project, no matter how minor the input may have been or how early or late the person got involved.

Leadership and business-related skills

Leadership coaches say that attitude is half the battle in any endeavor, but some measure of social skills and business savvy is an important part of forming ideals, finding practical ways to meet them, inspiring others to collaborate with you, and achieving success. Following are skill sets that are crucial to possess when greening business practices, whether you're in the top ranks of your business or trying to get your grassroots efforts in motion:

✔ **An understanding of risk/reward trade-offs:** High levels of risk can lead to big rewards, but not everyone can stomach this kind of business roulette. A sustainability champion isn't afraid of doing what it takes to make his working environment a little greener, even if that means taking a personal risk (like presenting Chapter 1's business case for sustainability to senior management) or taking a risk that's more far-reaching (such as agreeing to oversee the reconfiguration of the entire company's product packaging). When this person sees an opportunity for benefiting the triple bottom line (and often himself as well), he isn't afraid to take it.

✔ **A gift for selling an idea:** Sometimes what you say isn't as important as how you present it, or how you craft your case to meet potential resistance. A good sustainability champion can speak eloquently and persuasively. He also knows how deep to delve into an issue — being particularly conversant on the molecular structure of a toxin isn't important so long as you can make a sound case as to why the toxin shouldn't be in your company's product line in the first place.

✔ **A knack for building team spirit:** The old "my way or no way" philosophy doesn't fly in the world of sustainability. To truly make any ecosteps forward, both an understanding of the value of teamwork and the ability to bring like-minded folk together are essential. Sustainability champions typically have both in spades — and better yet, they tend to put these skills into action in fun and engaging ways. They seek allies from any rung of the company ladder, from the janitor to the CEO or majority shareholder.

✔ **A talent for project management:** Transitioning your business to a green model is the result of many activities — brainstorming the idea, planning for it, acquiring the capital needed to turn it into reality, implementing the idea, communicating the change to stakeholders, evaluating the impact the change has had on the company, and so many more. The sustainability advocate can usually balance all these parts — and see the holistic connection between them — because he can both see and communicate the bigger ecopicture.

✔ **An appreciation for incremental change:** Sweeping, all-encompassing green change usually results in a sustainability plan that falls flat. Because most people are resistant to change and often mistakenly see going green as a *huge* change, you need to take baby steps if you want better odds for success. A true sustainability champion knows to start small, build a history of successful initiatives, and keep all the research, lessons learned, and project-assessment data clear and accessible.

✔ **An ability to see the bigger picture:** Sustainability isn't limited to just one aspect or department of your business. That's why aligning sustainability priorities among departments is hugely important, as is the ability to design green initiatives that are easily replicable (with small modifications) in other areas of the company. Sustainability champions can take the task at hand to the next level. If, for example, that task is examining the ramifications of eliminating toxins from the office building and grounds, true sustainability champions can see the bigger picture and consider how to eliminate the toxins from *all* products and *all* processes.

✔ **An ability to think outside the box:** The old, standard ways of doing business are part of what has lead to today's global challenges and threats. Therefore, you can't rely on these old methods if you want to bring about ecochange. True sustainability champions aren't afraid to brainstorm their own ideas or research ways that other companies' solutions can be applied to the sustainability challenges facing their workplaces. They subscribe to the notion that sometimes pressing challenges must be addressed by revolutionary ideas.

Recognizing Common Frameworks for Sustainable Development

To help you form your green value system and inspire or institute change at your place of business, I present to you two *sustainability frameworks,* or sets of guiding green principles. Many large companies, such as Ikea and Volvo, have followed a sustainability framework as a way to align their business tactics with an overall sustainability strategy. When planning for new product lines, markets, facilities, or processes, the principles inherent in these frameworks channel your green team's energy toward identifying *how* to accomplish the task at hand while considering nature's constraints.

The Natural Step

The Natural Step (TNS) is a set of system conditions that outlines how business must align operations with ecological constraints in order to negotiate a place in the future. It was created in 1989 by Dr. Karl-Henrik Robèrt, a leading cancer scientist in Sweden, as an all-encompassing set of principles necessary for ecological and societal sustainability. The entire framework for making strategic sustainable business decisions according to TNS is encompassed by adhering to certain system conditions. You may suspect that this is a lengthy list. Au contraire! Although the Earth's ecosystem is extraordinarily complex, the ways in which humans (and businesses by default) are contributing to its destruction are deceptively simple.

The TNS framework helps guide you in examining how your business can become sustainable, and therefore prosper in the long term, by describing four system conditions that must be complied with in order to maintain a sustainable society:

- ✔ The Earth's biosphere isn't increasingly subjected to substances that are removed from the Earth's crust.

- ✔ The Earth's biosphere isn't increasingly subjected to substances produced by society.

- ✔ The Earth's biosphere isn't systematically impoverished by physical displacement, overharvesting, or other forms of ecosystem manipulation.

- ✔ Resources are disbursed fairly and efficiently in order to meet the basic needs of all members of the global population.

These conditions for sustainability are most readily applicable to product design (see Chapter 7 for more on this topic), but are used by many green business visionaries as guidance for decisions affecting daily operations, facilities, corporate strategy, governance, and the creation of competitive marketing advantage. Billion-dollar companies such as Volvo and Rohm and Haas subscribe wholeheartedly to TNS as their sustainability framework of choice, but the true beauty of TNS is found in its wide applicability to any size organization.

The following sections delve into the four system conditions of the TNS framework in more detail.

Minimizing usage of natural resources

The first system condition of TNS addresses the issue that mankind is removing natural resources from the Earth more quickly than they can be replaced. Think about it. The Earth took billions of years to create and sequester minerals, heavy metals, and fossil fuels in its crust. Now society is extracting these materials from the Earth's crust and redistributing them into the soil, water, and air at a rate faster than the ecosphere can absorb them, which is leading to the gradual destruction of the very ecosystems upon which society depends. For example, removing fossilized carbon (coal) and burning it is contributing to climate change, thereby accelerating biodiversity loss, intensifying natural disasters, and leading to less food security via desertification, flooding, and the like.

How does this system condition pertain to business? For business to flourish in the long term, the distribution of the Earth's natural resources must be regulated. Because natural resources have been used to power commercial facilities and manufacture products for years, the business world has boundless opportunities for creating a balance between what's taken out of the Earth and what goes back into it. Your company's choice of raw materials (new versus recycled and reused), choice of energy sources (renewable versus nonrenewable), method of product manufacturing and distribution (cradle to cradle or cradle to grave), and embrace of technological innovation to increase resource productivity can all make a difference.

Limiting production of harmful chemicals and excess waste

The advancement of human technology and the growth of the global population have lead to increased production of harmful substances and excess waste — which is precisely what the second system condition of TNS addresses. Nature has no experience in assimilating synthetic compounds produced by humans. Thus, the rate at which nonbiodegradable substances are being produced by humans far exceeds the Earth's capacity to incorporate them into living systems. Whole new families of toxins are being introduced into the Earth's rivers, air, soil, and seas — even at this very moment. Additionally, solid waste "disposal" (I use that term loosely; there's really no "away" when throwing trash away), whether the garbage is incinerated, dumped in the ocean, or sent to a landfill, is occurring with a frequency that's destabilizing natural systems at an alarming pace.

How does this system condition pertain to business? Any business owner has had experience with this system condition in the form of compliance with waste-disposal regulations. You know there's a financial price to pay if you don't follow the law. However, excess production of harmful chemicals and waste has hidden costs as well — negative health effects caused by persistent pollutants and increased insurance and capital costs. When combined, these costs add up to billions of dollars a year in unnecessary business expenses. So you can see that there are some specific, strategic advantages inherent in lessening (and eventually eliminating) your company's waste production.

Balancing consumption with rejuvenation

The third system condition of TNS focuses on the idea of balance and being grateful for what Mother Nature so generously provides. Just think about the vast array of products and services, valued at trillions of dollars per year, that comes from nature: Pharmaceuticals, food, pollination, flood and erosion control, topsoil, water, fibers, and timber are but a handful. Throughout history, mankind has taken advantage of these gifts, but particularly in the last century, society has operated with a "take, take, and take some more" mindset — without pausing to think about how these harmful consumption patterns are altering the very resources it depends on. As grasslands, wetlands, fisheries, and forests give way to sprawl, blacktop, monocultures, and the like, mankind is imperiling its own ability to survive.

How does this system condition pertain to business? This system condition is designed to engage you in taking better care of nature and rejuvenating it at every level and across every function of your organization. For example, if you use forest products in your catalogues, construction, or packaging, be sure to source from a vendor that practices sustainable harvesting. Likewise, when planning expansion activities of any sort, attach high importance to maintaining the integrity of natural ecosystems.

Treating the Earth's human resources equally

Sustainability isn't just about protecting the environment. A fundamental aspect of sustainability is the equal and humane treatment of all members of society. In today's world, however, overconsumers (citizens of developed nations) and underconsumers (citizens of developing nations) are far from equal — which is where the fourth TNS system condition comes into play. True sustainability can't be achieved without social transformation that acknowledges the value of each human life as equally valuable.

How does this system condition pertain to business? This fourth and final system condition challenges business to explore how it can increase positive human impact by providing solutions to the world's neediest. Some organizations are already making progress in this arena. For example, Grameen Bank has a specialized program to provide microcapital to beggars; Nike is actively working on enhancing youth athletic programs on Native American reservations; and Proctor & Gamble's new clothes rinse product sold to the rural poor radically reduces the amount of time women must spend finding and hauling water. Additionally, countless organizations are finding market value in designing products to meet developing countries' needs or in collaborating with nonprofits to lessen this gripping global crisis (see Chapter 12 for ways your company can partner with a nonprofit).

Natural Capitalism

Natural Capitalism was the first framework designed to show businesses how the new century's profits would be drawn from engaging in socially and environmentally responsible behaviors. Whereas TNS (described earlier in this chapter) is a science-based definition of how to sustain society, Natural Capitalism outlines how commerce can transform itself by enhancing value through capitalizing on green opportunities.

The sustainability framework of Natural Capitalism evolved out of a 1999 book of the same name penned by Paul Hawken, Amory Lovins, and L. Hunter Lovins. The basic premise of the framework is that not only must business quit depleting the Earth's *natural capital* (water, minerals, soil, and the like) but it must also reinvest in natural capital to replenish and mitigate the degradation of the past. Natural Capitalism is a meaningful framework that can help guide you in thinking strategically about your business, much like Interface, Inc. (the world's largest commercial flooring covering company), which swears by it.

This sustainability framework calls for four primary shifts in the way business operates:

- ✔ Use new technology to increase resource productivity.
- ✔ Rethink production processes.
- ✔ Move toward a service and flow business model.
- ✔ Invest in natural capital.

All four of these transformations are interdependent and equally vital to pursuing sustainable economic development. Together they recognize that business depends on environmental and human resources to flourish. The deep interrelationship of these resources with financial success is becoming increasingly clear. The question of whether to go green or value natural capital is being replaced with a new set of questions: How does my company make this transition — quickly, efficiently, and with the fewest economic costs?

I explain the four tenets of Natural Capitalism in greater detail in the following sections.

Using new technology to increase resource productivity

Natural capital essentially describes one or more of the natural resources you rely on to keep the wheels and cogs of your operation running. But because natural capital is being used faster than the Earth can replenish it, business must play a part in developing and employing technology that uses essential resources like water and wood products many more times efficiently than they currently are.

For example, instead of supplying your headquarters with water by powering pumps to draw even more water from a rapidly depleting aquifer, why not design or purchase a system to collect and recycle your rainwater in a constant stream? As a result, you'll have heating, cooling, and flushing capacity built into one system — which saves you money in operation and repair costs for fancy heating and cooling systems. These reduced costs (and accompanying profits!) accrue over time, providing your company with the funds needed to further propel innovation associated with increasing resource efficiency.

Rethinking production processes

If production processes more clearly emulated nature, there'd be no waste at all because nature recycles everything. Every element in nature serves a purpose. From tiny micro-organisms to *keystone species* (those at the top of the feeding chain), every species is part of the intricate and complex ecological web. Remove one cog in the wheel (or introduce a non-native species) and the biological machine disintegrates. For example, soil becomes sterile when nitrogen is removed by mass irrigation and the burning and clearing of grasslands and forests before planting (common practices in huge agricultural organizations).

Just imagine if your product was made entirely of recycled raw materials so that every part of it (including the packaging) could be recycled, resulting in zero waste. Strive to turn your business into a closed-loop system where no waste is generated by designing a product that can be fully used as raw material for another product at the end of its useful life. The savings inherent in this business model allow your company to push the sustainability envelope even further by challenging product designers to think up new ways to use recycled raw materials, thereby decreasing waste-removal expenses and raw materials costs.

Moving toward a service and flow business model

Modern society is overly concerned with owning goods, which leads to more goods being produced (and thus more natural capital being spent) than necessary. Is it really so important for a law firm to own the carpet in its commercial building, or do the partners just want the service that a floor covering provides? The idea behind a *service and flow economy* is that producers give consumers the service of an item rather than the product itself. The producer thus has all sorts of incentives to innovate and recycle, and the customer has none of the hassles and all of the utility.

To go about implementing this business model at your company, you first need to consider whether you sell products that you could really lease and whether you currently purchase any items for your business that you don't care to own and could lease instead. The benefit of this model is that both the producer's and the consumer's interests are aligned. For example, Pitney Bowes sells the service of processing your company's mail. The customer gets the desired service without owning assets that are unimportant to the core business strategy, and the producer has a reason to maximize the productivity of existing resources to increase profit.

Investing in natural capital

At one time, natural resource availability seemed boundless — clean water, timber, fish, minerals, and the like were harvested with abandon and appeared to replenish adequately for more taking. However, the per capita availability of all these resources is declining dangerously, putting a strain on commerce to find raw material sources to continue production. Capital investments in pollution and climate change mitigation, restoration of depleted and degraded biological systems, and the expansion of stocks of natural capital must occur for continued business sustainability.

Building a Green Team

Ask around any organization that's actively pursuing sustainability where this whole hullaballoo started, and I can guarantee you that many fingers will point to one person or a small team of people. You have much to gain by identifying these people within your company and bringing them together as members of a *green team,* which is a group of organizational stakeholders that establishes, communicates, and measures ecogoals. In a mid-sized company, a green team should have anywhere from 11 to 13 members; more than 13 becomes unmanageable, and less than 11 can make the effort feel thin and unimportant if meetings aren't fully attended. If you operate a smaller company, you'll need to adjust these numbers accordingly.

Building and fostering a green team is important for any business, from the smallest mom-and-pop shop to the largest of organizations, because employee participation is crucial to any long-term, core cultural change — which is precisely what transitioning to a green business is all about!

Unless someone within your business has sustainability expertise, or you're really super-tight on budget, your green team's kick-off meeting (and ideally its initial follow-up meeting too) should be facilitated by an external sustainability consultant. Many formal planning processes are facilitated by a consultant, so don't worry that this is an unusual request. *Note:* If budget limitations mean all you can afford is one session with the consultant, never fear — you're still getting a great start. One to two sessions will give your green team a great basis for continuing the sustainability-planning process on its own.

If you're lucky enough to have an in-house sustainability expert, you can forego hiring a consultant and use your internal expertise — and save some cash in the process.

The next three sections help you identify and develop change agents to promote social and environmental endeavors through proposed business solutions.

Choosing your green team members

Part of selecting your green team members involves knowing what types of people to look for, specifically those who are concerned with sustainability issues and who display the qualities and skills I outline at the beginning of this chapter, in the "Becoming a Sustainable Thinker" section. Keep in mind that these green leaders may come from any and all parts of your company. Sure, you may find them in such expected departments as environmental design or facilities, but you're just as likely to find them calculating in the accounting department or toiling away under a biohood in your research lab.

Both passion and position are important — which is more compelling depends on your business's size, corporate culture, structure (centralized versus decentralized), and a host of other organization-specific items. Regardless, the key isn't whether the person has passion or occupies a certain position but that he or she has the core personality traits and business-related skills of a sustainable thinker. Potential green team members' commonality lies in the fact that they're just as (if not more) concerned about your business's potential for doing environmental and societal good as they are about personal wealth or career advancement.

After you know what types of people to approach, grab an organizational chart of your company and sketch out your ideal participants for your green team. Try to sketch out positions rather than specific people. If you merely target employees who are proven leaders, your green team may not be an accurate reflection of your company, and you may overlook your sustainable thinkers. Also, by focusing on positions, you can spread the responsibility for achieving and maintaining sustainability throughout your company.

If your business is large enough to employ a few people in each of several departments, make sure that all business systems are represented (HR, accounting, marketing, investor relations, information technology, and so on). Operational areas, particularly facilities, purchasing, and product or service design, must have a presence as well. If you have managers in place in each department, ask them to nominate at least one person whom they supervise for membership on the green team. If no one responds to the department's call for volunteers, ask the department manager to serve as the department's green team representative.

Don't forget to ask one or two highly visible executives to participate. Having management onboard can lend credibility to your greening initiative by showing other green team members that top management has bought in to the endeavor and is supportive of the team's time commitment. If your executives are unavailable to participate (or perhaps in addition to your execs' support), consider asking a board member who has expressed an interest in pursuing sustainability to join the team. Just remember that even if the exec(s) and board member(s) can't commit to the full process, they should be present at the kick-off day, as well as at the initial follow-up meeting because green team members need to feel that their participation is recognized and supported by higher-ups.

Of course, if you employ only a few people (or if you're all you've got), then your options are a bit limited. In this case, you may have to rely on a passionate, proactive person to step up and initiate leadership in effecting green change, or you may be forced to mandate that everyone in the company must participate on the green team.

Convincing them to come onboard

Getting people to sign on the green dotted line can be a challenge. If your company doesn't have an ecohistory, people may be very unfamiliar and therefore unwilling to join the green team. If you're lucky enough to identify sustainable thinkers from your group, use their infectious energy — this is your key asset when roping in other green team members.

If you don't have a sustainability champion or top-management mandate, you need to garner interest in the green team by making joining seem

- ✔ **Enticing:** Try to make the project as relevant to overall corporate well-being (and by default, individual job security) as possible. Point to competitors or highly admired local companies that have already taken up the green torch as examples. Be prepared to offer a small incentive for participation in the effort (this expense is included in your sustainability-planning budget).

- ✔ **Easy:** Reassure hesitant green team prospects that the green team is a *steering committee* and that project teams for the implementation of initiatives will be made up of different people within the organization. For example, if the team identifies waste reduction as a *cluster group* (in other words, a sustainability priority area) during the planning process, a project team to spearhead initiatives aimed at assessing and then reducing solid waste would be separate from the original green team.

Certainly green team members may participate in project teams, but the two teams are *not* one and the same. Obviously, though, you must make the most of your resources, so if you have only a few business colleagues, you must distribute responsibilities however seems best for your particular situation.

✔ **Un-time-consuming:** Let people know you aren't forcing them to sign their lives away. Ask green team prospects for a nine-month commitment to the planning process — no more, no less.

Although the green team isn't stuck with implementing every idea, someone from within your organization must be willing to oversee the company's sustainability efforts and serve as the green team leader. Without an identified leader, many of these efforts start with great intentions and then fizzle out. The green team leader generally spends five hours less per week on his or her own job and must be passionate about sustainability planning.

Hiring a consultant to lead the way

A good sustainability consultant can offer your green team a broad educational overview, including providing an electronic presentation or handouts for posting on your company's intranet site. He or she can also work with your green team to start members thinking about the fit between sustainability and your organization. This sustainability expert will lead your green team through a SWOT (Strengths, Weaknesses, Opportunities, and Threats) analysis of your organization via a sustainability lens. (If your green team members have been involved in strategic planning before, they may be happy to once again get acquainted with this familiar tool, which I delve into in Chapter 4.)

If you aren't fortunate enough to have an in-house sustainability expert, never fear! Sustainability consultants are readily available in many areas of the U.S. (such as the Pacific Northwest, California, Illinois, and Vermont). In other places, however, tracking one down may be much more difficult. Unfortunately, there isn't one particular Web site organized by state for the purposes of helping business owners find sustainability consultants. There are, however, informal networks of people everywhere working toward sustainable business, lifestyles, governments, and communities. Tapping into one of these networks is guaranteed to lead you to an expanded web of other professionals committed to sustainability in your area.

If you prefer to let your fingers do the searching for you, check out these Internet search tips to get some leads as to who's who in sustainability in your neck of the woods:

✔ Type your state's name and "sustainability consultant" into your favorite Internet search engine and see what you get. Some states have hubs where consultants post their practices and client portfolios.

✔ Key the name of your area and "sustainable business council" or "local business alliance" into Google or another search engine. These types of groups are teeming with sustainability aficionados.

✔ Type your state's name and the phrase "businesses for social responsibility" into a search engine. BSR, an international sustainability research and consulting organization, has inspired regional networks in many states and may be a great resource for finding a sustainability consultant in your area.

In many cases, these Web searches may direct you to a university in your area that's working on sustainability projects. Contact the professor or department to network your way to someone who's in the know. I can almost bet that after you find someone who's active in the local sustainability scene, you can get the names of folks who may be interested in leading your green team through its kick-off and initial follow-up meetings as an external consultant.

If your company is housed in a large metropolitan area, one of the big four international accounting firms (Deloitte & Touche, Ernst & Young, Pricewaterhouse Coopers, and KPMG) may have a sustainability consulting division in your city. Get in touch with them to find out.

After you've done some research and identified potential consultant(s), make sure to do your due diligence by checking on references, asking to see any other educational information the prospect may have prepared, and giving his or her Web site a thorough once-over. Specifically, ask the following questions:

✔ How much real-life sustainability consultant experience does the candidate have?

✔ What are the candidate's references? Because no specific accrediting agency exists for sustainable business consultants, references and testimonials are particularly important. Look for projects similar in scope to yours.

✔ Is the candidate organized, professional, knowledgeable, and pleasant? Because this person will be facilitating a collaborative planning session, he or she should be likable, articulate, and knowledgeable about both sustainability and the planning process.

Budgeting for the Planning Process

When you're ready to take a shot at preparing a budget for the planning process, remember this fact: This budget isn't an implementation budget; it's a budget for the sustainability-planning process. Don't worry about trying to envision what sorts of initiatives you may want to develop or how much they'll cost. One step at a time!

When preparing the planning budget, you must consider two aspects that affect your business: the outright financial needs of the planning process and the cost of the green team members' time commitment to the effort. Not presenting a credible planning budget will most certainly undermine your efforts. Be thorough in your resource planning and be prepared to stick to it, especially if you must seek approval for your budget from higher-ups. You don't want to go back and ask the Powers That Be for more moola, so be forthright about what you need from the get-go.

Monetary costs

Planning to take your company in a new, green direction costs money. Period. When budgeting for the planning process, be sure to include the following:

- ✔ **Facility costs:** These expenses include renting a meeting room and bringing in a catering service to supply coffee and/or a meal. If your office or warehouse is large enough, you may be able to avoid the cost of renting a meeting space.

- ✔ **Incentive costs:** Plan to pay for small incentives for green team members. Don't break the bank, but do look for incentives that tie back into sustainability, like a gift certificate to an area restaurant that features locally grown foods.

- ✔ **Printing fees:** Of course, a sustainable planning session minimizes paper usage, but if you absolutely must have a few hard-copy handouts, be sure to factor in the cost of printing them.

- ✔ **Sustainability consultant–related charges:** Factor in the consultant's fees as well as travel and per diem.

- ✔ **Technology-related expenses:** You'll mostly likely need a computer, LCD panel, screen, and wireless access for the area, so be sure to budget in what the meeting site doesn't offer for free. Also, don't forget to ask your consultant what he or she needs to facilitate.

Time costs

Make sure to account for the following in your planning budget:

- ✔ **Time cost for meetings:** You absolutely have to be upfront and frank about green team members' time commitments. To figure out what those should be, multiply some reasonable hourly figure for an average employee's time by the number of hours you plan on having the green team meet per month. Use Figure 3-1 as your guide, based on the size of your business. Set a date for your first planning session and allow about a half day for it; then plan for a follow-up meeting of about three hours. After that, regular meetings should last about one and a half to two hours.

Time Commitment Required for Planning Process			
Size of Firm	Number of Meetings per Month	Hours per Meeting	Longevity of Planning Process
Micro (fewer than 25 employees)	2	1.5	4 months
Small (26-100 employees)	2	2	6-9 months
Mid (101-250 employees)	2	2	9 months

Figure 3-1:
Time-commitment recommendations for green team members.

✔ **Time cost for meeting preparation and follow-up:** Include a monthly allocation for administrative tasks — typing and distributing minutes, preparing for meetings, and so on. Also build in some time for people to collect *baseline data,* which is a current assessment of your company's state of sustainability in identified priority areas (see Chapter 4 for more information on determining priority areas).

✔ **Time cost for the team leader to fulfill leadership responsibilities:** The team leader is in charge of synthesizing information, serving as the coordinator between different cluster groups, working with the consultant and Webmaster, and presenting findings on an ongoing basis to executive management or the board. Typically, this person needs three to five hours per week to devote to these tasks.

Chapter 4

Creating Your Sustainability Plan

*S*ustainability is a journey, not a destination. But like any significant organizational undertaking, you absolutely have to have a plan in place. The purpose of sustainability planning is not only to assess the impact of global trends on your business but also to commit to sustainability as a creative strategy for dealing with the challenges and opportunities inherent in these trends. The result should be a comprehensive and practical tool that guides everyone in your company — from top management on down — in efforts to green the organization. This chapter helps you formulate your sustainability plan. (If you already have a sustainability plan in place for your organization and are looking for suggestions on implementing your prioritized goals, turn to Part II.)

There's no best place to start your greening efforts. In some organizations, sustainability naturally emanates from office practices, because someone in the office starts a recycling program and it grows. Sometimes a product engineer comes up with a new design concept that emphasizes green principles and the movement expands from there. Regardless of where your sustainability movement begins, everyone in your office should have a triple-bottom-line consciousness when going about daily office and administrative tasks. Thinking simultaneously about people, planet, and profit yields immediate cost savings (called *low-hanging fruit*) and sows the seeds for long-term shifts in organizational culture.

Laying the Foundation for Your Plan

Developing a sustainability plan is a far-reaching and often intense process. The prep work for it is demanding in and of itself, but it's crucial to your success. Trust me, the time you and your green team spend planning is well worth the enhanced efficiency of your greening efforts down the road (not to mention the impact this well-thought-out planning will have on your triple bottom line). Your sustainability plan does a great deal; it

✔ Outlines your areas of focus and your goals within those target areas

✔ Identifies the initiatives you're going to implement and details how to execute them

✔ Explains how to assess the success of your efforts, thereby allowing you to modify your plan based on those assessments

Before you dig in, though, you need to create a *green team,* a group of employees to help guide the planning process, and you need to draw up a planning budget to account for the monetary costs, as well as the time costs, of planning. Chapter 3 walks you through these early preparatory steps.

After you establish a green team and negotiate a budget, you need to follow these specific steps, in order, to successfully create an effective sustainability plan:

1. **Assess your business's current strengths, weaknesses, opportunities, and threats from a sustainability perspective.**

2. **Identify target cluster groups.**

3. **Set goals for each cluster group.**

4. **Choose key performance indicators.**

5. **Conduct a baseline assessment with the key performance indicators (using external factors as benchmarks for comparison purposes).**

6. **Prioritize your plan goals by assessing the goals' complexity and your current ability to achieve them.**

7. **Outline and prioritize specific initiatives, including approximate costs.**

8. **Communicate your plan to employees and other stakeholders.**

After implementing your sustainability plan, you need to spend time assessing the impact of your efforts so that you can modify and reprioritize your goals, indicators, and initiatives as necessary for the future. In doing so, you'll probably generate a series of suggestions that are more long-term in nature and can be tackled in phases — and that's a good thing!

Don't forget to share the results of your sustainability efforts with all of your stakeholders. Celebrate the steps your business has made toward sustainability; communicate the lessons learned from those initiatives that didn't produce as you'd hoped; and move on to the new and improved version of your sustainability plan.

After you go through at least one review cycle for each initiative, you should be able to see, pretty clearly, what's working and what isn't. For those projects that are wildly successful, propose formal policies or procedures through existing business-system channels to adopt your sustainability initiatives. Make sure to involve IT and accounting folk, particularly if your new initiative is something you want to scale up and deploy in a cross-departmental way (like a sustainable paper purchasing policy, for example).

Now it's time to jump right in with your green team, get your hands dirty, and start writing the plan that will put you on the ecopath to success!

Assessing Your Business's Current State of Sustainability

The first step in creating an effective sustainability plan is multifaceted. It involves getting a lay of your business's green (or not so green) land in order to identify which areas you're already making progress in and which items you can improve upon. Understanding where you're at today allows you to look back to this jumping-off point and measure your subsequent success accordingly.

For example, if you're making a case for installing energy-saving "smart strip" power strips throughout your office, you want to show that they've resulted in a decrease in monthly kilowatt usage. To do that, you have to establish a gauge (called a *baseline*) — today's energy usage. It's really the same with any plan, whether it's a weight-loss plan, a sustainability plan, or a training program for an athletic event. You have to know where you're coming from in order to have a sense for where you're going

The goal of your green team's first meeting is to develop a broad sustainability framework for your organization by conducting a *SWOT analysis.* This strategic-planning tool will help your green team think about the organization's Strengths, Weaknesses, Opportunities, and Threats as they relate to sustainability.

A well-executed SWOT analysis allows a green team to

✔ Assess the current state of organizational sustainability and produce a list of ecostrengths and ecoweaknesses

✔ Identify external factors that impact your organization's green status (for example, vendors', subcontractors', regulatory agents' and/or investors' policies and procedures) and whether they'll have a positive or negative effect on your business's overall sustainability plan

The following sections walk you through how to gather the information you need to begin your SWOT analysis, as well as how to use this strategic-planning tool with your green team.

Getting stakeholders' perception of your company's sustainability

So your green team is assembled, and you're all sitting around the Energy Star–certified laptop with Fair Trade Certified snacks, just looking at each other and wondering where to start. Here's a hint: Because your key stakeholders are the ones who'll be evaluating your sustainability progress, go on out there and ask them what their problems, concerns, and informational needs are.

But who exactly are your key stakeholders? The answer is simple: anyone and everyone who's impacted in any way by your company's operations, products, or facilities — whether inside your company or out. The people whom your business impacts the most are the people you want to mine for information and advice. They're not only your target audience but also your collaborators. Projects evolve with stakeholders as you bring them into the process. For example, you may decide to institute a project with suppliers to green your raw material lines, or to team up with your community's leaders to bring renewable energy sources to your area.

Asking people for their opinions implies that you're eventually going to adequately address their concerns — so don't ask if you don't have a vision for ensuring quality stakeholder engagement and aren't ready to follow through! No, a particular problem or issue won't automatically be off the ol' to-do list by next week, but by talking with both internal and external folks, you can better set targets to improve upon and come up with a reasonable way to measure how you're doing.

Deciding whom to talk to

You certainly can talk to just about anyone, but your results will be more effective if you brainstorm whom you think should be consulted within each of the following stakeholder groups:

- ✔ **Employees:** Are you going to approach *all* employees, including part-time, temporary, and fresh-in-the-door type folks? Or only full-timers with a year or more under their belts? Do you want to include independent contractors who do significant work for your company but aren't on the actual payroll, as well as trade union reps?

  Which specific employees you talk to isn't as important as ensuring you have far-reaching representation that includes employees who have varying influence levels and are from different departments. Because greening your business may impact many aspects of employees' work lives, you must solicit and value their opinions.

- ✔ **Suppliers:** Are you going to reach out to each and every one of your suppliers? Engaging your key suppliers in the input process is critical. You can determine who your key suppliers are by either setting an actual minimum dollar amount of annual business or establishing a percentage of inventory purchased from them. As you continue to grow your greening efforts, you may establish supplier programs that reward their green behavior.

- ✔ **Shareholders, investors, and creditors:** It may be too much to ask to approach every single shareholder, investor, and creditor, so how do you decide who to include? Anyone who has a material and vested financial interest in your organization should be party to the input stage. Who exactly that is is up to you to define. You can establish percentage of ownership (say 5 percent or greater) as the parameter, or you can consider how long they've held an investment in your company. If you don't have an inordinate number of shareholders, investors, or creditors, feel free to engage them all, as time permits.

- ✔ **Customers:** Do you approach everyone who's ever purchased a product or service from you, or only those who've been repeat customers? Again, you need to decide the scope of the input you want. If four or five customers constitute 70 percent of your revenue, that's pretty clear-cut. On the other hand, if your revenue base is comprised of thousands of smallish transactions, a random sample of your customers might be more appropriate. Ideally, you're already tuned in to your customers' needs and concerns regarding your company. But this is your chance to really expand that conversation and let them have some free-form dialogue surrounding what they want to see as far as your company's environmental and social performance.

- ✔ **Community members:** Are you planning on talking to your nonprofit partners, city government leaders, and local business organizations? What about business professors at universities and colleges in your town? (After all, kids in the classroom today will be businesspeople in your community very soon.) You can glean some very interesting information regarding your company's impact on the community that you do business in by engaging in dialogue with these folks.

Having a way to record and organize your chosen stakeholders' responses is important, too. Be sure to iron out the system that works for your green team before contacting anyone.

Getting what you need from them

After pulling together your working list of targeted key stakeholders, discuss your environmental and social goals with them so that they have some idea that you have a sustainability vision that holds their best interests (and the community's) paramount. By having everyone on the same page, your stakeholders can respond to you with confidence. Also, if your targeted stakeholders don't have a working knowledge of sustainable business performance, you may want to provide them with a list of potential key performance indicators (KPIs) and state what you're trying to accomplish by measuring each of them. Then ask stakeholders to rank the KPIs by importance or comment on them in a scaled format.

After educating these stakeholders a bit about sustainability, you can ask a variety of questions with the goal of getting the answer to one essential question: "What are *your* concerns regarding social, environmental, and economic issues as they relate to our company?"

You may need to draw stakeholders into the conversation by mentioning issues that have general social or environmental relevance. It's important, however, not to lead them by mentioning specific items of concern — doing so would invalidate the input process. So, even if water conservation is very important to you, don't guide stakeholders' input by asking, "Is water conservation an area of concern for you?"

Allow stakeholders enough time to answer questions that are applicable to your industry sector in regards to the triple bottom line. Also, be sure to offer them an opportunity to talk about any topic in a free-flow format.

If you have quite a large group of key stakeholders to chat with, you may want to provide them with an electronic copy of the questions so they can type out their key topics and concerns. If, however, you're a privately held company with, say, a working capital line of credit at the local bank, obviously this particular stakeholder dialogue would occur in a more informal setting. You want the bank's input on what sorts of performance indicators it may look to in order to assess how you're doing.

A combination of informal and formal surveys and focus groups may be the best way to gather customer input, specifically. You may be surprised to find out that a bunch of your customers want sustainable decking or fencing materials because they're tired of the upkeep on traditional products, or that more folks than you thought are willing to pay a premium for products made in North America.

Be sure to document your responses from the various stakeholder groups and take time to outline their main points of concern. You don't need to mention every single suggestion or complaint you received. Instead, focus on those points that were repeated enough times among the various groups to identify them as bona fide focus areas. **Note:** This is the summarized input you'll work from as you move into the SWOT-analysis process.

A quick follow-up after your stakeholder meeting is crucial. Make sure to thank each participant for his or her input. After all, engaging with stakeholders shows that you care about their concerns and rights; responding shows that you have a desire for them to flourish as a result of your operations.

Conducting a SWOT analysis with your green team

Every business consultant, sustainability-minded ones included, has a different style and technique for facilitating a SWOT analysis. The sustainability consultant you hire will probably lead your green team to consider each of the SWOT quadrants in an open and informal style and will likely use the chart shown in Figure 4-1 to get the group thinking about what's going on inside and outside the business from both positive and negative standpoints. If people are stumped and conversation dies down, the sustainability consultant can easily offer ideas to capture sustainable organizational attributes in each of the areas.

After the consultant has guided your group through this process, he or she will merge the summarized input from your stakeholders (which you gather as described in the earlier section "Getting stakeholders' perception of your company's sustainability") to the appropriate quadrants. The consultant will have had access to the stakeholders' results in advance of the meeting and will have compiled comments in a cohesive way to prepare for this analysis. What emerges is thus a visual synthesis of internal and external input.

A solid SWOT analysis is guaranteed to produce good ideas about where to target your company's sustainability endeavors. Your consultant will lead you through the quadrants with a solid explanation of how to define each item and what their differentiating characteristics are, but a brief definition of each quadrant follows:

- **Strengths:** Your organizational strengths are internally embedded attributes that will be helpful to achieving your sustainability goals, for example a corporate commitment to using nontoxic raw materials.

- **Weaknesses:** Your organizational weaknesses are internally embedded attributes that may be harmful to achieving your green objectives, such as significant investment in equipment that can't easily be converted to manufacture green products (think about automobile manufacturers trying to recalibrate production toward hybrids).

- **Opportunities:** Your organizational opportunities are external factors that will be helpful in achieving your sustainability goals, for example the ready availability of high-quality local raw materials as an alternative to materials that have to travel thousands of miles to your facility.

✔ **Threats:** Your organizational threats are external aspects that may be harmful to achieving your eco-objectives, for example, a lack of recycling facilities in your area.

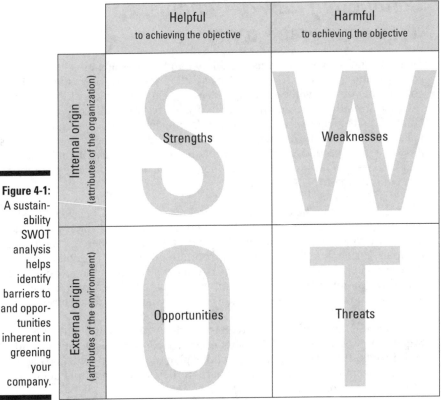

SWOT ANALYSIS

	Helpful to achieving the objective	Harmful to achieving the objective
Internal origin (attributes of the organization)	Strengths	Weaknesses
External origin (attributes of the environment)	Opportunities	Threats

Figure 4-1: A sustainability SWOT analysis helps identify barriers to and opportunities inherent in greening your company.

Identifying Target Cluster Groups

After you assess your business's current state of sustainability (head back to that earlier section if you skipped this important step), you need to identify *cluster groups,* also known as sustainability priority areas, that you want to target. These groups serve as a green framework for outlining your goals.

Each cluster group should be broadly identified, but designated with some forethought given to how you're going to assess performance in that arena. Following is a list of some common cluster groups, most of which are applicable to any business. Be careful, though, not to choose a cluster group from this list just because it's common — the groups you choose should be important to *your* company.

- ✔ Customers and community
- ✔ Employees and workplace
- ✔ Environmental impact
- ✔ Organizational governance
- ✔ Sustainability education and communication
- ✔ Supply chain management

Because every company is unique in its scope, location, operating environment, and limitations, you may find additional cluster groups that are appropriate to your line of business. The possibilities are limitless, which is why I can't offer all the suggestions. Simply consider the most common groups; if additional ideas spring to mind, add them. If not, don't try to force 'em.

Setting Goals within Each Cluster Group

If you have a good idea of the cluster groups you want to address, you can set specific goals within each of these priority areas. Think about what kind of goals you can set in relation to the cluster groups you've already identified for your organization. This is your (and your employees') chance to put your thought process into action — these goals will be the concrete catalysts for change within your organization.

If budget allows, you may choose to have the sustainability consultant walk you through this process as well. If resources are tight, have the consultant focus on facilitating your SWOT analysis (a process described earlier in this chapter).

Though setting a lot of sky-high goals is a swell way to spend an afternoon around the conference table, eventually you have to drill down to what's most important and achievable for your company. Make a final decision on goals based on what's attainable within your company's resources of time, talent, and treasure.

Your green team should be careful to include all pertinent goals, even if some of them feel very lofty or long-range or don't fit with other goals.

The SWOT analysis left you with four lists, one from each of the quadrants, focusing on your business's strengths, weaknesses, opportunities, and threats. Refer to these lists when considering solutions to the following four questions:

✔ **How can the internal strengths be used to set the sustainability agenda?** Build on the sustainable activities your business is already engaging in. For example, if one of your business's strengths is that your current product line already features complementary green products, "more rapidly expanding green product line" may be at the top of your sustainability to-do list.

✔ **How can the internal sustainability weaknesses be converted to strengths?** A typical weakness for companies that are just dipping their toes into ecowaters is a lack of knowledge about what exactly "going green" entails. If your green team identifies lack of employee knowledge as a weakness toward achieving your sustainability objective, counter that by deciding to set "developing employee sustainability education plan" as one of your paramount goals.

✔ **How can each external opportunity be expanded into action?** Look to the outside stimulus for ideas on how to expand your green plan. For example, if one opportunity is a strong community recycling program, reducing solid waste by 25 percent within 24 months may be a viable goal.

✔ **How can we creatively deflect each external threat?** External threats often come from city, state, and federal regulations, or demands from investors and shareholders. If your state is very close to instituting a carbon tax and you're a long way from being carbon neutral (like many businesses), brainstorm the kinds of immediate action can you take to reduce your company's carbon emissions by 15 percent within 24 months.

Because each organization's culture differs widely, only you know how readily the green team's sustainability ideas will be accepted by staff. Is your company into brainstorming sessions and creative visioning? If so, you're in luck — possibilities are darn near limitless and solutions may emerge quickly more often than not. Alternatively, is your business chock-full of the "we've always done it this way" folks? Then finding out your colleagues' concerns and using them as a basis for project development is essential (and something you should've already accomplished in the "Assessing Your Business's Current State of Sustainability" step).

If your green team has trouble thinking up sustainable goals and opportunities, suggest members tap into the best resource available — their co-workers! Some of the best ideas come from the folks on the front line. They see waste, inefficiencies, stakeholder dissatisfaction, and bear the burden of regulatory compliance. Ask them how they view the goals you've outlined. What would they change, add, delete? These folks can also be instrumental in helping your green team finalize goals before moving on.

Each goal must begin with an action verb to clearly identify that it's an active goal you want to pursue and not just a theoretical concept. Check out Figure 4-2 for some examples to get you thinking.

Sample Cluster Groups and Goals

Cluster Group	Goal
Customers and community	Pass on a conservation ethic to customers.
	Enhance quality of life for customers and community.
	Increase sustainability outreach to stakeholders.
Employees and workplace	Enhance employee health and well-being.
	Surpass labor/union standards.
	Engage in sustainable education and development of employees.
Environmental impact	Protect biodiversity.
	Reduce water usage and decrease waste output and carbon emissions.
	Optimize energy efficiency.
Organizational governance	Designate how a culture of corporate social responsibility is developed and who is accountable for tracking progress.
	Build in transparent communication modes.
	Link strategic analysis and financial performance with sustainability initiatives.
Sustainability education and communication	Identify techniques to train management and employees.
	Outline effective incentives.
	Develop tactics on how to inform stakeholders about greening efforts.
Supply chain management	Create programs to stimulate ecochange for supply chain partners.

Figure 4-2:
Your cluster groups and goals may look like this.

Conjuring up a name for your planning effort is a good idea at this point. Is it a Sustainability Strategic Plan or a Triple Bottom Line Plan? Whatever name you prefer, it should be something you imagine will resonate with all stakeholders.

Seeing whether your company has any peer groups that are engaged in sustainability planning or reporting is worthwhile — after all, they may be a source for great *benchmarks,* external factors against which to measure your performance. For example, if you're a small utility, check out Seattle City Light's Sustainability Plan. If you're a retailer, take a peek at Wal-Mart's published sustainability plan, complete with a sustainability progress update. To see who's doing what out there, look to your trade association's Web site and print materials, or do an Internet search on your industry and the phrase "sustainability plan."

Choosing Key Performance Indicators

The fourth step in creating your sustainability plan is all about determining your *key performance indicators* (KPIs), a series of metrics that your green team will use to help define and measure your business's progress toward each sustainability goal set in the third step (see the preceding section for more on goal-setting). Your company's KPIs should reflect the concerns stakeholders have expressed that may not yet be incorporated in the sustainability plan.

Identifying KPIs is consistent with the Global Reporting Initiative's (GRI) standards for sustainability reporting and will help you way down the road when you reach the point of reporting your sustainability progress. See Chapter 16 for more details on the GRI and sustainability reporting.

In the following sections, I familiarize you with some of the most common performance indicators, explain how to develop your broad list of options, show you how to select the right KPIs for your business, and help you figure out how to handle KPIs that seem to conflict with each other. Because of the lack of developed frameworks and systems in this area, you may find that you can soon add the title "trailblazer" to your résumé!

Recognizing common types of performance indicators

Performance indicators are often developed to help companies measure efforts toward broad organizational goals that are sometimes difficult to quantify. Typically, they fall into one of three main categories: ecological, social, and economic. As you strive to develop KPIs within each category, it may be easiest to think of them by mentally referencing traditional financial indicators. For example, a conventional economic objective is to increase shareholder wealth. Indicators of this objective are items such as net income and earnings per share.

I delve into the three categories of indicators as they relate to the triple bottom line in the next few sections.

Ecological indicators

Ecological indicators communicate your company's environmental dimension. They demonstrate whether your business is environmentally sustainable and gauge your level of impact on the Earth's ecological systems (biodiversity, water, air, and land). Ecological indicators are quantifiable and are generally based on scientific principles and guidance.

Your choice of ecological indicators is very dependent on your type of company, but should address (or at least acknowledge if you haven't started working on them yet) the following aspects:

- ✔ Energy, water, and waste
- ✔ Biodiversity
- ✔ Products and services
- ✔ Transportation of people and products
- ✔ Regulatory issues

Make sure to keep your ecological indicators highly relevant to stated stakeholder objectives. If reducing greenhouse gases weighs heavily on stakeholders' minds, state your objective as "reduction of carbon emissions by 15 percent by the year 2015." Your indicator would most likely be tons of carbon dioxide emitted or carbon emitted per dollar of sales.

Social indicators

Social indicators convey the impact of your organization on the social systems within which your business operates. They address your social sustainability and how your company contributes to society's quality of life, community improvement, and human rights enhancement. Social indicators are based on either quantitative or qualitative data and often are formulated in response to commentary from stakeholders.

Social indicators may address items such as the following:

- ✔ Organizational governance and transparency
- ✔ Diversity and equality in the workplace
- ✔ Health, safety, and welfare in the workplace
- ✔ Societal impact of operations
- ✔ Human rights
- ✔ Nonprofit collaborations
- ✔ Sustainable purchasing, including suppliers' ethics and green practices

Presenting your company's social performance on a scale is acceptable. For example, if your stakeholders tell you that a key area of concern is to increase employee work-life balance, your corresponding social indicator may be employee level of satisfaction. A score of 0 shows no satisfaction, whereas 4 reveals a very high level of satisfaction.

Economic indicators

Economic indicators communicate your company's ability to be financially sustainable and are generally based on quantitative data. This is where you look to financial beacons to tell your story. They're usually the most familiar to readers. Although individual organizational economic indicators, such as sales growth, net income, and market share, illustrate the primary economic impacts of your company, key stakeholders may be interested in a wide range of economic indicators that have broader sustainability implications, such as

- ✔ Percentage of inventory purchases that come from local suppliers.

- ✔ Percentage of gross or net income that you donate to your community. How does that compare to the last three years? What's your target for next year?

- ✔ The compensation matrix and how that fits with local living wage estimates.

- ✔ Government subsidies, credits, or programs that you're involved in.

- ✔ Supplier relations, including timely payment, long-term relationships, and supplier satisfaction with the relationship.

For example, how does your organization contribute to overall community economic development or industry-sector sustenance? If your cement plant is a key employer in your area, what are the future impacts of increased green-building techniques?

Developing your broad list of KPIs

Finding the most efficient KPIs and establishing the appropriate ones for your ecological, social, and economic goals may require some outside research and consultation in order to determine the metric option that works best for your company's needs. For example, say you operate a company in the Southwest. Chances are water usage bubbles up as one of your areas of concern. What's the best way to measure your company's current water usage? Is it charting your last 24 months of water bills on a spreadsheet? Or if you run a sales-focused operation out in the suburbs, how best can you approach calculating employees' emissions from company travel and commuting? On a per-employee basis? By carbon emitted per sales dollar? Research how other companies are measuring ratios of emissions to number of employees.

According to conventional wisdom, KPIs should meet a number of criteria referred to as SMART, which stands for

- ✔ **Specific:** They need to directly identify the metric. Something like "energy usage" is inadequate, whereas "average kilowatts used per month over prior 18 months" is appropriate.

✔ **Measurable:** They need to be broken into discrete areas that can be calculated. A KPI such as "human rights" should be broken down into something like "number of foreign manufacturing plants that have third-party certification."

✔ **Achievable:** They must look credible. If a KPI addresses the number of employees telecommuting, but there's no program in place to allow telecommuting, that isn't very achievable.

✔ **Realistic:** They should look authentic. Reducing water consumption to zero is probably unrealistic; reducing paper usage to zero may be entirely possible.

✔ **Timely:** Some KPIs need to specifically address the time period over which they'll be measured. In order to show triple-bottom-line trends, your accounting team may come up with metrics that can be measured over time such as

- Carbon emitted per unit sold

- Energy usage per square footage of facilities

- Greenhouse gas emissions per employee

- Miles traveled per unit of product sold

- Number of hours of volunteer service provided in the community

- Waste created per square footage of facilities

Feel free to jot down multiple KPIs for any given concern or issue. Your green team can winnow them down as it goes. For example, if a focus group of key supplier stakeholders has expressed concern that your company doesn't adequately source from certified minority and/or women-owned businesses, your task is to figure out what measurement ties directly into this objective. Number of certified suppliers? Dollars spent with these suppliers? Ratio of certified suppliers to all suppliers? Try on a few KPIs to see what fits best with your situation.

In my experience, economic KPIs are fairly easy to establish because that's what traditional business models are generally based on. Environmental KPIs are almost always wrapped around measuring water, waste, and energy usage. However, people seem to get stuck on how to develop social KPIs. Looking for ideas in existing documents and program plans may help. Check out your

✔ Employment policies and guidelines

✔ Programs you're implementing to improve verification of labor practices, particularly in foreign countries

✔ Plans to enhance the health and safety of your employees and supply chain

✔ Employee training, career advancement, and educational opportunities

✔ Formal diversity and tolerance policies (ratios are often a good way to present this data)

Consider having discussions with stakeholders as you go. For example, if you're trying to determine how to measure progress toward serving disadvantaged customers, try asking the customers who fall into that category. What do they believe would be indicative of success for that goal? More services? Expanded hours? Dedicated help lines? Use information gleaned from stakeholders to help direct the development of your KPIs.

Selecting your KPIs

The quality of your KPIs is critical, because these are the metrics you use to measure your success, so plan to spend more than one meeting selecting the KPIs you're going to incorporate into your sustainability plan.

The key to selecting the right KPIs from your broad list of possibilities is to make sure you're not overzealous when initially outlining them. Because each cluster group contains multiple goals, you may have more than one KPI per goal. However, fewer and well-thought-out KPIs are much more desirable than a whole litany of them. For a sample of how you can organize goals and KPIs in each cluster group, take a look at Figure 4-3. (As for using your KPIs to measure your company's progress, turn to Chapter 15.)

Cluster Groups, Goals, and Key Performance Indicators

Cluster Groups	Specific Goals	KPIs
Customers and community	Protect habitat and biodiversity.	Watershed habitat conservation plan developed in collaboration with stakeholders.
Employees and workplace	Engage in fair labor and hiring practices.	Diversity representative of community from which our employees are drawn.
		Percentage of managers who are from a minority population.
	Enhance quality-of-life initiatives.	Number of employees job sharing or telecommuting.
		Establishment of programs that support working parents.
Environmental impact	Increase fleet efficiency.	Fossil fuel consumed per year transporting product.
Organizational governance	Provide sustainable education to Board of Directors.	Attendance of board members at sustainability training.

Figure 4-3: Cluster groups, goals, and their corresponding KPIs may look like this.

The number of KPIs isn't nearly as important as making sure you have the right ones. Quality over quantity is the motto. There's no right or wrong here — the hope is that your green team members have generated significant discussion to flesh out the most important points and engaged in research when needed to get you to this point.

For expediency's sake, you may want to break your green team into two groups at this point, each tackling half of the cluster groups identified by the green team as a whole. Because your green team is *cross-functional* (meaning it features members from various departments), expect each department's representative to brainstorm ideas that relate to his or her respective area of expertise.

The KPIs your green team is generating aren't engraved in gold. They may change and evolve as the team delves further into the sustainability-planning process.

Addressing conflicting KPIs

As you start compiling a list of your chosen KPIs, situations can arise in which they're at odds. This occurrence means that a tactic designed to increase results from one KPI may adversely affect another one, and improving that one may mean impeding another's progress. In the following example, one KPI is market share percentage, and another is pounds of nonrecyclable packaging used. To increase the market share of your small microelectronics manufacturing firm, you have to scale up your distribution chain. Suppose a national big-box store wants to carry your product, but in order to ship it over long distances, you need to add a layer of protective packaging. Reduced packaging and increased market share is an example of conflicting KPIs.

Determining which KPI should be pursued may well be one of the first tests of your triple-bottom-line thinking. In a traditional business model, the decision that increases the economic bottom line is given more weight than other factors. However, a sustainable planning process necessitates that you have a more balanced approach to economic, social, and environmental indicators. When KPIs are at odds, look back to your evolving sustainability plan and attempt to balance your judgment with your stakeholders' input to see whether you can find a way to reconcile the benefits of each KPI.

Conducting a Baseline Assessment with Your Key Performance Indicators

The next step is gathering data and conducting a baseline assessment of your current performance in regard to each of your goals. This assessment is more specific than your SWOT analysis (which simply allows you to determine your business's strengths, weaknesses, opportunities, and threats as they relate to sustainability). In this step, you're using your chosen key performance indicators (KPIs) to provide an overview of your sustainability performance, thereby allowing you to identify which goals need the most attention and in what order.

At the same time, the baseline assessment helps you see whether the KPIs you've chosen are truly reliable. Assessing them is vital to your initial planning stage, because your KPIs are the cornerstone of your plan.

Gathering internal data for the assessment

Compiling baseline data may seem like an overwhelming process. If you're interested in enhancing work-life balance, you need to establish a baseline as to current level of satisfaction. If you want to push your locally made product line, understanding the level of customer interest is critical. In these scenarios, you have to gather data. In some instances, though, utilities or local waste management facilities are willing to conduct appraisals, assessments, or audits regarding water usage, waste output, or energy usage (usually for free).

When you gather data, make sure it's valid; you'll use it in the future for monitoring your progress and ultimately reporting on your results. (Chapter 15 explains how to ensure the validity of your data.)

If interest is starting to wane, or collection of data for all of your KPIs looks to be too great a task, then feel free to prioritize a few goals within each cluster group and go after the baseline data for the associated KPIs.

Chances are not all of your KPIs will have accessible quantitative data, so you have to build in time for the green team to accurately accumulate it. Be prepared to do the legwork or pay someone else to do the data mining for you.

If you decide not to gather baseline data for all KPIs, don't despair! The work you've already done identifying them won't be lost; it'll still be there for future development. Make sure to keep the planning process fluid and responsive to green team members' concerns relating to time or scope constraints so no one burns out.

Using external factors as benchmarks

As you gather data, you may run into some gold standards known as *benchmarks* — external factors (such as standards or performance parameters) against which you can measure your own company's results. After you name the benchmarks against which you're measuring your success, you can create some targets and goals in the short term (upcoming year) and interim targets for longer-term goals. By using external benchmarks, you can strive for results that are already out there and help your stakeholders see how you're doing in comparison to others.

For example, scientists from the Intergovernmental Panel on Climate Change (IPCC) agree that in order to stabilize the Earth's temperature, greenhouse gas emissions must be reduced by 80 percent by the year 2050. This is the benchmark you can use to evaluate your company's performance in reducing greenhouse gas emissions.

Many sustainability goals don't have specific benchmarks available because they're unique to your company. Depending on your industry sector, however, common benchmarks you may want to consider are as follows:

- Specific third-party certification of materials, processes, or products (for example, wood purchased from Forest Stewardship Council–certified sources or an Environmental Management System that's ISO14001 compliant)
- International greenhouse gas reduction standards
- Widely held goals such as zero waste
- Facilities standards such as LEED (U.S.) or Green Globe (Canada)
- Local or regional green awards or standards
- Regional data on employee performance, productivity, or healthfulness

Rating your performance according to your KPIs

After you identify a KPI and gather the data that pertains to it, you can score your organization's performance in that particular KPI via a simple scale. To make the rating objective, try to work out a mathematical score (see Figure 4-4 for an example). If you're not quite sure how your performance scores against a chosen benchmark, use your collective, albeit subjective, green team judgment to give it a score.

When you rate a KPI, use the following simple scale:

- 1 – Way below-average performance.
- 2 – Below-average performance, or no data available. (If no data is available for your indicator, give it a 2 [which is standard].)
- 3 – Average performance, complies with regulations. Used to establish baseline for first year and assumed to be on par with peer-group performance.

      ✔ 4 – Above-average performance.

      ✔ 5 – Superior performance.

Figure 4-4 identifies what sorts of benchmarks may be appropriate for your evaluation purposes and shows how you might rate and assess your KPIs. As you find benchmarks that can help you look more intimately at how your KPIs are performing, drop that info into the corresponding column. (**Note:** Benchmarks aren't necessarily available for each KPI you come up with.) In the next column, you should evaluate how your KPI is performing compared to your chosen benchmark. You can then rate each baseline assessment according to the previously provided scale. (If no benchmark exists, standard practice is to assign a rating of 2.0.)

Baseline Data and Company Performance Ratings

KPI	Benchmark	Baseline Data & Evaluation	Rating
Diversity representative of community from which our employees are drawn	Commnuity census shows demographics by ethnicity, gender, and age. This info is compared to employee data – both management and nonmanagement (give numbers).	Gender dispersion mirrors community (give numbers). Ethnic dispersion doesn't mirror community (give numbers). Age dispersion doesn't mirror community (give numbers) and shows a labor force heavily weighted in the 45 and older category. (Use numbers to estimate rating.)	3.6
Fossil fuel consumed per year transporting product	No benchmark available.	225,138 gallons of diesel fuel consumed in prior fiscal year. (Because you have baseline data with no prior record, assign a rating of 2.)	2.0
Attendance of board members at sustainability training	No benchmark available.	No board members attended sustainability training in prior fiscal year.	1.0
Watershed habitat conservation plan developed in collaboration with stakeholders	County X Watershed Conservation Plan guidelines.	Compliance with 3 of the 8 recommended environmental initiatives for facilities located in County X watershed. (Calculate as ⅜ x 5 [top possible score] to get the rating.)	1.9

Figure 4-4: The baseline assessment of your indicators may look like this.

Summarizing your findings

After you've gone through the rating process, average the ratings for each of the cluster groups and summarize your findings so you can include a brief snapshot of each in your final plan. The summary of your baseline assessment should show each cluster group with specific goals, KPIs, and current scores using those indicators. The format should look similar to what you see in Figure 4-5.

Summary of Scores for Cluster Groups & KPIs

Cluster Group I: Employees & Workplace
    Goal 1: Engage in fair labor and hiring practices.
        • **KPI 1:** Diversity representative of community from which our employees are drawn = 3.6
        • **KPI 2:** Managers who are from a minority population = 1.8
    Goal 2: [Insert next goal]

Summary Section for Cluster Group I

Average score of Goal 1 $= \frac{3.6 + 1.8}{2} = 2.7$
Average score of Goal 2 = [Insert calculation]
Average score of Cluster Group I = [Insert calculated average of all goals within cluster group]

Figure 4-5:
Your baseline assessment summary may look like this.

Prioritizing Your Goals

After conducting a baseline assessment of your key performance indicators (KPIs), your green team can easily see which goals take priority and demand immediate attention (those with the lowest score need the greatest amount of improvement). The order in which you plan to tackle them, however, doesn't solely depend on need for improvement.

When you prioritize your goals, you assess them from a holistic perspective by looking at their complexity, your current ability to achieve them, and other similar factors that provide a realistic vantage point. I suggest that you use a simple rating scale of 1 to 5, with 1 being "none or not at all" and 5 being "a lot or significant," to address the following questions:

✔ How much of the goal do you *think* can be accomplished with existing resources?

✔ How critical is this issue to your company's core mission?

✔ How much risk does your company incur if you *don't* move on this issue?

✔ How important is this issue to external stakeholders?

You may need to do some broad research to adequately answer this question. Choose three employees, three vendors, and three community members and provide them with a copy of your current KPIs and baseline data (without the scores) and ask them to first prioritize goals within each cluster group and then prioritize the cluster groups themselves.

Assigning scores based on this scale gives you a rudimentary prioritization of your sustainability goals, as well as a clear idea of how you're currently doing on each of those goals. Well done!

Identifying Specific Initiatives

If you've made it this far, you're in the home stretch of creating your sustainability plan. You've outlined and prioritized all of your goals, so now you just need to create and prioritize the specific initiatives you'll take to work toward those goals. Depending on the size of your organization, you may decide to tackle one cluster group thoroughly and split the prioritized goals among working groups. Or you may choose to target one or two goals in each of your cluster groups.

This decision is a tactical one that you must make based on your earlier prioritization of goals (see the preceding section), as well as your take on the culture in which you operate. For example, if you know you're going to get a lot of internal resistance to auditing foreign manufacturing firms for labor standards compliance, don't start there. If you've heard a ton of grumbling about needing to improve your office's energy efficiency, then *do* start there.

The next few sections explain how to brainstorm ideas for specific initiatives, work out the details of each one, and then prioritize them according to your company's needs.

Brainstorming ideas

My first piece of advice when brainstorming about specific programs and initiatives is to go for it — nothing is off limits, and nothing is too far out. My second piece of advice is to be realistic. Obviously, your company's set of initiatives will be unique to your organization in terms of scope and focus. So consider factors such as implementation costs and reaction from management and employees. How is it possible to consider both? Realistically, if you come forward right now with a series of recommendations that are going to cost a ton and seem pretty out there to your average Jane or Joe, they won't fly.

Keep cost in mind as you move into discussions at this stage, noting that today's far-fetched ideas may be attainable in a few years' time. Make sure you capture all the ideas on paper, even if some of them will clearly be tucked away until a later date. Recording every idea keeps your green team's synergy in motion.

Based on how many folks are on your green team and where the areas of interest are consolidated, split the team into two to three working groups to develop specific sustainability initiatives. Don't forget to include team members' individual knowledge bases when divvying people into groups. For example, your facilities person is the best person to address greenhouse gas emissions from your plant, whereas your HR rep is the best person to review your labor rights cluster group.

Prior to breaking into working groups, distribute a template for documenting initiative ideas and estimating the approximate costs and savings of those ideas. When you reunite to consolidate your ideas, everything will look the same in your word-processing software and spreadsheets.

Say for example, that two of your goals were flagged in the prioritization process and that the individual working group you're in is given the responsibility for suggesting initiatives that will help you to achieve these two specific goals. You can create a summary table of what you already know (like the one shown in Figure 4-6) to better evaluate which initiative ideas are most appropriate for immediate implementation.

Summary Table of Info Prior to Brainstorming Initiatives

Cluster Group	Goal	KPI	Benchmark	Baseline Data & Evaluation
Environmental impact	Increase of effciency of cluster fleet.	Fossil fuel consumed per year transporting product	No benchmark available.	225,138 gallons of diesel fuel consumed in prior fiscal year.
Organizational governance	Provide sustainable education to Board of Directors	Attendance of board members at sustainability training	No benchmark available.	No board members attended sustainability training in prior fiscal year.

Figure 4-6: In order to brainstorm initiatives effectively, you need this info at your fingertips.

After you take a look at the summarized information, determine where a good point of entry is. For example, if you have plans in place to upgrade your fleet, that's a great arena for easing your sustainability plan into action because you've already identified that action as a specific goal. If the goal doesn't coincide with current strategic priorities, establish ways to impact it within your resource constraints. For example, are there options to use rail or modify your logistics to minimize the distance needed to transport products?

Your working group members may or may not have any expertise in the area you've been assigned to investigate, so be ready to rely on further investigation or on the knowledge of other employees and stakeholders.

Continuing with the preceding example, if you do have the logistics person in your working group (lucky you!), he or she can provide an overview of the issues surrounding product transportation. If you don't have this internal expertise, your working group needs to bring the logistics person in for a consultation.

Be sure to consider the following when you're brainstorming possible initiatives:

- ✔ **Outline pertinent questions.** In this example, you may ask how many trucks, what kind of trucks, how many miles per year are driven, how many average miles does each unit of product travel, where are distribution centers, are there alternatives, what are the costs, and so on.

- ✔ **Research what other companies have done.** Check out big delivery companies' Web sites to view their sustainable transportation plans. Your working group should be creative in exploring ideas and suggesting where to make inquiries. Assign specific legs of research to different team members and then reassemble and share what you've discovered and the ideas you've come up with.

- ✔ **Set realistic expectations.** Clearly, you need to set interim targets for each year to attain long-term goals. If you're trying to reduce your greenhouse gas emissions, for example, begin by establishing modest percentage-reduction goals (such as 2 percent reduction per year) that are attainable through conservation and the use of today's technology, realizing that you're aiming toward targets farther down the road.

Sustainability initiatives shouldn't be long, convoluted, or important sounding. Instead, they should be quite concise and include very specific items like: "Replace current distribution fleet with hybrid alternatives over the next ten years." Keep your language simple upfront so you can then expound on the thought behind the initiative.

At this point, the diligent efforts of the various working groups will have resulted in small start-up projects. You should also have a list of more comprehensive initiatives for the identified priority goals.

Selecting the best initiatives from your brainstormed list

After you create a list of possible initiatives, you need to select those that will reap the most benefit for the triple bottom line because they're the ones you'll move forward with. The next two sections show you the two options most businesses use.

Getting a visual cue: Plotting cost against overall sustainability benefit

A rudimentary way to analyze sustainability projects is to construct a visual graph. Name the x-axis Cost and the y-axis Sustainability Impact. Then, based on estimated costs and perceived sustainability benefit, label where proposed projects belong on the graph. Finally, using the bubbles in Figure 4-7 as a guide, decide which initiatives to move forward with and when.

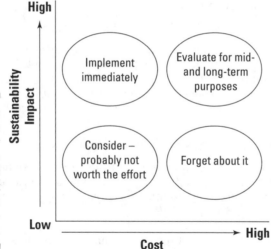

Figure 4-7: Plotting the cost of your sustainability initiatives against perceived performance.

Number crunching: Assessing the weighted average of the triple-bottom-line benefit

One good way of analyzing initiative options within the context of how they'll benefit the triple bottom line is to use a simple weighted-average criteria chart.

1. **Create a chart like the one in Figure 4-8 with the initiative options you're considering as the column heads following the TBL Criteria and Weight of TBL Criteria columns.**

   In this example, the three initiative options are meant to increase the efficiency of a business's fleet.

2. **Allocate a weight to each aspect of the triple bottom line (based on a 1 to 10 scale, with 1 being least important and 10 being most important) based on which aspect is of chief concern to your company for the particular initiative in question.**

   The business in this scenario determined that the impact on profit was its top concern, so they rated that a 10. Planet was the next concern for this efficiency-related goal, so it received a 7. The impact on people was important but not critical, so it got a 2 — reflective that in this example, there isn't much effect on people.

3. **Evaluate each option against the impact on people, planet, and profit, assigning a numerical score to each.**

   This score is obviously subjective, but it helps you to succinctly compare each of the three options to each other. When used in combination with the weight you place on each of the elements of the triple bottom line, you have a mathematically deeper analysis than just a simple straight ranking.

   Don't mire yourself down in statistical detail here. This chart is a forecast and, as such, is simply an educated guess.

4. **Multiply the weight of each TBL criteria by the weight of each option.**

   Record the result within the gray box that corresponds with that TBL criteria and the option in question. So, for example, People is assigned a weight of 2, and in Option 1, it's multiplied by 5 for a score of 10. In Option 2, the weight of People is multiplied by 0 to get 0, and in Option 3, it's multiplied by 10 to get 20. Work through the same process with the remaining TBL criteria.

5. **Add the numbers of the gray boxes within each column.**

   Enter the sum in the box for that option within the line designated Total. You wind up with the weighted average for each of the three options. This info allows you to compare the forecasted performance based on your assumptions.

You can easily see in Figure 4-8 that the most financially beneficial option doesn't maximize the triple bottom line. This weighted-average chart may be an uncomfortable model to use, but it should serve as a guide as you transition to a new and sustainable decision-making framework. The highest score is going to yield you the most desirable initiative according to the weight you assigned your criteria.

Outlining the details

To wind up with the specific initiatives you're going to proceed with, you need to outline the details involved with each option. Sustainability initiatives for each prioritized goal need to include the following details:

Weighted-Average Triple-Bottom-Line Evaluation

TBL Criteria	Weight of TBL Criteria	Option 1: Subcontract with dispatcher committed to green principles.	Option 2: Invest in logistics software to decrease miles driven with current fleet.	Option 3: Implement replacement policy that gives preference to fuel-efficient vehicles.
People	2	5	0	10
		10	0	20
Planet	7	10	7	10
		70	49	70
Profit	10	4	7	2
		40	70	20
Total		120	119	110

Figure 4-8:
Sample weighted-average triple-bottom-line evaluation of initiatives.

✔ **The significance that the initiative would have in contributing to the attainment of the sustainability goal:** No need to make this an intricate process. Simply state how the initiative contributes to attaining the overall goal. The more succinct your statement, the better.

✔ **An assessment of how complex it will be to implement the initiative:** Nothing fancy is involved here either. All you really need is a simple bulleted list of the steps required to implement the initiative. Your *project team* (the group charged with carrying out the initiative) can then determine the complexity of the project based on the outlined steps.

✔ **Which organizational units/business systems need to be involved:** Use common sense and your business acumen to identify which specific areas, such as HR, accounting, logistics, or marketing, need to be involved in the implementation of the initiative.

✔ **The internal capacity for implementing the action plan:** The most important piece of advice I can give you at this juncture is that you should make sure a particular person is responsible for spearheading implementation of each sustainability initiative. Ideally, this point person is the lead on the project team charged with overseeing that particular initiative. He or she should have a clear timetable, chain of command, and budget. Without this accountability, all the green team's planning work can collapse into a heap of good intentions.

You also need to determine whether you're going to ask outside stakeholders to participate on the project team to help guide the initiative through its implementation phase. Although project teams are typically made up primarily of employees, feel free to invite suppliers, investors, community members, and customers to come onboard.

✔ **A timetable for the initiative:** When setting the timetable, you need to establish whether there are going to be phases of implementation and whether you're going to measure results at the end of each phase. Without a set timetable, your initiative may never get off the ground.

✔ **A description of how results will be measured:** Build a solid assessment mechanism into your implementation plan and prepare either a formal or informal tool to determine how far you've come from your baseline assessment. Communicate your project's efforts far and wide as you go.

✔ **The budget impact of the initiative:** As in any planning endeavor, you must attach a budget to everything you do. As you think about resource needs, make sure to

- Identify which members of the organization would be ideal candidates to work on the project team charged with overseeing the initiative.

- Include the costs of outside consultants.

- Itemize required asset purchases and line out ongoing expenses needed to make the initiative fly.

- Identify savings that will accrue from reducing waste output, energy usage, and anything else associated with this project and net that out against the cost of implementing the initiative.

- Include a timetable for full implementation of your plan.

- Outline the chain of command that exists in your organization to apportion these resources.

Prioritizing your initiatives

As you look at different initiatives, compare the complexity of implementation against the urgency of taking action. Small but strong projects garner interest, so attack the easiest and most urgent first.

When you prioritize your initiatives based on complexity and urgency, the projects that make their way to the top of the to-do list are those that are easiest to implement and address a critical need. If you're trying to prioritize the remaining initiatives in the future, I suggest being patient and seeing how implementation of the first set of projects goes because follow-up or phased-in projects from your to-do list may naturally follow. For example, if you determine that conducting a carbon footprint evaluation is a priority goal, then projects to decrease emissions will follow.

Making far-fetched ideas seem reasonable

Sometimes a particular sustainability initiative seems unrealistic, whether that's due to its exorbitant costs, way-out technology requirements, a lack of resources for implementing it, or something else. Before you cross that idea off the list, try to figure out whether it can be presented in a different light.

For example, suppose that one of your initiatives is to replace your current distribution fleet with hybrid alternatives over the next ten years, but a lot of your research shows that current trucking logistics is transitioning toward a new generation of vehicle, and that hybrid 18-wheelers will be rolling off the assembly lines in 24 to 36 months. The projected cost of replacing

your fleet with these new rigs is $2.3 million. Do you scrap the idea completely, knowing that the cost would prohibit consideration? No, but your action plan to meet the goal of "increased fleet efficiency" could include a fleet-replacement initiative that calls for all *new* purchases to adhere to certain internal guidelines for carbon emissions.

If gathering age- and longevity-related data for each truck within your fleet is fairly easy, then you can propose the approximate time span within which this transition would occur, showing that over ten years you can be fully converted. Fuel savings from each new purchase may fund the next replacement and make the initiative look more viable to stakeholders or top management.

Spreading the Word about Your Plan

For your sustainability plan to work, you must be prepared to help your stakeholders understand *why* you prioritized your sustainability initiatives the way you did. Then you need to offer them a compelling case as to how this prioritization is going to strengthen the company, the community, and, yes, each person's individual well-being.

With a workable sustainability action plan, you can communicate to everybody, in an authentic manner, how you're positioning your business for the future. Showcase your work with local policymakers and media — let everyone know, for example, that you're crafting carbon-neutral commuting options. Take advantage of press releases and opinion pieces in the local paper to highlight your good work and reach out to the blogging world. See whether other businesses are interested in bringing a corporate car-share program to town. Who knows — other companies may even contact you to get ideas for their programs!

Communicating your green initiatives occurs whenever someone walks into your place of business, not just when the media reports on them or when they're described in marketing materials. Therefore, demonstrating a commitment to all of your stakeholders through daily activities goes a long way toward making the right impression and creating buy-in. (This approach applies to employees, too; I cover bringing them onboard in Chapter 13). Communicate the green team's progress, taking every opportunity to share all the ecoevents occurring in your company. Talk about your sustainable product rollout, the number of employees biking to work, or your new green advertising firm whenever and wherever you can!

If you need to communicate difficult subjects related to your sustainability plan, such as rolling out a preferred green supplier program that may require significant changes on the part of your existing vendors, couch them in a positive tone that stresses how going green is part of a long-range strategy. Tell folks how your plans to remain economically viable in the changing world are a benefit to them and focus on green collaborative potential.

Communication is a two-way street, so why not get stakeholders involved? Asking your stakeholders, particularly those from the community in which your business operates, to serve on a corporate sustainability advisory panel is a great way to get input and bring lots of different types of people together.

To ensure that the best practices become policy, make sure to formally follow through with your stakeholders. Set out a suggestion box. Engage stakeholders with sustainability training to make sure everyone's on the same page with the initiatives. Conduct check-ins as the initiative progresses to see whether it's on track. *Remember:* Creating your plan is only the first step in making sure all of your sustainability goals become reality — following up on it is the key to success.

Creating project teams to foster collaboration

To build excitement and buy-in potential, prepare a summary chart to reflect your working groups' efforts to see whether any initiatives offer coordination potential. For example, every working group is probably going to come up with ideas for dealing with greenhouse gas emission reductions. Do you want to create a project team to work on this issue that crosses over cluster-group boundaries? Figure out your strategy and create an easy-to-understand chart that lets everyone know his or her responsibilities.

Note: Depending on what venue you need to go through to obtain approval for the creation of project teams and approved budgets, setting up prospective project teams may very well be one of your green team's final roles. Transitioning to project teams that oversee the various elements of the sustainability plan begins with approval of the proposed initiatives.

Remember: Although potential project team members were identified by your green team during the creation of specific initiatives, you may still need input from advisors. Pull up your list of key stakeholders whom you may have had conversations with regarding the outcome of the SWOT analysis because these folks may make good external advisors as your project teams evolve.

The green team should plan on meeting quarterly with the project teams to review how implementation is functioning, as well as to examine the results and suggest modifications accordingly.

In your follow-up meetings, you may modify your key performance indicators after finding that more appropriate measurements exist for particular goals. Likewise, you may come up with new benchmarks to compare your business against after researching other organizations' work. Keep everything dynamic and open to change!

Chapter 5

Paying Attention to Public Policy and the Regulatory Realm

In This Chapter

▶ Recognizing the value of understanding the big green-policy picture

▶ Identifying how current and impending policies affect your business

▶ Deciding how to respond to and influence policymakers

Sustainable business development is a necessary model shift that demands operating within the Earth's sustainable carrying capacity. It requires more reliance on regional trade, financial incentives to value ecosystem services, greenhouse gas reduction policies, and an emphasis on equity in international relationships. The great news is that you can be a part of it! And quite honestly, you should, because the fiscal implication of these policies hits you where it counts: your wallet. Addressing the scope of acts being considered and passed is impossible, but suffice it to say that they're occurring at every level of government and will filter down the supply chain to affect every size business enterprise.

The Basics on the Green Movement and Public Policy

In order to bring about real change in response to the shifting global business model, public policies that guide participation in the green transformation are crucial. Many aspects of commercial trade will be affected as a result of these policies — taxation structures; free trade agreements; oil, gas, and other natural resource leases; and new markets (for carbon and green products). Realizing that umbrella solutions must exist under which every business and consumer can move ahead to face common challenges, all kinds of government agencies, investor groups, businesses, trade associations, and individuals are jumping into the policy game.

In the next few sections, I show you who the main players are, how their decisions and actions affect your business, and how you can respond.

Who's running the show

Many sustainability advocates believe that a combination of deep understanding, commitment, and concerted action from four key groups is the only real chance for coloring the global environment green. Each of these sectors must possess a keen willingness to be part of the change and recognize that it has a unique and equally potent role to play:

- **Business:** With most of the world's trade based on a capitalistic system, business is clearly a key driver in the transition to a sustainable global economy. Private enterprise encourages creativity, innovation, investment, and technological improvements. Sustainability adds a new way of thinking about all these things and is thus a crucial business model for the 21st century.

   Currently, capitalism doesn't integrate the full cost associated with production into the actual product. For example, the product prices of petroleum refining companies and timber companies reflect only the overhead associated with extracting the raw material, not the full cost, which includes mitigating climate change. Some economists believe that this skews the market, because the product is inappropriately priced.

   Thanks to a growing number of various green consumers (you can read all about them in Chapter 10), the demand for green product lines, service offerings, and business operations is growing. However, if businesses choose not to make the effort to meet this demand in favor of sticking to the old business model of short-term, purely profit-based thinking, the continued decimation of natural resources and the growth of global inequity will escalate, causing potentially irreversible damage to the planet and the world's population.

- **Government:** The influence of government at all levels is important as a unifying force to tip the playing field toward sustainable development. Why? Because fiscal policies, such as subsidies, taxes, and credits for research and development (R&D), as well as regulatory guidelines, are the responsibility of different government entities, and they can have intense impact on how businesses operate.

   On the micro level, a progressive local city council can spur innovative green neighborhood developments, which in turn spawn green builders, carpenters, planners, and landscapers. On the macro level, policies that move toward climate change mitigation and adaptation may require countries to limit carbon emissions or meet waste targets, requiring businesses and individuals to adapt quickly.

✔ **Nonprofits:** In many areas of public policy, nonprofits are leading the move for shifts toward a more sustainable future. Many nonprofits have even become large and powerful financial forces with international membership numbering in the tens of thousands.

When these organizations partner with companies, investors, and policymakers, their potential to inspire real change is significant. For example, the Sierra Club and the Citizens for Tax Justice partnered to expose subsidies to industry sectors that left taxpayers with clean-up costs, thereby reversing an alarming trend of citizens bailing out pollution remediation.

✔ **Individuals:** Of course, instilling values about environmental and social stewardship and purchasing power changes at the grassroots level are essential for true, widespread change. Particularly pertinent in the movement toward a global green economy is the influence of share-holders, both large and small.

Institutional investors, as well as individuals holding 50 shares of a company's stock in an IRA, have started to tap into the power of resolutions and activist agendas (see the later section "Targeting your efforts" for more on shareholder resolutions). Because of the changes effected by these initiatives, individuals are becoming recognized as a force to be reckoned with in the movement toward sustainable development.

How the greening of public policy affects business

A number of policy mechanisms can urge consumers and producers alike to change their behaviors toward sustainability, but what really comes first — the change in behaviors or the policies themselves? Opinions diverge when discussions dial in on incentivizing versus regulating. Some taxpayers believe that incentives, like tax credits and subsidies, encourage innovation without mandating particular ways of getting there. Others see newly imposed taxes as yet another impediment to maintaining a profit margin adequate to keep their businesses solvent.

Regulations such as imposing new taxes on old behaviors (like generating garbage) probably isn't the first place government would turn to effect change, because of business owners' natural resistance to new taxes. However, new fiscal policies actually institute change at no or low cost to businesses. For example, plastic bags used in retail outlets are being eliminated from entire cities, and even countries, by placing a surtax on them. The businesses aren't suffering because they have a new commodity to sell (reusable bags) and are completely eliminating the cost of providing plastic bags to customers.

If given enough time, incentive-based tax models are effective in bringing about green change in some scenarios. However, regulation often brings about immediate (albeit antagonistic) change. Many tax models are bandied about in policy circles these days, but a hybrid of the following is likely to yield the most efficient path toward sustainable development and innovation:

- **Tax shifting:** The premise of *tax shifting* is simple: Stop taxing positive behaviors (like earning income and accruing net worth) and start taxing negative behaviors that require society to bear the external costs (like generating pollution and waste). Named after economist Arthur Pigou, these *Pigovian taxes* are usually associated with ecotaxes or sin taxes. Some economists believe that this type of revenue-neutral tax shifting is more immediate and effective than regulation, because it offers continuing incentive to pollute less.

- **Credits and deductions that incentivize solutions:** In a divisive arena, almost every policymaker agrees that incentives must exist. These incentives normally take the form of tax deductions or tax credits, most often for practicing energy efficiency and using renewable energy. Tax credits are also available in different states for constructing green buildings, employing at-risk individuals, and using recycled materials. Some jurisdictions are even considering tax breaks for sustainable corporations that have voluntarily adopted the triple bottom line as part of their corporate policies.

The Database of State Incentives for Renewables & Efficiency (www. dsireusa.org) features a comprehensive listing of renewable energy and energy efficiency income and property tax breaks, by state, for individuals and companies. Check it out to see what incentives are offered where your company is headquartered.

Ways you can respond

Business owners and employees are generally fearful of impending government regulations and mandates, because the policymakers possess great collective power. But that doesn't mean you should sit submissively on the sidelines — ample opportunities exist to have an equally potent voice at the policymaking table. Joining trade associations or green business groups, attending local city council meetings, and supporting like-minded politicos are all viable avenues for influencing the development of green policies. But in order to play ball, you must understand the implications of the macro policies being discussed in your area and how they may impact the future of a particular business or industry sector.

Because businesses are uniquely poised to work with the other core groups (governments, nonprofits, and individuals) responsible for creating and implementing green policies, you have two options:

✔ **Position your company to deal with the policies being proposed.** You'll be better off in the long term if you pay attention to proposed policies, because if a particular regulation is approved, your company won't have to hustle to meet new requirements. In light of carbon-tax discussions, for example, you'd want to begin the process of lightening your carbon footprint slowly and with purpose instead of responding in a panic when new laws are passed.

✔ **Try to do your best to influence the policies.** By being a part of associations or groups that are working toward specific regulatory changes, you can advocate on behalf of policies that will be most beneficial for your business.

Every aspect of your business will be affected as sustainability-oriented policies, laws, and tax changes begin to unfold. I encourage you to be optimistic and look to the opportunity-laden side of the coin, regardless of where you personally stand on the issue of government regulations.

What Green Policies Focus On in the Business World

As you think about how public policies will affect the greening of your business practices, I imagine you're pretty concerned about one or more of the following:

✔ Corporate and partnership taxation

✔ International trade

✔ Energy security and renewable energy development

✔ Future availability and pricing of water

✔ Incentives to develop products or services for the green market

✔ Raw material accessibility

✔ Waste management models, including new disposal pricing modes

Government is now stepping up to the plate on these and other key issues. Because discussions surrounding many of these areas of concern are in the infancy stage, you can have a real hand, particularly at the local or state level, in crafting policies that have strategic importance for your business.

Policies to spur economic development through green-collar job growth, alternative transportation R&D, biofuels, solar and wind manufacturing, and other sustainable maneuvers are making their way to the forefront of legislative agendas. The vast number of pending bills range in focus from green chemistry to high-performing green buildings and the introduction of sustainability into higher-education institutions. You may find that one or more of these proposed bills directly affects your small or mid-sized enterprise.

The next several sections offer some insight into what's been done and what's on the upcoming roster regarding several areas of concern to the average business owner.

Natural resources usage

The usage of natural resources is a vast and complex field that will only continue to grow in importance as timber, water, and ore become more precious. No matter what size your organization is or what industry sector it's in, you undoubtedly use water, energy, and other natural resources. Therefore, continued access to and affordable pricing of these items are crucial to the long-term survival of your company.

If your business depends on any natural resource, you need to follow pending regional and federal legislation affecting the material in question. One policy model in particular — the shifting of subsidization from oil, chemicals, and corporate agriculture to renewable energy and alternative transportation — has received a lot of attention.

The scope of the policies at hand is too broad to address in this book, but you can use an Internet search engine and type in your state's name and the phrase "Department of Natural Resources" to connect to natural resource regulations in your state. Because energy law pertains to converting natural resources into energy and is such a hot topic, you should also check out the breadth of partnerships, programs, pending legislation, and initiatives listed by state at the Department of Energy's state-specific Web site (`apps1.eere.energy.gov/states`).

Energy sources

At the most fundamental level, practically all businesses are understandably concerned with the pricing, accessibility, volatility, and security of energy. Many companies, particularly small ones, operate on a razor-thin margin that's sorely strained with 10 and 20 percent hikes in key budget line items — namely utilities and transportation. Of course, raw materials also have increased energy costs embedded in them as well.

The scoop on minerals and water

If your company depends on minerals, such as titanium, or water to turn a profit, here are some special policies and initiatives to keep an eye out for:

✔ Businesses that rely on minerals for manufacturing need to follow proposed environmental regulations surrounding lighter-impact mining techniques, as well as how those regulations may impact your vendors, future pricing, and raw materials availability. Keeping tabs on the move in policy may also be a great impetus for your product development team to analyze alternative, more sustainable raw materials

that can be used in place of the mineral in question. See Chapter 7 for more details on greening your approach to product development.

✔ If water factors into your business needs, pay special attention to initiatives being considered by the U.S. Center for Strategic and International Studies (CSIS). It's brokering water and exporting it from Canada to the U.S. — despite the fact that Canada has its own regional shortages. International water brokering is going on behind the scenes and can have big implications for your business's water needs in the future.

Tremendous controversy surrounds federal- and state-level approaches to energy policy, and you need to know what your state's legislators, governor, and public utility commission are discussing. If you belong to a trade association, consider encouraging the development of a subcommittee to focus on energy policy and crafting a statement of support for the policy that you believe will best benefit your business. If your state is trying to deregulate (or regulate) energy and you have reason to believe the outcome won't be in your organization's best interest, show up at public hearings, write letters to your local paper and legislators, and do an Internet search for other like-minded business owners in your area.

Looking toward the future, green tags may one day be required as part of carbon-reduction strategies for business. *Green tags,* or *Renewable Energy Certificates,* represent one megawatt-hour (MWh) of renewably generated electricity. They can be traded, and the owner of the tag may accurately claim to have purchased renewable energy. I recommend staying on top of the development of green tags to better understand how the implementation of this greenhouse gas reduction policy may affect you down the line.

Currently, 25 states have Renewable Portfolio Standards, which require electric companies to procure a certain percent of their electricity from renewables by a certain year. For example, New York has a 24-percent requirement by the year 2013. Electric companies' compliance with Renewable Portfolio Standards is important to you as a business owner because to operate a truly sustainable business, you should source your electricity from renewable sources. Also, as more electric companies make the switch to renewable sources, your business's energy bills may be positively impacted.

Greenhouse gas emissions

In the U.S., more than 100 pieces of legislation are pending that contain climate change provisions. The Global Warming Pollution Reduction Act proposes cutting greenhouse gas emissions to 80 percent below 1990 levels by 2050, whereas the Climate Stewardship & Innovation Act of 2007 aims to cut them by 30 percent from 2000 to 2050. Many other proposals contain less sweeping language but still set big reduction goals, particularly considering the Earth's population is continuing to grow. Although these proposals aren't specifically targeting greenhouse gas emission reduction among corporations, the implications of such legislation should it pass are greatest for the business world.

On the proactive side, the U.S. Climate Action Partnership is applying pressure in Washington, D.C., to reduce greenhouse gas emissions and stabilize the climate. As more big corporations and nonprofits join, this effort will only continue. On a more local level, at last count, mayors representing almost 80 million citizens in 850 cities had signed the Mayors Climate Protection Act, a Kyoto Protocol–type treaty aimed at rolling back greenhouse gas emissions to 1990 levels. Many cities are also creating Sustainability Director positions to lead their local movements. (Chapter 11 explores this burgeoning movement to expand local economies and lessen reliance on products that travel thousands of miles, causing tons of carbon dioxide emissions in the process.)

In most parts of the developed world, climate change concerns have already resulted in far-reaching sustainability-oriented laws. Europe, Canada, and Australia are much more progressive than the U.S., and it looks like it may take a while to garner political consensus on how to proceed. The primary federal policy tools being explored include cap and trade and carbon taxing, both of which are explained in the following sections.

Setting a cap on carbon emissions allowed: Cap and trade

Cap and trade is a tool designed to regulate carbon emissions in absolute metric tons from any point of emission. There are three general ways to approach cap and trade:

TECHNICAL STUFF

Renewable energy policies around the U.S.

The potential for job growth and increased national security associated with developing renewable energy is great and will be an area that many smaller businesses will eventually be a part of. Your business may find itself purchasing renewable energy in the future (if you don't already) or being one of the many businesses that will be a part of the supply chain for these rapidly growing industry sectors. If you believe that renewable energy is an area that holds significant promise for energy security and reliability, consider this: The U.S. government allocates about $1.5 billion dollars annually for renewable energy R&D. This may sound like a big number, but consider that ExxonMobil generates that in revenues in just one and a half days.

The Energy Independence & Security Act of 2007 is focused on research in combined heat and power (CHP) fuels. It sets national goals, in billions of gallons of renewable fuels created through 2022, focusing on new technologies like advanced biofuels, waste recovery, and cellulosic ethanol. Examples of state-level progressive policies that have already been enacted include the following:

✔ California's Air Resource Board uses a combination of market mechanisms and regulations to ensure a 25-percent reduction in greenhouse gasses by the year 2020.

✔ Georgia launched *Conserve Georgia,* a marketing campaign aimed at getting residents and businesses to conserve water, energy, and land.

✔ Illinois and New York have laws requiring the use of green cleaning supplies within public schools.

✔ Montana requires plans from all government entities as to how they propose to reduce energy consumption 20 percent by the year 2010.

✔ Washington and Maine have product-stewardship laws that make electronics manufacturers responsible for taking back equipment at the end of its life.

Because of the magnitude of effort swelling up around new technologies, businesses need to start considering a shift toward using and developing them, thinking out of the box that oil won't always be the only main energy source. When it comes to renewable energy, start asking questions like, "Where can I buy it?", "How much will it cost?", and "How effective and reliable is it?"

Many individuals and companies purchase green power through green tags (described in the nearby "Energy sources" section). That doesn't mean the companies are directly getting power from a wind farm, for example, but it does mean that they've purchased one megawatt-hour of renewable energy from somewhere. You can accurately claim to be using 20 percent green power if you're buying green tags equal to 20 percent of your average monthly electricity usage. Go to apps3. eere.energy.gov/greenpower to find green tags to purchase in your area.

✔ **Allocation of tons of emission:** Companies receive a set number of tons, and if your company doesn't use them all, you have a sellable commodity. If you need more, you buy them. (The Chicago Climate Exchange can broker greenhouse gases for you.)

> ✓ **An auction of units of emissions:** A total number of tons of emission is calculated, and the government conducts an auction of sorts, where corporations bid for the carbon units.
>
> ✓ **Cap and dividend:** This approach is the same as the first method, where your company gets a set amount of emissions, but you receive a rebate if your company doesn't use its allocated amount.

The positive side of this policy model is that there's an absolute cap on the number of tons of emissions agreed upon by the policymakers. The target is widely known and ideally in line with the reductions needed to achieve climate neutrality. However, opponents of this policy claim that it provides little motivation to be creative about how to reduce emissions below pre-determined targets. They also argue that most companies that *do* reduce emissions below their targets will sell their unused emissions rather than let the share expire, thereby contributing unneeded greenhouse gases into the atmosphere.

Taxing for carbon emissions by the ton

A *carbon tax* is an example of a type of pollution tax. Each emitted ton of carbon (and other greenhouse gases) is taxed in an effort to encourage companies to reduce the amounts they emit. Some people believe these taxes could be most easily sold as an income tax rebate: Collect carbon taxes and then rebate them to taxpayers.

Proponents of the carbon tax point to the success of other pollution taxes in altering behavior. Naysayers, however, state that carbon taxes give corporations and individuals the *right* to pollute as long as they can afford it. Furthermore, many policymakers are justifiably nervous about the longevity of their careers when they utter the dread t-word, particularly in an election year.

One current example of a carbon tax is in British Columbia, where residents now pay a $10-per-ton tax on carbon-based fuels. This tax is applied to gasoline, diesel, natural gas, and home-heating fuel and is anticipated to increase $5 a ton per year until reaching a cap of $30 a ton in 2012. The government claims that income tax offsets for businesses and individuals make this a revenue-neutral policy. Yet this law is still new and will need to be analyzed in subsequent years to gauge its effectiveness in cutting net emissions.

Waste generation

Green policies regarding the generation of waste are currently all across the board. Thousands of "paying as you throw" (PAYT) programs are scattered across urban and rural North America. *PAYT* is a trash tax, meaning the more solid waste you generate, the more you pay. A full 25 percent of all communities nationwide have a PAYT system that converts trash disposal from a right to a fee-based service.

Greenhouse gas reduction initiatives in practice

Specific initiatives designed to reduce the amount of greenhouse gases being emitted include the following:

✔ Boulder, Colorado has a Green Points & Green Building ordinance that triggers changes in how residential building permits are granted based on energy efficiency and recycled-content usage, among other techniques.

✔ Chicago, Illinois is committed to using 20 percent renewable energy by 2010.

✔ Leaf Rapid, Manitoba no longer allows nonbiodegradable bags.

✔ Vancouver, British Columbia's recycling program recognizes that society bears the burden of cleanup and that the manufacturer should be the one to develop and submit a plan to manage certain products (like solvents, pesticides, paint, tires, and others) through their end of life. The incentive is now on the producer to use less harmful materials and to make them easy to remediate.

I personally like the approach used in East Hampton, New York: There is no trash service. Each resident and business owner must sort and prepare his or her recycling and trash and then haul it to the recycling center or dump as appropriate. Can you imagine how resourceful you'd become at eliminating trash if you had to personally handle it through its end of life?

In an industry-specific bend, Europe has recently passed legislation requiring electronics manufacturers to take responsibility for what happens to their products at the end of life. Because these items, called *e-waste,* contain heavy metals, e-waste is an arena that U.S. states are also regulating because of the potential groundwater leaching and hazardous material issues. (Turn to Chapter 6 for tips on disposing of your business's e-waste.)

Corporate social responsibility

Corporate social responsibility issues such as human rights violations, climate change, and executive compensation pepper the topics that spring up repeatedly in shareholder resolution filings. The Interfaith Center on Corporate Responsibility is a leader in this area. You can see the green focus of the topics that topped its most recent agenda by going to www.iccr.org and clicking the Shareholder Resolutions tab at the top of the page.

In terms of taxes, tax credits and other incentives aimed at growing the green economic sector will likely be passed in greater numbers in the future. So keep your eye on this area if your business is involved, currently or prospectively, with growth in wind or solar power, aquaculture, alternative transportation, or local food and/or landscaping so you can reap some well-deserved benefits for your greening efforts.

Additionally, economic think tanks and university studies alike have been claiming that North America will see significant growth in green-collar jobs in the upcoming decade. With any luck, these new jobs will provide employment for the myriad of people who've lost their jobs due to downsizing or outsourcing.

In 2007, the first federal piece of legislation targeting green-collar jobs was passed. The Green Jobs Act was included as part of a comprehensive energy bill; it's geared toward providing job training in renewable energy, flexible vehicles, and green construction. About 20 percent of the funds are earmarked for hard-to-hire folks like former prisoners, welfare recipients, and high-risk youth.

Cities and states are coming onboard as they begin to understand the opportunity inherent in developing this new economic niche. Oakland, California's Green Jobs Corps and the Richmond, Virginia job training program are both being heralded as innovative programs to develop at-risk citizens into employable green-collar workers. Additionally, Iowa has passed job-training bonds for biofuel job creation, and Oregon is focusing on training wind technicians.

How and Where to Make Your Voice Heard

In many ways, grassroots movements have shown a high degree of success in bringing about meaningful change. A classic example is the coalition of mothers in Niagra Falls, New York who banded together to hold a company liable for its negligent handling of toxic waste. The result of their union was the passage of the *Superfund Act,* which requires polluters to pay for the cleanup of toxic materials.

More so now than ever before, ecodriven grassroots movements are cropping up and influencing change for global benefit. Whether you're working individually or joining up with your local trade association, professional affiliate, or other small or mid-sized enterprises in your area, consider working to effect change in any of the following ways:

✔ Reward innovation in energy efficiency and renewable technologies.

✔ Implement policies to reduce solid waste and appropriately recycle e-waste.

✔ Pass a carbon policy to decrease future market risk surrounding this issue.

✔ Stop water brokering and encourage regional solutions to water problems.

✔ Incentivize the use of high-recycled content materials.

✔ Encourage innovative product design and certification.

✔ Require municipal and state government agencies to impose green procurement policies, decrease energy usage, and add sustainability training for all employees.

In the following sections, I help you find like-minded businesspeople to join forces with and show you how to take part in pressuring policymakers for green change that benefits you. I also outline the changes being made in green public policy through the involvement of various levels of government and influential stakeholders.

Joining with like-minded businesspeople

Businesses gain power when they join together with other businesses that have similar values and goals. Perhaps that's why a number of organizations proactively working on the greening of business (as opposed to waiting for lawmakers to step up to the plate) are out there just waiting for you to join:

✔ **Professional or trade associations:** My guess is that no matter what industry sector you're in, your professional or trade association is working on something green. For example, as fisheries declined significantly in the late 1990s, large fish product purchasers got together with the Marine Stewardship Council to design programs to certify that fish were harvested using sustainable methods. The companies involved not only crafted policy (instead of waiting for government regulations) but also began the critical steps necessary to preserve their long-term raw material source.

If you're not sure what kind of green projects your professional or trade association is up to, run a search within the group's Web site. If you're the chief partner in a law firm, you may be surprised to know that the American Bar Association has a Climate Change, Sustainable Development, and Ecosystems Committee that's in the process of crafting a model sustainability policy/implementation guide.

✔ **Sustainable business organizations:** Although a significant number of organizations are working to help businesses develop sustainably, here's a smattering of ones that can offer you a place to craft policy with other like-minded businesses:

• **Social Venture Network:** With a mission statement of "Transforming the way the world does business," the Social Venture Network is one of the grandfathers of the sustainable business movement. Its Web site (www.svn.org) has a searchable database of case studies and best practices, as well as an action page that can get you hooked up with other members to achieve carbon neutrality. The group also holds annual conferences that are great networking opportunities.

- **U.S. Business Council for Sustainable Development:** This heavy-hitting organization has five policy platforms — energy, water, byproduct synergy, value chain, and ecosystem services. You can get involved in the issue that's important to your company by visiting www.usbcsd.org.

- **Net Impact:** This group is focused on joining business leaders together to solve day-to-day sustainability challenges at the office and to effect change at higher-education institutions. Net Impact is a good fit for small and mid-sized enterprises. Visit www.netimpact.org to take a look at its focus initiatives.

Pressuring policymakers for change

Whenever a comprehensive carbon-reduction policy is negotiated by the federal government, companies that haven't been proactive in at least anticipating the effects of these policies will be left in the proverbial dust. Don't let your company meet this fate. Instead, make a stand for your business by pressuring lawmakers at all levels to institute the policies that work for both your company and the environment.

Following are two organizations that are working with lawmakers to stimulate change:

- ✔ **ICLEI-Local Governments for Sustainability:** This global organization helps local governments develop sustainably (check out www.iclei-usa.org/about-iclei to find out more). Getting involved as a key player in this group by providing input on discussions and proposing funding initiatives can be a very positive move for your company as you go green. After all, only you know which of the various legislative concerns are most important for your business. Whatever they may be, you can bet that any potential changes may affect your bottom line. So why not try to have a hand in helping local lawmakers craft policy rather than simply reacting to it?

- ✔ **Investor Network on Climate Risk:** Considered a rather influential group, INCR represents some of the biggest institutional investors in the U.S. Managing more than $6.5 billion in assets, INCR calls on legislators to fulfill three specific tasks in response to climate change:

  - **Reduce regulatory uncertainty.** Everyone knows that carbon will be regulated one day, but INCR thinks that the markets are bearing the uncertainty of what that's going to look like. After policymakers firmly commit to a set reduction and establish a system to promote reduction, business entities will respond and markets will adjust accordingly.

- **Reward solutions.** INCR wants legislators to propose a comprehensive bill that would provide incentives to companies implementing innovative ideas.

- **Minimize risk.** As other developed countries are changing their business modalities to reduce carbon, INCR believes the U.S. is becoming more exposed to future economic risk due to its lack of a cohesive policy.

Targeting your efforts

Where you invest your persuasive efforts is wholly dependent on what business you're in. In the following list, I outline ways the various levels of government and other influential folks are generally getting involved in the world of sustainability. Consult your state or province's congressional Web site to see a list of pending legislation. If you're really committed, call or e-mail your representative or senator directly to obtain a specific list of green legislation you can use to help determine where your energies are best directed.

✔ **Federal government:** The U.S. and Canadian governments officially recognize climate change and stable energy as prevailing national security and economic issues. Accordingly, hundreds of pieces of legislation are pending in both Congress and Parliament.

The easiest place to follow federal legislative activity in the U.S. is to go to `thomas.loc.gov` and key in "green" or "sustainable." To track Canada's federal, provincial, and territorial legislative status on sustainability-oriented issues, join EcoLog Environmental Resources Group at `www.ecolog.com/sustainability`.

✔ **State government:** Many states are aggressively pursuing the transition to sustainability, whereas others are doing little. Sustainable purchasing policies and energy efficiency are areas of interest for many state agencies that are going green, but specific policies really tend to run the gamut.

A comprehensive list of states working on greening efforts isn't available, so plug in the name of your state and "sustainable" or "green" into an Internet search engine to see what's going on in your neck of the woods.

Don't forget about powerful state coalitions working on a host of issues. The Western Governors Association, for example, is committed to sound water, energy, and climate change policies; the Northeast Governors are looking to increase rail capacity as a cornerstone of sustainable development.

✔ **City councils and such:** Even cities are jumping on the green bandwagon. Across North America, mayoral leadership is generating business and community support for policies that encourage sustainable economies and cut greenhouse gas emissions. With environmentally preferable purchasing policies arising from many of these efforts, look for increased opportunities for your green business to serve government agencies.

✔ **Shareholders:** Although shareholder resolutions have showed up on dockets for almost 40 years, the scope and intensity with which they're shaping sustainable corporate policy agendas of late is truly amazing. The U.S. Securities and Exchange Commission allows any stockholder who holds at least $2,000 in stock for a minimum of one year to file a shareholder resolution. (Obviously, however, there's more impact if individuals collaborate.) Most resolutions are generally filed in order to raise public awareness and effect change in environmental or human rights practices.

Even though many resolutions fail, and often the ones that pass aren't generally binding, they bring a lot of attention, sometimes adversely, to the company. Fortunately, after management grasps the inherent marketing and image-enhancement value in making some of the changes contained in the resolution, the triple-bottom-line impact of shareholder resolutions can shine through. For example, a major computer/electronics firm committed to removing all persistent toxic chemicals from its product line as the result of a shareholder resolution suit. This decision resulted in a plethora of free press spotlighting the company's progressiveness compared to its competitors and a reduction in the company's need for expensive hazardous material disposal.

Shareholder resolutions and proxies may not *directly* impact your business, but as sustainability increasingly becomes the business model for larger corporations, the trickle-down effect is inevitable. Sometime soon, your key customers will be asking for *your* sustainability plan or awarding points to *your* bid based on green agenda items.

Though these scenarios typically occur for companies that are publicly held, overall community awareness is growing, creating new opportunities for your small or mid-sized enterprise to do sustainable business with the big guys. Identify which of your value chain members are going green and see how you can serve their needs.

Part II
Pushing Up Your Green Sleeves: Implementation

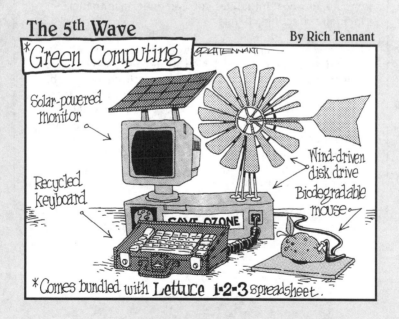

The 5th Wave   By Rich Tennant

*Green Computing

Solar-powered monitor

Recycled keyboard

SAVE OZONE

Wind-driven disk drive

Biodegradable mouse

* Comes bundled with Lettuce 1-2-3 spreadsheet.

In this part . . .

The most effective way to green a business is to look at the big picture and then roll up your sleeves and craft small, achievable goals for each functional area. That's why this part takes you through the basics of greening some of your business's most integral functional areas, starting with your daily office practices. From offering tips on handling e-waste to showing employees how altering paper margins can result in reduced paper waste, here I clue you in to the many opportunities for high-impact, low-cost initiatives you can undertake to incrementally effect big change.

Engaging in sustainable product development, which is geared toward modifying design strategies to encompass new thinking, is another way you can institute sustainability at your company. Eking more out of natural resources, reducing waste, and minimizing energy and materials usage are all core values of green design. Facilities management and accounting practices are some of the other key organizational areas in which you can effect eco-change, perhaps by implementing some of the suggestions I offer in the following pages.

Chapter 6

Small Steps, Big Change: Office Practices

*L*ooking at your daily routines, as incorporated in office policies and procedures, is often a visible and tangible way to begin the transition to a green business model. Greening your office practices deepens employee knowledge, saves you money, and serves as an integral part of overall company ecoimprovements. As is true in all comprehensive cultural shifts, small daily behavior modifications add up to sweeping changes and potentially big cost savings. In this chapter, I introduce you to the breadth of the most common changes in the office practices arena and show you how to implement these changes while getting your colleagues onboard.

Greening Office Practices: What You Can Do and Why You Should Do It

Sustainability efforts in the office usually center on key areas such as energy efficiency, waste reduction, purchasing practices, and company travel policies. Most action items in the office arena, as well as organizational areas, have multiple layers of positive impact. For example, engaging in a paper-reduction policy saves energy and reduces waste. Establishing new procurement parameters for office equipment enhances energy efficiency and contributes to easier recycling of electronic waste, or *e-waste*. Moving to nontoxic office cleaners improves indoor air quality and provides a more healthful work environment for your employees.

If you want to take sustainable steps in other areas of your operation, then you absolutely need to make some basic green changes in your daily office practices. After all, how can you expect stakeholders to get onboard with progressive changes like sustainable product design if you don't recycle or practice temperature control in the office? By making the commitment to green your internal practices as well as those that affect external stakeholders, you're letting all stakeholders know that sustainability is here to stay at your company.

Because most employees (unless they're at a remote site) will be engaged in some way with office greening efforts, this is a great way to bring everyone onboard and introduce the opportunities inherent in practicing green behaviors in the workplace. Not only can you secure staff's buy-in but you can also begin looking for those ecominded individuals who might be good candidates for furthering green change throughout your organization. (For help spotting the characteristics of a sustainable thinker, see Chapter 3.)

Where to Begin? Getting the Lay of the Land

Projecting triple-bottom-line benefits from individual initiatives may help guide you in what to do first. However, prioritization in office sustainability efforts is based on the location and culture of your organization, the nature of your operations, and the structure under which you operate. Prices for energy vary greatly among different geographic areas. For example, some company cultures might easily embrace a change to corporate travel policy, whereas others might be very resistant. You have to be able to decide in which areas change will be the most visible and the most well received.

With all that said, however, most companies begin greening their office practices by promoting energy conservation. Because of the tremendous amount of personal and commercial concern as to energy prices and volatility — as well as the immediate impact on utility bills — improving energy efficiency through tactics like lightening up on your lighting usage and greening your IT department is an easy way to start greening your office practices. Picking the low-hanging fruit by introducing energy-usage-reduction projects is often a way to showcase immediate economic savings. These great starter projects allow opportunities for outreach to employees and help bring them onboard with the green movement. Many times, energy-reduction projects generate additional cash from utility savings, and those funds can provide seed capital for further work.

Simplifying sustainability initiatives in the office environment is the key to successfully implementing change in your office practices. You can't overwhelm your employees with a big long list of mandates (If you do, you'll likely be managing a small-scale revolt rather than generating interest in greening your office.) The best approach is to ease people into working sustainably by making the changes small, easy, and rewarding. Then, as you introduce the more complex or high-barrier ideas, your team will (theoretically, at least) be less resistant and on track with the bigger picture.

Here are my recommendations on what to do when you're first starting to green your daily office practices:

✔ Ensure that the cost-benefit analysis makes sense (for example, in some rural areas, recycling glass isn't environmentally sound because a solid reuse market doesn't exist).

✔ Find easy-to-implement practices first.

✔ Be able to show a cost savings from early efforts.

✔ Don't require tons of behavior changes early on.

Ultimately, increasing office sustainability benefits the *triple bottom line* (people, planet, and profit; see Chapter 1 for more on the triple bottom line). Be prepared, however, to justify initial outlays of capital for some of these projects, realizing that savings generated over the long term will more than amply provide for your original upfront expenditure. Depending on how resource allocation works in your company (which is highly dependent on your organization's size and corporate structure), you may be running expenditure requests through your direct superior, the finance director, or executive management.

Increasing Energy Efficiency

These days, you can't enter a room without spotting at least one electrical outlet on a wall. What you don't see is that a majority of those outlets are powered by coal plants that emit a disturbing amount of carbon dioxide, which is a major contributor to climate change. Good energy management is good business. Depending on your industry sector, energy costs, and geographic location, utility bills can be a significant line item on your Profit & Loss Statement. Even a small percentage reduction can have big dollar impact.

Consequently, it's not surprising that reducing energy usage is on the global business population's mind lately. You can take steps toward decreasing your business's greenhouse gas emissions (and its resulting effect on climate change) and increasing your cash flow by setting up a well-crafted, long-term energy conservation plan for your office that focuses on eventually becoming carbon neutral. To achieve this status, you need to develop a three-pronged approach:

- ✓ **Practice energy conservation.** This term refers to becoming more efficient with the energy you currently use. Depending on how efficient your facilities and operations have been in the past, aggressive energy management efforts can, in certain parts of the country, yield up to 30 percent savings, according to the U.S. Environmental Protection Agency.

- ✓ **Convert all or a part of your usage to renewable energy sources.** However aggressive your energy-conservation initiatives may be, you'll still have *some* energy needs. Because of the uncertainty surrounding carbon taxes and restrictions in the future (see Chapter 5 for more on pending policy discussions), all businesses need to be thinking about ways to reduce greenhouse gas emissions. Position yourself for the future by turning to renewable energy sources as much as possible. (See Chapter 8 for the scoop on renewable energy sources.) Most parts of the U.S. have some renewable energy that can be purchased, with prices varying widely depending on your geographic location. Although renewable energy may cost you more now, you're beginning the process of weaning your company off of oil and coal, which sets you up for stability in the future.

- ✓ **Offset any traditional energy that you can't convert to renewables.** This step, known as *carbon offsetting,* refers to purchasing an instrument to absorb any carbon you continue to emit, despite your efficiency and conservation efforts.

Why not plan for the future while you're at it? Make sure to expressly request that any savings generated by increased energy efficiency at your office be allocated to future sustainability efforts, which may require more seed capital than the easy and obvious projects described in the following sections.

Finding out the amount of energy you currently use

To practice energy efficiency effectively, you first need to get a handle on the amount of energy you currently use. You may think this amount is fairly obvious, but I'm going to let you in on the dirty little secret about office energy: Most of those machines plugged into your walls are sucking power even when they aren't in use.

The best way to start gauging your current energy usage is to gather a rudimentary baseline assessment. Using the last 12 to 24 months of energy bills, enter your kilowatt usage and total electricity cost per month on a simple spreadsheet. Doing so gives you an idea what your utility usage patterns are and provides you with a jumping-off point as you begin to implement ideas from the next few sections.

Traditional 8-to-5 companies use the most electricity when rates are at their highest. This is called your *peak amount.* If you're charged a *demand rate* on your electric bill, you pay a fee based on your peak amount of electricity consumption. Lowering your peak rate of usage can save you some big-time cash. ***Note:*** Peak times are unique to certain parts of the country, so you may not have to deal with this issue at all.

When you pull your utility bill, look for surcharges or demand rate add-ons. Call your utility company to clarify if you don't understand certain charges.

As you plan your energy-conservation measures, make sure to keep a keen eye out for any energy-sucking operations or tasks that could be repositioned at another time of day. When you look at your next 12 months of energy bills after implementing some of these simple measures (with all other variables being equal, of course), you should see a decrease in kilowatt usage compared to the same month in the prior year.

For extra impact, use a carbon calculator to convert kilowatts to tons of carbon emitted per month. The resulting number will serve as the basis for assessing the success of your energy-reduction efforts. A great carbon calculator to use is currently available at `www.safeclimate.net/calculator/biz_calc_form1.php`. The best one isn't up and running yet as of this writing, but keep checking the U.S. Environmental Protection Agency's (EPA) Web site (`www.epa.gov`) and searching for its Office Carbon Footprint Calculator.

Your baseline assessment of office energy usage gives you glimpses of the canvas, but by no means does it paint the full picture of your organizational impact on climate change. To comprehensively catalog your business's greenhouse gas emissions, a full inventory is your next step. Inventorying greenhouse gases is a fairly time-consuming and complex task, and goes much further than baseline energy assessments.

Conducting a full inventory of your company's greenhouse gas emissions is generally only desirable for small to mid-sized businesses if

✔ You're really serious about significantly reducing your business's environmental impact and you want to establish a baseline assessment because you intend to expand your market into areas or niches that will make purchasing choices based on your efforts. (See Chapter 10 for a run-down on the various types of green consumers who might base their purchasing decisions on your initiatives.)

✔ A key customer has asked for it as part of greening its supply chain.

✔ You're anxious to market your greening efforts and want to share data with stakeholders as to your overall greenhouse gas reduction goals and accomplishments.

The big six greenhouse gases are carbon dioxide, nitrous oxide, methane, hydrofluorocarbons, perfluorocarbons, and sulphur hexafluoride. Reduction targets are outlined in the *Kyoto Protocol,* a global greenhouse gas reduction treaty signed by more than 180 countries since 1997. It voluntarily calls on signatory countries to reduce their greenhouse gas levels to at or below 1990 emissions.

Most power companies are willing to conduct a once-in-a-lifetime free energy audit of each building that they service in their area. I recommend finding out whether yours does and getting on its waiting list now. If your power company doesn't offer this service, a private company in your area may be willing to perform this function for a fee. However, there's no reason to do both: Use the free audit if you can and turn to the fee-for-service option if you must.

A professional audit should include an evaluation of your utility bills and current energy-conservation methods via interviews and observation. It should also include an analysis conducted with specialized equipment such as blower doors (which measure air leaks in the building envelope) and possibly infrared cameras that can identify hard-to-spot air pockets or missing insulation. The output should be an analysis that identifies specific projects, including cost estimates and related energy savings.

After the audit is complete, you'll receive a report (each report differs based on the unique company that issues it) that offers some energy-saving tips and gives suggestions as to how you can

✔ Increase the efficiency of the energy-consuming systems you have in place

✔ Conserve energy by sealing external air leaks, adding insulation, and implementing weatherization measures

✔ Purchase green power to offset the traditional energy you use

Starting with the low-hanging fruit

Prioritize the energy-conservation ideas that seem easiest and least costly to implement and get going on 'em. These low-hanging fruits are an easy sell to the higher-ups and provide tangible and immediate savings in the form of reduced utility bills. They also have impact on employees. Some of the projects mentioned in this section involve minor disruptions; others may constitute (in certain individuals' minds) sincere sacrifice.

Counting your company's carbon emissions with the GHG Protocol

Ten years ago, the World Resources Institute joined forces with the World Business Council for Sustainable Development to create the Greenhouse Gas Protocol (GHG Protocol) as a way to help government and business leaders comprehend, measure, and manage greenhouse gas emissions. After scads of industry input, the GHG Protocol working group has released a user-friendly tool that's both non-technical and consistent with proposals by the Intergovernmental Panel on Climate Change (IPCC) for greenhouse gas emission inventorying. It provides greenhouse gas standards, including some industry-specific calculation tools.

You can check out the wide array of good calculation tools by registering (a simple and free two-minute process) and then accessing the information at this Web site: `www.ghg` `protocol.org/calculation-tools`. Unlike the many Web sites out there that claim to be carbon calculators for businesses but are actually sales tools for carbon offsets, the calculators published by the GHG Protocol are the real deal.

What's neat about the tools is that you can calculate one facet of your company at a time, if that's the approach you've designated. For example, if you've identified business travel as an area of concern, there's a calculator to help you understand your company's impact from that activity. The same goes for employee commuting or purchased electricity.

The GHG Protocol also has a great resource for small, office-based organizations that includes spreadsheets and guidance. You can find it here: `www.ghgprotocol.org/down` `loads/calcs/working9-5.pdf`.

Because all fundamental shifts come with some amount of sacrifice, make sure your employees see that the burden is spread equitably among all levels of employees. Model efficiency in all that you do and spearhead the communication effort, continually emphasizing how important it is that your company takes responsibility for its own energy future. Acknowledge that some of the changes may be frustrating at first, but will soon become routine.

Following are some examples of simple tasks you can do that require minimal time and effort:

- **Install "smart strip" power strips.** These savvy little energy-saving power strips work between your main device (such as your PC) and the main outlet. All of your PC's peripherals (like scanner, fax, printer, and PDA) plug into the other receptacles of the "smart strip." When the main device is off, all other energy flow is stopped, saving up to 75 percent of the previously wasted energy. Although relatively new to the market, bloggers and marketers alike are saying that these $30 to $40 gadgets can pay for themselves in just six short weeks.

✔ **Turn off lights in unused spaces, including restrooms, breakrooms, and boardrooms.** This idea sounds pretty basic, but make a mental note in your daily life to flip lights off as you exit a room. You'll start to notice how many uninhabited spaces are lit. Ridiculous, huh? The amount of energy and cash you can save by keeping uninhabited spaces unlit is worth adding this task to your routine.

✔ **Impose a policy of turning all computers and lights off at night.** Even though most new computers have sleep or hibernate modes, the officials who provide Energy Star ratings (see the later section "Replacing old equipment with green alternatives" for more on Energy Star certification) still assert that turning off your computer at night maximizes energy savings. Even in sleep mode, a computer uses about 3 watts per hour, so shut it off completely on weekends and at night. Assign a different person each week (or month) to make sure all computers and lights are turned off at night until the practice becomes a habit for everyone. You can certainly mandate that all PCs and desktops be turned off even though servers may need to be on for backup purposes.

✔ **Moderate the thermostats by a few degrees.** Optimal temperature in your office depends, of course, on what part of the country you operate in. However, the suggested "responsible" indoor temperatures for commercial and residential facilities are 64 degrees Fahrenheit in the winter and 78 degrees Fahrenheit in the summer. Energy savings can be dramatic for even a one or two degree shift in average indoor temperature. Make sure to let staff know that tweaking the temp is an integral part of your business's overall energy-efficiency efforts. They'll figure out how to dress appropriately pretty quickly.

Always be sure to evaluate the impact implementing an energy-efficiency idea will have on your organization as a whole — including your employees. Potential problems arise when the response to a new temperature policy yields a rash of under-the-desk space heaters. Depending on the type of personal space heater, these devices can suck more energy than you're saving with a facility-wide temperature reduction. Policing the office for violations gets awkward, so save yourself the potential frustration and definite expenses by consistently directing green messaging toward your employees.

To make the green sell easier to your staff, show them the summarized results of your baseline energy audit (described in the preceding section) and track the progress you're making together toward reducing monthly kilowatt usage on a chart in the breakroom or in the monthly newsletter. People tend to feel great when they can see the results of their efforts. Tie the reduced energy usage into cost savings and reiterate that your company is positioning itself for the future by becoming less reliant on volatile energy. Take some of the savings and host a quarterly get-together to celebrate your group efforts. In any event, continually reinforce that together, as a group, you're making your company stronger by your efforts.

Lightening up on your lighting

Looking at the lighting in your office space as a platform for increasing sustainability can yield some real triple-bottom-line results. In an average office building, lighting can consume up to 50 percent of total energy used. The impact, therefore, of conserving energy through lighting retrofits can be quite significant. Also, increased worker productivity due to decreased eye strain from natural lighting (a key component of sustainable lighting) is another key benefit. The triple-bottom-line impact is rounded out by reduced carbon emissions from more efficient lighting.

If the idea of sustainable lighting increasing worker productivity seems a bit hard to swallow, consider that when furniture company Herman Miller built its new LEED-certified furniture plant in Zeeland, Michigan, the lighting (featuring daylighting and state-of-the-art sustainable lighting) was widely given credit for increased employee productivity in the ensuing year. Although productivity can be difficult to measure accurately, one statistic stands tall: More than 50 percent of the employees had perfect attendance records in the subsequent year. With the combined productivity increase and cost savings from a green building, the facility paid for itself within the first year of operations. At $525 per square foot, that wasn't a small feat!

Not up for a major office overhaul at this point? Don't worry. The easiest way to lessen energy expended by lighting, without major retrofitting, is to encourage habit-changing behaviors in everyone down the corridor. Lowering wattage and reducing the amount of time lights are actually on are the two most effective energy-reduction techniques that can be made, according to the American Lighting Association.

Check out the following list to get some additional ideas of minor lighting conversions that pack a big energy-savings punch:

- ✔ **Replacing incandescent light bulbs with compact fluorescent light bulbs (CFLs):** This advice may sound trite, but changing out your old incandescents for CFLs immediately reduces your expended lighting energy by 50 to 80 percent. Additionally, a single 18-watt CFL (replacing a 75-watt incandescent) generates a $45 lifetime savings (assuming an 8-cent-per-killowatt-hour energy cost). When multiplied by the number of standard bulbs in your company, my guess is that savings tallies to a significant number.

- ✔ **Adding dimmers, motion sensors, or automatic shut-offs on existing lights:** Don't feel like relying on yourself or your staff to turn off lights? Hand the task over to technology! These lighting controls don't increase the energy required to operate the unit, but (depending on the specifics of what you install) they can reduce the amount of time any given light is on, thereby increasing efficiency.

✔ **Converting desk lamps to cutting-edge LED lamps:** This new lighting technology, which relies on *light-emitting diodes,* is even more highly efficient than compact fluorescents. It's also coming down in price and widening in availability. In the old days, LEDs were only used as indicator lights. However, as the materials used in LEDs have grown more sophisticated, LEDs have become bright enough to be used for illumination in lamps and other lighting fixtures.

✔ **Decreasing lighting used in overlit areas:** Simply switching from four-lamp fixtures to three- or even two-lamp fixtures can reduce both energy inefficiencies and their associated costs.

Selecting the most efficient lighting for your office requires balancing a complicated stew of ingredients, which include lamp ballast platform performance (as measured in lumens per watt), color-rendering indices, task assessment, lamp life, and, oh yeah — cost!

Ousting old office equipment

It's fairly common knowledge that commercial buildings contribute significantly to carbon dioxide emissions in North America. What you may not realize is that the office equipment within them represents the third largest energy draw within these structures, after lighting and heating, ventilation, and air conditioning (HVAC) systems. Additionally, if the building isn't vented properly, the heat all this equipment produces ramps up the structure's air conditioning requirements significantly.

What office isn't virtually humming with PCs, servers, printers, and peripherals? Office equipment is an area of tremendous energy drain with big cost implications. The American Council for an Energy Efficient Economy states that the daily workhorses in society's offices directly consume 7 percent of total commercial electric energy, which translates to an astounding $1.8 billion in electricity costs to businesses annually.

The Energy Star labeling program has identified the following pieces of equipment as high-priority items: computers, monitors, printers, fax machines, copiers, scanners, and multifunction devices. Identifying which exact piece in your office is ripe for replacement is completely dependent on the age, make, and usage of that item. Copiers use more energy per unit that any other piece of office equipment, so set it to sleep mode, if you have that option, when you close the office for the day.

In the next two sections, I help you figure out how to turn your energy-guzzling office equipment into active components of your overall sustainability plan.

A quick primer on choosing and disposing of CFLs

If there's one icon of the green movement, it's the swirly, ice cream cone–looking compact fluorescent light bulb (CFL). This little guy can cut your energy expenses by up to 80 percent simply by installing it. Shopping for anything, whether it's for personal or professional life, is always a little daunting the first go around. Because CFLs have only been on the scene a few years, I provide you with some guidance as to what you should be looking for in the sea of new lighting lingo and labels:

✔ **Choose the color temperature of the bulb.** Around 2700K is a warm white (which looks just like an incandescent), and around 5000K constitutes a cool white (which gives off a white-blue light).

✔ **Choose the appropriate number of watts.** *Watts* measure energy used, whereas *lumens* measure light strength. A quick rule of thumb when converting incandescent wattage to CFL wattage is to divide by four. So, for example, if you want to switch from a 100-watt incandescent, you'll be safe with about a 25-watt CFL.

✔ **Choose the right shape for your fixture.** CFLs are available in a variety of shapes to fit a range of lamps and lighting fixtures.

✔ **Find a local place to recycle CFLs.** These efficient little bulbs have one problem — they contain trace amounts of mercury. Recycling is available at IKEA (find the store closest to you at www.ikea.com) and possibly at your local hardware store or recycling center.

Making a list of life-expectancy expiration dates

If you have an idea of when computers, faxes, copy machines, and the like may be on their way out the door, you can more easily construct a green replacement strategy, which is then reflected in your new purchasing policies.

Start by pulling an inventory of your office equipment as it stands today. The easiest way to acquire this info is probably by grabbing it from the depreciation schedule (typically housed with accounting staff) or from your purchasing manager, if he or she is charged with asset management. (If you operate a very small business, turn to your tax returns for this info instead.) Then assign an estimated life expectancy to each asset based on the date the equipment was purchased so that you can efficiently plan for green replacements in your budget. *Note:* This step will likely require a conversation with the office manager, purchasing guru, or company accountant — all of whom should have the appropriate records if you don't.

Taking stock of your current office equipment's expiration dates can also help you get a grasp on your e-waste volume and address the own-or-lease question outlined in the later "Opting for utility over ownership" section.

Replacing old equipment with green alternatives

Your primary purchasing policy modification may mandate an office equipment replacement policy that requires obsolete office pieces (think the junky copier that only works three days out of the week, or the fax machine that long since stopped printing every page) be replaced with a certified Energy Star equivalent. Products with Energy Star ratings, on average, use 25 to 50 percent less energy than their traditional counterparts. And depending on the item in question, this energy savings can quickly offer a significant contribution to the return on your capital investment.

Of course, choosing a model that meets your operational needs varies as widely as the type of tasks you're asking the equipment to perform. When comparing costs of certified versus noncertified equipment, keep in mind that Energy Star–labeled computers, monitors, fax machines, copiers, or printers usually save more than $80 per product, per year.

If you're prioritizing replacement by projected savings, consider the following high-impact change-outs:

✔ **Copiers:** These gluttons use more energy per unit than any other piece of office equipment. Without power management, most of the energy is expended when the copier is inactive. To receive Energy Star certification, a copier must have automatic duplexing capabilities because it takes ten times as much energy to produce a piece of paper as it does to place an image on one.

✔ **Computers:** Consider requiring that all new computer purchases be Energy Star–certified. Because of the huge amount of hours computers are used every day, the EPA's requirements for computers and their peripherals are very demanding. The Energy Star logo assures you that energy savings are embodied in a qualifying computer's stand-by, sleep, and active modes, and that more efficient internal power supplies are used.

✔ **Monitors:** More than 50 percent of energy expended on a desktop computer system is attributable to the monitor. An Energy Star–qualified monitor uses 90 percent less electricity than a monitor without power management.

✔ **Printers and fax machines:** Printers can only be assessed based on which category they belong to. Each category yields a wide range of energy-consumption patterns. For instance, laser and LED printers with power-management systems can use less than half the energy of a conventional laser model. But the real efficient worker is the old-fashioned ink jet, which uses less energy because it doesn't require heat fusion to function. In general, printers that have earned the Energy Star certification use 60 percent less energy than their competitors.

Decoding Energy Star and EPEAT

As you investigate more sustainable office equipment and products, you're probably going to run across the terms *Energy Star* and *EPEAT* quite frequently. Here's what they mean and why they're relevant:

✔ **Energy Star** is an ecolabeling program developed and administered by the U.S. Environmental Protection Agency (EPA). The logo, which you can read more about and see in Chapter 10, is now used in many countries. It signifies that the item in question possesses a high level of energy efficiency. The Energy Star rating is available in more than 50 product categories, including appliances, computers/peripherals, buildings, and many consumer products.

✔ **EPEAT** is a system developed by the Institute of Electrical and Electronics Engineers to help purchasers assess desktops, monitors, and notebooks. Check out the EPEAT Registered Products Search Tool found at www.epeat.net to see at a glance how the listed product categories match up with three tiers of environmental performance.

Don't be fooled by the abundance of pseudo Energy Star logos ("energy smart," "energy solutions," and so on) that may trick you into thinking an item has complied with EPA energy-reduction parameters. The only EPA-sanctioned logo is Energy Star. Visit www.energystar.gov, click the Buildings & Plants link, and then click the Purchasing & Procurement link in the Quick Finder box on the right-hand side of the page. From there, simply click the Office Products link to find Energy Star–certified items you can use in your office.

Greening your IT department

For companies with an IT department, a ton of opportunities exist to radically reduce energy consumption — and save money in the process. Involving your IT professional in a discussion surrounding any comprehensive mid- and long-term design strategies is imperative if you want to green the department successfully.

Here are some questions you can pose to IT pros to get the conversation flowing:

✔ **Do we need the server on 24/7?** Actively managing your server for energy efficiency may be an energy-reduction target area for you. The average server costs $700 per year to run in a low utility rate area, according to Ken Brill with the Uptime Institute. Between 10 and 30 percent of the energy consumption in a typical data center is for servers and storage that most businesses don't actively manage.

> ✔ **Where is the data center housed?** Heat management in data centers is a trying issue for all companies. Analyze it from both facilities' and IT's requirement standpoints to ensure that the location within the facility optimizes the HVAC system as well as IT needs.

There's a whole new movement of IT professionals collaborating on how to maximize computing performance while reducing environmental impact. To catch the wave (or to find such an IT pro if you don't already have one onboard), check out the Association of Information Technology Professionals at `www.aitp.org`. One the group's annual conferences was centered around two days of sustainability-oriented discussions. Also, try signing up for *Greener Computing* (`www.greenercomputing.com`), a free weekly e-news-letter that offers a column and access to all the current green techie journal articles you can possibly ingest.

Reducing Waste

As your company begins to recognize that reducing usage on the front end also reduces the need to manage waste on the back end, your costs will begin to decrease. Cost considerations include employee/contractor time for folks who manage recycling efforts and the cost of receptacles, as well as the opportunity cost of space dedicated to recycling (if it takes potential workspace). Also, purchasing nondisposable items, such as office and breakroom supplies, for example) may cost more upfront, but doing so yields savings in the long term.

Office waste is often heavily made up of paper, nonfunctional electronics, disposable supplies, and packaging. Cutting down on all that miscellaneous waste requires figuring out ways to reuse products, reduce absolute usage (as well as reliance on disposable products), and recycle those objects that can't be reused or cut back on as easily. In the following sections, I show you how to zero in on the amount of waste currently generated at your office and how to cut that number down through waste-reduction and recycling efforts.

Obviously, some money will need to be thrown into this effort, but keeping it to a minimum is a good idea. When considering the design of a recycling center, for example, you don't need the most expensive, heavy-duty bins if your center is located inside the building. Also, sometimes recycling services provide complimentary bins. If yours doesn't, you can use large cardboard appliance boxes; these serve the receptacle purpose perfectly well.

Behavior change is one thing, more work is another. The more convenient you make behavior change for your employees, the more likely they'll climb onboard the waste-reduction train and come up with innovative ways to decrease your company's waste stream. Diffusing resistance to change isn't always easy. The best advice I can give is to ease into changes slowly and offer lots of accolades for the efforts being made. Keep communicating about the importance of becoming a green company that's poised to function in the new ecoera.

Use the following tips to expand your communication efforts to new and existing employees:

- **Train new employees.** Communicate your expectations that resources should be used carefully and that each person should fully participate in waste-reduction programs. Explain how to prevent waste and recycle materials.

- **Use employee events and gatherings to promote waste reduction.** Show what's being done well and what areas need improvement.

- **Solicit ideas from employees.** Involve your workforce in the company's waste-reduction efforts to give them ownership of the program.

- **Ask employees to sign a waste-reduction pledge.** Research shows that when a person signs his or her name to something, that individual has a higher propensity to carry through with the action.

Conducting a waste assessment

Getting a grasp on where to look for areas where you can cut back your waste is simpler than you may think. Start by compiling a list of all the different places waste originates (taking a close look at workrooms, restrooms, cafeterias, breakrooms, and individual offices), specifically addressing

- Discarded office supplies, packaging, and other general personal waste. Look at the contents of central collection bins where individual baskets are dumped.

- Obsolete equipment and furniture and fixtures.

- Lawn and garden detritus. Try to get an idea of the quantity and size of leaves, grass, and other trimmings that are dumped. How many bags per week are dumped, and how many weeks per year does this dumping occur?

The key to lassoing in the amount of waste generated in your office is to first figure out the source point: Where is waste generated?

You may want to actually take a close peek at your facility's dumpsters to get a preliminary idea as to what's in 'em. Figure 6-1 offers a sample worksheet you can use to fill in what you see.

After you know how much waste your business is generating, determine how much of it is potentially recyclable. This amount will be specific to your locale and may require a call to your waste-removal provider or recycling service to get a list of potential recyclables. Additionally, many communities have a special center for lawn trimmings. You may consider letting grass trimming mulch rather than wasting costly and unnecessary lawn bags, as well as landfill space.

Figure 6-1:
An easy way to compile rough data regarding dumpster contents.

| Monitoring Sheet | | | | | | | | |
| Observer: | | | | | | | | |

Estimated Percentage of Garbage from Each Source in Dumpsters

	Approximate Depth of Garbage	Paper	Cardboard	Aluminum Cans	Plastic Bottles	Lawn Waste	Other Plastic	Food Waste	Other
Dumpster 1 (Location)									
Dumpster 2 (Location)									
Dumpster 3 (Location)									

Exploring quick and easy waste-reducing actions

Not all waste-reduction projects are time-intensive. Some general tips of the trade for reducing office waste (and causing an immediate impact on your triple bottom line!) include

- **Reducing business junk mail:** You can start by checking out the resources found at the Business Junk Mail Reduction Project (your. kingcounty.gov/solidwaste/nwpc; click the Reduce Business Junk Mail link). You can also register your company's name and mailing address to get employees who've left your organization off of mailing lists via the EcoLogical Mail Coalition's Web site (www.ecological mail.org). The service is free, but be prepared to give it six months before you see a direct reduction in business junk mail.

- **Banning colored papers, high-gloss products, and the like that aren't recyclable:** Notice that many product tags, labels, and inserts, as well as marketing materials, are now imprinted on unbleached, recycled paper.

- **Making cloth tote bags available so that plastic bags aren't needed for office shopping trips:** Depending on how many quick trips you make from your office, you could wind up saving quite a few bags every month.

- **Ridding the office of disposable items:** Compostable alternatives are available for many disposable breakroom products, such as paper plates, napkins, plastic cutlery, and cups. Office supplies, such as refillable pens, are much greener than throwaways. Batteries should be rechargeable; 15 billion batteries are produced a year and a large majority of them are alkaline disposables. Question anything that's disposable and ask your vendor or office supply store if there are any reusable or compostable alternatives to the product in question.

✔ **Ending your supply of Styrofoam cups for coffee and asking employees to bring their own coffee mugs:** You'll be reducing your business's footprint and encouraging staff to actively engage in a greening effort that's easy and feels good.

✔ **Removing bottled water from vending machines and office refrigerators:** Interestingly enough, the Environmental Protection Agency's standards for tap water are *more* stringent than standards set forth by the Food & Drug Administration for bottled water, so get rid of the bottled water and return to good old water from the tap. If your company is located in a place where tap water doesn't taste good or may be of a suspicious quality, install a faucet filter to remove trace chemicals and bacteria.

The amount of fossil fuels consumed in the extraction, production, packaging, and transportation of bottled water is truly stunning. Then there's that nasty disposal problem. Estimates on the number of disposable water bottles that wind up in American landfills range from 10 to 28 billion (yes, with a *b*). Peter Gleick, a water policy expert and director at the Pacific Institute, estimates that when you add up the energy impact of the entire life cycle of a bottle of water, it's like "filling up a quarter of every bottle with oil." Additionally, it takes approximately 3 liters of extracted water to produce 1 actual liter of bottled water.

Have a local vendor make hard-plastic water bottles with your logo and company name on them and give 'em out as Christmas presents. Make sure they're the new Bisphenol A (BPA) free bottles, available from a prominent outdoor hydration company.

Minimizing paper waste

As you're looking to decrease usage of natural capital in your daily office life, minimizing paper used plays an important role. Those reams of paper come from trees that sequester carbon dioxide, which helps to minimize the effects of greenhouse gas emissions. Fewer trees mean more carbon in the atmosphere. In addition, milling, packaging, and transporting paper are all highly energy-intensive activities. For example, the Palo Alto Research Center's study shows that it takes the equivalent of 60 watt-hours of energy to produce one single sheet of paper. That's for production only — not for transporting that sheet or imprinting an image on it. The real shocker comes from the nonprofit Conservatree (www.conservatree.com): A ton of (non-recycled) printing and office paper uses 24 trees (a mix of softwood and hardwood trees standing 40 feet tall and 6 to 8 inches in diameter).

Recycling paper saves trees and uses 60 percent less energy than manufacturing paper from virgin timber. In addition, producing recycled paper causes 74 percent less air pollution and 35 percent less water pollution, and it creates five times the number of jobs as producing virgin paper does.

Despite the benefits of recycling paper, make reducing your paper use your true goal. Why? Because recycling paper is still energy intensive. Whether you establish a company-wide goal or ask each department for a reduction goal depends on your company size and organizational culture.

To help identify your opportunities for reducing paper waste, ask for three to five specific paper-reduction strategies from each department of the company so you can investigate the ideas for potential. After all, most managers know intuitively where the majority of their paper usage is concentrated. If HR still runs paper paychecks, this department may submit "converting to electronic checks" as one of its ideas. Likewise, marketing may have long considered changing up its advertising mix to focus more on an online presence and less on largely ineffective, paper-wasting mass mailers.

Want to get the ball rolling without waiting for the feedback of various departments? Try implementing some of these simple ways to decrease the amount of paper generated in your office:

- **Edit documents on your PC rather than on hard copies.** This is an easy and efficient way to save paper. In fact, the more you do it, the easier it becomes.

- **Take paper that has been printed on one side and convert it to note pads.** By doing so, you get two lives out of one piece of paper. If printing hard copies is absolutely necessary, you can also print drafts of documents on the back sides of printed paper. When you're done with the draft, recycle it instead of trashing it.

- **Require ½-inch margins on all documents.** This move can save up to one page for every three pages printed. Pretty impressive for a couple clicks of a mouse! The easiest way to make this change is to adjust the defaults to Narrow if you're using *Microsoft Word.* Doing so sets margins to a ½ inch on the top, bottom, left, and right portions of the page. In other programs, look for the screen to set margins in and choose Custom. The view may take a bit to get used to because there's more text on the page, but after a month, you'll feel like your documents have always looked this way.

- **Print on both sides of the paper.** Double-sided printing is a no-brainer and deserves to be a mandatory policy in your office. Review your printer's manual to make sure it can automatically handle *duplex printing* (a fancy term for *double-sided*). Alternatively, you can check out the print dialog area in word-processing documents. Click the Properties menu, review the options, and scan for Duplex Printing or Two-Sided Printing. If you see either term, then your printer is configured to handle automatic duplex printing. (*Note:* If you have several printers, you need to check out each one individually to assess its automatic double-sided copying potential. However, if your printer also functions as a copier and is capable of double-sided copying, you're probably good to go for automatic duplexing.)

If your printer isn't equipped for automatic duplexing, you'll have to do your double-sided printing manually — meaning you first send a print job and print the odd-numbered pages Then you flip those pages over and print the even-numbered pages. To do this, go to the print dialog box and check Manual Duplex. It may take a few practice sessions to figure out how to pull the paper out and flip it so that the second page is right side up on the back of the first page. After you've figured it out for your printer, post a note nearby so that everyone in your office can easily see how to manually print double-sided.

Certain older printers don't support duplex printing in any format. When you send this printer to e-waste heaven, make sure that your procurement policy states that all future printers must be capable of duplex printing.

✔ **Invest in green printing software.** Some printers are now being bundled with green printing software called *GreenPrint*. This program neatly identifies and eliminates unnecessary pages (like those containing only a legal disclaimer, URL address, or Web banners) and converts files automatically to PDF format for easy document sharing. It also tracks the number of pages and associated costs so you can capture the savings and toot your own green horn. The average savings per user is about $90 and 1,400 pieces of paper annually. You can check out the details at www.printgreener.com.

Purchasing environmentally friendly goods

You may be hesitant to lay out more money upfront for a green product that doesn't appear to enhance business value in the short term. But as you move toward triple-bottom-line thinking, you'll start to see the value in measuring purchases in longer time frames and by their impact on people, planet, and profit. Purchasing products that don't end up in your waste stream and need to be repurchased again and again is clearly beneficial to all three bottom lines.

Following are some environmentally friendly office products for your consideration. *Note:* It doesn't matter which of these items you start using first; using any of 'em is an important ecostep in the right direction!

✔ **Solar-power devices:** These solar chargers can contribute to reducing waste from disposed batteries and nonrenewable energy usage. They sport onboard battery packs that juice up while the solar cells are harvesting those wonderful renewable rays. The battery packs then deliver the power, on demand, to your device of choice. The options for on-the-go solar power are growing, so be sure to check them out carefully.

These devices are new to the market, but you can keep abreast of new discussion out there in cyberspace at blogs.consumerreports.org/electronics. Just type "solar power mobile" (or whatever particular device you're interested in seeing others' opinions of) into the search engine and see who's saying what.

✔ **Rechargeable electronics and a battery charger:** By investing in rechargeables, you can eliminate an unnecessary source of office waste in a snap. After all, just consider the number of office products that require batteries: cell phones, office tools, Bluetooth devices, laptops, digital and video camcorders, and PDAs.

✔ **Recycled toner cartridges:** Lots of outlets sell toner and offer price breaks on new cartridges for trading in the old ones. The old cartridges are then refilled and sold at a discount. The number of times a particular type of cartridge can be refilled is limited. For example, laser printers come with a drum that in most cases can only be refilled once or twice.

Unfortunately, using refilled cartridges in new equipment will void the manufacturer's warranty should a problem arise, so you may want to wait until a printer's warranty expires to begin using recycled cartridges. In the meantime, save your spent cartridges because they can be refilled and used when the warranty is up.

✔ **Undated and erasable wall calendars:** Forget those disposable paper calendars and make the one-time investment in an item that virtually never needs to be replaced. This is a super-easy to eliminate waste at your office.

✔ **Paper that's responsibly produced:** The three most important factors to look at when seeking out responsibly produced office paper include the following:

- **Post-consumer waste (PCW) paper:** Based on your printing volume and the price differential, begin the transition to PCW paper. This may be something you phase into. For example, a transitional period may include a plan to immediately institute a minimum PCW content of 50 percent, with 100 percent as the goal within 12 months. Always look for unbleached paper.

- **Forest Stewardship Council (FSC) certification:** The Council is a nonprofit organization that certifies forest products that use responsibly harvested fibers. When purchasing virgin paper, look for the FSC stamp (shown in Chapter 10). However, purchasing recycled paper over virgin paper should always be a priority.

- **Bleaching method:** When purchasing white paper, look for non-chlorine-based bleaches. PCF (which stands for processed chlorine free) is the most desirable for recycled fiber; TCF (which stands for totally chlorine free) is the way to go for virgin fiber.

Developing an office recycling program

When it comes to starting up an office recycling program, first and foremost, you have to solicit senior management's buy-in to the whole recycling scene. Not only do you require their support but you also need to garner their budget approval for your start-up costs. Resource allocation is a must, with the goal being to grow the organizational and environmental impact as the plan increases in scope. Office recycling is an imperative program when your company is greening, and it's easy to tie in from a mission-congruence standpoint (less waste, better for the environment).

The next few sections outline how you can design a comprehensive recycling program for your place of business.

Identifying your recycling program's leadership

To have a successful office recycling program, you need to appoint a recycling coordinator who can manage all facets of the effort. The most critical criterion in selecting this person is that he or she is truly interested in the program. The obvious place to look within your organization is the facilities department, but that's not mandatory. The recycling coordinator can come from any department, but be aware that as the program grows, it may be necessary to modify this person's job description accordingly. Try using encouraging phrases like "This is a great opportunity to demonstrate leadership skills" and offering incentivizing caveats when you begin recruiting for your program's leadership.

The recycling coordinator may need to organize a recycling task force. Depending on the size of your organization, this task force may include representation from each department within the company. Make sure to get the building custodians' input and concerns right upfront. They're the ones who'll have the skinny on content, process, and ways to streamline any preliminary ideas, because they're mostly in charge of the day-to-day waste handling.

Designing a collection system for recyclables

An efficient and effective office recycling program also requires a game plan. That's why designing an internal collection system for recyclables within your organization is essential. Your system will vary based on the size of your organization and whether you occupy seven floors in a Manhattan high rise; are disbursed over two office campuses in Puget Sound; or are a small, remote, rural operation north of El Paso. The person who designs the system will also depend on your individual organization's characteristics. If your business is quite small, then the recycling coordinator designs the program; if your business is midsized, you can probably have the whole recycling task force chip in.

Regardless, the primary consideration for all entities is the same: You need to make recycling as convenient as possible for both the employees and the collection staff.

Carefully consider the following:

- ✔ **What you're going to collect the recyclable materials in:** As you conduct your waste assessment (see the earlier related section within this chapter), notice the volume of each type of recyclable and attempt to identify what sort of receptacle may be appropriate, according to size and ease of use. Office paper requires a different bin than broken-down boxes. Some considerations include

- How much space you have available

- How many of each type of bin will be necessary

✔ **Where the containers are going to be located:** Placement is paramount, so locate recycling bins close to individual workstations as well as within areas of concentrated waste generation — cafeterias, breakrooms, and copying/printing centers. Make sure to use the space efficiently. Too many bins are a waste of space; not enough bins results in chronically full tubs and a lack of employee participation.

✔ **How you'll instruct staff to separate the landfill-bound office debris from the recyclable stuff, and the different types of recyclables from one another:** Signage by recycling bins is very important, because the collection area is an important space to display educational materials. Tell people what can and can't go into each bin. Lots of folks simply don't know that paper clips don't belong in office-paper recycling or that plastic bottles need to be emptied of all liquids before chucking them in the container.

✔ **Who's responsible for the collection and how often will collection take place:** For example, who's going to move the recycling containers from workstations, the cafeteria, the lawn maintenance area, and the like to the centralized storage area for collection or delivery? (See the later section "Designating a centralized storage area for the collection" for more on assigning your centralized spot.) The other side of the equation is the frequency of your collection. Try to coordinate pickups when the bins have reached their capacity, knowing that the timing may vary by time of year or location.

✔ **How you'll get recyclables to their final destination:** Depending on where your company is located, some materials will be picked up curbside, and some will need to be processed (bundled, shredded, or crushed) in preparation for the end users. Does this processing require any specialized equipment? How often do these tasks need to be performed? Who will do that, and after the materials are ready to move on to recycling heaven, how are they moved there? These are all questions you'll need to think about so that your recycling efforts can be the shining green star in your office's ecoefforts.

Modifications to your system will be necessary, so don't be discouraged when the need arises to make some.

Designating a centralized storage area for the collection

Most recycling services pick up from one area, so you need to designate a specific spot as the go-to point for your recycling efforts. Will this recycling center be located inside your facility or outside of it? If inside, allocate ample space for the selected receptacles. If outside, make sure the bins have covers to provide security against local critters. Depending on your part of the country, anything from bears or raccoons to rats can invade your recycling stash, leaving a less-than-pretty sight in its wake.

Pitching the idea to the higher-ups

Unfortunately, an officewide recycling program isn't the easiest project to sell upper management on. Setting up such a program often requires initial capital outlay, ongoing maintenance, an internal person (or team) committed to getting it going, and behavioral changes. However, if you've already picked some of the low-hanging fruit from the energy-conservation tree (see the section "Starting with the low-hanging fruit," earlier in this chapter), you can point to those savings to fund the initial resources needed to get the office recycling gig going.

Or you can always attempt to sway management with some real-life success stories, like that of Ben Franklin Press in Napa, California. This company instituted a program to distribute leftover paper/scrap to local schools and recycle all cardboard and uncoated paper. Its waste-reduction efforts reduced the company's waste-disposal fees by $500 per month *and* benefitted local schoolchildren. Talk about a triple-bottom-line winner!

Following are some tips to help you pitch your recycling program idea:

- ✔ **Get your foot in the door.** Meeting with the right people is critical and usually doable in a small business. In mid-sized organizations, the right folks aren't always apparent, so you have to seek them out.

- ✔ **Determine which decision-makers are crucial to your waste-reduction program.** Depending on your company's size, the CEO, owner, or other senior managers have the ability to make decisions about operations, purchasing, products, packaging, and services. Figure out who makes those calls in your company and start there.

- ✔ **Network.** If you don't have direct access to the decision-makers, find people in your organization who do. Ask for their suggestions on approach. For example, ask whether you should make a presentation. If so, should that presentation contain details or a mere overview? (Some managers like to approve general concepts; others want statistics and research before considering a new idea).

- ✔ **Make your presentation clear, factual, and persuasive.** Stress the fact that if waste can't be reduced voluntarily today, the business may face mandated changes in the future.

As you implement your plan, incrementally or in total, make sure to leave room for assessing its performance. Use a formal evaluation tool that asks maintenance staff, accounting folks, employees, and waste managers (processors, haulers, or end users) to help you calculate the percentage of waste reduction the program has generated. You should have an idea of what your company's waste volume looks like on a weekly basis thanks to your baseline assessment (see the earlier section "Conducting a waste assessment" if you skipped this step). *Anything* being recycled and diverted from the landfill should be considered a success!

Arranging for end-of-life recycling for electronics

A critical piece of analyzing the environmental footprint of your office is to consider in advance what's going to happen to your office electronics when you're done using them. Electronic waste (known as *e-waste*) now poses the fastest growing element of manufacturing waste in North America due to a number of unique problems. Circuit boards, batteries, monitors, color cathode ray tubes (CRTs), and batteries all contain heavy metals such as mercury, hexavalent chromium, and lead. When these metals are improperly disposed of (that is, thrown in a landfill), toxins may leach into groundwater or be released into the air.

As the volume of e-waste (and society's understanding of its negative impact) has mounted, more businesses are trying to figure out how to responsibly handle this new waste stream. In the European Union, for example, a new directive mandated that the producers of electronic products take them back and deal with their end-of-life liability issues. Guess what happened in the EU in response? The focus of product design for electronics shifted to easy disassembly and recyclability, because disposal of heavy, metal-laden articles is no longer an option.

Ask your office equipment vendor whether it has a *take-back policy,* a type of voluntary policy (or a law in some states) that requires a manufacturer to take back its products at the end of their useful lives, thereby placing the onus for disposal on the original producer.

You can also consider taking advantage of the booming electronics recycling business. But before you hand off your e-waste, be sure to research the collection firm. Many of these so-called recycling businesses are selling the old electronics to e-waste "brokers." The discarded electronics are then shipped to developing countries with negligible environmental standards (primarily India, Kenya, and China) where 25-cent-per-hour laborers (often children) remove valuable parts like circuit boards and burn off the plastic on electrical cords over charcoal fires to harvest the copper wire. The remaining worthless parts are dumped and remain to contaminate the local area. These "recyclers" are in fact expending a ton of fossil fuels to move heavy metals from North American landfills to the "disposal sites" of the developing world.

To find a reputable e-waste recycler, go to the list of e-stewards found at the Basel Action Network (BAN) Web site (www.ban.org). BAN is a nonprofit group that monitors the global toxic waste trade, providing a qualified list of North American recyclers called *e-stewards* — responsible recyclers that have signed the BAN pledge and met all disassembly and recycling environmental regulations. Many of these organizations have mail-in service for electronics recycling. (***Note:*** Recycling e-waste is a budgetary line item. I'm not going to kid you about that. It should be incorporated in the IT budget.)

Changing Purchasing Practices for Office Supplies

Implementing green office purchasing policies goes a long way toward reducing your office's carbon footprint. Major water, waste, and energy-reduction initiatives can all be driven in large part by your company's purchasing policies. Chapter 7 offers detailed coverage of how your company can green its supply chain, so suffice it to say that many of the action items referred to in *this* chapter (such as rethinking whether ownership of office equipment is necessary and adopting sustainable office supply purchasing policies) originate from within your company rather than from without.

In very small organizations, one or two people may purchase the office supplies. In a mid-sized organization, however, you can probably find a centralized purchasing department. Modifications in procurement policy play a big role in either setup.

Opting for utility over ownership

One of the four premises of Natural Capitalism (see Chapter 3 for a more in-depth explanation of this sustainability framework) is converting a product-based economy to a service and flow economy. A *service and flow economy* contributes to increased value for the customer and betters the bottom line for the vendor, because both parties' interests are now aligned. Basically, it favors the concept of opting for utility over ownership.

Ownership of many items that businesses rely on to conduct operations isn't necessarily desirable. Often what businesses want are the services that the items provide. For example, many small and mid-sized enterprises aren't necessarily interested in owning copiers, faxes, computers, HVAC units, commercial carpets, or office furniture. Instead, they want the *utility* of those items — they desire the functions these objects can provide for their businesses.

Transferring responsibilities of ownership to the company that produces the goods you need changes all the rules of the game. Suddenly, these companies are intimately vested in producing high-quality, durable products that efficiently provide the services they're intended to. Additionally, companies become interested in their products' end-of-life liability issues, disposal costs, recyclability, and so on.

Just look at what one company was able to do. Ray Anderson, president of the international flooring systems company Interface, Inc., was a visionary in reconfiguring the company's primary product — commercial carpet tiles — into a service. Instead of selling commercial carpeting, Interface leases the tiles, replacing high-traffic-area tiles as they wear out. The old tiles are remanufactured into new tiles as part of the lease costs. In this closed-loop system, raw material use decreases dramatically and zero waste becomes an achievable goal. In short, everyone wins!

Ask your vendors about leasing programs or actively solicit new vendors that engage in them.

An added bonus of opting for utility over ownership is that the customer thus converts a capital expenditure (which is written off over time through depreciation expense) into an immediate deduction, thereby decreasing his taxable income and reducing his corporate tax bill. Doing more with less doesn't sound half bad now, huh?

Considering the source of your supplies

One aspect of sustainability includes the source of products or services, in an environmental capacity as well as a socially responsible capacity. Acquiring your office supplies from a sustainable vendor counts just as much toward positioning yourself as a truly green business as the sustainability of the end product you offer your customers. Fortunately, you have control over the sourcing of your office supplies.

- ✓ **Choose to source your office supplies as close to home as possible.** Ideally, your office essentials should come from your local region or from within North America. If you require a certain item that has to come from far away, make sure to look for sweatshop-free designations, usually offered by reputable third parties.

- ✓ **Incorporate specific sustainability requirements when requesting bids.** Depending on what it is you're sourcing, identify what green attributes you want to see incorporated in that product or service and specify that in the bid. For example, tell office equipment vendors that you want a fax machine that handles PCW paper or insist that your lawn care company use natural fertilizers.

- ✓ **Specify Energy Star–certified or EPEAT–qualified products in your contracts or purchase orders.** The Energy Star rating signifies that the item in question possesses a high level of energy efficiency. EPEAT provides a similar assessment for computers (both desktop and laptop) and monitors.

It may be helpful to award your office contracts based on a point system. Of course, that leads to the question of how many points do you allocate for green product attributes and how many do you give to a vendor that actively practices corporate social responsibility. The answer is truly up to you and your individual business needs and preferences. Depending on what you decide you want to emphasize and how your procurement system works, assigning additional points for desirable attributes can be a way to lean toward selecting greener suppliers.

Shelling out for sustainable and nontoxic office items

Purchasing environmentally sound office products, both for daily use (supplies) as well as long-term use (furniture and fixtures) is an important part of greening your office. The costs may be higher for some of these products. However, as the number of suppliers and available alternatives increase, prices are decreasing for many items. In each of the next few sections, I cover the specific cost-benefit issues related to common office items that you can replace with green alternatives. Of course, any recycled-content or local purchases you make are an integral part of messaging your company as one that isn't just thinking sustainably but is also acting accordingly.

Ecofriendly office décor

When considering decorating your office with sustainable purchases, you may find that seemingly similar items cost more upfront. But at the same time, the overall costs are less because that bamboo bookcase will last longer than its cheaper, foreign alternative. Consequently, you'll get more lifetime usage from it, thereby decreasing the item's overall costs. Additionally, depending on the particulars of the product, green office décor items don't contribute to poor indoor air quality through the distribution of volatile organic compounds (VOCs).

Textiles should be from a readily renewable and natural source (such as bamboo, hemp, wool, or organic cotton). Picture frames should be made from recyclable parts and be easy to disassemble and recycle. (Wood frames in particular should be certified by the Forest Stewardship Council.) Glues, foams, adhesives, coatings, and solvents should be water- or biobased, meaning they're nontoxic and don't release VOCs.

Lots of companies are jumping onboard and touting green pieces in their product lines, so when shopping for sustainable office décor, make sure to ask questions to protect yourself against *greenwashing* (when a business states that it's green without taking the actions necessary to back up that statement). Probe as to third-party certifications and what specific attributes make a product sustainable.

Green cleaning supplies

Environmentally friendly office cleaning supplies were forever fairly obscure, very expensive, and often not as effective as their chemically based counterparts. Luckily, this product group has evolved dramatically — in large part due to the nasty side effects of toxins and VOCs found in traditional cleaning supplies, which read like a laundry list of health hazards.

Purchasing green cleaning products is an issue that's making a big splash in the media of late. You may be questioning why your business would want to spend the extra money to purchase these items. Consider the following triple-bottom-line ramifications:

- **Worker safety and health issues:** The list of hazardous chemicals contained in traditional cleaning supplies is truly staggering. Exposure to these toxins, particularly if your office facilities don't have adequate ventilation, can directly affect workers' health, productivity, and morale. So clearly switching to green cleaning supplies is a boon for the people part of the triple bottom line.

- **Disposal costs:** This one affects both the planet and profit aspects of the triple bottom line. Any leftover toxic office products must be disposed of in an approved manner. You can't pour them down the drain, into storm sewers, or in the trash because of the polluting compounds they're made of. Recycling and disposing of hazardous materials isn't free, but with nontoxic cleaning supplies, these costs disappear.

Raising the bar on office furniture

Herman Miller has won a number of design awards, including a Smithsonian National Design Award, for its beautiful, green office furniture. This furniture manufacturer, with more than $1.5 billion in annual revenues, produces its furniture in a LEED-certified green building in Zeeland, Michigan. The company's sustainability efforts are encompassed in its "Perfect Vision Program: 2020" — an internal deadline to achieve an ambitious range of sustainability targets, including zero landfill impact, zero hazardous waste generation, zero carbon emissions from manufacturing, and a minimum LEED Silver certification for all facilities.

Herman Miller already uses 100-percent green energy to meet its power needs and has formally instituted a Design for the Environment product evaluation method (see Chapter 7 for more on this approach to product design). Its protocol for sustainability looks at each proposed product in terms of material chemistry, ease of disassembly, recyclability, and recycled content.

The company's award winning Mirra chair is 96-percent recyclable and contains 42-percent recycled material. It has no polyvinyl chloride (PVC) and is produced using green energy. The textile is hemp, which doesn't require pesticides. New work surface materials were introduced in 2004, including bamboo veneer. Herman Miller's quest for sustainability is apparent in everything it does and is a real inspiration to all companies looking to increase their greening efforts.

Herman Miller has been honored with *Business Ethics* magazine's 100 Best Corporate Citizens designation and has been repeatedly cited by *Fortune* magazine as the Most Admired company in its industry. The laundry list of awards it has received is a testament to how well Herman Miller's greening efforts have served its corporate image. You can see this list for yourself by going to www.hermanmiller.com, clicking the About Us link (in the Just browsing column), clicking the Who We Are link, and then clicking the Awards and Recognition link on the right-hand side of the page.

So what exactly are natural cleaners?

✔ They're made from natural, renewable resources such as citrus oils, coconuts, and other plant-based materials.

✔ Their ingredients are all biodegradable.

✔ They're cruelty free, meaning no animals were used in their testing.

✔ They're completely (or almost completely) free of petroleum, and they're totally free of phosphorus and bleach.

✔ They don't use aerosols.

If your cleaning supplies manufacturer claims that its components are organic, sustainably harvested, toxin free, and/or recyclable, great! But who says so? Always double-check that all certifications are legit. If your inquiries provoke discomfort or a downright blank look, you can feel reasonably sure that this line of supposed green products is a marketing tactic and not the real deal. If your vendor is comfortable giving you frank answers, you can use those responses to determine the credibility of product claims and compare the product with others on the market.

If you really want to verify the authenticity of green cleaning supplies, look for the Green Seal. This certification, provided by the organization of the same name, is the stamp of authenticity when it comes to toxin-free cleaning products. All products bearing the Green Seal have been scientifically evaluated for their health impacts. Go to `www.greenseal.org/findaproduct/cleaners.cfm` to access the organization's list of certified cleaning products.

Cutting the Carbon Impact of Company Travel

Business travel significantly contributes to carbon emissions, so cutting down on your business's carbon impact by revamping your company travel policies — including employee commuting — is valuable for profits, people, and the planet. After all, global airfare prices are on the rise; so are the costs of hotels, restaurants, and rental vehicles.

Companies of all sizes are building up their corporate social responsibility efforts by purchasing carbon offsets (which I explain in the "Increasing Energy Efficiency" section, earlier in this chapter) to diminish the impact of business travel. The investment firm Sustainable Asset Management is working toward complete elimination of business travel emissions — a fact it's touting on all of its marketing materials! Although that good PR isn't directly measurable, it's an integral part of the company's overall green image.

Because carbon offsets cost additional dollars, the financial benefits from greening your company's travel primarily accrue from reduction efforts (for instance, engaging in telecommuting or train travel rather than air travel).

I delve into different green travel-related policies you can explore within the following sections.

Conferencing electronically instead of in person

Certainly much can be said about the networking that transpires when people physically meet and engage in business transactions and events at a personal level. But is this in-person networking necessary every time? Not at all. The potential for significantly reducing your office's carbon footprint by using telephone-based and Internet-based conferencing rather than jumping on a plane is significant. If your company is engaged in significant long-distance air travel (particularly international), it may not take long for you to recoup the costs of this additional technology.

If the sale of teleconferencing equipment is any indication (with two large suppliers reporting a 40 to 60 percent annual increase in sales), same-time communication via phone, audio, or Web conferencing systems is a modality that's becoming a highly accepted alternative to traditional business travel.

Triple-bottom-line benefits of teleconferencing include

- **A reduced environmental footprint:** The more meetings you hold by phone or Internet, the less people have to hop on a train or plane that emits greenhouse gases. The planetary benefits on this one are a no-brainer!

- **Increased productivity from employees:** Employees who don't have to spend as much time traveling can spend that newly found time working instead.

- **Reduced travel costs:** Travel is often cited as one of the top five expenses of doing business, depending on your industry sector, size, and location. Clearly anything you can do to cut back on this expense is a boon on the profit side of your Profit & Loss Statement.

The increased capabilities of Web conferencing, including sharing applications, VOIP (voice over internet protocol, such as Skype), electronic whiteboards, and text chat for live Q & A sessions has led many companies to consider teleconferencing as a green alternative to physical travel.

Want to make an impact on your company's travel policies? Check out the costs associated with purchasing the necessary telecommunications equipment and compare that to the associated travel savings. You can then use your findings to show that conferencing electronically is a clear triple-bottom-line winner on all counts.

Investing in sustainable company cars

If your company owns or leases a fleet of automobiles (for salespeople or for executives), considering a sustainable fleet-replacement policy may be important. As these cars come up for replacement, will you purchase more of the same, or is it time to rethink the corporate fleet?

The real debate is whether making the change from traditional cars to green ones is worth the effort. Consider that single-passenger vehicles (particularly full-size ones that aren't fuel efficient) aren't ecofriendly. Vehicles are estimated to supply 25 percent of greenhouse gas emissions that significantly contribute to climate change. In 1950, there were 50 million cars on the road; now, more than 700 million dot the globe — a number that's growing exponentially with the increased affluence of citizens in the developing world. According to the *Earth Island Journal*, the world's car population is increasing *five times as fast* as the human population.

To effectively determine whether switching to fuel-efficient company cars is right for your business, do some quick math to calculate your potential total savings annually.

1. **Determine the average number of miles your current fleet vehicle gets and subtract that from the number of miles per gallon the average hybrid car gets.**

   So if your average fleet vehicle gets 24 miles per gallon and your company autos travel 30,000 miles per year, how many gallons per year will you save if you convert to a hybrid (assuming this vehicle gets 50 miles to the gallon)? In this example, you'd save 26 (50 – 24) miles per gallon.

2. **Divide that total by the total number of miles traveled by all fleet vehicles per year and multiply your answer by the average regional price for a gallon of gas in your area.**

   Sticking with the previous example, here's how the equation would look:

   30,000 ÷ 26 = 1,154 Gallons × Average Regional Price for a Gallon of Gas = $_____ in Total Annual Savings

   Assuming static gas prices, you can then easily calculate how long it will take to pay for any sticker-price differential between a hybrid and a traditional vehicle.

Reducing your company's carbon footprint is dependent on your staff's driving habits, the region where the cars are traveling, and how the vehicles are maintained. However, a rough estimate is that one mile driven in an average, well-maintained hybrid vehicle emits about one pound of carbon dioxide. So not only do you double your efficiency by making the switch to fuel-efficient company cars but you also halve your business's carbon footprint.

Instituting green corporate travel policies

When employees must travel, craft sustainable travel policies to guide them when they're out of the office.

- ✔ **Mandate fuel-efficient rentals if car rental is absolutely necessary.** These vehicles now comprise 50 percent of two major car rental agencies' rentals. Look for hybrids to join the ranks soon.

- ✔ **Prioritize mass transit as the transportation mode of choice in metro areas instead of renting individual passenger vehicles.** If employees are going to a conference, meeting, or event, consider requiring mass transit to transport them between the airport or train station and the hotel and event location.

- ✔ **Require travel by train rather than by plane when feasible.** Planes' emissions have a particularly strong impact on climate change due to the altitude at which they're released.

- ✔ **Book rooms at hotels that belong to the "Green" Hotels Association (or are Green Seal–certified).** You can find these hotels at `www.green hotels.com` or at `www.greenseal.org/programs/lodging.cfm`, respectively.

On a side note, if you're planning on holding a conference at a hotel, be sure to ask whether it has ecofriendly meeting rooms available. Characteristics of ecofriendly meeting spaces include in-room recycling bins, compact fluorescent light bulbs, and the use of china and cutlery rather than disposable products.

Chapter 7

Lean Green Product Development Machine

*D*eveloping new products for the green market is an exciting challenge for businesses new to sustainability. Designing a product with ecoattributes as its driving force will stimulate lots of new discussions about your product line. Great products are a result of superior design; extraordinary green products take that stellar design to the next level.

As your organization increases its commitment to sustainability, prodding your product design team to transition to sustainably oriented thinking will edge its way to the top of your to-do list. Now is a great time to start capitalizing on green product opportunities while reducing your company's exposure to external threats, such as increased raw material costs and changing markets, posed by your less-than-sustainable merchandise.

In this chapter, I preview the variety of ways you can green your product design practices, explain why greening your product line is an important part of your business's overall sustainability plan, and show you how to make changes, from simple yet effective ones to more concerted efforts.

Surveying the Three Main Aspects of Sustainable Product Development

One of the goals of sustainable product design is to create a comprehensive bill of materials through a green lens, which means looking at your products' content by measuring greenhouse gas emissions, recycled content, virgin natural resource requirements, water usage, waste produced, packaging per unit, and the like. Of course, your suppliers will be assessed in this light as well, because most companies rely on other companies to provide input for their products and services. You'll also want to review the effects of the various production processes on the *triple bottom line* (benefits to people, planet, and profit, as described in Chapter 1).

Both raw material inputs and production processes used are of grave importance when looking holistically at sustainable product design. They're viewed as a package rather than independent units because production processes rely on the raw materials that constitute the input.

Products

The paramount thing to understand about sustainable product design is that it isn't an add-on concept. Rather, it's a "be all" strategy. Modifying existing products to tack on elements of sustainability is *not* what the whole idea's about. Truly green products are designed from the get-go with ecological sustainability as a driving force. You have to constantly pose questions as to how to minimize inputs, reduce reliance on virgin raw materials, decrease impact during the period the product is being used, and extend responsibility (as the producer) through the item's end of life. The intent of green design is that a product will either be recycled into *compostable* (biological) nutrients or upcycled into another product at the end of its useful life, without any harmful waste being generated. (*Upcycled* refers to using waste material as components of new and viable products.)

Developing sustainable products also means giving ongoing attention to deleting any harmful items from the bill of materials and keeping an eye out for ways to innovate natural products. Just consider the case of a small pet care products business that incorporated sustainable thinking into its design phase and came up with the idea of using a fuzzy stuffing for its pet beds that's made of recycled plastic soda bottles rather than the synthetic alternative. This design consideration not only saves money but it also greatly reduces the company's carbon footprint and diverts hundreds of tons of plastic bottles from landfills. It has also managed to stimulate other ecofriendly pet products as well.

Simply put, sustainable product design looks to minimize raw materials input and the processing needed to convert raw materials into a final product. It also looks to create products that are less harmful to people and the environment and can be used for the betterment of society. Ultimately, it envisions what the product's next life will look like.

Consider another example: Rohner Textil AG, a textile mill in the Swiss Alps, was formerly under pressure from Swiss regulatory agencies to clean up the toxins found in its factory trimmings. The company opted to collaborate with DesignTex (a U.S. furniture products operation) in order to analyze all of its 1,600 dyes for toxic content. By the end of the analysis, only 16 dyes were identified as nontoxic; Rohner proceeded to eliminate all the hazardous dyes from its inventory. The resulting natural fabric produced by the company has earned DesignTex and Rohner many awards, and the water leaving the Swiss factory is now actually cleaner than the water entering the plant. Because the tailings are now nontoxic, they can be used as a byproduct in other textile operations.

Putting green product design at the forefront is imperative because it can lead to simplification of both inputs needed and processes required. Doing so can also save you money and showcase your company as a leader in its field. Green product design is manifested through

- **Materials choices:** Reducing packaging and virgin raw materials is a key consideration, as is having an emphasis on using local products whenever possible. Selecting biobased and nontoxic materials in exchange for synthetic and hazardous materials is also key. (Many flooring choices, such as synthetic carpets and linoleum, have toxic components that as a whole can't be upcycled because the next generation of product won't want to mix toxic and nontoxic materials.)

- **Foregoing unnecessary bells and whistles:** Such add-ons require more tools, machine calibration, and processing, yet add little real value for the end user. It's best to just cut them out of your design process wherever possible.

- **Creating products with longer lives and more adaptability to a wide variety of needs:** This approach results in a more sustainable manufacturing process, because if your products are more far-reaching in their usability and last longer, you can create fewer of them. Patagonia perfected this notion in that its products are meant to have very long lives and be layered for different levels of activity, without being trendy or mod.

- **How the product's structure will affect its lifelong sustainability:** Analysis includes how much energy it will take to get the product in consumers' hands, how easy replacement parts are to access, how durable the prodcut is, and how long its useful life will be. For example, cars manufactured on heavy chassis don't get good mileage throughout their lives —no matter how efficiently the motor functions — because of the weight. An Energy Star–rated dishwasher takes just as much raw materials (casing, sensors, pump, and the like) as a traditional dishwasher, but during its life cycle, the true sustainability attribute shines through because it uses much less energy and water.

Only products that truly add value to customers' lives are envisioned in the green product design process. Disposable, feel-good-for-a-moment items that quickly become obsolete or require an inordinate amount of materials or processing are undesirable ideas; discard these concepts immediately.

Talk about a leader in green product development: Nike took the lead in sustainable shoe design by challenging its product engineers with some revolutionary design parameters. According to these new mandates, Nike shoes can no longer contain PVC or incorporate toxic ingredients in the formulation of their rubber shoe soles. The shoes now have to be designed so that they can either be recycled or become a new product at their end of life — all without losing any element of performance *or* increasing the shoes' final price point.

As a result of rethinking product engineering, Nike designed a line of shoes, named Considered, that was the first major design of its type to commit to water-based adhesives (thereby eliminating volatile organic compounds). The company also launched Nike Grind, a program that slices shoes into three components at their end of life: rubber, foam, and fabric. All of these end-of-life products circle back into production as flooring, baseball fields, tennis courts, and padding under hardwood basketball floors.

Processes

Many industrial manufacturing processes aren't configured to maximize efficiency because they rely on outdated design. Whole industrial parks are now designed to employ the concept of *closed-loop manufacturing,* which creates new products from reused materials in perpetuity. With physical proximity of raw material production/extraction to the assembly line, transportation costs are negligible.

For example, powder coat tailings from an industrial painting process can be used as a dye in greeting cards. Fly ash, a byproduct of producing coal, is used as a strengthening component in construction-grade cement. Spent grain from a brewery provides a growing medium for mushrooms. Concurrently, the used mushroom substrate becomes worm fodder, which is used to manufacture biodegradable detergents and is also packaged and sold in home composting kits.

Eliminating or lessening environmental harm

Much of the work being done on sustainable process development revolves around reducing energy used (and therefore greenhouse gases emitted) and toxins released from a particular course of action. A sustainable manufacturing process is one that has maximized energy efficiency through equipment selection, facilities layout, materials handling systems, and supply chain control.

If you use toxic materials in your current production process, eliminating their use in future designs is critical. If dangerous materials are part of your industry and natural alternatives aren't available, you need to consider the safe manufacture, transportation, and disposal of them.

Minimizing water and atmospheric pollution is also an important consideration — and one that has ongoing regulatory compliance issues for most manufacturing entities. Future product and process design discussions should consider ways to enhance your company's opportunity to purify the water it uses and cut greenhouse gas emissions through reduced energy usage.

Reducing waste

From a manufacturing standpoint, all waste is an expenditure that adds no value and therefore should be eliminated. Clearly, reducing waste has triple-bottom-line effects because if a particular material isn't incorporated into the next loop of manufacturing, it's either incinerated or diverted to a landfill. Some waste streams (like e-waste, which I cover in Chapter 6) have strident impacts on people in other countries (where the process of extracting valuable metals occurs in a way that's harmful to human health.)

Lean manufacturing, or *lean production,* is a sustainable manufacturing model in which sustainable product engineers look at waste elimination when analyzing processes. Any use of resources that doesn't create value for the consumer is considered economically and environmentally unsound and is automatically a red flag area to target for improvement. Technological capacity is increasing every day, and new materials, coatings, machine-cutting tools, and finishing processes are being innovated to focus on waste-reduction methods as a result.

Increasing resource productivity

In crafting your new product design paradigm, you should analyze every input (think energy, water, and raw materials) for the potential to eke more productivity out of fewer resources. Fortunately, technology has the capacity to increase the utility of natural resources 5, 10, or even 100 times more than what it is currently. Advances in refrigeration technology in the last 30 years have increased energy efficiency an astounding 98 percent. New lighting technology, such as LEDs and compact fluorescent light bulbs, has decreased energy usage tremendously in homes, plants, and offices.

Electric motors are widespread throughout many industry sectors. They move materials, power pumps, and energize grinders, compressors, and mills — and account for tremendous costs and emissions for lots of companies. By investing in more efficient motors, or by retrofitting existing ones to decrease energy used per unit of output, your company has significant capacity to reduce inefficiencies and yield savings.

Ways to envision increasing resource productivity include looking at

- **How much more output can be achieved from one unit of energy:** For example, a Rocky Mountain microbrewery captures steam emitted from the brewing process to heat its building. In the Midwest, pumps in an industrial process have been reconfigured to minimize energy usage without impacting production quality or quantity.

- **How materials input used can be reduced (which almost always reduces energy used as well):** The wood products industry offers a stellar example of this consideration thanks to a new honeycomb-type design that creates structural support equivalent to that of solid wood, without requiring as much virgin material. Also, less energy is needed to transport this lighter material. If you require further inspiration, consider how new solar technology is poised to manufacture nonsilicon solar panels by imprinting a thin layer of microscopic solar cells onto aluminum foil-like metal sheets. The result is a lighter weight, more efficient solar panel.

Supply chain

Extended product responsibility is based on the concept that everyone — suppliers, manufacturers, and consumers — shares the responsibility for reducing the environmental impacts of a product throughout its life cycle. As you dial into each of your raw material sources, asking your suppliers whether they're having the same conversations with their product design teams is prudent. In many cases, reducing toxins in your final product requires in-depth conversations with suppliers about how they're approaching their materials throughout the whole spectrum: manufacture, use, distribution, and disposal.

You may be surprised at how many companies (particularly if you source from large multinational organizations) are already deep into greening their product design. For example, a gigantic chemical company is spending millions to research biotechnology alternatives to synthetic chemicals. An international furniture company is working as a key member of the Sustainable Packaging Coalition to minimize packing materials and use only recycled ones.

Consider requiring your suppliers to judiciously label all materials for their recyclability (particularly plastics) so that end users can see how components may have different recycling or upcycling capacity. Also, make sure your suppliers are forthright as to the content of the raw materials you purchase from them.

Recognizing the Value of Sustainable Product Development

Nothing speaks more loudly about your company than your product line. As more media attention is lavished on products that are adversely affecting the planet, as well as on those that are helping to rejuvenate it, more and more people will start caring where *your* company stands on the topic of green product development. Depending on where your company is in the sustainability-planning process (which I outline in Chapter 4), greening your product design efforts will have an effect on public relations, networking potential, and new customer growth.

Following are the major potential benefits you can accrue by greening your product line. Of course, you may not see all of these benefits from each product design modification.

- **Reduced expenses:** Well-designed products minimize use of raw materials by squeaking out the most productivity possible from each unit of input. Modifying your design process so that manufacturing, materials movement, storage, and distribution decrease energy usage and either minimize or eliminate waste are expense-reducing maneuvers. Waste is an unnecessary business expense and a burden on the environment; many times it's also toxic to the community. Reduced waste-disposal expenses on one hand and decreased raw material costs on the other make zero-waste design a triple-bottom-line winner.

  Of course, reduced expenses also add up to increased savings. A stellar example of this savings involves Interface Ltd. When the company built its factory in Shanghai, China, it was able to reduce a particular industrial process that required 14 pumps. It redesigned the system from small pipes and big pumps to big pipes and small pumps, increasing energy efficiency by 92 percent and saving tons of capital investment.

- **Additional revenue:** Identifying a second-hand use for waste can effectively give you another product, possibly generating additional revenues. For example, sawdust byproduct from a mill can be used to manufacture pressboard, lyocell fabric, and other items, thereby creating a second market for what was previously treated as waste.

✔ **Business position within green supply chains:** Your small or mid-sized enterprise may not feel very influential in the larger commercial world where the power of your influence seems pretty limited. But consider how your products play into the needs of the many large corporations that are going green. Look at your key customers and analyze where they're heading. Check out these examples to see what I mean:

- When a company such as Ford Motor Company (with more than $100 billion in annual purchase orders) announces the greening of its supply chain, you can bet tens of thousands of vendors down the supply chain are taking notice and reconsidering how they can make compliant products.

- Seventh Generation assesses its manufacturers' processes with an audit-type tool, giving preference to the organizations that can provide sustainable materials and services. This tactic is called *environmentally preferable purchasing.* Determining whether any of your key customers are heading toward these policies is definitely worthwhile.

✔ **Expanded customer base and increased customer satisfaction:** Developing products with a keen eye toward the emerging green market offers you tons of creative opportunities because the market for green products is exploding. The value of sustainable product/service purchasing is estimated at more than $200 billion in the U.S. alone. Yet a 2007 National Technology Readiness Survey shows that 42 percent of adults have difficulty finding the green products and services that they're interested in buying! That's a big disparity. (Turn to Chapter 10 for a peek at the minds and behaviors of the burgeoning green consumer base.)

Additionally, business value accrues to organizations that employ *Cradle to Cradle,* a high-visibility approach to product design that promotes strong customer relationships that arise from superior, safe, and durable products that reduce product liability exposure and material input. I go into greater detail about this approach later in this chapter.

✔ **Reduced legal risk:** Activist shareholder lawsuits are on the rise. These lawsuits center on everything from workers' rights to product liability to environmental degradation and ethics violations. Domini Mutual Funds alone has filed more than 140 shareholder resolutions with more than 60 corporations. These lawsuits are targeted toward such topics as product safety, natural resource protection, and energy conservation. Because sustainable product design takes engineers through the process of looking at many of these design aspects, it reduces your overall legal exposure.

Bottom line: Litigation from hazardous materials (either those materials used in production or those created as a byproduct of it) eats up a tremendous amount of financial resources. Why waste funds and time (and cause yourself a lot of angst in the process) when you can instead explore and develop natural alternatives to your components to alleviate this concern completely?

✔ **Less negative publicity:** News of mistreated employees litigating, hazardous material cleanup efforts gone awry, international labor violations, or other insidious business transactions can undo the effects of positive advertising dollars. Remember how Greenpeace launched a mock Apple Web site highlighting egregious amounts of waste associated with iPod production and packaging? This move created scads of negative press for Apple right before the tech giant's biggest product start in years.

Taking Stock of Your Current Product Line: Three Approaches

To create energy-efficient, sustainable products, you may need to administer a radical dose of rethinking to the design of your product and production process. Although sustainable product design aspires to much more than bare-bones compliance, approaches to sustainable design can be a good jumping-off point for analyzing how your products and processes can not only conform but also add value. Luckily, some very well-respected systems can guide you in developing innovative new products. The next few sections identify some of the approaches you can use when brainstorming ways to revamp your product line. They include the following:

✔ **Life cycle assessment (LCA):** LCA refers to the analysis of each phase of your product's life for its *environmental load,* which means quantifying greenhouse gas emissions, waterborne emissions, solid wastes, raw materials, and energy required. This technique can be used to analyze existing products and develop new products. Companies like Sony, Volvo, and Xerox have been using the LCA approach for years to reduce emissions, lower energy requirements, and decrease ecological impact.

LCA is a fairly complex assessment requiring materials or energy specialists to flesh out where exactly the carbon footprint, for example, lies in your production process. If you make postcards for the tourism industry, how much carbon is involved in making and transporting the paper? Obtaining the photos? Embossing the photos on the paper? Transporting the postcards to various shops? Sending the postcard (that is, using the product)? Disposing of the product? You get the idea.

✔ **Cradle to Cradle (C2C) design:** This is a product design strategy that stretches the innovator to think of the product design system as a whole rather than the sum of its parts. It encourages design engineers to pre-think where the product will end up at the end of its useful life. So many products currently on the market are intended to end up in the landfill. In this zero-waste model, that thinking becomes obsolete. At the end of a product's life cycle, all of its components have a new life, and no part of the product is considered waste. The ultimate goal of the C2C design approach is a zero-waste product.

> ✔ **Design for the Environment (DfE):** This is an EPA program that works with different industry sectors to select technologies, materials, and processes that reduce energy used and chemical risk involved. These industry sector and government partnerships cover the gamut, from nail salons and low-VOC adhesive companies to wire/cable insulation companies and industrial and institutional laundromats.

Good design requires thoughtful analysis of a product's entire life cycle. Analyze a product from inception to disposal to see where energy inefficiencies exist or where waste is produced and create steps to change the unsustainable practices.

Considering each phase of a product's life cycle: Life cycle assessment (LCA)

The objective of conducting a life cycle assessment (LCA; see the basics of this tactic in the preceding section) is to decrease total environmental burden by *quantitatively* determining where the highest-impact improvements on reducing inefficiencies can be found. Conducting an LCA (including an analysis of your supply chain) allows you to easily see which areas should be addressed first so you can focus on producing the highest results and then move progressively through other identified areas to reduce impacts. LCA produces a list that quantifies the pollutants at each of the product's life stages, as well as the amount of energy and materials used.

By looking at the life cycle phases of your product when reviewing product design, you can easily see which design considerations to prioritize. Stages that have the highest negative environmental impact are given priority for change and design modifications. For example, say you ship assembled powertrain units from China to Washington, but you know that shipping them from Kentucky to Washington causes fewer atmospheric and waterborne emissions. LCA gets you thinking about whether the shipping weight can be reduced, whether you can tighten distribution to eliminate such long-distance shipping requirements, and whether you have any options for alternate assembly locations.

Cutting overall emissions, for example, requires identifying carbon dioxide equivalent emissions at every stage of a product's life because looking at one total emission number for a unit of product isn't helpful in assessing where to begin decreasing that number. Only when you can see the parts that make up the sum can you easily pigeonhole where the highest-impact areas are.

Often the results of your LCA may be surprising: Your product may have most of its impact in a stage other than the one you imagined, giving you fodder for creative ideas on how to minimize emissions at that stage of the life cycle.

Conducting the analysis

The standard life cycle phases that you should look at are as follows:

- **Extracting or producing the product's raw materials:** This phase takes you all the way back to the start of your product's story. For example, if the product in question is a cotton shirt in a typical chain store, your company may identify the cotton as having come from Uzbekistan. The cotton is a heavily fertilized crop (and the fertilizer contains petroleum, so there's some negative environmental impact there) and has been shipped across Asia to a manufacturing plant (again requiring the use of fossil fuels, but this time for transportation). There's also a negative impact on the groundwater in the valley in Uzbekistan due to runoff from overfertilized soil. Additionally, you have a possible violation of workers' rights laws because children are being employed to harvest the cotton.

- **Manufacturing or assembling the product:** This phase looks at and documents the aspects of the processing stage that are potentially harmful to the environment. Say your cotton has arrived in Korea (which causes atmospheric pollution because of the fossil fuels used to ship it there). The environmental laws in Korea may not require scrubbers on the stack that fuels the plant, resulting in significant emissions during conversion of the raw materials into the final product. Additionally, some toxins are included in the finish that's applied to the product, and they're packaged in layers of plastic for shipping.

- **Distributing the product:** This phase requires reviewing how the product is disbursed to its final markets. This distribution may be multistep via warehouses, or it may be directly to the end consumer. Because final distribution of the cotton shirts is in the U.S. (and therefore rail isn't an option), the shirts are most likely put on container ships that run on fossil fuels and have many negative impacts on oceanic health.

- **Using the product:** This phase involves determining what the final user is intent on doing with the product and what the potential effects of that use are on the environment. The cotton shirt may have a life of only two years, considering it's an animal of the fashion world and is designed to have a short life. In that time frame, it'll be washed 40 times, which means using water, energy, and detergents that possibly contain phosphates (which have negative watershed implications).

- **Disposing of the product:** This phase is all about figuring out the environmental impact of the product's end of life process. The shirt may see a second life in the rag bag in your consumer's home, or it may end up in a second-hand shop; most likely it'll go the landfill where it will become part of methane emissions.

You should assess each life cycle phase in regard to these three considerations. *Note:* These categories may be different among companies and may pertain regionally to appropriate issues such as smog or water toxicity.

> ✔ Where the most energy is embodied (and carbon emitted)
>
> ✔ Where the most waste is expended
>
> ✔ Where other environmental load may be created

Because LCA is a tool to help decision-makers better understand the full impact of a product, you should use it with other decision criteria, such as cost, price, and performance, to make the best product development decisions possible.

Comparing results of the analysis

After you've gathered raw data through your assessment, you may convert it to categories that allow comparison between areas of impact. For example, the toxic impact of different heavy metals on soil needs to be expressed in common terms. Likewise, the effect of all sorts of greenhouse gasses should be expressed as carbon dioxide equivalents. Although a full-blown LCA can be quite complex and costly (and may require the assistance of an external expert), application of the principles in the form of a simple chart (for each of the five life cycle stages) may easily and graphically illustrate for your management team which areas of focus will yield the greatest improvement in product design.

Even without an LCA expert, a simple compilation of all the information outlined in the preceding section provides an overview of where the problem areas are, allowing your design team to visualize where its energies should be used in order to have the highest impact.

You can also use a chart to gauge products in comparison to one another. One of your products may be very energy intensive in the production stage but relatively benign in all other stages and get a bad rap simply because production is a high-visibility area. When doing LCA, you may find that another product that has little waste and relatively light emissions at the production stage turns out to have heavy impact on the raw materials extraction stage, a fact that doesn't automatically jump out of corporate data.

Figure 7-1 illustrates each stage of the life cycle of two hypothetical products and analyzes current and proposed emissions from both. Notice how this chart takes a visual snapshot of the stages of a product's life and lets designers, managers, suppliers, and employees all easily see where design modifications should focus as they pertain to carbon dioxide emissions. The same sort of analysis can be done for waterborne pollution, heavy metal release, and so on.

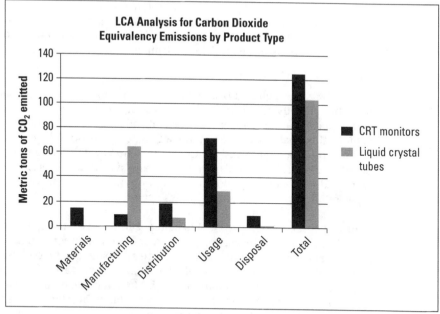

LCA Analysis for Carbon Dioxide Equivalency Emissions by Product Type

Metric tons of CO_2 emitted

- CRT monitors
- Liquid crystal tubes

Materials · Manufacturing · Distribution · Usage · Disposal · Total

Figure 7-1: An LCA of two types of monitors' life cycles and carbon dioxide emissions.

Rethinking how products are designed: Cradle to Cradle (C2C)

To understand William McDonough and Michael Braungart's Cradle to Cradle (C2C) design paradigm, you have to understand that traditional product design theory has long relied on a linear, extract-consume-dispose model called *cradle to grave.* This model seemed perfectly acceptable in the 1800s and 1900s because raw materials such as minerals, timber, coal, land, water, and so on appeared inexhaustible and fossil fuels for processing were cheap and readily available. Now, however, many natural resources are limited, and the planet is warming, which I explain in more detail in Chapter 2.

Some studies show that 90 percent of all extracted materials go to waste in producing durable goods in North America, leaving a scant 10 percent for actual consumption. Historically, many companies have even built in obsolescence during the product design phase by creating new-generation technology that requires upgrading to current models and throwing away the old items. Additionally, chemicals used in many household products release carcinogenic compounds and weaken human immune systems.

According to McDonough and Braungart, manufacturers' response to most of these problems has centered on reducing or minimizing the amount of pollutants or the impact of the product. McDonough is famously quoted as saying "less bad is not good." Decreasing pollutants, for example, still results in pollution.

Instead, McDonough and Braungart suggest that product design as a whole must be radically rethought in order to minimize environmental impact with a particular eye to what happens at the end of a product's life cycle. To achieve this goal, they recommend segregating a product's materials into two major types: biological and technical nutrients. *Biological nutrients* decompose organically; *technical nutrients,* usually synthetics or ores, can be easily extracted and become part of a closed-loop manufacturing system. Both types of nutrients are used in endless cycles.

Today, the C2C design protocol is being used for everything from packaging materials to toys to the reconfiguration of complex integrated manufacturing plants. Packaging materials that eliminate all toxins can be endlessly recycled and need not ever become part of a landfill. Toys that are made from sustainably harvested wood and painted with biologically based dyes can be cycled through a continuous loop. In the context of manufacturing processes, C2C gives product design folks an overview of how to configure facilities so that waste from one process serves as food (in other words, an input) for another while minimizing energy required and retooling machines to work with new materials that contain no toxins.

Although relatively new on the green scene, C2C is a concept that some very old processes are built on. *Permaculture,* an agricultural method that uses shade from one plant to protect another, natural pest control, and sophisticated rotation methods to preserve soil integrity, is a grand example of C2C that has worked for centuries. All the end products are endlessly looped backed into the next generation of products.

In Europe, many manufacturers are already responsible for what happens at the end of their products' lives. Not so — yet — in the U.S., but stay tuned. Chapter 5 addresses the changing regulatory environment in greater detail.

Assessing overall environmental impact: Design for the Environment (DfE)

Begun by the U.S. Environmental Protection Agency (EPA), the Design for the Environment (DfE) program is a practical approach to product design that looks at decreasing the overall environmental impact of a product throughout its life cycle as well as eliminating chemicals as much as possible. The EPA uses this program to work with industry sectors to reduce chemical exposure risk and improve energy efficiency. Because it is so industry specific, the practical methods used to decrease environmental impact (primarily through reduced emissions) and chemical risk vary by industry.

One DfE program works with detergent manufacturers to reduce the amount of unsafe surfactants (nonylphenol ethoxylates) contained in traditional detergents. Under the Safer Detergents Stewardship Initiative, the EPA recognizes those companies committed to using safe surfactants that are nonpolluting (and therefore have minimal impact on groundwater and aquatic life). In partnering with the dry cleaning industry, the EPA has helped provoke research about natural alternatives to traditional chemicals and encouraged folks to share technologies and research progress.

The DfE program offers industry partners access to expertise and research models, unique technical tools, and a scientific review team in order to effect change in manufacturing processes and products. The program has partnered with 200,000 business facilities and more than 2 million workers to date. In 2006, the DfE program had successfully reduced the use of persistent chemicals by approximately 183 million pounds.

Any product bearing the DfE label, as shown in Figure 7-2, has undergone a thorough EPA review and contains only those chemical ingredients that are the least problematic in their class.

Figure 7-2:
Working with the EPA's DfE program can earn your products this label.

Partnerships with the EPA usually originate through trade associations or a coalition of industry leaders, research institutions, universities, and nonprofit groups that need technical support for an industry-wide issue that impacts human or environmental health. Go to www.epa.gov/oppt/dfe and click the Partnership Projects link on the left-hand side to see whether your industry sector currently has a working partnership with the EPA.

If your company thinks that the whole industry can benefit from a collaboration with the EPA, gauge the interest of your trade or technical association by contacting the officers and putting forth an informal member e-mail survey. If member interest seems hopeful, contact the DfE program for information on proposing a partnership and submitting a proposal to the governing group of your trade association.

Biomimicry: Letting nature stimulate design

Over a decade ago, Janine Benyus (a natural sciences writer by trade) proposed bringing biologists and ecologists to the table with product designers. Why? Because she believed that inspiration for creating products and solving human problems lies in looking deeply at all the genius found in the natural world. Product designers that subscribe to biomimicry (and there are now thousands of them linked through The Biomimicry Institute) are coming up with amazing ideas based on the study of nature. After all, each of today's living organisms is the result of 4 billion years of adaptation!

Biomimicry is a term coined from *bios* (life) and *mimesi* (imitate), and the concept is gaining international acceptance as a design order that studies nature's best ideas and then emulates them. The idea is that for mankind to continue to occupy this planet in a sustainable manner, people must become more attuned to natural processes and use them for bioinspired design.

The Biomimicry Institute houses a growing database (check it out at www.biomimicry institute.org/case-studies) of more than 2,100 biomimicry-inspired innovations. Choosing just a few to highlight is a challenge, but here are some of my favorites:

- **Flipper power:** The bumps on a humpback whale's flippers allow the creature to streamline a tremendous amount of energy. This natural feature is thus being incorporated into the design of fans, propellers, and wind turbines to increase aerodynamic efficiency.

- **Like a lung:** Product engineers are working to design filters that eliminate 90 percent of carbon dioxide from flue stacks by using technology that imitates the human pulmonary process.

- **Quiet like a kingfisher:** The bullet train in West Japan was designed to reduce noise (and electricity usage) by shaping its "nose" like a kingfisher's beak. Nakatsu, the chief engineer on the project, was inspired after watching a kingfisher dive into the water at great speeds and yet create very little splash.

- **Weeds and seeds:** Velcro was invented when a Swiss engineer closely examined the burrs sticking to him and his dog after a hike in the Alps. After seeing hundreds of tiny hooks, he invented the well-known hook-and-loop fastening system.

- **Repellants without chemicals:** By copying the tiny bumps on a lotus leaf's surface, shields applied to paints, glass, and textiles reduce the need to use harmful chemicals to keep the surfaces clean. Water is repelled so effectively that it pulls attached dirt off of these surfaces as it goes.

Worldwide interest in biomimicry is growing, and the body of research in bioinspired design is likewise expanding. In order to facilitate shared research, The Biomimicry Institute is planning a portal (which is currently in the prototype phase but accessible if you go to www.biomimicry institute.org and click the Design Portal link on the left-hand side) to catalogue how nature's systems meet global design challenges and allow international collaboration to enhance the progress of design work. Keep your eye on this site, which is intended to connect people around the world engaged in sustainable design based on biomimicry.

Beginning to Green Your Product Line: The First Steps

You may be wondering how you can possibly start redesigning your products and rethinking your product development process to align with your company's sustainability vision. Think of all steps in the green direction as progress! Although reworking your existing product line may not be in the immediate future, consider a review of what you already have on the market (using one of the approaches outlined earlier in this chapter, if appropriate to your industry). Also, begin rethinking the design of new products in the pipeline.

Involving *everyone* in your new sustainable product design venture is an important part of gaining buy-in. When you sit down to analyze a new or existing product through a green lens, bringing together customers, distributors, employees, and product designers increases creative potential exponentially. Consider holding a *charrette,* a way of getting input on your design process from a multitude of stakeholders. Charrettes are usually multiday, beginning with a big group meeting and then splitting off into smaller groups for design brainstorming. Each subgroup then presents its work to the full group as material for future dialogue. Because of the different perspectives brought to the table, charrettes are growing in popularity as a way to build synergy around green product design.

Of course, any time you facilitate a group, costs are involved for food, rooms, and facilitators. If you want to hold a charette, you must budget for it. Because the possible benefits of creating new green products are intangible, base the costs of your charette on the future benefits that may result from ecoefficiencies and enhanced revenue from new products.

Your design ambitions must be matched by your demonstrated commitment to growing your staff's capacity to see your product line through new eyes. All product design folks know, for example, that matter doesn't disappear — it simply changes form (incinerated waste generates air pollutants; landfill waste becomes methane). Unfortunately, in a traditional capitalist system, this transformation is inconsequential. As long as the company isn't directly responsible for the cost of waste disposal or toxin remediation, those costs aren't a concern when designing new product. Exposing your employees to a new and greener way of thinking opens them up to the full life cycle design approach. See Chapter 13 for more thorough coverage of training your employees in sustainability and providing incentives for action.

In the following sections, I walk you through the process of gathering and brainstorming ideas you can use to enhance the sustainability of your product line. I also present the value of crafting new guidelines that challenge your product design folks to consider the ecological effects of all aspects of product design.

Gathering ideas from outside resources

Don't waste time reinventing the wheel or struggling to find resources that are already out there. Consider the following organizations as a jumping-off point for gathering all kinds of ideas related to implementing sustainable product design at your company:

- **The Biomimicry Guild:** Closely linked with The Biomimicry Institute, the Biomimicry Guild conducts workshops, coordinates research, and engages in consulting in order to help product developers figure out how to think about design by examining ecosystem models. It offers corporate education with deliverables, including a feasibility analysis and implementation plan for companies interested in pursuing bioinspired design. Go to www.biomimicryguild.com and click the Services link at the top of the page. Then click the Complete List of Services link on the left-hand side of the page that follows.

- **Centre for Sustainable Design:** An initiative of the University for Creative Arts in England, the Centre for Sustainable Design is considered an informational clearinghouse. It brings together international research on sustainable design in easy-to-read white papers and reports and has served as a catalyst for some of western Europe's finest sustainable design work. This organization offers educational materials and online networking capability at its Web site, www.cfsd.org.uk.

- **Engineers for a Sustainable World:** This organization's aim is to promote sustainable thinking in all the young engineers coming of age today. This group has a presence on college campuses; it also hosts an annual national conference to network engineers who are interested in sustainable design. The ESW's influence can be seen in programs at Cornell, the Rochester Institute of Technology, the University of Texas, and Stanford, to name a few. Visit www.eswusa.org to find out more about the ESW.

- **MBDC:** This organization, founded by Cradle to Cradle creators William McDonough and Michael Braungart, offers workshop training to educate product design teams and green-minded folks on how to approach sustainable design. Get the scoop on these educational opportunities at www.mbdc.com/train/index.htm.

- **Specific professional associations:** Depending on your particular industry, trade associations can have significant political, regulatory, and business power. They can also serve to unite like-minded professionals in the field. Associations such as the American Institute of Chemical Engineers (AIChE), the American Institute of Architects (AIA), and the American Society of Mechanical Engineers (ASME) are involved in education and outreach to their members in the form of virtual seminars and networking opportunities regarding sustainable product design efforts. Look for similar movements within your own industry niche.

> ✔ **The U.S. Environmental Protection Agency:** The EPA annually sponsors a National Sustainable Design Expo to showcase work done by student groups at universities across the U.S. These student groups partner with government, private agencies, and nonprofits to facilitate their research. For ideas on some of the newest technology, visit es.epa.gov/ncer/ p3/expo.

Establishing new green guidelines for product design

Establishing additional or new guidelines for designers to consider can help jump-start a green product design process. In addition to existing product design standards, think about what new guidelines you may want to give your engineers or suppliers to work with. The first section in this chapter, "Surveying the Three Main Aspects of Sustainable Product Development," provides several guidelines to get you started. Essentially, you should challenge your in-house engineers or parts suppliers to minimize waste, reduce energy, reduce water, and consider nontoxic materials. Your company may already incorporate industrial engineering techniques, inventory systems, or business-efficiency theories (such as Total Quality Management, Six Sigma, or Just in Time) that already contribute to reduced environmental impact by increasing production efficiency. If so, seeing the fit between continuous improvement inherent in these models and designing green products is quite easy.

Including new design parameters in your company's research and development process doesn't happen overnight. Your design team is going to need training opportunities and the ability to network with other product designers who are working through the same issues, so see Chapter 13 for the scoop on HR's role in designing sustainability-oriented training sessions.

Above all, foster a can-do attitude. Your company absolutely must encourage and reward innovative, out-of-the-box thinking to help your product design team transition to sustainability. So many folks seem quicker to toss out a hundred reasons why something can't be done differently than to identify the one way change can actually happen. Seek out sustainably minded thinkers within your organization and benefit from their ecopassion and ecoknowledge. (Turn to Chapter 3 for tips on identifying these thinkers within your company.)

Brainstorming ideas

As you brainstorm ideas for greening your product development process, let your new quality and sustainability parameters guide your thinking in ways that may have not been on the table before. Try using your new model as the driving force behind your product design team's strategy session for your next project and see what comes out of it. Let your designers explore out-of-the-box ideas and see what sorts of new discussions arise. Envisioning the future doesn't mean all proposed ideas are realistic today, but it does encourage product developers to dream about what a perfect product looks like to them.

How about posing queries such as the following to help get those creative juices flowing?

✔ **How can we minimize waste at every stage?** Finding uses for manufacturing byproducts is a great way to reduce waste. Think about where your waste may be useful. Can it be used to create energy or serve as a raw material input to another process? Can a product design or process be slightly changed to make previously unusable waste ready for a future life? For example, a dairy farm in western Montana installed two 30,000-gallon anaerobic digester tanks to create its own energy. Additionally, the digested outputs are nitrogen-rich and sold as soil amendments. Quite a story for manure!

When considering ways to cut down on waste, consider reducing or eliminating your product packaging. Either move is a great way to cut down on your company's waste. And don't forget about the resources and research available when you become a member of the Sustainable Packaging Coalition (see www.sustainablepackaging.org).

✔ **Can we explore new materials, particularly recycled or post-consumer waste materials? If so, by what percentage?** This is an important question to put out there because closed-loop manufacturing (a core component of sustainable product design) is all about using recycled and reclaimed raw materials rather than virgin materials and feeding the product in question into another cycle at its end of life. Continuous recycling of materials is the goal. Responding to growth in the natural lawn and garden market, TerraCycle sells plant food composed of worm detritus. The product is packaged in reused plastic bottles and shipped in boxes that other companies would chuck out.

✔ **Are the technical and biological nutrients easily separable?** As explained in the earlier "Rethinking how products are designed: Cradle to Cradle (C2C)" section, considering a product's end of life is critical, and the need to easily separate components for their next lives is a core concept of extended product responsibility and C2C thinking. Can you easily distinguish the biological and technical components in your products? How might you look at your design process if you knew you *had* to segregate out these two elements at the end of life?

✔ **Is our product easy to disassemble and therefore able to serve as a component for another like-kind product or the next generation of a similar product?** An office chair constructed of natural fibers and fillers that are grafted to postindustrial steel tubing can easily be disassembled at life's end because of the attachment choices made in the design phases (the natural coverings attach to the steel tubing with a snap system). At end of life, the natural fabrics are detached and sent to the compost bin, and the steel tubing is reused for the next generation of office furniture.

Don't forget about hazardous waste and e-waste issues. Think of ways to mitigate hazardous waste issues by using more natural alternatives and consider the recyclability of any electronics you use and/or produce. Disposing of hazardous waste is incredibly expensive, and eliminating this step will almost always decrease costs for your company.

✔ **Can we cut greenhouse gas emissions as part of the manufacturing process?** Decreasing energy used is obviously very important. Consider ways your company can decrease weight for shipping purposes and think about where you can decrease the need for heating, cooling, machining, and the like. Also look at whether you have the capability to generate renewable energy in order to decrease your reliance on fossil fuels. For example, a Rocky Mountain brewery uses 100-percent wind power to run its operations. It analyzed the difference in carbon dioxide emissions between using wind power and capturing and reusing heat generated via its fermentation process and found that wind had six times the capacity to reduce emissions than the recycled heat did.

✔ **How can we minimize transportation costs?** Exploring whether opportunities exist to source alternative raw materials closer to your area is well worth it. You can also look at the other side of the equation and determine that distributing final products to far-away places isn't desirable and thus step up your efforts to develop regional markets, acknowledging that serving customers across the globe will become increasingly more expensive as energy prices continue to rise. Or you may address materials handling and find that processing your product in stages at different locations is unwise from a transportation standpoint.

✔ **Which of our vendors may be willing to partner with us in innovative ways?** Explore whether there are any ways that existing vendors might increase their market share by filling your company's green needs. For example, your local telecommunications co-op may find that your commitment to reducing corporate travel (see Chapter 6 for more on greening this particular office practice) generates a need for video conferencing. Consequently, your vendor decides that interactive video applications will be growing as more companies cut air travel and their product line development focuses on video conferencing.

✔ **Do our current products and processes put us at risk legally?** Prethinking and rethinking how you create products that are environmentally and socially regenerative keeps bad press off your back and can in fact lead to really positive press if you're truly visionary. So perform a critical review of potential legal issues and make any necessary changes to avoid getting into potential hot water. *Note:* This is particularly pertinent to producers that handle toxic materials, dispose of hazardous waste, engage in production processes that may impact water and air pollution, and use subcontractors that operate in foreign countries with potential human rights issues.

You may own or manage a small, privately owned company and not feel exposed to legal risks related to the environmental and social impacts of your products, but take a peek up your supply chain. Who do you design products for, and do *they* have any big potential problems on the horizon?

For example, if you're involved in supplying catalogue copy or doing graphic design work for one of the companies targeted by the Forest Ethic's campaign to cut virgin timber used for catalogues, your business may be imperiled. Home Depot's wood suppliers felt the pressure when the chain store was targeted by the Rainforest Alliance to remove wood products that were unsustainably harvested. Often the ramifications of this type of pressure for the supply chain can be very broad in scope.

On the flip side, an eye toward reducing litigation exposure may lead you to fall into obvious new sustainable product lines. NaturaLawn, founded by one of the old field managers for Chemlawn, capitalizes on customers' desires to eliminate pesticides from their lawns and has more than 50,000 clients in 25 states.

Chapter 8

Looking Closely at the Brick and Mortar: Facilities

. . . .

In This Chapter

▶ Understanding the benefits and challenges of greening your facility

▶ Deciding whether to build or renovate and figuring out whose help you need

▶ Determining whether to certify your project

▶ Incorporating sustainable design

▶ Finding opportunities for small green renovations to your existing space

. . . .

The intense interest surrounding green construction arguably gives it one of the highest profiles of all green business initiatives. Whether you're considering upgrading minor aspects of your facility to green what you have, remodeling your existing space, or building a brand-new sustainable facility, this chapter gives you what you need. It presents the various aspects you must consider, from the systems you can target and professionals you need to involve to the factors that determine how extensive your changes are — and then some! (If concern about financial resources immediately springs to mind, head to Chapter 9, where I provide coverage on accessing ecocapital for sustainability efforts.) First, however, I expound on the myriad benefits of greening your facility.

Why Greening Your Facility Is a Good Idea

With *natural capital* (water, mineral, soils, and the like) depleting rapidly, and the availability of future nonrenewable energy very much up in the air (no pun intended), the need to include sustainable facilities design in your overall green business plan has never been stronger. Consider these facts:

- ✔ The life cycle of a building (construction, operation, renovation, and deconstruction) is responsible for 45 percent of the world's carbon dioxide emissions — believe it or not, that's more than automobiles!

- ✔ Buildings use around 15 percent of the annual global water supply.

- ✔ Construction waste makes up 40 percent of landfill space, and a quarter of the globe's virgin wood goes to fuel the world's construction industry.

- ✔ A shocking 60 percent of the United States' electricity consumption occurs in commercial buildings.

The biggest argument for greening your building, quite simply, is that you can't afford not to! When you consider how long you plan on being in your commercial office space, distribution center, or manufacturing plant, you can see pretty quickly that occupying a high-performing space that generates annual savings on energy, waste, and water will result in substantial savings over the next 75 to 100 years.

On the present-day end of the spectrum, productivity and performance studies show an increase in employee output and satisfaction among individuals who work in a sustainable facility. Additionally, a green building (depending on its particular features) yields immediate reductions in operating costs through savings in water, energy, and waste disposal bills. Green buildings retain their asset value much more than their inefficient counterparts do.

Furthermore, depending on location, structure, and other variables, green buildings can be up to 30 percent more energy efficient, on average, than traditional buildings. If your current utility charges are 8 cents per kilowatt hour, simply reducing energy consumption by 30 percent knocks your costs down to 30 cents per square foot per year. Now *that* packs a punch for the ol' corporate pocketbook!

The advantages of green buildings include

- ✔ **An excellent return on your investment:** Depending on your building's original costs, utility infrastructure, and location, the *payback period* (how long it takes you to recoup your additional investment with the dollars you've saved through ownership and maintenance costs) required to retrofit old buildings or construct new ones can run from one to seven years. After the payback period, you can enjoy some green gravy!

- ✔ **Enhanced employee health, happiness, and productivity:** Because green buildings employ natural daylighting, employee morale is improved and absenteeism is reduced. Additionally, the increased indoor air quality found in green buildings and the decreased eye strain associated with natural lighting contribute dramatically to enhanced employee productivity. Extracting data on the correlation between employee health and sustainable buildings is difficult, but literally hundreds of articles and reports have found a lower rate of illness (particularly fewer cases of respiratory sickness, allergies, and asthma) in green buildings.

✔ **An opportunity to certify your green efforts and garner recognition from environmental leaders:** If you want to get some free publicity and credit for your company's sustainable facility, and show your stakeholders that your company practices what it preaches, acquiring official green-building certification is invaluable. Not only can individual components of your green building be certified as sustainable (wood, adhesives, wall coverings, paints, and carpets, to name a few) but also the entire building can be accredited by the U.S. Green Building Council as a Leadership in Energy and Environmental Design structure — more commonly known as a *LEED building*. More and more people are growing familiar with this terminology as cities and universities in the U.S. and Canada start adopting green-building requirements as the norm for their facilities. (I delve into the details of certification in this chapter's "LEED-certification specifics" sidebar.)

✔ **Piqued stakeholder interest and increased stakeholder respect:** News of a glistening new headquarters or renovated production facility is sure to arouse the curiosity of your stakeholders. In fact, many businesses with LEED-certified buildings, including banks, production facilities, and retail outlets, report that leading tours of their sustainable buildings is practically a full-time job. Not a bad way to get customers, investors, and other stakeholders in the door to educate them about your company's green vision, huh?

As consumers become more knowledgeable about green living and business, their attention increasingly turns to trading with and investing in businesses that are recognized for their sustainable facilities. Perhaps that's because green buildings help stakeholders feel good about a company's commitment to corporate social responsibility. Regardless, investors are increasingly assessing companies based on their preparedness for the future and are clearly interested in how they're mitigating exposure to energy volatility. Green construction is such a compelling part of the solution to many of the crises facing the global community today (and has so much media exposure) that it's an easily understandable way to showcase your sustainability efforts to stakeholders.

Making Preliminary Decisions

If your company's green business initiatives include improving the performance of your facilities, you essentially have three options: make greener choices with what you have, renovate certain areas or systems in your building, or build a new facility altogether. In Chapter 6, I present options for greening your office practices and instituting other small-scale changes, like incorporating energy-efficient lighting fixtures. Here, I help you decide whether renovating your current facility or building a brand-new one is in your company's best interests.

Another decision you have to make is whether you want to certify your new or renovated facility as a Leadership in Energy and Environmental Design (LEED) building. This certification is a widely recognizable stamp of authenticity that your company is the real green deal and not simply engaged in *greenwashing* (stating that your business is green without taking the actions necessary to back up that statement).

To renovate, or to build?

Analyzing whether to engage in one or more green renovation projects on your existing structure(s) or to jump into the fire with both feet and build a new facility requires an understanding of what's really involved in a remodel or new building project.

Remodeling requires fewer materials and therefore produces a lighter carbon footprint than new construction (although deconstruction waste can be significant). Remodeling thus allows you to incrementally green your current business abode by analyzing its performance and identifying projects within your scope. Stringing projects together year after year may be a perfectly viable alternative to building a brand-new structure.

If you do decide to build a new green facility, whether it be a coffee shop on a walking mall or a mid-sized dental instrumentation production facility, it'll be a significant effort for your company. Your image is reflected in your new building, and the time and financial commitment inherent in this process goes without saying. Among other factors, you must consider cost, business interruption, and the chaos of construction, not to mention a plethora of choices: building materials, site selection, energy and water efficiencies, waste reduction, and indoor air quality.

In green construction, the costs of a facility's entire life cycle are weighed against the upfront capital outlay necessary to get the project started. Green construction decreases ownership and maintenance costs over a building's life. So although the initial costs of building or remodeling sustainably may be higher, these costs are recouped (and often quickly!), which provides a triple-bottom-line win for people, planet, and profit. How so? Not only are your total ownership and maintenance costs decreased but also your business gets to leave a lighter carbon footprint, and your employees get to work in an environment that sports high indoor air quality and natural daylighting.

After you've looked at all the angles affecting your decision (both internal and external, as explained in the following sections), communicate your decision to renovate or build adequately to all of your stakeholders. Don't forget investors, employees, customers, and community members.

Assessing your internal capabilities

Environmentally sound design requires thinking in broad brush strokes about what it is you're designing and how that fits into your long-term, strategic green plan. Designing a green building thus means thinking upfront about materials, natural resources usage, site selection, and the handling of waste.

In order to effectively evaluate your internal capabilities to determine whether renovating or building makes the most sense, you need to revisit your long-term business plan and thoroughly analyze the performance of your current facility.

Also, try taking a stab at answering these questions, being careful to work from the top of the list (the most important questions) on down:

- **How is your building's current performance?** Do you have any impending issues like major structural deficiencies, hazardous material problems, or environmental remediation that need to be addressed? If so, you may be better off starting from scratch with a new green facility than trying to remediate these problems to make them code-worthy and sustainable.

- **What does your forecasted growth look like?** If you have aggressive growth plans for your company, retrofitting your existing building to incorporate green features may not be worth the investment if you're poised to outgrow it within ten years. On the other hand, if you can accommodate moderate growth by renovating and adding on to an existing structure, your costs and carbon footprint will be less to stay in the current building If you're unsure about *what* your projected growth looks like, revisit your business plan to concoct solid forecasts before moving on.

- **What are your future plans regarding the sales potential of the business itself?** If your goal is to turn the business over to new owners within five to seven years, you may not recoup the front-loaded costs of a new green building. You may, however, easily see a return on green remodeling endeavors.

- **What will the impact on your cash flow be?** Specifically, you should consider how likely you'd be able to make debt payments for either type of project — a renovation or a new facility. Have your accountant run some rough numbers based on rudimentary projections. This approach gives you an idea what your payments may be based on loan length, project cost, and interest rates.

Energy systems in new construction are obviously of paramount interest. Both wind and solar energy, for example, have come down significantly in price in the last few years, and many people project the price will continue to decline — so these two options are good ones to consider. If you decide to revamp your energy sources, though, make sure to compare costs per kilowatt hour (multiplied by your new building's estimated monthly requirements) against the price differential for installing the different options.

✔ **Are any loan or grant programs available to subsidize your green-building costs?** The Energy Security and Independence Act of 2007 provides the U.S. Small Business Administration (SBA) with funds designated to help small businesses purchase renewable energy systems. Contact your state SBA branch for more info. Also, a growing number of states are implementing grant and loan programs for sustainable commercial building features. Use the Internet search engine of your choice and type in your state's name and "loans grants green commercial building" to see what's available in your area. Each program is different, so make sure to ascertain whether grant money is attainable for new construction and/or renovations.

✔ **What will your workforce look like in the future?** Do you need to build *more* office space, or should you invite discussion about alternative employment models? (See Chapter 13 for details on these models, such as telecommuting.) If you foresee a shift away from 8-to-5 workers, you may not want all that extra workspace down the road, making renovation a more desirable option. Try to find out what digital capabilities exist for workers in your industry sector.

✔ **Are there any areas of concern specific to your business?** Making the decision to move your business to a new facility has some pretty extensive costs associated with it, particularly depending on the number of people you employ. If your business involves a couple of CPAs and paraprofessionals who rely on computers to perform their daily tasks, moving them is more cost efficient than moving a manufacturing facility, for example.

Don't forget to factor in the costs of moving the physical contents of your building when you're making this very important decision, as well as how long your business will be interrupted during the move or remodel. Lost revenue from days of downtime during the renovation or construction process should be clearly calculated into the project's total cost.

If you've been playing with the idea of new construction for a while, you may feel overwhelmed with all the information bombarding you about building green. If your organization is making the transition to a sustainable business model and you feel like you only have so much cash to invest in ecoendeavors at this time, you may want to consider the following: The true principles of sustainability aren't about buying the newest hot technology or having the flashiest facility; they're about doing more with less and conserving wherever possible.

Don't feel pressured into investing in a new green building to meet your mission of being a sustainable business — that may be an oxymoron! Many existing structures have tons of potential with well-thought-out remodels. You can be just as sustainable if you remodel the right way, plus you'll have spent less money (leaving more money to invest in other areas of your business) and used fewer raw materials and natural resources.

Considering external factors that affect your decisions

As you debate the value of renovating or constructing a new green facility, you need to have a big picture of the opportunities, resource availability, and threats that may impact your decision. Primary factors to look at, from most important on down, include

- **Your location:** The location of your facility affects both the availability and effectiveness of the various sustainability options you have to work with. For example, in regard to renewable energy, a lot of neat technology is in the works, but storage and distribution issues make much of it unavailable in many areas. Also, some types of renewable energy work better in certain geographical areas than others. For instance, solar power is most effective in the southwestern U.S., and hydropower is only available around dams. If your current building isn't situated to tap into passive solar energy and that's a viable method in your area, that may be a strike against renovating if solar energy is the wave of the energy future.

- **Your city's master planning initiatives:** What kinds of transportation plans are in the works, where are the majority of your employees coming from, and what sorts of zoning ordinances are on the table? The answers to these questions may very well affect your renovation or construction plans. Availability of alternative transportation and access to raw materials and distribution channels (if applicable) are important considerations as well when deciding whether you should rebuild. If you're guaranteed access to sustainable transportation where you're at now, you may want to stay put. If, however, that's an issue for you currently and your region's master plan contains caveats that may enhance access for you if you relocate your operation, then constructing a new, sustainable facility in a different location may be a better plan.

- **Tax credit availability:** Research available property and income tax incentives for building green in your area. Make sure to look at state, county, and city possibilities. Some tax credits exist for renovation efforts as well, so make sure to compare them in your particular state.

- **Plans for new industrial or business parks, green or otherwise:** If your business can be a part of a planned green neighborhood that's zoned for multiuse, or if it can be considered as the anchor in a new green shopping area, now may be a good time to seriously look at the opportunity to build a green facility.

- **What sorts of business models might be incorporated into future plans:** If you're in the business of selling retail products or services, think about whether putting up brick-and-mortar storefronts is an absolute necessity. Other sales strategies, such as Internet or catalogue sales, may be more sustainable. (And even if you don't necessarily *want* to be Internet-based, the market you're in may drive you that direction.) If you go with either of these strategies, renovating your current space rather than building and maintaining new square footage may be wise.

✔ **Potential resale value:** Future real estate market considerations are always important, whether you want to renovate or build new. Think about whether the area you're currently in is on its way out of popularity or whether it's coming into its own because of its proximity to the city's new light rail system. The answer may help drive your decision to green your existing facility or look for a new location that's more in line with your sustainable vision.

If your business has geographically scattered buildings, factor increasing fuel costs into your future strategy. Businesses strewn over multiple locales must analyze the movement of people and products between facilities. New green distribution centers and warehouses may reduce operational costs, but they won't cut your exposure to volatile fossil fuel costs.

LEED-certification specifics

The LEED rating system has evolved at a very rapid pace to feature new categories for different types of green construction projects. Currently, the available certification options include

✔ LEED-CI (for commercial interiors)

✔ LEED-CS (for core and shell)

✔ LEED-EB (for existing buildings)

✔ LEED-H (for homes)

✔ LEED-NC (for new construction and major renovation)

✔ LEED-ND (for neighborhood development)

✔ LEED-R (for retail)

The U.S. Green Building Council determines a project's LEED-certification status level by dividing attainable points into six categories. There are various options for attaining points within each of these categories:

✔ Sustainable siting

✔ Water conservation

✔ Energy and atmosphere

✔ Materials and resources

✔ Indoor environmental quality

✔ Green design innovation

The number of points earned per category on a project drives the level of certification your project receives. (To see a full list of how points can be gained in each category, go to www. usgbc.org.) Based on the points you attain, your building may be recognized as one of the following:

✔ LEED Certified

✔ LEED Silver

✔ LEED Gold

✔ LEED Platinum

If the LEED-certification waters still seem murky, know that you can get help from a LEED Accredited Professional (AP). LEED APs have undergone rigorous testing on sustainable design and construction and understand the LEED rating system. To see a list of APs, visit www.gbci.org and click the LEED AP Directory link at the top of the page.

Hot off the press: Tweaks to LEED certification for 2009 involve a point system that reflects regional differences, such as drought, which helps to address one of the main points of concern from the green-building community.

To certify, or not to certify?

Although green-building certification programs are popping up all over the place, LEED is by far the most widely recognized one in the U.S. In Canada, the same may be said for Green Globes. Pursuing LEED certification is something you should think about carefully in advance of deciding whether to renovate your existing facility or construct a new green one. Because you want a specialist in all LEED plans from the get-go, and because certification can add costs, the decision to pursue LEED certification must be a consideration from the beginning.

Strategically, LEED certification means your facility gets listed on a national registry of all LEED-certified buildings. For your efforts and expenses, you receive a plaque bearing the LEED logo, as well as free publicity and increased respect from your green-minded stakeholders. Also, by inviting the U.S. Green Building Council (which provides the stamp of approval on all LEED certifications) in to certify your efforts, public perception is that your commitment to transparency will carry over to other facets of your operations.

Note that pursuing LEED certification is a financial decision as well as a strategic one. Aside from standardized costs, such as registering a project, the price of obtaining certification varies according to the various types of LEED-certifiable construction projects (described in the nearby sidebar). Because some of the costs necessary to attain the higher levels of certification are a bit exorbitant (and are mostly associated with jumping through paperwork hoops like a trained terrier), some companies are opting to simply construct their buildings according to LEED guidelines and *not* spend the money for certification.

So is going for LEED-certified status worth it for you and your company? Ask yourself the following:

- **What percentage of your total budget is applicable to the LEED-certification process?** For example, $15,000 may seem like a daunting figure, but it may be only 2 percent of your project's total cost. When expressed as a percentage, this certification cost may appear less fearsome.

- **What will a LEED-registered project do for your mortgage-negotiation capabilities?** Chapter 9 pursues this question in more depth, but consider that many lenders view a LEED-certified building as a less-risky investment and may be amenable to negotiating based on that.

- **How much free publicity might LEED certification garner for your organization?** In my community, two financial institutions almost simultaneously announced that they were pursuing LEED projects. I can't even begin to tell you the number of articles, awards, and accolades these companies have accrued based on their projects. Always factor in the value of free press when considering the cost of pursuing LEED certification.

✓ **What sort of increased value might LEED certification add to your building?** Because LEED is a widely recognized certification system that identifies your building as energy, water, and waste efficient, consider how your facility's future fair market value may be impacted by the rising costs associated with energy and other natural resources.

Surveying Your Options: Specifics You Can Target

If you're like most businesspeople, when you begin strategizing ways to make your facility (or parts of it) sustainable, you're not quite sure where to begin. The next few sections give you an overview of the five defining characteristics of green buildings: sustainable materials, water conservation, energy conservation, renewable energy sourcing, and enhanced indoor air quality. Which characteristic(s) you pick depends on your overall goals and the resources you have available. I help you make decisions in light of those factors earlier in this chapter (see the "Making Preliminary Decisions" section); here, I simply lay out your options.

Waste reduction is, of course, a very important component of constructing and running a green building, but I cover it in Chapter 6. There, I explain how to reduce solid waste in an office space, as well as how to design and where to locate in-house recycling centers to handle appropriate recyclable materials within your facility. When it comes to construction waste, reducing waste on-site is primarily achieved by employing a construction-site recycling firm to reuse and recycle construction and demolition debris.

Choosing sustainable materials

Before you can start renovating or building, you must first identify which characteristics from the following list are most important to you when selecting sustainable materials:

✓ Harvested or manufactured locally

✓ Sustainably grown or harvested

✓ Nontoxic and natural

✓ High recycled content

✓ Easily recycled at its end of life

✓ Low or no ongoing maintenance

Sometimes you can only afford to focus on one characteristic, so you need to have an idea of what's available, what your contractor knows how to work with and find, your budget, and your aesthetic goals before you really start researching materials.

The vast array of green building materials coming onto the market daily makes any attempt at listing them grossly incomplete. However, there are some big-ticket items in your building that should be addressed:

✔ **Framing:** Depending on your particular project, you may be choosing between steel, engineered lumber, and traditional wood framing. Each of these materials has different environmental considerations and long-term impact on your building's operations and maintenance. For example, steel is extremely energy intensive to manufacture, but is very easy to recycle. Wood comes from trees, and you want to keep trees standing because they're carbon eaters.

If you do go with solid wood, make sure it's certified by the Forest Stewardship Council (FSC), an international agency that independently certifies forest products as harvested from sustainably managed forests. Go to www.fsc.org to see the particulars of FSC-certified wood and look for the seal shown in Figure 8-1 on all of your wood products, including framing lumber, trim, and plywood.

Figure 8-1:
Look for
this Forest
Stewardship
Council seal
on all wood
products.

The FSC Logo identifies products which contain wood from well-managed forests certified in accordance with the rules of the Forest Stewardship Council ©1996 Forest Stewardship Council A.C.

✔ **Roofing:** Your choice of roofing can have a strong impact on the overall energy efficiency of your building. Dark roofs absorb and emanate much more heat than their light-colored counterparts, greatly increasing cooling costs for your building. When identifying roofing possibilities, consider high recycled content, recycled rubber shingles, spray-on foam, and solar shingles.

✔ **Walls:** Consider using either 100-percent recycled gypsum or recycled-content drywall paper for your walls. Structured Insulated Panels (SIPs) are another option. These panels come to a worksite precut; are highly durable; won't crack, buckle, or warp; and contain an expanded core of insulation bound on both sides by oriented strand board or plywood "skins." Make sure that the SIP you select uses formaldehyde-free foam insulation cores.

✔ **Insulation:** A key component of an energy-efficient building is insulation — and a ton of it. Many new types of formaldehyde-free and recycled-content insulation are out there (including shredded blue jeans, recycled newspaper, cellulose, and recycled cotton), so check out commercial-grade green insulation materials.

✔ **Flooring:** Toss away the notion that your facility's floor needs to look like all other commercial facilities' floors. Based on your business's specific needs, you can choose your flooring from a multitude of options that include reclaimed wood, bamboo, cork, PVC-free carpet tiles, and colored concrete.

Conserving water

Water conservation in and around your building is of paramount concern. Most outdoor water planning issues have to do with maintaining your commercial landscaping and managing stormwater. Inside your facility, you'll be most concerned with designing your internal plumbing, fixtures, and water-transfer system.

You may not have the funds or desire to incorporate all of the following water-conservation methods, but at least consider which one(s) might benefit your business the most:

✔ **Water-conserving plumbing fixtures:** Certain plumbing fixtures can conserve as much as 50 percent of water used for that particular feature. For example, dual-flush toilets allow you to control the water that flushes out of and into your tank to limit needless water use. Low-flow faucets or shower heads (if you have an in-house gym or showering facility) are also important contributors to lowering water usage.

✔ **Water-efficient landscaping:** Native landscaping reduces the need for energy- and water-intensive sprinkler systems. Landscaping for outdoor buildings should emphasize water-efficient plants, trees, and shrubs. Turf should only be used where absolutely necessary (such as in a play area for an on-site day care). If you must water turf, make sure to do so at night, when evaporation potential is low.

✔ **A used-water recycling system:** A variety of methods are out there for collecting and purifying used water from commercial buildings (but not from toilets or cafeterias). These various systems recycle the used water for flushing toilets, running appliances, watering landscaping, or maintaining production processes.

Commonly referred to as living machines, *hydroponic ponds* are systems that recycle *graywater* (used water from restroom sinks and showers, for example) and process stormwater runoff polluted by pesticides, petroleum residues, and other toxins. Through a series of ponds, bacteria, snails, and plants act like a natural wetland to cleanse and recycle these waters into clean liquid. Not only is a hydroponic pond incredibly water efficient but it's also aesthetically beautiful. It can be built outdoors in warmer climates and in a greenhouse in colder areas. (As an added bonus, the interest level in and free press generated by hydroponic ponds is extraordinarily high.)

✔ **Rainwater harvesting:** By combining roof and gutter design with cisterns to harvest and store rainwater, April showers can be used in and around commercial buildings. Recycled rainwater can be used for functions such as watering landscaping and flushing toilets.

✔ **A water-conserving procurement policy:** This is a purchasing policy that states that as any appliance or plumbing fixture wears out, it must be replaced with a water-saving model.

Reducing energy usage

Energy conservation is embodied in every aspect of a green building, and you may be surprised by how much you can dramatically reduce energy by employing green-building techniques aimed at energy conservation. Your team of hired, professional advisors (see the later section "Professional Help You May Need" for more on these folks) can work with you to prioritize the features that will yield the greatest energy savings for your building.

Plan on having lengthy conversations surrounding the

✔ **Building envelope:** Optimal energy performance comes from a solid infrastructure, or *building envelope* (wall systems, windows, doors, insulation, and roofing components). A building envelope that provides adequate ventilation for indoor air quality while maximizing energy conservation is key to a high-performing building.

✔ **Lighting system:** An energy-efficient lighting system includes dimmers, timers, bulbs, ballasts, task-specific lighting, and integrated natural daylight.

✔ **Heat-recovery systems:** Depending on how much hot water your facility uses, this feature can be a no-brainer. A heat-recovery system is a coil installed in the water outflow drain that absorbs heat from hot water and circulates it back into the building where it can be used in radiant floor heating or manufacturing processes.

✔ **Heating and cooling systems:** A full 60 to 70 percent of your building's energy may be expended to keep it at the proper temperature. Nonrenewable energy systems, including gas and electricity, are the most common methods for heating water and air and powering the pumps and fans used to heat and cool your building.

If you need to go with a traditional mechanical system, be sure to choose one that's Energy Star–certified. Of course, conduct a thorough cost-benefit analysis of ground source heat pumps (that use underground water's naturally modulated temperature to reduce the amount of energy needed) and radiant floor heating before making a final choice.

Getting energy from renewable sources

Many entrepreneurs, owners, and managers are beginning to realize that oil addiction will soon require a serious 12-step program. But contrary to the theory on how to wean a person from a substance, going cold turkey simply isn't an option when it comes to fossil fuels. Instead, you have to limit energy usage where you can and then consider the next step — ensuring that whatever energy *does* need to be expended relies heavily on renewable resources. *Renewable energy* refers to energy from resources that can't be depleted, such as wind, sunlight, biomass, heat stored beneath the Earth's surface, and flowing and/or hot water. These natural energy sources can be converted into mechanical, electrical, or chemical energy.

Unlike fossil fuels, which emit carbon dioxide into the air and contribute to everything from biodiversity loss to coral bleaching to climate change (see Chapter 2 for more details), renewables are clean and don't emit greenhouse gases. So which one is best to use?

The future of energy conservation: Demand-response technology

Facilities of the future will most likely include *demand-response technology*. These are systems designed to protect businesses against energy interruption and maximize energy efficiency. Demand-response technology allows the existing electrical grid to "talk" to your business's computers, appliances, and other power-sucking devices — even asking them to respond to peak energy-consumption periods by adjusting your building's temperatures and lighting to avoid brownouts. On the supply side, the *smart power grid* refers to the use of communication software to make the current electrical power grid operate more efficiently.

You can actually view your facility's energy consumption through a smart-grid meter.

Already rolled out in housing markets in Toronto and coming in 2009 to Boulder, Colorado, demand-response technology may be worth investigating for your business. See how you can be a part of it by visiting www.gridwise.pnl.gov for an overview of a Department of Energy–funded pilot project going on in the northwest United States.

Often, the best renewable energy portfolio choice is a mix of several options.

✔ **Wind:** Wind is the world's fastest growing renewable. Wind turbines convert the kinetic energy of the wind into electricity. As turbine capacity grows, the cost of wind power decreases, making wind more attractive as a renewable energy source. The indications are that pursuit of wind power will accelerate in the next three to five years in the U.S. and Canada, further driving down the price.

✔ **Solar:** By almost any measure, sunlight is the greenest of the renewable energies. It's perpetually available, produces no emissions or waste, and can be converted into either heat or electricity. Also, it's being harvested, stored, and distributed in new and innovative ways, including the use of solar shingles that combine solar cells with slate, metal, or asphalt roofing. You can benefit from solar power through both active methods (such as using silicon wafers) and passive methods (like orienting your facility to absorb and use direct sunlight).

The capability to manufacture solar cells is growing globally. Silicon wafer production facilities are springing up in North America, adding to the significant manufacturing capacity already found in Germany and Japan. As this capacity continues ramping up to meet demand, the price of solar energy will fall, causing many energy brokers to predict that solar energy will outpace wind power within a decade.

✔ **Biomass:** Plant matter or biodegradable waste used to generate electricity (or produce biofuels) is referred to as *biomass energy*. Of particular promise in the U.S. is the use of wood biomass in timber-intensive states.

✔ **Geothermal:** Generating power from heat that's naturally stored beneath the Earth's surface is a promising source of renewable energy. Ground source heat pumps harvest this energy to heat and cool buildings. The great thing about geothermal energy is that you can supply your building with warm water by using the byproduct of the energy-generation process. There's a lot of interest in geothermal systems due to their reasonable cost of installation and maintenance, as well as their energy-efficient properties.

✔ **Hydropower:** Hydropower refers to energy derived from the force of moving water. Turbines located in the water flow harness this energy for use in many capacities. Hydropower is a significantly developed source of energy in the U.S. and Canada already and is very reasonably priced.

Certain challenges are inherent in using almost every type of renewable energy. Early wind turbines were tied to migratory bird deaths; hydropower is currently controversial for its impact on wild fisheries; and ethanol is partially responsible for an escalating global food crisis. Make sure to do your homework on the pros and cons of the renewable energy source you're considering using.

Introducing living buildings and green roofs

Some visionary designers are already looking past green buildings to the next generation of structures — *living buildings.* This holistic type of architecture applies to buildings that act like natural organisms, with components that sense and react to differing levels of temperature, carbon dioxide, water runoff, and other ecological occurrences. The structures themselves are self sustaining and even give back to the environment. Imagine a building that's actually ecologically restorative! Think of structures that capture and recycle rainwater endlessly, using it to create a rooftop habitat that increases biodiversity in urban areas. Sound far-fetched and hopelessly futuristic? Think again — such structures are already here! To find out more about living buildings, visit the Cascadia Region Green Building Council's Web site at www.cascadiagbc.org/lbc.

Some design ideas already being explored will surely be incorporated into living buildings of the future:

✔ **Smart shades:** Made of metal composites that are highly sensitive to thermal changes, these shades curl up in the winter and expand for full coverage in the summer, thereby controlling a building's interior solar rays depending on the season.

✔ **Windows embedded with carbon dioxide–sensitive sensors:** An electric current activated by carbon dioxide causes a contraction of wires that slightly open slits etched into the window. When proper ventilation is achieved, the electric current subsides, the slits close, and the sensitive wires return to normal.

Green, or living, roofs are a very progressive alternative you may want to consider as well. Green roofs have been incorporated in projects ranging from urban office spaces to the huge, industrialized Ford Rouge River revitalization project taking place in Dearborn, Michigan. Living roofs have a multitude of benefits:

✔ Reduced heating and cooling costs (during winter months, a green roof can reduce heat loss by 25 percent or more)

✔ A longer life span than their conventional counterparts

✔ Provision of a natural habitat and consumption of carbon dioxide

✔ Significant decrease in stormwater runoff

✔ Aesthetic beauty that can add value to your facility, including providing a habitat for butterflies and birds

Although the individual design of green roofs may vary, they all share basic similarities. Check out www.greenroofs.com for the latest in technology, new projects, consultants, and other resources related to green roofs.

Cleaning up indoor air quality

Providing good indoor air quality is essential if you want to be considered a socially responsible corporation and have healthy, productive employees. Poor indoor air leads to Sick Building Syndrome (SBS). People with this condition complain of acute health discomfort. Complaints consist primarily of headaches; difficulty concentrating; irritation in the eyes, nose, or throat; dry coughs; itchy skin; dizziness; nausea; fatigue; and ultra-sensitivity to odors.

If an unprecedented number of your employees complain of these health issues, your building may be giving them SBS. What can cause this condition?

- ✔ **Inadequate ventilation:** If your original building design didn't contain provisions for adequate ventilation, contaminated indoor air has nowhere to go. Proper ventilation is a key element of sustainable design. Be sure to incorporate a mechanical engineer's advice on providing for an adequate mix of indoor and outdoor air.

- ✔ **Chemical contaminants from indoor sources:** From the glues and adhesives in flooring to the textiles in your office furniture and the paint on the walls, *volatile organic compounds* (VOCs) are swirling around most indoor work environments. These VOCs, including formaldehyde, are toxic indoor pollutants. Considering most people spend 80 percent of their lives indoors, improving indoor air quality is one of the most compelling social benefits of greening your facility.

- ✔ **Chemical contaminants from outdoor sources:** The outdoor air that enters a building can contain pollutants from motor vehicle exhausts, plumbing vents, and building exhausts (found primarily in restrooms and cafeterias).

- ✔ **Biological contaminants:** Unseen nasties like bacteria, molds, pollen, and viruses may be hiding in your building's ducts, or any place that water has permeated, such as carpeting, insulation, or ceiling tiles. Biological contaminants can also emanate from insect, bird, or rodent droppings.

Any of these items can act together to intensify the effect of SBS on human health. However, this condition can be difficult to diagnose, and even when it *is* diagnosed, pinpointing the specific source of the complaint, much less remediating the problem, is even more challenging.

One step you can take to combat SBS, especially if you can't afford a brand-new building right now, is to ensure that your adhesives, paints, flooring, and wall coverings contain few or no VOCs. Look for the GREENGUARD certification, shown in Figure 8-2, on these products or their packaging.

Figure 8-2:
The GREEN GUARD certification ensures few or no-VOCs are included in a variety of building materials.

Professional Help You May Need

If you determine that constructing a new, green facility, or renovating an existing space, is in fact the best tactic for your company, keep in mind that you aren't embarking on this journey alone. You're going to have a team of experienced sustainable building professionals working for you and guiding you through the process of designing and constructing your green facility or remodel.

The following sections highlight some of the folks you may need to consult, depending on the type and breadth of the greening you want to do. And of course you'll want to make sure these pros understand that your facility is a core part of your green strategy and your organization's commitment to a sound sustainability policy.

Always perform the following due diligence on prospective members of your green-building team before finalizing your selections:

- ✔ **Request a reference list and make calls.** Follow a prepared script of questions that delves into how well the candidate stuck to budgets and timelines, how he or she managed a worksite, how pleasant the candidate was to work with, and especially how well he or she listened and responded to client needs. Ask the referrals direct questions relating to the depth and breadth of the candidate's sustainable design knowledge. If feasible, go visit the sites and see the candidate's work for yourself.

- ✔ **Interview each prospective candidate.** Ask specific questions pertaining to green building — how many ecoprojects the candidate has been involved with, how much continuing education has he or she received in sustainable construction/design, and what are his or her greatest green accomplishments. Provide a brief description of your project and ask for ideas upfront about what sorts of sustainability-oriented features the candidate recommends.

Architect

Whether or not to hire an architect is arguably one of the most important decisions you'll make because an architect can guide you through design, contractor negotiations, and a myriad of other critical steps in your project. The different services an architect provides depend on your individual situation and the extent of your remodeling or new construction project. Cost and internal expertise will drive your decision as to whether to hire an architect for these sorts of projects.

By law, you must have an architect onboard if your proposed renovation will impact the building inhabitants' safety, such as structural modifications or changes to entrances and exits. If your renovation project won't put anyone's safety in danger, the decision to hire an architect is completely up to you.

Architects offer a wide set of services. You may contract an architect to

- **Conduct a sustainability assessment of your current facility:** This assessment involves conducting energy modeling on the structure to evaluate interventions and see how well they might perform. An effective assessment measures potential energy savings against the cost of upgrades that may be available in a retrofit situation and is a valuable tool for analyzing your current facility's performance.

- **Make general suggestions and provide counsel on the direction of a project:** Architects are a great resource for reigning in or encouraging your company's vision. They can offer practical guidance (as well as advice based on zoning regulations) on issues such as parking, accessibility, and the positioning of your facility on the property.

- **Create a full set of drawings:** Architects can transpose preliminary sketches into full-scale architectural drafts, including product specifications.

An architect's advice is essential during the site-selection process, so if you're thinking about hiring an architect, plan on interviewing and hiring him or her *way* in advance of your anticipated project start-up date.

A good starting point in locating a commercial architect who understands sustainable design is to scan a list of LEED-certified commercial buildings in your region. In many areas of the U.S., only a handful of firms tend to spearhead green-building projects, so they'll jump off the page at you. In other parts of the country, you may have a plethora of firms to choose from.

To legally call oneself an architect, a person must be licensed by his or her state's licensure agency. This designation indicates that the person passed a rigorous test and possesses a standardized level of competency. Unfortunately, sometimes people use the term "architectural draftsperson" without having undergone state licensure. To ensure that the person you're considering for your project has been appropriately recognized as a bona fide architect, go to your preferred Internet search engine and type in "licensed architects" and your state's name.

The best current indicator that a person has exposure to green-building concepts is the LEED Accredited Professional (AP) certification (see the earlier "LEED-certification specifics" sidebar for tips on finding a LEED AP). This is, however, a generalist accreditation and doesn't necessarily address specific competencies such as energy modeling or passive solar assessment.

Belonging to the American Institute of Architects (AIA), although professionally enriching to the individual, simply means that the person has paid his or her dues to the national association. In no way does AIA membership indicate the architect in question is competent or experienced.

Ask your architect whether his or her firm includes a landscape architect and/ or a biomechanical engineer. If an architectural firm is indeed tapped into sustainable design, it either directly employs this expertise or subcontracts for it. If the firm doesn't seem to have a handle on this level of expertise, consider that a red flag and look to the next architect on your list.

Contractor

Your contractor, or builder, takes the design work prepared by your architect and converts that pretty paper or digital picture into your new physical space by coordinating materials purchasing and delivery, supplier payment, worksite safety, subcontracted labor, and the like.

If your remodel is small and tightly scoped, you may not need a general contractor, who usually adds 10 percent onto the subcontractors' bids. After all, do you really want to incur that extra surcharge on a highly specific sustainable renovation project, such as adding insulation and a metal roof? On bigger, more complex remodels and additions, however, you may be working with 20 or more different subcontractors. In this scenario, the extra fees of a general contractor who can oversee all the subs are worthwhile.

In the absence of a general contractor, you, as the building owner, become the de facto general contractor.

If and when you're ready to start the contractor hunt, gather a list of contractors in your area who've been involved in commercial green-building projects. Solicit referrals from your architect and do your own research as well by contacting your county or city building department to inquire whether a green-builder education program is available in your area. If one is, obtain a list of certified green builders from the program's facilitator.

After you've whittled down your prospects to a list of three to six contractors (depending on the size and complexity of your project), ask each candidate to price out the project both with and without individual sustainable features. For example, solar panels, graywater recycling systems, or ground source heat pumps are features that should be lined out on the bid sheet individually. This proposal method allows you to prioritize which green attributes are most important to your company if the total project numbers come in higher than your expectations. It also provides you with the opportunity to see more clearly how individual components contribute to total project costs.

Also, ask which subcontractors your general contractor prospects use for the mechanical, electrical, and plumbing (MEP) work. The American Subcontractors Association gives out annual awards for "Best MEP," so ask your candidate whether he or she knows of any subs who've received this award. Or check it out for yourself by searching for "American Subcontractors Association" and your area's name on the Internet and see whether that particular region provides a list of recent recipients.

Don't make your final choice based on price alone. Particularly with green construction, less is by no means the best. The bids you receive from your narrowed list of potential contractors should be pretty tightly clustered. If one bid is significantly below the others (by say 15 to 20 percent or more), make sure that the contractor understood the specs or didn't forget to include something big. Otherwise you could end up with a subpar job or miss out on a sustainable feature you really wanted to incorporate.

Interior designer

Although sustainably harvested wood and a ground source heat pump are crucial components of your green building, most of your clients, employees, and other stakeholders don't see 'em. What they *do* see is your office furniture, cabinetry, restrooms, cafeteria, breakroom, floors, and window coverings. Choosing an interior designer who understands sustainable design is a critical finishing touch to your green building.

Some projects will necessarily involve an interior designer. For example, if you're interested in renovating a large, open work area that's going to be refurnished, you'll need help designing workflow and lighting. In this case, you may go right to an interior designer without first hiring an architect or contractor.

On more comprehensive projects, you may want to hire an interior designer to give you an overview of what your design considerations entail. Full-service consultation includes not only a design plan but also a professional to liaise with vendors, coordinate purchases, and make recommendations to fulfill your sustainable interior needs.

If you have in-house expertise and want to save on professional fees, you may want to contract for an interior-design consultation and the production of a design plan. This way you get the benefit of expert guidance *and* save money by implementing the plan internally.

Be sure to test out your prospective interior designer's green knowledge by asking about his or her prior experience with PVC-free and natural carpets and floor coverings, organic textiles, low-VOC paints/finishes, and recycled/reclaimed woods. If your questions solicit a look of incomprehension, you may want to rethink your choice.

Getting Down to Business

Assessing your renovation needs requires considering what specifically is mandated by law and what's guided by aesthetic desire. If you're changing any corridors that affect exiting, modifying points of access, or structurally altering any part of your building, you must have an architect onboard to guide you through the process (see the earlier "Architect" section for help hiring one). If you're replacing windows and doors, painting, changing out plumbing, or doing cosmetic renovation without an architect, you may take your renovations one step at a time.

What goes on in the space around your building is just as important as what goes on inside it. Visit different undeveloped and commercial tracts of land, parcels in business parks, urban areas ripe for transformation, and even *brownfield sites* (contaminated areas usually available at a good price because of the associated clean-up costs). Imagine the different ways you could build your facility to complement existing wind and solar patterns, water flow, and biological elements.

Of course, green building and remodeling present some interesting challenges. As with anything innovative, you're better off acknowledging these challenges upfront and preparing for them accordingly. Here are some of the most common challenges you may run into:

- **Mechanical features in a green building may not respond to manual change as quickly as employees are used to.** Some of the switches and gauges in green buildings may not provide results as quickly as the systems you currently use. For example, HVAC units that rely on radiant heat or natural cooling won't immediately adjust the temperature the moment an employee touches a dial. Alert employees to expect some slowdown in certain areas so they're not disappointed if the office's new green features don't provide the immediate satisfaction they're accustomed to.

- **Some aspects of greening your facility require mitigating their adverse effects.** Green construction has special challenges. For example, siting a building to maximize daylighting requires adding other features to reduce the resulting glare. Likewise, installing a living roof (see the earlier sidebar) requires adding more structural support to the building. Being aware of the pros and cons to any specific features or systems you're installing helps you prepare building inhabitants (and executive management) for what to expect.

✔ **New green products may require staff training.** Sustainable products, such as dual-flush toilets and solar hot water heaters, don't function like their traditional counterparts — a fact that may cause anxiety for users. If you're looking at such products, have a plan in place to train staff in the use of your building's new green features.

✔ **Certain sustainable features may look odd to the unaccustomed eye.** Not all green features are going to appear familiar to your customers, employees, and investors. For example, most people are used to seeing uniform, freshly mown lawns surrounding office buildings. By contrast, native landscaping (like long grass prairie) may appear scruffy or untended. You may want to place placards around and about these areas that explain how much water and energy this landscaping saves, as well as the fact that it's free of pesticides. Using placards simultaneously generates interest in the project and provides educational value.

The best way to address any challenges associated with green features is to be prepared to openly address them and help stakeholders understand that new technology sometimes takes a while to get used to.

Picking renovation projects

If you've chosen to renovate certain aspects of your existing facility, you can benefit from two good assessment tools designed to help you identify your building's key performance problems, as well as solutions that may help you maintain and improve its long-term performance. After you have the results of one of the following assessment tools, you can begin prioritizing what's most crucial to deal with first:

✔ **Green Globes Continual Improvement Tool for Existing Buildings (Green Globes-CIEB)** is a Web-based tool that guides you through the creation of a baseline of your building's performance and identification of persistent problems. In an interactive way, you can walk through potential improvement scenarios and plan for and monitor the success of your prioritized green remodeling projects. This tool has been used in Canada for years and is just being introduced to the U.S. To see a free teaser version, go to www.thegbi.org/lp/freetrial.asp.

✔ **LEED for Existing Building: Operations & Maintenance** is administered by the U.S. Green Building Council and incorporates the organization's trademark rating system to help building owners create a plan to transition their current structure to a high-performing one. This tool captures physical systems (like mechanical systems and land use) and the manner in which the building is used (waste stream and commuting programs) in developing a plan to enhance the building's sustainable performance potential. Check out what this tool looks like by going to www.usgbc.org/leed, clicking the LEED Rating Systems link at the top of the page, and then clicking the Existing Buildings: Operations & Maintenance link on the right-hand side.

Alternatively, you can browse this list of different projects for some initial remodeling ideas. Just make sure you always analyze the costs versus the benefits. For example, a new heating and air conditioning system is a big-ticket remodel, but it may yield a payback within three to five years.

- ✔ Install water-efficient plumbing fixtures such as dual-flush toilets, waterless urinals, or low-flow faucets.

- ✔ Install *on-demand water heaters* (meaning the water is only heated when it's needed) or solar water heaters.

- ✔ Retrofit lighting systems incrementally (via programmable timers and compact fluorescent light bulbs) or in totality.

- ✔ Replace floor coverings with carpet tiles or commercial-grade bamboo.

- ✔ Install energy-pinching mechanical systems such as an Energy Star furnace, air conditioning system, or solar hot water heater.

- ✔ Upgrade windows and doors to high-efficiency models to reduce heating and cooling loss.

- ✔ Blow in more recycled content or natural insulation.

- ✔ Install programmable thermostats.

- ✔ Update roofing material from heat-absorbing asphalt shingles to high-recycled content metal or other recycled-content shingles.

- ✔ Add automated shades to maximize daylighting while reducing glare.

- ✔ Weatherize existing windows.

- ✔ Trade out your pesticide-laden, water-intensive lawn for native landscaping to add visual interest and habitat on your commercial grounds.

Planning the site for your new building

Site planning takes an aesthetic eye as well as technical expertise, usually in the form of a biomechanical or bioclimatic engineer. When planning out a new location for your facility, pay close attention to

- ✔ **Biodiversity needs:** Retaining as much natural native vegetation as possible is always the best way to preserve existing biodiversity. Aim high — set goals to *increase* habitat availability. As much as possible, incorporate existing trees and native landscaping.

✔ **Wind, water, thermal, and solar patterns:** In warmer climates, design your site to augment cooling breezes; likewise, in colder areas, design your site to block arctic winds. If you're in a part of the country with good solar potential, site your building so you can harness this free and renewable energy (south facing exposures are great for solar panels or shingles, for example). Heat energy can be stored in materials referred to as thermal mass, such as masonry and water, and you should consider this info when outlining the materials you want to use and the angle at which you want to place your new construction.

✔ **Access to the property:** Predetermine the easiest ways to get to and from your facility by methods other than single-passenger vehicles. Can supplies, inventory, customers, and employees easily access your facility by using alternative transportation? If that's not feasible in all cases, strive to shorten the length of road you need to construct.

✔ **Minimization of stormwater runoff:** Stormwater runoff is accelerated in many commercial buildings because of the large square footage of parking lots. As the water hits the asphalt and runs off, it accumulates pollutants on the ground that mix together in a pretty toxic stew. Managing this flow naturally is part of your site-planning process and can be done by using some fairly simple (and very ancient) methods. Also, asphalt contributes to heat islands and is made from petroleum, so minimizing its usage is an important consideration in green construction.

✔ **Security:** This consideration depends on the exposure of your facility to potential security breaches. If your organization has high-profile security needs, you may want to engage an architect who has experience in designing buildings that have antiterrorist characteristics, for example.

✔ **Noise barriers:** Natural noise barriers, like berms and plantings, may decrease noise marginally. However, the only true way to decrease noise is by distance, which may or may not be a feasible variable in your situation.

✔ **Daylighting potential:** Early on in the design phase, it's important to understand building orientation as it pertains to the location of doors and windows that will serve as shade providers. Increased daylighting reduces the need for artificial lighting, may result in lower heating and cooling costs, and is a gentler, more pleasant light to work under.

✔ **Views:** Siting a building to maximize your view is valuable, albeit secondary to most of the previously listed considerations.

Sustainable deconstruction

Most renovations generate a tremendous amount of waste, and disposing of that waste costs money. Because you're a good environmental steward, when deconstructing part of an existing building with the anticipation of remodeling, decide what can be reused in the remodel effort. Lots of components, including cabinetry, beams, flooring, shingles, and so on, can be reused.

Think you'll need a hand developing a good construction-waste-elimination plan? Run an Internet search using the name of your town and "deconstruction services" to see what resources you can find. The cost of recycling on-site often offsets conventional waste-disposal costs.

When refurbishing an existing facility, consider the following:

✔ **Make sure your general contractor and subcontractors understand sustainability.** From the subs on-site to the designers and project planners, everyone on the project needs to know the importance of reducing waste.

✔ **Use a crusher on-site to recycle shingles, concrete, stone, and the like.** Reprocess existing demolished materials for reuse as landscaping and roadfill.

✔ **Use excavated materials for contouring and landscaping.** As an added bonus, you can create sound and privacy barriers by using these materials.

✔ **Reuse deconstructed material creatively.** The only limit to using deconstructed material is one's imagination, so think outside the box. Old brick can be used as an interesting component in garden pathways; old wood can live anew as flooring or cabinetry fronts.

✔ **Work with suppliers and contractors who have a take-back policy.** Look for people on your building team who accept surplus supplies. Don't expect a credit for the returned goods but know that, from a sustainability standpoint, ensuring the materials are used in another project is better than letting them go into a landfill.

Chapter 9

Greening Your Accounting Practices

....

In This Chapter

▶ Gauging a financial institution's sustainability

▶ Understanding the green financial services and investment opportunities available to you

▶ Figuring out where to turn for start-up capital for your green projects

....

*N*egotiating sustainable financing and leasing packages, developing green banking relationships, and repositioning your portfolio to feature socially responsible companies offer tons of sustainable development opportunities. Engaging in such green accounting practices also provides access to new and creative financing instruments, chances to develop partnerships with other forward-thinking businesspeople, and occasions to enhance your company's image as a green business and elevate your branding efforts.

Moving your money, loans, credit cards, and investment portfolio to sustainable counterparts isn't something you can accomplish overnight. But that doesn't mean you shouldn't prioritize these tasks, all of which fall on your accounting team. In this chapter, I outline the various sustainable accounting and financing options available and explain their value so you can decide how you want to incorporate them into your business structure.

Understanding What Green Finances Entail

Green financial service providers exhibit evidence of triple-bottom-line manifestation in their operations, products, and policies. If you work with a particular financial institution and don't observe examples that specifically address all three aspects of the *triple bottom line* (people, planet, and profit; see Chapter 1 for more on the triple bottom line), then you should reconsider whether working with that institution is really in your business's best interest.

Following are some hallmarks of green financial service providers:

- **People:** To serve the people aspect of the triple bottom line, financial service providers mandate employee/customer policies that center on sustainable ideals. Examples of such policies and programs include

  - Helping lower-income folks purchase their first homes through *Individual Development Accounts* (IDAs), which operate like an IRA.

  - Participating in other community-development programs, such as donating 1 percent of net income to philanthropic causes.

  - Having a stringent policy against *predatory lending* — programs such as pay-day or car title loans that have extremely high interest rates and potentially devastating results on low-income earners.

  - Matching employees' charitable dollars or volunteer hours up to a certain limit.

  - Giving a percentage of bank-sponsored credit card transaction fees to local environmental organizations.

- **Planet:** Financial institutions may engage in the following environmentally conscious activities:

  - Providing debit and credit cards made from biobased raw materials.

  - Offering online banking and other green options, such as direct deposit of paychecks and new ATMs that don't use envelopes or receipts.

  - Issuing bank statements, financial statements, and sustainability reports online instead of in hard-copy form.

  - Renovating existing facilities to employ green-building concepts rather than using virgin resources to build new structures.

  - Implementing greener operational strategies with the aim of becoming carbon neutral.

  - Offering green accounts, mortgages, credit cards, and other services.

  - Providing financial support for green projects and organizations through the bank's foundation.

- **Profit:** Clearly, the traditional bottom line also needs to be addressed. Green financial institutions focus on supporting organizations and projects that merge environmental and social concerns with profit enhancement by

  - Sanctioning projects that have the triple bottom line embedded in their proposals and working with noncompliant companies and organizations to bring them up to green speed.

- Focusing on *relocalization,* which is a fancy way of saying looking to your local vendors and distributors for products and services. The financial institution supports relocalization by creating new, locally owned, independent businesses in your community to keep profits circulating in your area. (Because relocalization is the cornerstone of many sustainable business practices, I've devoted a whole chapter to it; see Chapter 11 for more information on this hot topic.)

Working with a green financial service provider not only showcases true commitment to greening *your* organization but it also contributes to enhancement of societal benefits.

Why Green Your Accounting Practices?

So what's in it for you and your business when it comes to greening your corporate accounting practices? Connections for one thing! Bankers and financial institutions that have a keen eye toward the emerging green sector can serve as powerful liaisons for you to meet other like-minded businesspeople.

You may be surprised how delving into new financial relationships based on green parameters draws you into a whole new circle of people who can enhance your business's sustainability potential. When you begin meeting your community's green-finance players, the networking possibilities become endless because of the number of other local businesses they deal with. These new ecocontacts — think up-and-coming green marketing firms, sustainable builders, and other businesses that are transitioning to green practices — have the potential to develop into good partners for your business.

Another big reason is the perception stakeholders get when the Chief Financial Officer of an organization announces that corporate accounting is going green. Even though the budget doesn't just emanate from the accounting team, such an announcement allows your outside ecoimage to tie together. When customers and employees see not only green products and sustainable operations but also alliances with green financial institutions and credit card companies, the cohesiveness of a truly green organization is readily apparent.

Tracking sustainable companies' performance in the financial markets

The flow of capital into companies formed to market sustainable products, technologies, and services has gone from a trickle to a deluge in the last couple years. One can only imagine that even more formalized markets will emerge in response to this groundswell of interest.

Here are some of the avenues through which you can follow the performance of ecocompanies that are firmly committed to a sustainable business model:

✔ **Dow Jones Sustainability North America Index:** This index tracks more than 100 of the 600 largest organizations in North America in terms of sustainable operations. Based on the Dow Jones World Sustainability Index, this index started its North American performance tracking in 2005. Visit www. sustainability-index.com to see a list of tracked companies and an encouraging comparison of these companies' performance over time compared to other major market indices.

✔ **The Green Exchange:** This exchange has recently commenced operations as part of the New York Mercantile Exchange (NYMEX). With big investment brokerage firms partnering with the NYMEX, the Green Exchange will provide trading capacity for environmental products, specifically those designed to deal with pollution reduction, renewable energy technologies, and climate change damage mitigation.

Looking to the future, keep an eye out for the BX public stock exchange, which is currently in the works. This exchange is a creation of B Lab, a nonprofit organization that provides a company-wide certification for sustainable businesses known as B Corporation certification (which I describe in much greater detail in Chapter 14). The B Lab cofounders are modeling the BX public stock exchange on the United Kingdom's Social Stock Exchange and are deeply committed to developing a private stock exchange that will evolve into a public marketplace with only value-congruent companies listed. Not only are they working with some high-profile financial institutions, venture capitalists, and investment intermediaries to make this exchange a reality but they're also helping these companies to become B Corporations themselves, thus adding more credence to companies pursuing a socially responsible model.

How to Green Your Accounting Practices: The Basics

Regardless of the size of your business, in order to effectively implement green accounting policies and practices, someone — whether that's one person or a team of folks from your business service area — must understand the importance of developing new financial relationships and decision-making tools to support your company's broader greening endeavors. The accounting staff is responsible for communicating how sustainable decision-making considers triple-bottom-line layers of impact instead of focusing on traditional short-term profit.

In annual budget preparation, for example, the accounting team can generate conversation about how investing in big-ticket items today (like renewable energy technologies for your plant) has triple-bottom-line payoffs later due to reduced total ownership and maintenance costs, increased environmental stewardship, and creation of local green-collar jobs.

Budgeting in most companies is based on existing organizational structure — department, geographic area, or product line, for example. Creating a mentality (and system) for incentivizing managers to consider budget requests that can benefit the whole company and are based on measurable data and resulting sustainability improvements is a feat that should rest with your accounting folks. After all, with the various measurements they've created for the numerous facets of your organization's sustainability operations, they're the ones who have the closest relationship to your data and your budget.

Your accounting team doesn't operate in a vacuum, though, and it isn't necessarily the gatekeeper of all things budgetary. Don't be afraid to spark your own creative thoughts on how to incentivize green behavior and then track interdepartmental impacts. Try some of these ideas on for size:

- Paying for managers to attend sustainability training may come out of the HR budget and yet provoke your lead engineer to design your next best-selling product because she became intrigued with *biomimicry* (emulating nature in product design). How do you track this? Follow up the training in six months with a questionnaire asking for direct work-related changes attributable to the training sessions. Craft a colorful chart highlighting sustainability accomplishments that arose from the training, with dollars spent per employee training hour translated into economic gain and increased employee satisfaction.

- Engaging third-party certifiers to assess your supply chain partners' sustainability comes out of the production budget. But sales increase because a new distributor is interested in carrying your authentic green product line. Data presentation should link the new expense with the increased sales and illustrate the percentage of supply chain partners now authenticated.

- The budget for cleaning up a *brownfield* (contaminated site) you own comes out of your Environmental Management budget, but corporate commercial liability insurance premiums decrease 8 percent due to decreased risk exposure. Getting managers together quarterly to discuss ripple effects of sustainability initiatives will flesh this out.

Budgeting for sustainability initiatives gets caught up in the ripple effect that occurs between departments. That's why you should cross-departmentally track benefits that accrue from sustainability investments as much as possible. Doing so gives you what you need to go back to the higher-ups, showcase results, and ask for green capital in the future!

When you're ready to green your company's accounting team, do so in phases instead of issuing a blanket list of transformative mandates. Also, focus on one or two of the goals that seem most relevant to your business based on what's already on the company's future workplan. For example, if your lease is coming due in the next year, that may be a good place to center the accounting department's green efforts (see the later "Encouraging your lender to offer green mortgages" sidebar for related tips). If you have some additional credit or refinancing projects that you're looking at in the next operating cycle, those projects may be good places to start implementing green accounting practices. *Where* you begin greening your accounting practices isn't nearly as important as actually jumping in and starting to effect change.

Choosing Green Financial Institutions

Greening your banking involves transitioning to a socially and environmentally responsible financial institution, capitalizing on financing opportunities for your sustainability efforts, and making your money work harder by choosing financial products that embody triple-bottom-line benefits. You may even want to consider moving your money to local financial institutions as part of focusing on a core sustainability principle: buying local (more on that topic in Chapter 11.)

In the following sections, I survey the facets of sustainable financial relationships so you can evaluate both current and prospective business partners and decide whether you'll make changes to your day-to-day financial relationships (and if so, how you'll go about doing that). If, after this cursory glance, you're not feeling satisfied with your current financial institution's sustainability efforts, maybe it's time to look at other banking options (preferably within your local area) by adding these questions to all the typical economic evaluative criteria you always use when choosing a bank.

Focusing on practices

How can you assess whether a financial institution's values are green? Start by typing in "green" or "sustainable" on the internal search engine of your bank's Web site and see whether anything pops up. Then do some background research on the company to find answers to these questions:

✔ Does the institution have a formal sustainability or corporate social responsibility plan?

✔ What percentage of the bank's loans (specifically those being made with *your* company's deposits) is local?

✔ Which company does the institution use to administer its credit card (see the later "Green credit cards" section for guidance on progressive green financial institutions)?

✔ Does the bank have a policy restricting its portfolio investments from funding unethical endeavors (like companies that engage in animal testing or the manufacturing of weapons of mass destruction)?

✔ Has the institution engaged in predatory lending practices? Find out by searching the Center for Responsible Lending's Web site (www. responsiblelending.org), which provides an updated list of these financial institutions. (***Remember:*** Like anything, the presence of an institution on this list is a red flag, not a definitive sign to cross the bank off your list. This is one consideration you really need to think about to decide whether you're comfortable with your bank engaging in such practices.)

Considering investment locale

Because a core concept of sustainability is using local vendors (including financial institutions) as much as possible, you should always give your community banks and credit unions the first shot at your business. The biggest benefit is that you're channeling your money where your mouth is. You're also engaging in yet another tangible ecoaction to convey your green commitment to your stakeholders. Local banks lend to other local businesses, thereby expanding your sphere of green influence and contributing directly to the triple bottom line of one of your primary stakeholders — your local community. Community finance has virtually no drawbacks and with the collapse of several reputable national and international institutions, many organizations are feeling that local finance is a much less risky place to park their capital.

If you want to bank locally, you have two options: Community Development Banks (CDBs) and Community Development Credit Unions (CDCUs). These institutions may look and feel like the big bank next door, but their business models focus on permanent, long-term economic development of low- and moderate-income members of the community.

✔ **Community Development Banks:** *CDBs* offer all the products and services that the giant conglomerates do (cash management, commercial checking accounts, certificates of deposit, lending, FDIC-insured money market accounts, and the like), but they provide one important additional service — programs geared toward enhancing economic justice for all in the community. They do this by designing specific programs targeted at community development, advocating at the state legislature to eliminate the availability of predatory funds, and listening and responding to your region's unique capital needs.

✔ **Community Development Credit Unions:** *CDCUs,* which are nonprofit organizations owned by members (residents of a particular town or employees of a select employer), offer another sustainable option to super-sized financial institutions. They regularly rate high on consumer satisfaction surveys for their low fees, friendly service, and community commitment.

CDCUs may earn a few extra sustainability points because being member-owned allows a wide constituency to participate in the benefits of ownership, compared with CDBs in which a few shareholders may own all the stock.

Credit unions may also specialize in ethically sound investments or use social and environmental screens to aid in their loan decisions. For example, Co-operative Financial Services (CFS) in the United Kingdom works with the local prison population to teach prisoners basic financial skills. It also places fee-free ATMs in low-income neighborhoods. Both programs were developed to maximize the credit union's triple bottom line — and they've succeeded. CFS contributes to empowering socially impoverished people, offers opportunities to access financial services without travel, and increases profitability while developing a very loyal customer base.

You may have tapped into a network of fiscal progressives in the process of asking questions about a particular financial institution's sustainability practices (see the preceding section). If so, these folks should be able to direct you to regional sources of sustainably minded financiers.

If you like a particular bank chain that's not a CDB or CDCU and you want to know whether it keeps its money local, try taking a look at where that chain is headquartered. If its HQ is in your community, odds are good its money is staying there.

Finding Green Lenders and Financial Services

By and large, the sustainable financial products available today come in the form of green mortgages and credit cards, although green bank accounts are increasingly popular offerings.

When evaluating a particular financial institution's green products, you may want to find out whether it's familiar with green mortgages and whether it offers them or can link you to a mortgagor that can. You may also want to ask whether the institution provides information on or directly administers one of the new sustainable credit card programs that are springing up these days. Both products promote your business's own sustainability efforts.

Green bank accounts are primarily a means for the financial institution to incorporate sustainable operations — most of which center on carbon-reducing operational practices such as offering paperless statements and free online banking (although these perks are becoming much more status quo in traditional accounts). Some progressive banks, such as Umpqua in Portland, Oregon, are offering customers a chance to willingly donate interest from their checking accounts to an environmental organization, so keep your eyes open for emerging opportunities along these lines.

If you're in need of financing for a particular green initiative —whether that's retrofitting your building, converting your packaging line to a new sustainable material, or prototyping a new green product — lots of sustainably oriented loan programs are available through numerous banks and credit unions. Financial institutions such as Good Capital, ShoreBank Pacific, and New Resource Bank lead the way in traditional bank financing for green projects.

For now though, I focus on the two sustainable financial products you're most likely to encounter — green mortgages and green credit cards.

Green mortgages

If your company is looking into sustainable building or remodeling, or if you're thinking about purchasing a green facility, you may be a great fit for a green mortgage. Although many in the financing field are still scrambling to define a *green mortgage,* the generally accepted concept is that lenders give better rates for homes that are either already green (meaning the structure is energy efficient and has other sustainable design features) or are going to be newly built to incorporate such sustainable features. If you're considering building or buying a LEED (Leadership in Energy and Environmental Design) structure, or if you're remodeling with the intent of obtaining LEED certification, you may have a number of financing options in addition to your traditional ones. Chapter 8 covers LEED in greater detail.

Almost all green mortgages require the building in question to be highly energy efficient due to the immediate financial savings involved. The decreased operating costs inherent in owning an energy-efficient building make a green mortgage less risky due to the increased cash flow to the mortgagee because of his or her decreased utility costs. Anytime a mortgagee's operating expenses are reduced, cash flow is increased, and the mortgagee's ability to repay the debt is enhanced. (Flip to Chapter 8 for more on green buildings.)

The EcoBroker designation certifies that a licensed real estate agent has fulfilled a set of requirements that include training in energy and environmental issues, as well as marketing. A real estate agent with this designation should have liaisons within the green mortgage industry. To find an EcoBroker–certified realtor in your area, go to www.ecobroker.com and click the Find Your Local EcoBroker link in the column on the left-hand side of the page.

Encouraging your lender to offer green mortgages

If your lender isn't currently onboard with green mortgages, encourage her to explore this new market by explaining that going green is shifting the industry. Her bank can ecoblaze a trail for others in the area to follow — and gain recognition for it. Because of these perceived benefits to the mortgagor, your negotiating power increases. Use these talking points to buy down the origination fee or interest rate for a mortgage, or to garner other loan concessions:

✔ Green buildings have enhanced value retention because of their extraordinarily high quality.

✔ Sustainable buildings have lower lifetime operating costs. Therefore, the mortgagee has increased solvency to make debt payments.

✔ A higher percentage of LEED-certified buildings are owner occupied, reducing risk to the mortgagor.

✔ Many analysts believe that the green capital market is poised to shift very quickly as oil prices continue to rise, energy and water worries escalate, and skepticism about the North American real estate market continues to grow. (As an added tidbit, share that in late 2007, Wells Fargo publicly released a statement that it had a cumulative portfolio of $1 billion in green commercial loans.)

Green credit cards

If your company uses credit cards for any purpose, you have yet another golden opportunity to get your green on. Not only are the physical green credit cards typically made of corn-based materials but they also offer an easy way to incorporate sustainability into the accounting functions of your company through at least one of the following ways:

✔ Banking miles to donate to environmental causes

✔ Participating in green-power projects

✔ Buying carbon offsets

✔ Contributing a percentage of each transaction to a philanthropic activity

If your current institution offers green credit cards, great! If not, the availability (or lack thereof) of green credit cards isn't something on which to solely base your banking-relationship decisions. After all, there aren't many green credit cards out there yet, which means there's no monitoring or certifying agency. Consider greening your banking relationship based on a financial institution's sustainable practices and whether it keeps its money in the local community (by using the info found earlier in this chapter) and simply picking up a green credit card wherever you can get one.

You may want to consider one of the following green credit card options:

✔ **Brighter Planet Visa:** Offered by Bright Planet (in partnership with Bank of America), this card is aimed at fighting climate change.

✔ **GreenCard Visa:** Offered by Repay International through its ClimaCount program, this card actually calculates the amount of carbon embedded in your purchases. Then, for no extra cost, the company offsets those emissions by planting trees. You have to pay a one-time start-up fee, but after that, you benefit from no annual fees and competitive interest rates. The GreenCard Visa recently expanded into the U.S. market from its home base in Holland.

All about green leases

If you're truly striving for sustainability, then the space your business occupies needs to reflect an alignment with your organization's ecovalues. So hats off to you if you decide to rent a green space! Look for the landlord to structure the rental agreement in a manner that encourages you to occupy the space in a way that aligns with the building's design strategy.

Building owners and managers are just beginning to create templates for green leases that address issues such as:

✔ Using and maintaining energy systems in an appropriate manner

✔ Maintaining indoor air quality by requiring natural cleaning products to be used so that volatile organic compounds (VOCs) are kept out of the air flow

✔ Promoting tenant recycling

✔ Requiring that any *leasehold* improvements (changes to convert the space to a tenant's specific needs) by renters be submitted for LEED-CI certification (you can read up on this specific LEED certification in Chapter 8)

For an in-depth look at green lease terms, check out `www.squarefootage.net/pdfs/articles/8_25_06_Green_Lease.pdf`.

If you're leasing your business facility and it doesn't incorporate sustainable design, you may not be able to renovate, but you can ask for specific provisions to ensure that the building will be operated in an environmentally sound manner. Many landlords of traditional buildings are willing to negotiate sustainable lease provisions with the understanding that these issues enhance the building's value and their reputation as well. Think about the following items when negotiating specific facets of your lease:

✔ Ask to be submetered for electricity use so that savings from green leasehold improvements accrue to you.

✔ Create a space (especially if the building is made up of shared space) for a recycling center.

✔ Ask for bike racks and prime parking spots for hybrids, electric cars, scooters, and motorcycles.

✔ Discuss a building upgrade plan and investigate whether the landlord is willing to consider phasing in efficient lighting or replacing carpets with PVC-free floor coverings.

Advocating on behalf of a green lease is usually an educational experience. The more you can illuminate your landlord, the more likely he or she is to see the benefits that accrue to landlords as a result of green leases.

You can keep abreast of what's going on in the green credit card world at `blogs.creditcards.com`. With the addition of MasterCard green cards, look for the other big credit card corporations to follow suit. In fact, a couple major companies are planning to release an ecocard that will directly target projects that reduce greenhouse gas emissions.

See where your current corporate credit card stands in Green America's interesting e-article on the social and environmental performance of megabanks that sponsor credit cards: `www.coopamerica.org/pubs/realmoney/articles/ResponsibleCreditCards.cfm`.

Putting Your Money Where Your Mouth Is: Investing Responsibly

Your controller or CFO probably has an investment committee that helps him or her manage your company's extra cash. Analyzing your investments through an ecolens establishes your company as the real green deal and shows that you're contributing to the trillion-dollar sector known as *socially responsible investing*, which helps grow other green businesses. How's that for triple-bottom-line benefits?

Based on the investment parameters that you work with, you may have a little or a lot of latitude as to what your company's investment portfolio can participate in. At the bare minimum, you should employ negative screens that eliminate any companies or funds related to products or services that

- ✔ Employ child, slave, or penal labor
- ✔ Sell tobacco, pornography, alcohol, or firearms
- ✔ Profit from war or other human misery
- ✔ Have a shoddy environmental history

If your company happens to allow for direct investing in other companies, look into businesses that are traded on The Green Exchange or tracked on the Dow Jones Sustainability North America Index. Otherwise, green mutual funds may be worthwhile for a portion of your business's portfolio.

Green mutual funds are offering lots of options to invest in products that regenerate the environment, eradicate poverty, alleviate global health concerns, or contribute to climate change adaptation and mitigation. Almost all major fund families have added at least one sustainability-oriented fund in response to investor requests. Of course, doing all the usual research is still important, so investigate fees, performance, managers, and the fund's objectives and goals. Comparing socially responsible funds can be a challenge because in addition to traditional comparative features, you want to ascertain whether the fund is *really* as socially responsible as it claims. After all, its parameters may not be the same as yours.

Natural Investments's Social Ratings are helpful for seeing how your prospective mutual fund rates. Emulating Morningstar's mutual fund rating based on one to five stars, Natural Investments assigns one to five hearts. Ratings can be found on the firm's Web site at www.naturalinvesting.com.

Many funds say they're green without taking the actions necessary to back up that statement, so beware of such *greenwashing.* For example, shunning investment in the oil sands of Alberta while propping up a corporation that makes gaming machines may not be as socially responsible as you'd prefer.

Convert your company's investment portfolio incrementally. Start with a small amount, tightly analyze the investment's performance, ensure that it's an appropriate mix in your portfolio, and then set target percentages for greening your investment portfolio annually.

Accessing Seed Capital for Your Sustainability Efforts

If you're doing something green and innovative, or if you're in need of funds to position your company for a sustainable future, accessing capital pools specifically designed for companies that are pursuing sustainability may be easier than you think. Businesses rolling out green products, particularly those that contribute to solving some of the biggest global challenges, have a unique opportunity to access the new capital sources sprouting up everywhere.

External seed capital primarily comes from two sources: venture capitalists and green angel investors, both of which I explain in the following sections.

Venture capitalists

A *venture capitalist* (also known as a VC) is an investment firm or individual person that invests in companies poised for high growth or expansion, typically in return for a majority ownership. The companies that VCs invest in are past the "sweat equity" stage (in which friends, family, and credit cards fund their startup) but are too early on to raise capital in public markets. VCs usually look for an exit strategy within five years and bring managerial and technical expertise to their investments, typically commanding a significant board presence.

Many say that *Pratt's Guide to Private Equity & Venture Capital Sources* (published by Venture Economics; editions updated annually) is an invaluable asset for anyone seeking VC funding, but it's quite pricy. For a cheaper way of finding VCs who might be interested in funding your operation, try doing an Internet search for your specific region and "venture capital." (If you're in Austin, Texas; Chicago, Illinois; or California's Silicon Valley, then you're in luck — these areas are home to clusters of intense venture-capital action.) Starting with regional firms is often best to cut down on your travel expenses; it's also often easier to sell your story to someone who understands the regional market you're in.

Because of the number of unsolicited business plans that many VCs receive, consider seeking a reference from a business advisor, such as an accountant, attorney, insurance or financial products counselor, or banker, to help get your business plan reviewed.

Venture capital conferences bring together a plethora of young companies looking for capital with the organizations that fund these sorts of upstarts. Conferences can be the result of university collaborations or independent endeavors by many VCs that have gotten together in a particular region or specific industry sector.

The sheer volume of upcoming venture capital conferences is fairly staggering. See for yourself by visiting www.greenvc.org/conference_and_ events_greentech_cleantech/index.html. The site's home page is an e-letter with scads of info on the clean tech venture capital world. After you find a conference you want to target, delve into this Web site to see whether there's a prescreening process for your business plan and whether you need to submit an executive summary of your business plan or complete a standard application because procedures tend to differ by conference.

Green angel investors

Many small communities are finding, to their great surprise and delight, a proliferation of *green angel investors,* philanthropists and investors who pool their funds to provide the very earliest seed capital for local green projects. This money is finding its way into small social and environmental ventures in diverse areas such as local foods, wineries and breweries, healthcare, community finance, renewable energy, alternative transportation, and local media, to name a few.

Unfortunately, green angel investors aren't organized in an easy-to-search database, so if you find one, consider that your lucky day. Although many of these people remain fairly low-key, you can try searching for them by tapping into every sustainable business network, alliance, and trade association you can in your area. These groups are fabulous resources for introductions into the world of sustainability, and their events usually feature local fare and fun, drawing you ever farther down the path toward sustainability.

Part III
Involving Stakeholders in Your Sustainability Efforts

The 5th Wave   By Rich Tennant

"Dick has been really popular since he implemented that telecommuting option, and let's face it, that big white hat doesn't hurt either."

In this part . . .

Involving all of your company's stakeholders — consumers, employees, shareholders, and more — is an important part of corporate stewardship. Your overall marketing strategy dictates how you communicate to many of these stakeholders, and educating them through your marketing initiatives is a core component of a sustainable business. But you must shift your marketing and messaging carefully due to the inordinate amount of misleading green information out there. I guide you through that process in this part.

I also show you how to help revitalize your local economy by collaborating with other businesses to encourage community members to buy local for the benefit of everyone in your area. And if you've never before considered partnering with a nonprofit organization as a way to effect change in your community, I introduce you to the ecobenefits involved in such a relationship. Finally, because recruiting, training, retaining, and evaluating your employees through a green lens depends in large part on your Human Resource team's efforts, here I help you identify how to make steps in that direction.

Chapter 10

Marketing to a Greener World

. . . .

In This Chapter

▶ Coloring your existing marketing model green

▶ Segmenting customers into shades of green so you can target them

▶ Educating customers about why green goods cost more and why that expense is worth it

▶ Finding distribution channels that work

▶ Telling the world you've gone green — or at least that your product or service has

. . . .

*Y*ou're on track with a sustainability plan and boy are you motivated to let the word out that you're going green! You want to talk about your green goods or services, differentiate yourself from the competition, and showcase your socially and environmentally responsible operations through your marketing message, which you can do through the classic marketing mix.

✓ **Product:** The product you're providing needs to be convenient, perform well, and meet a need.

✓ **Price:** The price needs to reflect your product's perceived value.

✓ **Place:** The point of purchase must be convenient and accessible for consumers.

✓ **Promotion:** The promotion efforts should encompass your company's brand image and offer product-differentiation messaging.

This four-fold marketing strategy takes on a new look when viewed through the lens of sustainability. After you feel confident that you've addressed all the traditional aspects of the marketing mix, you can begin to focus on each aspect with an eye to its green attributes. Sustainable marketing isn't so much about creating a new strategy as it is about considering what you already do from a green perspective.

In doing so, you want to take into account how your customers feel about your environmentally friendly business practices, educate consumers enough to bring them onboard with your new green product or service line, and spread the word about your environmental efforts. Not sure how to proceed? Never fear! I clue you in on these tactics and much more in this chapter.

Greening Your Marketing Model: The Basics

Taking your business to the next level requires understanding the complexities of the evolving green marketplace. Although recent marketing surveys indicate a definitive shift toward sustainability, many open-ended questions still remain as to how to incorporate it into your marketing model.

That's why you have to consider the following:

- ✔ **How green your customer base is and what options your company has for going green:** Who exactly is a green consumer, and does this person come in different shades? What makes a product or service green? What sort of premium will consumers pay for these attributes? Where are consumers shopping for sustainable products, and where are they turning for sustainable services?

- ✔ **What to focus your marketing on:** Should you promote your company's social and environmental responsibility efforts, the green products and services themselves, or both?

- ✔ **How integrally to embed your green messaging within your overall marketing plan:** Are you trying to find your green self, or do you already know you're 100 percent strategically committed to this initiative? Has your board and/or top management issued a "go for it" directive, or are you feeling them out?

- ✔ **How you'll communicate your green message:** Will you be layering a green message on top of your existing marketing efforts or crafting a whole new marketing message? Will your labeling and packaging reflect a new direction, or are you taking the add-on approach? Should you use your traditional labeling and materials but design a defining look for the green product line so as to tie the new with the old?

However you proceed with greening your marketing model, make sure to actively engage in consumer education and outreach in your messaging efforts so that your customers see how and why your green product or service offering is different and how it's making a contribution to solving social or environmental problems.

Color-Coding Your Customers by Their Shade of Green

Your job when engaging in marketing is to anticipate where consumer demand is heading. But to do that, you first need to understand your customer base's current green leanings. Then you must decide whether you're trying to position your green products and services to appeal to the full range of potential customers or only the segments already interested in or committed to sustainable purchasing. This decision impacts all facets of the classic marketing mix: which product to develop, how to price it, where to sell it, and how to promote it. (See Chapter 7 for in-depth coverage on the product development process.)

You can expect to have a smallish percentage of hard-core green consumers asking the tough questions and rewarding you with their purchasing power if your products or services truly meet their green screen. A larger percentage of your customers may fall in the middle ground, a group that enjoys exploring the idea of sustainability. A much larger segment of your customer base is likely the group that doesn't remotely identify social or environmental concerns as a relevant part of a purchasing decision. Your job is thus to determine: Where do your existing consumers lie? Where will you position your newly greened products or services?

In the following sections, I delve into ways you can find the answers to these questions and outline the most current demographic data about green consumers. With this information, you can begin to get a feel for where your existing customer base falls and start thinking about how that relates to your planned sustainability initiatives. The challenges you face when determining which groups of consumers to target are clear, but the rewards will be well worth your efforts if you can craft a strategy that meets the needs of one or more of these consumer segments.

Conducting green marketing research

Before you can assign a shade of green to your existing (or desired) customer base, you first need to figure out how these people are thinking. Lucky for you there are tons of ways to do just that.

If you have the cash but not the time to conduct your own research, you may be happy to know that green marketing research is now available for purchase. But buying marketing data gets expensive, and with this particular market poised to explode, purchasing green data is no exception. To find a wide variety of segmented reports, check out the LOHAS Consumer Reports at www.lohas.com.

For a cheaper way to get a feel for green consumers and where your products and services may fit best in the market, take advantage of others' observations. You can easily do this secondary research by

- ✔ Subscribing to a credible marketing journal, such as the *Journal of Marketing,* where a quick search revealed 17 green articles in the prior 12 months; or a tightly scoped green marketing journal, such as the *LOHAS Journal*

- ✔ Joining a blog focused on green marketing like `sustainablemarketing.com/blog`

- ✔ Perusing a prominent daily newspaper, such as *The Wall Street Journal* or *The New York Times* online, and searching for green articles

Conducting primary research is an option that allows you to gather either qualitative or quantitative data. A good way to gather qualitative consumer input is to hold a focus group made up of a slice of your customers (commercial, individual, online, and so on). *Focus groups* usually consist of approximately 6 to 12 individuals and a facilitator who administers a set of questions and solicits comments and responses from the participants.

To get the most from your focus group, consider having participants

- ✔ Define a green product, including identifying specific attributes and benefits

- ✔ Denote green features they'd find desirable if added to your current product line

- ✔ Identify what premium (as a percentage) they'd be willing to pay for the desirable attributes

- ✔ Indicate how they'd like to see your green products positioned in a shop — next to other green products or alongside traditional products (for the sake of comparison and comfort)

- ✔ Describe their purchasing behaviors toward companies that are perceived as being socially responsible (or not!)

Pine Greens: The uber-informed consumer

LOHAS (Lifestyle of Health and Sustainability) is the acronym for the estimated 60 to 70 million American consumers who make purchasing decisions due to a product's sustainable or healthful characteristics. Call 'em the *Pine Greens* — individuals who are very well educated about environmental and social issues and require honest and comprehensive product information. They want data on

- How your product is made

- What type of energy is used to make it

- How much recycled content is embedded in it

- What laborers' working conditions are

- Whether your product contains toxins, petroleum, or harmful ingredients

- Whether it is locally grown

- Whether it is tested on animals

The Pine Greens are the core folks behind the rise in organic foods, ecotourism, hybrid cars, and natural body and bath products. Oddly enough, some people in this group don't actually know they're in it. In other words, I may choose a solar-powered water heater over the conventional alternative because I'm worried about future energy prices or availability. Although I may not consider myself a Pine Green consumer (or even know what the heck that means), an underlying reason that I bought the appliance is that it relies on renewable energy, and I'm concerned about a volatile energy future.

The major marketing challenge is that this group employs a sophisticated purchasing screen and isn't bogged down by too much information. Au contraire! Pine Greens can sniff out a false claim of being green faster than a hound can tree a cat. Nor are they interested in the general term *green;* they want your product or service to showcase specific ecoattributes. So the more info you have out there about your product, the better for these folks.

Jungle Greens: The trendy, ecofriendly consumer

The *Jungle Greens* are a market ripe for the picking, because they're interested but not fully engaged in the sustainability scene. This group perceives green as trendy, but may not know exactly why it's so popular. Generally, they're okay with

- **Doing the supposed "right thing" — as long as it's easy:** Because this demographic is heavily weighted in the thirtysomething professional category, the Jungle Greens want the convenience of a strip mall, but with local products. Think fast-food drive-throughs with tasty organic tidbits in compostable packaging.

- **Finding out about what makes a business green:** They don't need anything technical — just some easy-to-read signage. A poster that points out the dangers of perchloroethylene (perc) — and by the way, can you smell how fresh it is in here? — is perfect in a dry cleaning shop that's trying to go green.

> ✔ **Paying a premium if you tell 'em why it's necessary:** Your Fair Trade Certified coffee may be $1 more expensive per pound than the competition's, but if you tell Jungle Greens that the Guatemalan farmers producing it are making a living wage and sending the first generation of kids in that region to school, then you've just scored a new customer base.

Jungle Greens may have general environmental and social concerns and are looking for easy solutions. Your task is to teach them why green is good and offer solutions to everyday problems. This group wants to

✔ Find out more about your product and its green features

✔ Understand the gist of why these features matter

✔ See the environmental benefit of purchasing your product and feel that it is significant

✔ Understand whether the green features change your product's performance

✔ Know how to find out more information

Above all, you want to help Jungle Greens equate their choices and lifestyle to being socially and environmentally responsible. These are smart people, so make your product plugs subtle but smart as well.

The primary challenge with this group is convincing Jungle Greens to change purchasing patterns that include sacrificing time. Shopping at a farmers' market eats up most of your Saturday morning. But buying green power by checking a box online the next time you pay your energy bill is feel-good and quick. Although it may mean a 5 to 8 percent increase in monthly energy expenditures, it's exactly the type of behavior change these folks want to green-drop into the conversation over pomegranate martinis at happy hour.

Moss Greens: The environmentally apathetic consumer

The *Moss Greens* either believe the seriousness of the environmental state of affairs is overplayed or that it's someone else's problem to fix. Your challenge is to convince them that considering green products and services is in their best interest.

These folks are primarily concerned with bargains and convenience. Any interest that they have in sustainability is solely tied up in how it impacts their finances and their time. It's not that Moss Greens don't have a conscience; they're just generally guided in their purchases by the demands of everyday existence. Demographics also indicate these folks are clustered quite easily by geographic and ethnic concentration, as well as socioeconomic status.

Spotting common ground among green consumers

An abundance of green market research data is out there, along with numerous ways to slice and dice consumer profiles. Attempts to apply standard demographic analysis often fall short of the mark, because green consumers are found across all typical segments, such as age, religion, income, and geography. So take any analysis you find concerning green consumer demographics for what it is — a blurry snapshot of an evolving scene.

However, a few interesting commonalities within the green marketplace have been reported:

✔ Women are much more likely than men to respond to environmentally charged marketing campaigns.

✔ "Wanting to make a difference" ranks consistently high as a driving force behind buying green. People feel overwhelmed with environmental and societal problems and see using their cash as a tangible way to be a part of the solution.

✔ Overall willingness to pay a premium for green products is growing, but a disparity still exists between how much consumers say they're willing to pay for green products and how much they actually cough up at the cash register.

Studies show that although consumers are increasingly indicating an interest in green goods and services, many can't explain what green is. But guess what? This finding shows you have tremendous marketing and educational opportunities as you dive into the world of green business.

To really sell your product or service to this group, you need to make Moss Greens

✔ **See a true financial benefit to going green:** Showing the cash conveniences of sustainability is growing easier because increasing energy costs are embedded in almost every product or service imaginable. Compact fluorescent light bulbs, cold water detergents, and hand-push mowers are flying off the shelves everywhere. Focus on cost savings, but engage in education at the same time, because deep down even the most frugal consumer wants to be part of saving the planet.

✔ **Understand what they may be losing or missing out on by not already using your product or service:** Moss Greens don't seek out environmentally related details, so if you want them to know that your green cleaning products make a home smell citrusy (instead of like a high school chem lab) *and* that they keep customers from having to worry about babies and pets being affected by those hard-to-pronounce toxic components, then you have to get out there and tell them that.

✔ **Recognize that obtaining your product or service is as convenient as purchasing traditional products:** This consumer group isn't going to go out of its way to find sustainable products or services. You need to bring 'em to them. Locate your green goods or services in a convenient outlet where Moss Greens are already stopping for other items (think big-box, one-stop store).

Because competitive cost is your biggest challenge with Moss Greens, you need to be very sure they understand that a price point above that of non-green products actually yields them proportionate savings in the long run. So instead of merely saying, "You'll spend 30 percent less on electricity over the life of this dishwasher," translate that savings into how much money the end user will save monthly on his or her electric bill. After factoring in these electricity savings, the consumer should net a savings when comparing payments on your dishwasher to payments on your competitor's.

Using the buy-local and buy-organic movements to your marketing advantage

Often your ecominded customers face a dilemma when packing up the hybrid car and heading out for a day of shopping: Buy local or buy organic? To solve this conundrum, they try to determine whether it's more important to

✔ Keep dollars circulating in the local economy, even though the product may not be certified as organic or sustainable by a third party

✔ Buy sustainably certified products that are being mass marketed at big-box stores

How you make use of your customers' buy-local versus buy-organic dilemma depends on whether you're involved in a franchise or global business or you're a small business owner. Obviously, you can't claim to be a local store if you're owned by a conglomerate in Holland, but you can feature local products in your store (if your franchise allows it). Buy-local campaigns are growing in numbers and influence, and the concept of building regional self-reliance is a strong marketing thread for many local businesses.

For example, food is, of course, the biggest buy-local push in North America today. Restaurants, coffee shops, and even whole events featuring local food are growing in number and visibility. If you're undertaking marketing for a food-centered organization, you should have a keen understanding that folks want assurance of the origination of their foodstuffs. After all, recent studies show that the 16 most common crops grown in a Midwestern state travel about 1,500 miles as an *import* to chain groceries in that state. Consequently, the average item on your dinner plate, even if it was grown in your home state, has journeyed out of state to a processing plant, then to a distribution center elsewhere, and then back to the place you purchased it from near your home. So even when you buy local, the item you buy may still have traveled a long way to get to you! Imagine being a Nebraskan sitting down to a dinner of Chilean beef. Weird, huh?

Balancing Premium Pricing with Consumer Demand

A great deal of confusion tends to surround the question of how products that contain *less* (think fewer pesticides, no preservatives, less packaging, and the like) can possibly cost *more*. The quick-and-dirty answer is that many sustainable products aren't mass-produced or mass-marketed, so the overhead captured in them may be significantly more on a per-unit basis. This fact requires you to educate your consumers at every turn so that they know *why* they're paying more for your product or service.

Say you sell kids' clothing and lots of these clothes are made from cotton, one of the most heavily fertilized and water-intensive crops known to mankind. Oh yeah, and lots of cotton is picked by young children in the developing world who are, well, picking cotton rather than going to school. So you decide to carry an organic line of cotton clothing, grown and harvested in the country. The problem is that your new trendy tots line prices out at about 45 percent more than the not-so-earth-friendly alternatives. Is that necessarily bad? Breathe deep and repeat after me: "No, it's not."

Although many people say they'll pay a premium for a green product, most can't name a single brand that they consider to be green. Add that to the fact that the only consistent thread in green marketing surveys is that consumers insist they want to make a difference with their purchases. The result? You now have an awesome opportunity to build an image in consumers' minds that your products and services are green and that purchasing them positively impacts the world.

When introducing a new green product or service, your marketing approach should be to make sure your messaging conveys quality while giving you an opportunity to educate consumers on the environmental pluses of choosing the very features that make your product or service sustainable. You may be a bit worried about pushing your product because your customers are price conscious, and you don't honestly know whether they're full-fledged Pine Greens or not (here's where doing your market research helps; see the earlier section "Color-Coding Your Customers by Their Shade of Green" for more info).

Don't try to explain the premium away. Instead, showcase the product or service as part of a new and forward-thinking line that complements what you already carry or provide by doing the following:

✔ **Place a placard spotlighting the issue next to your in-store display.** The placard should be pretty simple and highlight the main green attributes of the product or service and the connection to why those are good. Signage decrying "Made with 50-percent renewable energy" should be tied to verbiage like "Climate-friendly" or "Do your part in reducing global warming." If you're in the food business, you may prefer signage that states "Slate harvested within 50-mile radius," which links to "Providing jobs for your neighbors" or "Less distance — less fuel — less cost – more Earth-friendly." The purpose of your placard is to make the connection for your customers.

✔ **Highlight your new product or service in your monthly newspaper spot or your electronic newsletter.** Education is the key here as well. Don't just tout the green features of your product. Use your precious promotional space to concisely convey how the green attributes of your product or service make a positive impact on the environment in easy-to-remember bullets. This isn't the place for displaying lengthy climate change stats, but it _is_ the place for dropping tidbits on sustainable bamboo harvesting and its impact on the habitat of panda bears.

✔ **Encourage your employees to tell the product or service's story to browsing consumers.** Of course, it helps if your employees are well educated about your product or service. I can't tell you how many times I've been eager to learn about bamboo (a highly renewable floor covering) or inquired about a locally made artisanal cheese only to have a disinterested employee grunt, "I dunno," in response to my question.

You can't be all things to all people, but if consumers associate paying a premium with making a difference, you've established yourself as a business that understands sustainability and market trends. Pat yourself on the back for that one!

Recognizing That Placement Is Paramount

Where your sustainable products are distributed is an incredibly important factor in getting your green products to market. Although the actual distribution of them is logistically a supply chain management function, determining distribution channels is primarily a marketing decision. You need to consider whether you (as the producer) are going to market your green goods straight to consumers or whether you're going to move your items through a retailer or wholesaler-retailer partnership. I share what you need to keep in mind during this decision-making process in the following sections.

Channeling sustainable products through a retailer

Distributing your product through a retailer is a common way to reach consumers in a comfortable and traditional manner, but it's only effective if you find the right retailer to work with, leaving you with some options to consider. Are you going all-out green by marketing your holistic pet food products exclusively through a natural foods store, or do you think that a traditional, intensive distribution mode is best?

Try to find a connection that gives a retailer a reason to carry your product line. For instance, your green wedding products may fit nicely with the local floral shop, or your organic table linens may provide a natural enhancement at an organic foods store. Don't forget to look into mainstream stores that are featuring sustainable counterparts to existing products.

Focusing on the retail locations where your target customers are more likely to shop is another good move. Although little formal research is available on this topic, you can rest assured that the Pine Greens congregate at the pure-green retailers, whereas the Moss Greens frequent the chain stores. Jungle Greens go either way, with higher-income consumers gravitating toward pure-green and hybrid retailers and those with lighter wallets visiting the chain stores in search of organic foods, textiles, and toys.

Check out the next several sections for help making your decision on which distributor is most appropriate for your product and target market.

Distributing through pure-green retailers

Many dedicated green retailers, both online and storefront, have emerged in response to the growing green market. Additionally, many stores featuring natural landscaping products, sustainably harvested home furnishings and textiles, and the like are receptive to products that embody green living. You just have to figure out how to get into them.

Pine Green consumers, motivated by the desire to purchase healthful and sustainable items, actively seek out organizations that feature products and services that reflect their values. If you anticipate these folks being a key component of your market, check out some of the existing online-based green retailers. Pick up a copy of the green version of The Purple Book (not-so-surprisingly found at www.thepurplebook.com) for a comprehensive overview of ecofriendly online shopping.

Distributing through hybrid retailers

Hybrid retailers are those traditional retail outlets that have branched out to distribute some green product lines. They don't deal in green goods exclusively, which in my opinion makes them prime hunting grounds for Jungle

Green shoppers. Your choices, and they certainly aren't mutually exclusive, for distributing sustainable goods to the Jungle Greens are

- ✔ General online merchandisers that feature a green section within their existing lineup
- ✔ General retailers that integrate green products with existing products
- ✔ General retailers that segregate green products into discrete sections of the store

If you already have existing relationships with these retailers, that will get you in the door to talk about your new sustainable product line. Many traditional retailers that are looking at greener business models themselves are actively prospecting for innovative green products and would be happy to hear your pitch.

Distributing through the big-box chain stores

Many big-box stores are now developing their own green lines to ecocomplement existing products. Because of their bargain prices and easy accessibility, these ultra-large, big-box stores provide the only likely outlet for capturing the Moss Greens. And with the tightening of many consumers' budgets, you may even find more Jungle Greens knocking at these doors as well.

Of course, you can always try to influence change by pitching your product to the big-box big guys (see the nearby sidebar for tips). If your product is made in the local area or in the country, however, you may be excited to know that some chain stores are allocating square footage to locally made products. Firsthand research is really important in this category, so rely on your own observations. The folks that manage these stores respond to consumer interest by carrying products to meet these demands.

Look for evidence that the shift toward sustainability has begun in your community by being observant as you make your daily forays into shops. Ask questions everywhere you go and engage managers and employees in dialogue. For example, while the employee at the seafood counter wraps up your fresh fish, inquire about Marine Stewardship Council Certified seafood and ask whether a mercury content chart is posted somewhere. Popping into a home improvement shop? Ask whether it carries ecofriendly paints and "smart strip" power strips. Believe me, the more customers inquire about sustainability-related items, the wider the door will open for green goods and services.

Repeat requests for sustainable alternatives can make an impact. If you want to receive more calls from big-box stores for distributing your product, encourage friends and family to remind their favorite large retailer that they were the ones asking for the toxin-free glue or 100-percent organic hand towels.

Pitching your product to the big-box bigwigs

If you have an idea, product line, or prototype and want to get it in the hands of big-box retailers, start by searching your target nationwide or global company's Web site for a sustainability creed, a policy on corporate social responsibility, or a job title in the organizational chart like

✔ Sustainability Director

✔ VP of Corporate Social Responsibility

✔ Environmental Management Officer

Often the job of screening green products and processes for inclusion in the chain's lineup goes to these big shots. **Remember:** Persistence is the key here. Don't be put off by their secretary telling you that the retailer doesn't take new, unsolicited product ideas. Instead, conduct a search on its Web site for press releases related to "green" or "sustainability" and see who the internal corporate players are so you can contact them directly. See whether the retailer has any job postings for interns or positions related to sustainability and follow that line. Companies *are* seeking out ways to go green — convince them you're a part of their solution!

Some of these companies are releasing visionary plans for future stores, like including wind turbines in parking lots to harvest clean energy and charge the batteries of customers' electric

cars while they shop. Your job? Convince these big-box retailers that your ecoconscious product line is *exactly* what they're looking for.

When pitching your product, make sure you're clear on the exact green product attributes you're offering. Do your homework on how your product compares to its traditional counterparts for price point, performance, and convenience. A short and concise presentation should include a

✔ Quick lesson in green demographics. Consider sharing the info in the earlier "Color-Coding Your Customers by Their Shade of Green" section and definitely throw out the current size of the LOHAS (Pine Green) market and its growth expectations.

✔ Snapshot of which group your product is positioned to target.

✔ Value comparison between your product and the primary competitors.

✔ Wrap-up that features a quick reference to how the business case for sustainability means a partnership between your company and the big-box retailer makes sense for the triple bottom line. (Refer to Chapter 1 for thorough coverage of this topic.)

Selling directly to consumers

If you directly channel your products and services to consumers — through a storefront, catalogue operation, or online shop — you have a particular ability to control your customer relationships. Such control is rather attractive from an educational perspective because you have a dedicated opportunity to develop your consumers' green knowledge. As is true of almost all aspects of a green business, some rule-bending comes into play regarding the innovative ideas emerging in product placement for sustainable items.

Although no longer epitomized by two neighbors chatting across a fence, word-of-mouth advertising is still an incredibly effective way to market. In fact, many companies hoping to spread their green message are using YouTube, blogs, social networking Web sites, and environmentally and socially oriented online forums to generate a buzz about their sustainable behaviors and products. Companies are banding together online to offer free samples of green products, highlight ethical behaviors, share knowledge, and draw attention to companies engaged in *greenwashing* (stating that they're green without taking the actions necessary to back up that statement). So if you dabble in this practice, watch out because dodgy claims will only be exposed more frequently on consumer blogs and Web sites as time marches on.

Rethinking your inventory: Do you need one of everything to make the sale?

One of the prevalent ideas behind sustainability is using fewer resources to accomplish the same results. To this end, interest is growing in heating, cooling, and lighting small, smartly designed storefronts that showcase only one or two items of each featured product rather than maintaining square footage sufficient to carry an entire product line.

If you have a full product line, ask yourself whether you really need to carry inventory representing every item in every conceivable color and size. Instead, consider inventive ways to sell your product in a smaller environment. For example, in an ecochic boutique, the customer may touch, try on, cuddle with, or generally connect with the tangible item. Then an in-house interactive digital display illustrates the sizes, styles, and colors that the product's available in. The customer can order on the spot and receive the product by mail.

Slashing your on-hand inventory may be appropriate for your business if

- ✔ The items you sell aren't something your customer needs to use right now
- ✔ A small number of higher-end pieces allows your customer to get a feel for your full range of products
- ✔ Your distribution facility's costs and natural resource efficiency are significantly lower than your retail counterparts

Determining where to locate your display space: To integrate, or to segregate?

Where you place your product display within a store goes a long way toward arousing consumers' interest. After all, securing placement for your products in retail outlets, as well as cyberspace, is a significant part of the success or demise of a product.

When marketing green goods, you have three options:

✔ Design a separate, segregated green spot to showcase sustainable products.

✔ Integrate your sustainable products with existing product lines.

✔ Engage in a hybrid of the two tactics.

Table 10-1 provides further insight into what you get out of segregating or integrating your selling space.

Table 10-1	Segregation versus Integration and the Potential Effect on Green Goods' Sales	
Segregation	**Integration**	
You have lots of educational opportunities to showcase your company's social and environmental responsibility, along with the products themselves.	Customers don't have to actively seek out a new area of the store; they'll probably just happen through the area where your green goods are being sold.	
Customers are enticed to check out the new kid on the block, and it may feel like an adventure to visit this area of the store. The look, feel, and labeling information will probably be brand-new to many of your customers.	You don't have to worry about displays looking unfamiliar and being ignored.	
Green products can stand on their own merit, giving consumers a chance to process the benefits they may be buying for the premium price.	Consumers can compare sustainable products to their traditional counterparts on a side-by-side basis.	
Photo shoots for marketing pieces are easy to do.	If you have limited store space, you don't have to worry about coming up with a dedicated green area.	

Individual experiences are very valuable when trying to explore the pros and cons of integration versus segregation. Some members of your focus group (see the "Conducting green marketing research" section earlier in this chapter for the basics on focus groups) may have favorite stores with wonderful areas devoted to sustainable products that they seek out purposefully. Others may want to see solar tubes in the same section as incandescent lighting so they can compare features and pricing. At any rate, you're guaranteed to capture a wide range of opinions from the members of your focus group. Just remember that it's your job to translate the findings from your focus group into a product-placement plan for your sustainably oriented merchandise.

Product placement is something to think out very carefully. As you go about your daily life, check out how sustainable products are displayed, particularly in supermarkets and building supply stores. Does your supermarket display its organic produce separately or side by side? Are the low-VOC paints displayed next to the traditional paints at your local hardware store? If they are, is the price differential great enough to scare off all but the most dedicated green consumers?

You can create a lot of value by educating your customers about the merits of green products, but in order to do so, you have to get them to read the label, check out the locally made placard, or ask why your green product's worth the extra money when they just want to get a job done.

 I believe that the best way to sell your customers on your green product is to get them immersed in the experience of a green product display area that engages them in touching products, reading educational materials, and finding out the story behind your innovative new product line. For suggestions on how to accomplish this task, see "Balancing Premium Pricing with Consumer Demand" earlier in this chapter.

Considering rebranding

Outlining the objectives of your green message is critical if you want consumers to get it. Is your goal to introduce a product, showcase your sustainability plan, or change your marketing strategy completely? When you've reached the point of rebranding, you've ascertained that there's no time like the present to show your sustainable side. Now all you need to do is convince your consumers that you have the solutions to what they need.

The purpose of *branding* (name, mark, or logo) is to create a distinctive identity for your firm and to secure brand loyalty from your customers. You can identify your entire group of products, as well as your company, as green in a comprehensive approach, or you can individually brand your green products without a full company-wide rebranding endeavor.

When considering whether rebranding is right to better promote your product or service, you may find that you want to go all the way — differentiating your company and its operations and products by going all green. Or you may feel more comfortable transitioning slowly into the green market. At any rate, I'm willing to bet you can explore expansion into more sustainable product lines within your own business, because many industry sectors are experiencing an explosion in the green niche of larger, established markets. Just try doing an Internet search for your product line and sustainability. You'll be surprised to see what surfaces. Try "shoes and sustainability" or "weddings and sustainability" or "roofing materials and sustainability" — well, you get the point!

Warning: Deciding whether to take the green rebranding plunge can easily be one of your most critical decisions because doing so also has big risks. If you're going whole-hog green, make sure that your intent is to stay the sustainable course. A gigantic oil company recently engaged in a nine-figure green energy rebranding campaign, only to find that when the original visionary leader stepped down and was replaced, the company's focus reverted back to petroleum. The adverse press has been crippling.

Branding far surpasses simply showcasing your products or company; it embodies all perceptions that cause consumers to form expectations and mental associations about your organization. Heady stuff, huh? Decisions to reinvent your brand image should thus never be taken lightly.

Some very high-profile companies in industry sectors as diverse as autos, consumer products, and energy are rebranding themselves as environmentally and socially astute, complete with new logos, slogans, and marketing blitzes. Such comprehensive rebranding is only appropriate if these circumstances are in place:

✔ **You have strong commitment from your board and executive management team.** For a sizable company, this sort of endeavor usually emanates from a farsighted leader willing to convince shareholders and the public that his or her vision will take the company into the future. Small or privately owned companies in this category don't have as many stakeholders to pull along, so often personal charisma and vision drive the marketing and branding efforts.

✔ **You have a significant allocation of financial resources to comprehensively green your product line and internal operations.** Rebranding your business as green may well require hiring an outside company to guide you through the PR aspect of the rebranding process, something that's a bit beyond most companies' internal scope.

Remember: Quite a few different internal procedures and processes require an overhaul to match up to the mission of corporate sustainability. After all, finding new ways of doing business — reconfiguring delivery routes to minimize fuel usage or finding new sustainable vendors, just to name two — doesn't just happen overnight. So as you weigh the pros and cons of rebranding, keep in mind that testing the green waters within your industry sector by rolling out a few green products or services and assessing customer response is perfectly acceptable.

Rebranding your entire organization as green can have some big rewards. If you're already a recognized brand, your rebranding effort should be harmonious with the current perception of your organization. Rebranding in this manner helps consumers judge your new products based on their experiences with your prior products. Some of the rewards you may receive for your efforts include being seen as a forerunner in the sustainable movement and being able to clearly differentiate your business from the competition.

Promoting Your Green Product or Service

In the broadest sense, getting your green message out there should be geared toward developing and maintaining a positive relationship between your company and its stakeholders. Note that I didn't just say customers. Your marketing endeavors should facilitate warm fuzzies with all sorts of groups from investors and customers to employees and community organizations. Ensuring that your message is forthright ("We're just starting on this new sustainability thing") and resonates with credibility ("This is a path we're on, and we've got a lot of learning to do") is important.

One of the essential elements of starting down the green path is to repeatedly communicate your ecoinitiatives, big and small alike. Many companies balk at this step, thinking that what they're doing is insignificant or uninteresting to shareholders, vendors, and customers. Nothing could be farther from the truth. In fact, increasingly these groups are looking at the greenness of your company before they make the decision to do business with you.

In the next few sections, I reveal how to spread the word positively and avoid green marketing pitfalls.

Deciding what to focus on

Educating your consumers about what you're doing to make your company carbon neutral or more socially responsible isn't going to happen by Saturday, because it's an evolutionary process. But as your firm balances economic return with social responsibility, you'll notice that increased profits, media recognition, and satisfied customers and employees are but a few of the benefits of pursuing sustainability.

Whether you're showcasing corporate social responsibility or environmentally friendly products and services, use the activities you're already engaging in as a jumping-off point (and score some great PR to boot). For example, let everyone know that your Employee of the Year award includes a 12-month free train or bus pass. Or use trade shows as an opportunity to distribute recycled or locally made items featuring your logo. Believe me, these items stand out in a sea of disposable, logo-laden, plastic throwaways *and* reinforce your green image.

Stating ambitious goals is fine, but make sure to focus on what you've actually accomplished today versus what's in the hopper. Keep your customers posted on your progress. Celebrate your successes, focus on areas of improvement, and always be truthful.

The following sections offer some tips on how to effectively maximize your message, depending on your focus.

Playing up product attributes

As you work with suppliers to build a product line that sustains natural and human resources, educating consumers along the way is critical. Present human and environmental health impacts in a nonjudgmental way. Don't patronize or lecture. Instead, help your customers understand why the laptop without heavy metals is the obvious choice for their middle-schooler. Bring them down the ecopath with you by enticing them with the tidbits of knowledge embedded in your message.

The kind of clear-cut product differentiation that you're after revolves around promoting what makes you different from other products that essentially do the same thing. Focus on the following:

✔ Educating consumers about the connection between your product and how it lowers their costs

✔ Encouraging your customers to question whether the features they love about their favorite nongreen products are really better compared to your environmentally healthy offering

✔ Identifying your product's attributes that stand out from a competitor's that customers don't see as terribly different

✔ Underscoring the harmony between your company's social or environmental responsibility and your finished product

In playing up your product's attributes, you want to be making a link in your customers' minds between your product and the triple bottom line. As identified in Chapter 1, the *triple bottom line* refers to maximizing the benefits of your business decisions on people, the planet, and your profit.

For example, say your focus group results show that all that polystyrene packaging your frames come in just gets thrown away. So you decide to convert to recycled, unbleached cardboard for protective-packaging purposes. An insert in each frame box can then highlight the key points — that you've changed up your packaging, that this move is good for the environment, and that your customers can do their own research to find out more about sustainable packaging:

> Our new packaging contains 80 percent fewer resources. Packaging is a major source of landfill waste. Reduced packaging helps us keep our prices low. Packaging has no impact on performance. Check out www. sustainablepackaging.org for more info.

Be careful with your messaging if you're rolling out a green alternative to an existing product or service. After all, you don't want to compromise the position of your current products or services. For example, if your print shop introduces a green alternative, will you risk making your regular printing services look downright irresponsible because you don't offer 100-percent post-consumer-waste paper, recyclable bindings, and nonvolatile inks on all jobs? Be clear on what benefits the green option provides and carefully track your consumers' responses.

Conveying corporate social responsibility

Corporate social responsibility (CSR) refers to an organization's attempt to balance the needs of all its stakeholders while enhancing commercial success. CSR was once purely synonymous with corporate philanthropy, but in today's reality, charitable giving is only a blip on the CSR screen. Aside from direct giving, CSR refers to a company's efforts at promoting community development, enhancing stakeholders' quality of life, contributing to a sound ethical marketplace, and building a strong environment. Proponents of CSR also point out that as businesses craft solid ethical foundations, government is less likely to intervene and regulate behaviors.

From a marketing perspective, CSR is a brand-differentiation tactic. It's all about what sets you aside from the other roofers, hair stylists, or grocers in your area. Building your business based on strong ethical values, although an intangible asset for sure, adds value in many ways. So focus your CSR messaging on

- ✔ Linking your company with corporate concern for employee and environmental health and community involvement
- ✔ Letting consumers know that your business is committed to transparency and making progress in areas that need work
- ✔ Establishing a strong link between the economic and social facets of the triple bottom line
- ✔ Offering specific sustainability traits of both your product or service and your operations by letting the public know that your company's different and explaining why that's the case

Whatever your marketing focus is, ensure that it's congruent with your internal, employee-oriented messaging. Although your short-term thinking is small, your long-term plans are larger, so you want all of your media (both internal and external) to tie together.

Lending validity to your message with ecolabeling certification

What's natural about a chicken whose beak has been removed, or what makes the phosphate-based detergent in a PVC-laced container planet friendly? These are valid consumer questions that clearly require truth-in-advertising guidelines as well as (in some cases) third-party certification.

Ecolabeling certification, which conveys compliance with various organizations' environmental and/or social standards, looks to become a real hotbed of activity in the future. As companies increasingly tout their social and environmental responsibility and resulting product attributes, collective consumer suspicion heightens. Advocacy groups anxious to curb false green marketing, fickle consumers, and organizations dedicated to corporate accountability, among others, are aspiring to develop various ecolabeling certification schemes.

For a quick-and-dirty look at the groups working to standardize claims like "energy efficient," "ecofriendly," and "sustainably harvested," as well as the various ecolabels these organizations provide, check out Table 10-2.

Table 10-2   **Ecolabeling Certifications and Organizations**

Name of Organization and Web Site	Certification	Logo	Industry Sector	Certification Meaning
U.S. Green Building Council `www.usgbc.org`	Leadership in Energy & Environmental Design (LEED)		Construction	Point-based rating system for green building. Buildings are assigned points based on green-building categories and number of points accumulated. Four levels of certification are available: platinum, gold, silver, and certified.
EPA `www.energy star.gov`	Energy Star		New homes, appliances, electronics	Homes are rated on a Home Energy Rating System (HERS), and appliances/ electronics are given ratings based on attaining high energy-efficiency levels.
Green Seal `www.greenseal. org`	Green Seal Certification Mark		Cleaners, floor care products, windows/ doors	Assurance that certified products have been scientifically evaluated for their environmental impact. Based on Guiding Principles and Procedures for Type I Environmental Labeling adopted by the International Organization for Standardization (ISO).
Coalition for Consumer Information on Cosmetics `www.leaping bunny.org`	Cruelty-free standards		Cosmetics, personal care, house- hold products	Assurance that no animal testing is done in any phase of product development by the company or its supply chain.

(continued)

Table 10-2 (continued)

Name of Organization and Web Site	Certification	Logo	Industry Sector	Certification Meaning
USDA www.ams.usda.gov/nop	Certified organic (COG)	USDA ORGANIC	Agricultural products	Products originate at certified organic farms/facilities.
Marine Stewardship Council eng.msc.org	MSC Certified	MARINE STEWARDSHIP COUNCIL ™	Seafood products	Product was captured in the wild using sustainable fisheries practices.
Forest Stewardship Council www.fsc.org	FSC certification	© FSC	Forests and wood products	Provides three kinds of certification relating to forestry management practices and forest-related products.
TransFair USA www.transfair usa.org	Fair Trade certification	FAIR TRADE CERTIFIED™	Agricultural products, flowers, indigo	Strict economic, social, and environmental criteria were met in production and trade.

If you decide to go the ecolabeling route, be an involved participant with the sponsoring organization. Pooled resources spent on a cruelty-free or buy-local campaign have the potential to yield big green — in more ways than one! You can also rest assured that banding together with like-minded organizations offers more media and marketing opportunities, including lots of educational and promotional activities, than what you can accomplish on your own.

Some research suggests that consumers may already be struggling with green fatigue, so make sure to frame your message in a way that ties in your claims with believable and provable statements. For example, although Energy Star is a bona fide EPA ecocertification given to appliances and homes that meet certain standards, claiming that something is "Energy Smart" means nothing.

Touting recyclability is another green marketing boon. If you want to promote your product or its packaging as recyclable or reusable, let your consumers know about that characteristic in an easy way by imprinting a recycling symbol on the product packaging and in your marketing materials.

Optimizing effectiveness with a positive tone

The way in which you say something makes all the difference in what your listener hears. With all the news about global warming, the disappearance of natural resources, and the overfilling of landfills, some consumers may easily take your green message as a slap on the wrist or a guilt trip rather than the empowering and educational sales pitch you want it to be. That's why communicating your green message in a positive way is paramount.

Your challenge? Being optimistic and realistic all at once. Building credibility involves transparency, and that includes acknowledging your shortcomings. However, the fact that you're fleshing out solutions to those issues is what sets you apart.

✔ Craft a green vision statement and offer it up for all to see.

✔ Let folks know if you're accessing outside standards to guide your green journey. (See Chapter 14 for the most widely recognized agencies offering sustainability standards.)

✔ Provide concrete examples that your company and/or specific products are getting greener. Always emphasize that it's a journey; you're not there yet, but you're working on it.

✔ Highlight how your internal actions reinforce the message of sustainability (your new recycling plan, purchasing 20-percent locally generated wind power, and the like).

Table 10-3 highlights some of the steps you should and shouldn't take when talking to your customers.

Table 10-3	The Do's and Don'ts of Positive Green Communication
Do	**Don't**
Accentuate the positive aspect of environmental and social stewardship.	Play to the fear factor of environmental disaster or social calamity.
Showcase your company's or product's accomplishments.	Overstate your undertakings.
Engage in education and outreach.	Ply consumers with a full social and environmental manifesto.
Talk about why your green products or services are superior.	Talk about how horrible traditional counterpart products are.
Bring your consumers into the fold with a "we can make a difference together" type of approach.	Preach to your customers.

Never underestimate your customers. Even though they may not have a high level of sophistication with green product attributes or triple-bottom-line theory, they do know when they're being fed a line. If the '70s taught society anything, other than how bad disco could really be, it was that false environmental claims (like stating something is biodegradable when it actually has polystyrene content) are bad PR and can be potentially fatal for a company's greening efforts.

Building consumers' trust

To build customers' trust in your product or service, be sure to always tell the truth when it comes to your green business practices. Your company's marketing materials should reflect your commitment to sustainability and should never make claims that can't be substantiated or that exaggerate the impact of a program you've implemented.

The fastest way to turn off customers is to raise suspicions that you aren't really doing what you say you are. Self-identifying as a green corporation or claiming to be the model of corporate social responsibility are difficult assertions to uphold. Releasing ads featuring a new sustainable product line or highlighting sponsorship of employee diversity training is much more believable. These tactics show that you're on the same striving-to-be-greener journey as your customers.

You also want to be sure to practice what you preach, in all situations. If you want to discourage consumers from purchasing your competitor's product by spilling the beans that the competitor leaves a high *carbon footprint,* (the environmental impact defined by the amount of greenhouse gases emitted by an entity), be sure you know your own company's carbon footprint first. Or when attending environmental events to promote your service, consider showing up in an environmentally friendly vehicle or on a bike rather than in a super-sized SUV.

Affairs like trade shows are a bit tougher, because you don't get to control the logistics of the event — you just show up. But in this situation, ensure that any giveaways imprinted with your name (think pens and shopping totes) are utilitarian and made of recycled materials.

If you aren't careful to always communicate the truth and practice what you preach, you can fall into the trap of greenwashing all too easily. *Greenwashing* comes in several shapes and forms:

- ✔ Actively misrepresenting your company's environmental or social behaviors or products.

- ✔ Telling outright lies or blatantly exaggerating the positive impact of your product or service on the environment.

- ✔ Offering hazy product descriptions, like "holistic" or "natural" that leave consumers confused.

- ✔ Making a naturally dangerous product appear healthy. Can you say organic cigarettes?

- ✔ Leaving key info out of the picture, such as not mentioning that although your hybrid SUV gets 17 miles to the gallon rather than 14, categorizing any gas-guzzler as ecofriendly is still very difficult.

As sustainability continues to grow as a trendy proposition, the inclination to greenwash consumers will only increase. Not only is greenwashing bad karma, but trying to pull the ecofriendly wool over increasingly savvy consumers' eyes can only hurt your credibility in the long term. Report after report shows that the public would much rather know about what your challenges are on the road to corporate social responsibility than have you gloss over them.

Highlighting Overall Sustainability Results in Your Marketing Materials

Your marketing materials (brochures, tip sheets, Web pages, flyers, and so on) are excellent ways to educate consumers and showcase your sustainability results. Consider the trusty brochure as an example. This is the place to synthesize some of the key points from your sustainability report in a clear, understandable, bulleted list–type format.

Like your sustainability report (which I give you the tools to compile in Chapter 16), your marketing material should be suited for all the folks who are new to sustainability. The kinds of factors it should address are:

- ✔ **What are your core commitments, specifically as they pertain to the triple bottom line**? You want your marketing pieces to be educational, and the easy way to do that is to tell folks how your greening efforts have improved people, planet, and profit. How are you specifically attempting to reduce your carbon footprint and combat social inequalities?

- ✔ **How are you doing with achieving objectives in each of these areas?** Choose a few highlights and don't overwhelm your readers with a ton of scientific benchmarks or compliance standards. Tell them, for example, that you set a goal of increasing the diversity of management recruits to emulate the region in which you operate. Then present a very simple table showing demographic breakdown versus your employment data. Maybe include some bullets underneath your table to indicate how you plan on improving next year.

You also want to guarantee your pieces are eye-catching yet informative. You can achieve that by

- ✔ **Publishing photographs:** Pictures can easily clarify ecoconcepts that may be more difficult to understand with words alone. If you want to tout the living machine at your factory, be sure to show it because simply describing sewage-loving bacteria and hydroponic plants isn't going to be clear to most folks.

- ✔ **Filling readers in on any specific programs you've developed:** Provide the programs' highlights and be brutally honest as to their challenges and successes.

Not everyone wants to read the full text; some people just want the short version. Make it easy for them to get just the info they really need, and you'll be rewarded with buzz *and* new customers.

Chapter 11

Revitalizing Your Local Economy

*I*n response to the forest of chain stores peppering the landscape of any U.S. town in which people outnumber livestock, an exploding number of self-described independent businesses are popping up. Those that have weathered chain-store mania are banding together to create their own retail force to be reckoned with. From community groups to whole regional areas, hometown teams are committed to revitalizing their local economies. In fact, independent business alliances across the U.S. are predicting that buy-local movements will make as big of an impact as buy-organic movements have in recent years. Buying local may seem like a rather quaint idea, much like typewriters and poodle skirts. Au contraire! It's more than a movement; it's a revolution — an opportunity that's loaded with potential and serves as a key component of a sustainable business model.

By infusing their local economies with a surge of enthusiasm and committing to using one another as resources, hometown businesses are bringing the focus back to Main Street. You can harness the same local enthusiasm by offering a wide variety of products and services that are produced and/or distributed by independent entrepreneurs. After you have an idea of what relocalization means to you and your community, you can employ education and outreach efforts (such as community-based social marketing campaigns oriented toward changing behaviors) to help get consumers onboard. In this chapter, I show you how to make your business part of the buy-local movement and how to encourage your stakeholders to jump onboard.

What Relocalization Means and Why It Matters

Relocalization is a big word to describe the return to a very old concept: looking to your local vendors and distributors for products and services. Depending on the size of your community, *local* may be defined as 50 percent or more community ownership and a location within a 50-mile radius of the community. (Of course, this definition may not be very relevant in a sprawling urban area. In that situation, a more expansive definition may be desirable.) Buy-local movements are garnering ever-expanding interest as more and more consumers express concerns about foreign products (particularly foodstuffs and children's toys) and the outflow of dollars and profits to out-of-area interests.

A localized economy has lots of different meanings and connotations, but generally it has the following characteristics:

- **Local ownership:** Businesses that participate are majority owned by local citizens.

- **Direct control:** The business owners have the right to choose their suppliers and vendors, marketing campaigns, store design, and product lines. This freedom of choice is important because one of the basic premises of relocalization is that businesses purchase as much as possible from local vendors. After all, buying local accounting services and local media time stimulates local economic development. Also, the business owners have the freedom to offer products that your specific community's consumers demand, as opposed to some nationally mandated product mix.

- **Regional sourcing:** As much product as possible is sourced regionally, recognizing that some items aren't available in the region or even country and so they must come from foreign shores.

When it works well, relocalization can change the retail power structure of a community back to the mom-and-pop stores. Relocalization efforts encourage people to realize that the majority of North American businesses are human-scale and local — and that most jobs and innovation arise from these enterprises. That's why the concept of relocalization is vital not only to small communities but also to the well-being of the U.S. economy at large.

All efforts that you're making to green your business should fit into the triple-bottom-line model of considering the impact of your business on people, planet, and profit. (Flip to Chapter 1 for the full scoop on the triple bottom line.) Relocalization fits this model well because both the buyers and sellers who participate in it can contribute to the triple bottom line — socially, environmentally, and financially.

✔ **People:** From a social standpoint, sustaining a vibrant, local economy increases the quality of life of your employees, customers, and other key stakeholders. This improvement is the direct result of reduced sprawl and congestion, community building through the establishment of consumer relationships with vendors, and a sense of connectedness that occurs when shopping in smaller, more specialized environments.

✔ **Planet:** From an environmental standpoint, local products use fewer fossil fuels to transport and store products, thereby emitting less carbon dioxide, which causes global warming. Local products also often require less packaging and therefore don't contribute as much refuse to landfills. Additionally, local businesses are generally located close to hubs of alternative transportation so that customers can shop without getting into single-passenger vehicles and contributing to traffic congestion and carbon dioxide emissions.

✔ **Profit:** From a financial standpoint, keeping commerce at the local level results in the *multiplier effect,* whereby dollars are recycled through the community instead of being removed from it. Consequently, profit comes back to your store again and again. Chalk one up for a truly local economy!

What's all the buzz about big-box stores?

When big-box stores came on the scene in the late '80s, no one predicted the U.S. would transform from a nation of shop owners into a nation of clerks. Likewise, no one knew that formulas dictated from far-away corporate headquarters would determine what products you'd buy; how the outskirts of your town would look; or that the printing, accounting, and banking would all be done in distant lands. People generally didn't think about these things because the allure of lots and lots of choices at uber-low prices in big, gleaming stores was, well, cool!

Unfortunately, many towns have seen the demise of their homegrown enterprises as a result of the big-box model. Studies show that about 1.4 jobs are lost in the local retail sector for every one job gained when the biggest of the big-box stores comes to town. Not only that, but some studies show downward pressure on all wages from the proliferation of big-box stores.

The controversy surrounding the seemingly endless glut of big-box stores and the impact on locally owned businesses is one that's likely to continue into the future. On one hand, there appears to be widespread belief that big-box stores add jobs and tax revenue to a community and significantly support local charitable organizations. On the other hand, studies have shown that net jobs actually *decrease* as the finite retail pie is reallocated to big-box stores, meaning local stores eventually go out of business.

There's also the issue of big-box blight. Millions of empty square feet of chronically vacant chain store space are unsightly and costly. Between 1990 and 2005, the amount of retail space per capita in the U.S. doubled, whereas income grew by just about 28 percent. At some point, market saturation occurs, which is apparently the stage the U.S. is in now.

A substantial part of relocalization efforts, *buy-local* campaigns are primarily geared toward two actions: increasing customer awareness about all the upsides of choosing local products and then getting customers to modify their purchasing behavior accordingly. Certainly you can list many items in daily life that simply can't be procured from your local environment. So your goal should be to get your customers asking "Can I buy this item locally?" as they go about their daily lives.

The relocalization trend has been incredibly effective for the buy-local food market. If your customers have heard any buy-local buzz, it's most likely surrounding local sustainable agriculture. See the later sidebar "Sustainable strides for agriculture" for more information on this topic.

How to Become a Buy-Local Business

Some businesses have a natural fit that encourages consumers to buy locally. For instance, if you own a ranching supply shop in Wyoming, you're selling a product that meets a need for your community. Same goes for an optometry service in a Florida retirement community, a beachwear boutique in Orange County, California, or a rock 'n' roll music store in Cleveland, Ohio. But then again, maybe the company you're greening doesn't have a clear-cut link. Does that mean buying local isn't a part of your sustainability plan? Certainly not! It just means you can find your buy-local power by associating and cooperating with other like-minded entrepreneurs. Becoming a buy-local business means joining with others to build awareness and opportunity for locally based consumer behavior, as well as purchasing your supplies and services from local businesses when possible.

The cornerstone of relocalization is getting involved with other business owners. After all, capitalizing on buy-local momentum isn't a job you can do all by yourself. Think of your fellow business owners as a lovely little chain of islands that together make one great, sunny destination. You can join forces with your fellow local business owners in several ways:

> ✔ **Become part of an independent business alliance.** An *independent business alliance* is a network of locally owned businesses committed to consumer education in order to alter purchasing behavior to favor goods and services from the local community. From small towns to big cities, businesses are banding together to create vital city centers and healthy economies reliant on preserving community character. Currently, more than 30 independent business alliances are operating in the U.S.

✔ **Join a local living economy network.** A *local living economy network* is a vibrant, healthy community that relies on community-based capital, local businesses, environment-protecting incentives, and active community members — all of which are held legally accountable by a democratically elected government. These networks are working toward developing local human-scale economies that rely on independent businesses that respect all of their stakeholders. To date, the U.S. is home to more than 50 local living economy networks comprised of more than 15,000 entrepreneurs.

✔ **Participate in a co-operative, or co-op.** A *co-op* is a buy-local model that involves the cooperation of several different kinds of groups and retailers; the term refers to similar businesses joining together to take advantage of the purchasing-power benefits that come from buying in volume. Co-ops can be formalized (such as a well-known hardware group whereby each locale has an individual owner but a shared brand and combined purchasing power) or informal (like a group of farmers coming together to sell local food).

In the following sections, I share the how-to info you need to start collaborating with like-minded businesses, as well as suggestions for incorporating local resources into your business.

Joining or starting an independent business alliance

If becoming part of an independent business alliance sounds right for you, start investigating whether one already exists in your community. To find one, check out the organizations listed in the next section or try doing an Internet search using keywords such as "sustainable," "green," "network," or "business," plus the name of your local area.

Can't track down a local alliance? Get on the stick and get one going! More formal alliances and associations help you relocalize your economy and develop greener business practices.

The first step in forming a local alliance is to pull together an initial steering committee to create a buy-local network for your community. Make sure to include representatives from all the different industry sectors and geographical parts of town. After you have a solid steering committee in place, you can delve into the nitty-gritty details I present in the following sections.

Obtaining guidance from official organizations

As you work to get your independent business alliance off the ground, you may find it helpful to seek guidance from an official organization that can focus your efforts and offer some best practices. Although joining up with such a group costs money, doing so can save you time trying to figure out what works and what doesn't. Trust me, that alone is well worth your fledgling group's hard-earned start-up capital.

Check out these organizations and consider becoming a card-carrying member:

- **AMIBA:** The American Independent Business Alliance is a nonprofit group that helps citizens launch and then operate independent business alliances. An AMIBA representative will come to your area and hold a workshop for interested parties to kick-start the burgeoning interest in your community. Membership includes templates, checklists, and all the how-to-get-it-off-the-ground info you can ingest. For more info, visit www.amiba.net.

- **BALLE:** The Business Alliance for Local Living Economies is the world's fastest-growing network of sustainable businesses. BALLE's core group focuses on increasing the number of communities committed to going local, providing network opportunities, and catalyzing members new to the concepts of sustainable and just economies. To find out more about BALLE, visit www.livingeconomies.org.

Gathering info for a collective brainstorming session

To ensure your independent business alliance has a successful first brainstorming session (described in the following section), you may want to assign some of these early research tasks to your steering committee members:

- Investigate whether your community has a buy-local food movement that can give you momentum and advice and share its membership data. The food industry is almost always where the first seeds of a buy-local movement are sown, so it's a great place to start seeking out resources and info.

- Examine what other like-sized and like-minded communities have done to relocalize their economies. (**Note:** Approaches tend to differ by the area of the country you're in, so keep that in mind when seeking out examples.)

- See whether any regional opportunities exist in your area's emerging green economy. These sorts of opportunities (think biomass conversion plants, photovoltaic silicon chip manufacturing, aquaculture, and so on) may be incorporated in regional or statewide economic development plans. Places to begin asking about sustainable development opportunities in your area may include

  - Your local community development corporation
  - Your local Chamber of Commerce

- Community financial institutions

- Downtown associations

Make sure to split up the task of going out into the community to talk to different folks about your ideas among every steering committee member, because everyone has unique connections and insight. Also, provide each member with clear direction on documenting the conversations so that they can be easily brought back to the group. If you live in a metro area, make sure to hit all the different geographic areas where local indie businesses are clustered, not just the traditional downtown area.

Your research may point you in interesting directions, so stay open to making connections happen. For example, your emerging buy-local group may find that the proposed small-scale wind farm in your area could readily meet the needs of the new whole foods store. What about the local community college's curriculum incorporating green-collar job training, including wind-turbine mechanics? The sky's the limit when considering all the possibilities!

Creating a vision and brainstorming ideas for implementation

Because the goal of your independent business alliance is to promote place-based consumer behavior, you must develop an outreach campaign aimed at broadening awareness within your community about who's local and why local is good. Armed with the results of your research (see the preceding section for tips on acquiring info if you haven't done so already), find a place to meet and keep your agenda focused on getting everyone's initial ideas as to what "buy local" is and how there might be commercial strength in your numbers.

In the early days of getting together and talking about your alliance's direction, you want to come up with a group definition of the benefits of local enterprise in your community. Also, make sure to do the following:

✔ **Define what "local" means.** The definition may seem self-evident, but it's an important distinction. Many retailers are independently owned and locally operated, but they don't carry locally made items. For example, your local bookstore probably doesn't print and bind the books it sells; nonetheless, the bookstore can be considered local. Some franchises are locally owned but their vendors, accounting, advertising, and the like are all contracted by out-of-state franchise agreements. Additionally, some seemingly local businesses may be owned in large part by out-of-state parties.

The definition of "local" gets much more complicated with food, where "local agriculture" can mean food grown anywhere from a 50- to 250-mile radius, depending on which expert you're quoting.

✔ **Determine whether you're including a reference to sustainability in your buy-local group.** If you are, everyone must be in agreement as to what sustainability means and how the alliance will assess whether a business is committed to sustainable business practices. One way to assess a company's sustainability is by providing a checklist or assessment instrument that the business can use to identify ways it's practicing sustainability. After all, paying dues and saying "I'm green" doesn't qualify an organization as sustainable.

✔ **Settle on what your membership fee structure is going to look like.** Consider whether you want to price membership on a sliding-fee scale based on revenue or number of employees, or whether you want to have different fees for nonprofits versus entrepreneurial shops. Also, determine whether you want fees to be paid in kind or in cash.

✔ **Figure out what your initial focus will be.** Identify how your buy-local campaign will set you, as an aligned group, apart from the competition. For example, have everyone come up with some speaking points that define *why* consumers should buy from a group of local shops instead of going to the big-box stores or the mall. Examine what benefits your member organizations will realize and use that list as the jumping-off point to help you hone in on your alliance's primary mission.

✔ **Assign start-up tasks or form subcommittees.** An organized independent business alliance is an effective one. Right off the bat, determine who's going to apply for nonprofit status; where your marketing plan and list of membership benefits will come from; who's going to approach prospective members, bill them, and then collect from them; and who's responsible for preparing a rough fundraising plan. These preliminary steps will save you time in the long run so you can spend more time engaging in member outreach and community education and less time making things up as you go.

Finding a level playing field on Uncle Sam's turf

Locally owned independent businesses have found out the hard way that not only do their cities and states often fail to offer incentives for local enterprises but also that many governments actually *create* laws to relieve local business' big-box competitors of tax burdens. This loophole, which in some states allows chain stores to transfer their income to out-of-state subsidiaries (thereby reducing their taxable income and state income tax liability), creates an unfair competitive advantage for the chain stores.

Without getting thigh-high into tax theory, the good news is that a number of states are now closing this loophole and requiring that businesses follow a combined reporting method that doesn't allow for this reduction in taxable profit. Vermont led the way in 2004, with four more states following in 2006. A number of states are now considering this major reform in corporate income tax law.

Local independent business alliances have helped bring these tax inequities to policymakers' attention of late and been part of effecting the tax changes. This action levels the playing field, from an income-tax standpoint at least, between locally owned businesses and chain stores.

Forming a local living economy network

Because local living economy networks often start with a hearty independent business alliance movement, forming such a network may be a "down the road" goal for your community. But if you live in a very progressive community (such as Boulder, Colorado or Austin, Texas) that has nailed the buy-local movement through independent business alliances and is ready to move on to the next step, contact the Business Alliance for Local Living Economies about its advanced program. This program welcomes folks who are interested in strategizing about holistic concepts such as community-based finance and local economic development. Go to www.livingeconomies.org and click the Find a Network button to search for a network in your regional area.

Different kinds of people coming together with a common goal is great stuff. But it also brings diverse thoughts and approaches to the same table, and that means disagreements are bound to occur. For example, the owner of your local spa and pool company may not be completely on the same page as the manager of the downtown electrical engineering firm. Focus on what binds you together —the drive to revitalize your local economy — not what differentiates you.

Combining your product or service with others' as a package deal: Co-ops

Co-ops are a type of entity that's owned by more than one person and that relies on the group for decision-making. The co-op is a wonderful business model that uses all members' skills to harness larger rewards than a single business would be able to achieve alone. It also shares the risks of business ownership unilaterally. You may choose to incorporate a consensual style of decision-making rather than the traditional "majority wins" democratic-style format. Joint marketing efforts, volume-discount buying, and the opportunity to take advantage of each member's skills are the three key benefits of participating in a co-op.

Most people associate co-ops with food. Credit unions are another commonly recognized form of co-op in that one person equates to one ownership share and thus one vote. The co-op concept is centered on the traditional buy-local motive: keep local capital in the community in which it operates. (Financial co-ops are a big part of European and Australian financial systems, and they're springing up everywhere, including the U.S.)

If you're not a farmer or banker, don't sweat it. Get creative and find a way to incorporate your business into a cooperative model. You're local, so think about

- ✔ **The connections between your business and the unique history and culture of the community in which you operate:** For example, look for multigenerational businesses or ones that build on your area's unique culture or resources. If several businesses in your community specialize in selling Eastern European products or serving Cubano food and drinks, take advantage of that heritage.

- ✔ **Ways to pool your business's and other local businesses' limited marketing resources and create a brand around them:** Many businesses that join a co-op don't have the financial capacity to buy media spots on a solo basis. Hence, one of the major benefits of co-ops is providing members with a chance to go more high-profile than they'd be able to alone. Make sure that the marketing efforts focus on what you have in common to help promote a homegrown food, locally spun wool clothing, or ethnically unique artesian household items branding opportunity.

As in all collaborative efforts, circumstances can always go awry. Watch out for these common co-op problems:

- ✔ Going into business with too many folks or people you don't have strong background knowledge of can sometimes yield nasty surprises. Protect your business by doing your research on potential collaborators.

- ✔ Businesses in the co-op can have differing visions for the entity. Encourage a representative of each member business to come to the table as you craft your co-op's mission statement together in a fluid and fun way.

- ✔ Marketing and purchasing power sometimes don't seem worth the time and effort necessary to participate in the co-op. Be realistic about the true volume-discount purchasing potential.

Sustainable strides for agriculture

If you're engaged in a business that's impacted by food in any way, you're probably aware that the buy-local food movement has truly arrived. Emphasis on regional food is making quite a comeback, particularly due to widespread consumer dissatisfaction with tainted meat and poisoned produce. As this local-food emphasis has grown, so has the number of farmers' markets and other cooperative models. The number of farmers' markets has almost doubled from 1996 to 2008, an indication that people are very interested in having a personal relationship with the producers of their food.

Find out how your local farmers have organized (and believe me, they have) and how you can tap into their efforts by checking out the following Web sites:

✔ **www.slowfood.com:** This Web site celebrates a return to *slow food* (the antithesis of fast food) by sponsoring tasting events and workshops, supporting slow food in schools, and linking producers and coproducers.

✔ **www.localharvest.org:** This Web site provides the state-by-state scoop on

the folks involved in community-supported agriculture from grocers and restaurants to farms and farmers' markets.

✔ **www.leopold.iastate.edu:** This Web site has tons of great info about alternatives to current farming practices and why sustainable agriculture is the way to go.

If you're feeling adventurous, just type your community's name and the phrase "local food" into your favorite search engine and wait to see what the Internet spits out.

Incorporating local goods and services into your business operations

As more companies become committed to sustainability in their own operations, they'll strive to green their supply chains as a part of developing greener business-to-business practices. Finding sustainable sources for raw materials naturally requires businesses to look locally. If the raw material doesn't exist in your region now, is there the potential to develop it? Often businesses coexist in the same town for years and are unaware of the possibility for materials exchanges or that they can meet many of their purchasing needs without reaching beyond the local area.

You can always make use of the services and products your fellow community members offer. Food is a particularly easy means for local sourcing. For example, if you run a day care, hotel, brewery, airport, nursing home, school, gym, hospital, restaurant, coffee shop, or bar, you may consider featuring about 10 or 20 percent locally and sustainably produced food. As your relationships grow with your community's sustainable food producers, you may think of new and innovative ways to partner with folks in your local agricultural scene to increase your reliance on locally grown food. Suddenly, everyone is in on the local-food-buying game, creating stronger relationships throughout the community.

How else can your business relocalize its supply chain? First, I suggest you check out the Internet and see whether a search for your area's name and the phrase "business material exchange" yields any results. What you find may be limited, because the buy-local movement is a relatively new concept in most areas of the U.S. (and it's usually driven by a small number of people who craft concepts specific to their own towns). But don't let that discourage you! You can also take a gander at the supplies and raw materials you use in your organization and then search online for vendors in your area.

The more you can show your customers that you're on the buy-local band-wagon, the more they'll evaluate you in a positive light and ask the same of your competitors.

Increasingly, city and even state governments are mandating buy-local procurement policies, meaning that preference or points (if a bid system is in place) are given to regional or local vendors. This practice recognizes that even though a locally made product may cost a bit more, the long-term net financial impact for the government is more favorable.

Convincing Consumers to Buy Locally

Relocalization is all about putting the power of purchasing back into the hands of consumers who are willing to spend their dollars locally. Thanks to the dominance of big-box retailers in today's markets, convincing consumers to turn away from chain retailers and service providers in favor of their local counterparts has become a two-part process. All the grassroots marketing ideas in the world won't work unless you can impart a strong, unified message to your customers by combining education with your marketing efforts for a powerful punch.

Educating consumers on their buying habits and showing them how buying locally can change those habits for the better is essential, so think carefully about what you want prospective buyers to know about the fundamentals of buying local. Because many consumers have no idea of the true costs of spending a significant portion of their budget on big-box store items, perhaps making that connection for them is the best place for you to start the education process.

Doing so isn't easy considering many folks' purchasing decisions are motivated primarily by cost. For example, an Iowan who visits a regional supermarket and finds peaches from Mexico priced 25 cents less per pound than the peaches grown 15 miles from his hometown is usually going to go with the cheaper option. Your job is to convince this shopper that even though he saved a quarter today, by buying fruit shipped in from another country, he's going to pay for that savings both environmentally (through more fossil fuels consumed) and financially (through a reduced local tax base) in the long run.

Of course, including plenty of information about the benefits to the community and environment is great, but discussing the direct benefits to the consumer is just as important. In other words, force yourself to answer the question, "What's in it for the customer?" Purchasing decisions are ultimately based on this notion of "what's in it for me," and rightfully so. Be prepared to answer triple-bottom-line questions, but also be ready to talk about the benefits of buying local to everyone, including the end user.

The following sections prepare you to successfully engage your employees in the buy-local movement (after all, they're the ones making the sales to your customers), use community-based social marketing to develop a targeted buy-local campaign, and make behavior change as easy as possible for customers.

Getting your employees fired up for the community

One of the most important tools in your buy-local education and marketing campaign is the team of people working for you. Whether that's just you and your spouse, or you plus 50 faithful employees, you have a valuable marketing arsenal on your hands — but only if you get your employees onboard, motivated, and even downright giddy about the buy-local agenda.

Here are some more quick and easy ways to build excitement within your team:

- ✔ Include "why buy local" information in employee training sessions.

- ✔ Each month, train employees on a featured local product so that they can discuss it thoroughly and excitedly with customers. (I *always* ask to see local or American-made products in a store and am astounded how very few clerks can point me in the right direction.)

- ✔ Spotlight stories about the successes of buy-local campaigns in company newsletters and on your corporate Web site.

- ✔ Sponsor an employee competition and reward whoever gets the most people to sign a pledge to buy local with a gift certificate for a massage or other service from a local provider.

- ✔ Give a couple hours per month of compensated time to employees who want to be more involved with your town's local independent business alliance.

However you decide to pump up employees' enthusiasm for buying local, just be sure to do it. Because you aren't necessarily going to be the one behind the cash register for every sale, or the one providing every service, you absolutely need everyone in your organization to smile and say, "Thanks, Mrs. Jones, for buying locally today." (If you're into pieces of flair like the restaurant manager in *Office Space,* you can even make 'em wear a "Think local, buy local" pin.) Show that buying local is something you're behind 110 percent and that you expect everyone to join you in evangelizing the concept. People tend to have a lot on their minds, so you need to keep the buy-local idea front and center in all that you do.

Attracting consumers with a targeted buy-local campaign

Encouraging consumers to change their behaviors, including their purchasing choices, is the primary goal of *community-based social marketing,* which focuses on using social norms and influences to get people to commit to a desired activity. As you probably know, changing someone's ingrained behaviors is difficult. Frankly, sometimes even getting folks to *question* where they purchase their daily items can be a stretch.

Community-based social marketing is a response to historical evidence that mass media campaigns have often failed to provoke significant social and environmental change. Asking people to alter their behaviors (and getting responses) requires a clever blend of subtly overcoming their objections to the behavior change while getting them to commit to the desirable activity. Folks also need to feel that the behavior is more socially acceptable in the targeted community than the current behavior.

Instead of throwing your hands in the air in despair, take the following steps to help you develop a targeted campaign that entices community members to engage in buying locally:

1. **Identify consumers' barriers to buying local.**

   You can't get people to buy locally if you don't understand *why* they aren't buying local in the first place. According to informal studies, many consumers simply don't know what buying local really means, which leads them to perhaps mistakenly perceive "local" big-box stores to be cheaper, have better selections, or be more convenient. But don't just take my word for it. Ask a random sampling of residents around your community simple questions like

   - What's the number one reason you choose to shop at a particular store? (Ask this question first so you don't lead the person into the buy-local answer!)

   - Do you ever consider buying locally first?

   - Would you consider buying locally first if I told you . . . ? (Rattle off a few compelling statistics here, like the ones in the following section.)

2. **Develop a strategy that encourages customers to identify with "being local."**

   Information campaigns alone rarely bring about behavior change. Yes, education is an important component, but community-based social marketing asks you to go beyond that and get your customers to identify with "being" something and to proactively commit to taking action. (A written commitment is more effective than a verbal one if you can get it.)

The key is to get people to perceive that what you're asking them to do — in this case, to buy local — is the norm. If Joe the Plumber sees other people asking about the availability of locally produced goods, he's more likely to think, "Hey this is the norm; I should behave like that." Work to combat consumers' barriers to buying local by doing something like printing buy-local totes and asking high-profile community members to commit to carrying them on their shopping forays around town. The more consumers who are hesitant about buying local see others sending the message that it's a socially acceptable thing to do, the more likely they'll be to start buying local themselves. When it gets to the point that asking for plastic or paper bags at the store seems ridiculous, you know your community-based social marketing has triumphed!

3 Pilot your buy-local strategy within a small segment of your community.

Hand out flyers about what buying local means at the local farmers' market, or give out coupon books featuring independent businesses and ask people to commit to finding a local outlet for their needs. Get people to agree to try buying local and then follow up with them to find out what their experience was. Ascertain what you want to scale up and what doesn't appear to be working.

4. Evaluate the impact of your buy-local program after it has been implemented across a community.

Try to determine how many people have heard of your campaign, how many randomly chosen community members now think about buying local because of your efforts, and how many of them are actually doing it. Share your impressive results with your key stakeholders and keep at it!

The more you focus your buy-local campaign on the benefits of buying local, as opposed to the downsides of shopping big-box stores, the more you dominate the conversation. Keep your campaign positive and focused on why buying local is such a good thing, as well as on what you are, not what you aren't. Never ever engage in putting down the big-box stores. Instead, talk about what ties you to all of your different kinds of customers — the fact that you all call your local community home. Keep Main Street on the minds of your customers, and they won't have time to think about shopping at the local price club.

After you have the outline of your buy-local marketing strategy ready to go, you need to start filling in the details. The next couple sections offer facts you can share with consumers as well as some media and public relations techniques you can implement as part of your campaign.

Arming consumers with some basic buy-local facts

Wondering how to pitch the relocalization message to consumers? Focus on the benefits to both your customers and the community at large. Let your customers know that

✔ Small businesses are the largest employer in North America. (That alone is a powerful statement.)

✔ Local businesses are owned by people vested in the community (like you!). These people are more likely to stay in the community and feel a part of its future. In fact, studies show that entrepreneurs and skilled workers have more of a tendency to settle in a community that's tied to preserving its distinctive character.

✔ Hometown entrepreneurs contribute up to 2.5 times as much to local nonprofits as chain stores.

✔ About 45 percent of money spent at a local business stays in the community compared to only 14 percent of dollars spent at a big-box store. These dollars not only cycle through the community many times but they also produce tax revenues to fund schools and safe streets. (Local businesses do much more to enhance the local economy than big-box stores, contrary to all the media blitz you may have seen.)

✔ The unique shops and services available in your community are part of what brings tourists and their checkbooks to your locale.

✔ Local businesses quite often hire employees with better product knowledge and more interest in getting to know the customers.

Spreading your marketing message here, there, and everywhere

Buy-local messaging isn't a one-time endeavor. You want your customers to see these facts and figures repeatedly — on brochures, bookmarks, blogs, Web sites, posters, and so on. Take your buy-local message, complete with a quick-and-dirty list of *why* buying local is advantageous, to anyone who'll listen.

Reaping the benefits of big-box stores acknowledging relocalization strategies

As consumers begin to change their buying habits to accommodate growing interest in local products and services, you may notice your local big-box competition reaching out to local vendors and asking whether it can feature the vendors' locally made goods in its stores. For example, an unnamed humongous chain store regularly reserves some space for local products in each of its stores as part of its strategic operational plan. This acknowledgement of relocalization strategies creates more opportunities for local products to reach mass markets and hopefully spark consumer interest in further exploring local products. You may want to approach your big-box competitors and ask for an opportunity to showcase your local wares in their locations. If they come to you, then you know you have a righteous movement on your hands.

In order to get your customers thinking (or rethinking) about where they buy basic necessity items, particularly building products, clothing, and food, tap into the wonders of free media. The buy-local movement is gaining prominence in many communities, and local media folks are eager to join the fray not only for the value of local, feel-good news but also because they too have faced the realities of larger corporations taking over the local beat.

Consider tapping into these free media opportunities to spread the buy-local word:

- ✔ **Pen an Op-Ed to your local newspaper.** If you're a good writer, or if you know someone who knows someone who's a good writer, sharpen up the #2 pencils and get yourself front and center in the daily rag. Make sure to sprinkle your articulate argument *for* an economy based on local business (that means no harsh judgments on big-box stores, regardless of how you may feel) with facts and figures as to how buying local benefits everyone in the community.

- ✔ **Create a short program featuring local vendors on a community access TV show.** Community access TV allows programming initiated in and of interest to the local community to be broadcast to the public. To find your local community access TV station, check out www.community media.se/cat/linksus.htm.

- ✔ **Be a guest on a local talk show.** Many communities have an early morning radio show that welcomes local guests for the purpose of discussing community events and the like. Identify a partner to join you. I bet if you call up your local farmers' market coordinator and say, "Let's partner on Ruth's a.m. show at KGRN to talk about buying local," that he or she would jump at the chance.

- ✔ **Spotlight all of your events on TV and radio community calendars.** Take advantage of community calendars to promote your holiday buy-local campaign or to tout your Independence Day celebration of American-made goods.

- ✔ **Issue a Public Service Announcement.** PSAs are forms of free advertising and usually are part of a bigger public awareness campaign about an issue that affects your community, such as the importance of buying local. They can be released on radio or TV (or both); now you can even find them on youtube.com. Although the media time for PSAs is free, producing them isn't. However, PSAs can be powerful components of your buy-local messaging thread.

You can also launch a grassroots buy-local public relations campaign to tie in to your media relations efforts. Band together with other local businesses (like the members of your independent business alliance or co-op; see the earlier related sections in this chapter for more details on these groups) to take advantage of cross-marketing opportunities. Offer a flyer at every store that advertises everyone in the co-op or alliance and make handing it out and talking about it part of the checkout experience. Or you can design a logo for window clings and posters that are easy to spot in order to inform potential customers that your shop is independently and locally owned.

Don't forget about the influence of your city council. Request that your city government purchase locally when it can, serve locally grown food at events, and get its green power from the local wind farm. Make yourself heard, have your buy-local fact sheet in hand, and go for it. (If you want to go even further and try to impact local policies, check out Chapter 5 for specific tips on targeting your efforts.)

Making consumer behavior change easy and enticing

In order to encourage consumers to change their shopping habits and support local businesses, you need to make doing so easy for them. Take the guesswork out of finding out about the local co-ops, farm stands, and hometown retailers with ideas like the following:

- ✔ **Offer a green-mart (lucky you if it can be open year-round) and advertise it liberally.** In *green-marts,* folks shop at local companies that model sustainable business practices. Instead of sitting in traffic to get to a big-box store to purchase products made in a far-away place, imagine a green multiuse building that's easily accessible by alternative transportation. Green-marts house many local businesses, which provides customers with one-stop shopping for organic food, natural body products, and sustainable building materials, as well as green pet products, books, and baked goods.

   Green-marts aren't impossible visions; people all over the U.S. are pursuing this idea. Join forces with them and dare to dream big. Make the green-mart just as obvious to consumers as the local grocery store.

- ✔ **Provide car service to the local green-mart and/or sustainable retailers for customers who can't drive themselves.** Organize a green taxi service made up of hybrids or a ride-share program to your sustainable business outlet. Anything you can do to get people out into the independent business alliance's stores is valuable. It also helps you share community with your fellow citizens and feel pretty progressive while doing so.

✔ **Put together a coupon book featuring all the organizations that have joined your buy-local network.** Consumers who are new to your buy-local campaign need guidance. What better way to provide that than to offer an easy-to-reference booklet of participating organizations. Often companies that join a buy-local alliance give small discounts to fellow member organizations or to consumers who are consciously trying to modify their purchasing behaviors by buying local.

After all that hard work, you may still get the response, "I love the idea of buying local, but it's so time consuming/expensive/hard to find everything I need." Bring in the big guns and find even more ways to make buying local really enticing. Make it downright sexy, patriotic, moral, or whatever else you think will appeal most to your customer base. You can

✔ **Create special offers that directly benefit consumers.** Offer a "buy one meal, get one free" night at the local diner that features local produce, brews, and meats. Work out a deal with your co-op buddies to offer a deal to consumers for shopping at their stores. The possibilities are endless.

✔ **Make free samples part of the local shopping experience.** Give out samples at the local green mart, artesian craft co-op, or farm stand.

✔ **Consider creating a local gift card redeemable at every business that's participating in the community's local independent business alliance.** Show your customers how this idea gives recipients a wide variety of options as to where to spend instead of limiting them to one chain store. Time your efforts to coincide with big consumer-spending rushes such as back-to-school or holiday shopping.

✔ **Get well-respected local celebs (even if your best local celebrity is the high school football coach) to buy local and appear in some of your marketing efforts.** Make the connection between the local celeb in the ad and the fact that more local purchasing lines the community's coffers and enhances the parks and libraries that everyone enjoys.

✔ **Feature second- and third-generation businesses (ideally with historical pictures) in materials that are linked to the buy-local campaign.** This tactic highlights your unique community and the role commerce has played in its history.

✔ **Get people to feel a sense of common purpose by asking them to sign a pledge to buy local.** Such a pledge is typically a short statement of commitment to consider local vendors first.

✔ **Provide actual results in your marketing campaign.** For example, you can say that thanks to buy-local consumers, your town decreased its overall carbon footprint by 20 percent in the last year. Celebrate triple-bottom-line successes any time you can!

Buy-local movements are a proven success

Outreach campaigns aimed at educating consumers about supporting independent, unique businesses are *really* working. The following anecdotal evidence provides a pretty telling story:

Prior to the local independent business alliance's Think Local First campaign, many Bellingham, Washington residents couldn't even define what buying local meant. Even fewer residents bothered to consider local alternatives first when making purchasing decisions. After four years of the campaign, 69 percent of Bellingham residents cited familiarity with the program, and three out of five households indicated that they'd changed their purchasing behavior because of the crusade. Not only are individual consumers in this community buying in to buying local but also 89 percent of participating businesses say they now "always" or "often" consider whether a product or business is locally made, grown, or owned when deciding on a purchase. Talk about a significant cultural shift!

Here's another great example: The Independent Business Forum conducted a nationwide survey of 1,382 independent retailers and reported that a desire to support locally owned businesses is emerging as a key aspect of consumers' shopping choices. Retailers in cities with active buy-local campaigns reported much larger increases in holiday sales on average than those in cities without such campaigns. *Independent retailers* (meaning non-big-box retailers) in cities with buy-local campaigns reported an average gain in sales of about 2 percent over the prior holiday season, whereas those in cities without such campaigns saw an increase of less than 0.5 percent.

Chapter 12

Partnering with a Nonprofit

- -

In This Chapter

▶ Understanding why partnering with the right nonprofit is a win-win situation

▶ Identifying strong partnership opportunities and picking the best partner

▶ Securing a mutually beneficial partnership and spreading the word about it

▶ Ensuring your partnership will stand the test of time

- -

*T*he old model of the rich, evil corporation and the benevolent nonprofit is a thing of the past. Identifying collaborative projects and partnerships with nonprofit organizations is a cornerstone of forming a sustainable business. Doing so not only builds your corporation's image of sustainability but it also contributes to society's well-being. Both for-profits and nonprofits are seeing phenomenal success because partnering magnifies each side's potential for positive social, environmental, and economic impact. The big pluses for you? You get free press, which in turn magnifies your work and garners attention, and you help build community around your sustainability efforts and those of your partner nonprofit.

Partnering with a nonprofit is a way of doing business that involves engaging with a chosen organization to accomplish both parties' interests. Financial contributions *may* be a part of the picture, but they definitely aren't the whole painting. Being a good partner organization means being proactive in leading your company to meet the societal expectations customers exceedingly have of who they buy from, not just throwing money at a cause. It also means being smart and ensuring that the issue you choose to tackle has an immediate and relevant tie-in to your product or service.

The Form and Function of a Successful Collaboration

In order to fully understand the value that a traditional business-nonprofit partnership brings, and to decide whether a partnership is right for your business, you need to know what such a partnership entails. Both parties' responsibilities are crucial to fostering mutual benefits — if one party doesn't fulfill its duties, the partnership doesn't work.

The vital tasks for long-term success are finding and building upon a partnership that will be synergistic and contribute to enhanced capacity for both parties. (*Synergy* is that great creative energy that's unleashed when two parties bring mutually advantageous talents to the table; it drives them to be better than the sum of their parts.) Both partners should harness synergy to leverage each other's resources and elevate each other's respective capacities to a new level. A sustainability-oriented partnership is all about enhancing the triple bottom line.

For example, say you operate a regional energy company and decide to partner with a local agency that prepares at-risk teenagers to transition into adulthood. Your contribution is to teach the teens how to conduct energy audits. The *triple-bottom-line results* (as in the benefits to people, planet, and profit; see Chapter 1 for more details on the triple bottom line) are evident everywhere. Here's how they break down:

- ✔ **People:** You're providing a specific vocational skill for teenagers who might not otherwise gain it.
- ✔ **Planet:** You're taking part in the reduction of future carbon emissions.
- ✔ **Profit:** You're simultaneously training your next workforce generation and reaping the rewards of publicity surrounding your nonprofit collaboration.

To see some real-life examples at work (and the benefits therein), check out these high-profile partnerships:

- ✔ Greenpeace and Coca-Cola are working to eliminate hydrofluorocarbons and chlorofluorocarbons from refrigerators. Benefits accrue to both parties: Greenpeace is attaining its environmental goals, and Coca-Cola is garnering invaluable free press. Note that both partners bring specific competencies and/or resources to the table. Greenpeace has environmental scientists and skills, whereas Coca-Cola has a captive audience and significant resources dedicated to furthering social and environmental initiatives.

✔ The Rainforest Alliance and Chiquita are working to greatly improve labor conditions in Latin America. Value accrues to the nonprofit because its mission includes ecological preservation through transforming land-use practices, and Chiquita has a happier and more productive workforce.

The following sections delve into greater detail about what each of you (the for-profit business and the nonprofit organization) bring to the partnership table.

How you help the nonprofit

Many nonprofits (which are sometimes referred to as *nongovernmental organizations,* or NGOs) are finding that access to additional revenue streams through partnerships with for-profit organizations is an integral part of a sustainable fundraising plan. After spending countless hours planning annual events that barely break even, or after receiving the dismal news that a significant grant source is drying up, many nonprofit leaders turn to the idea of partnering with for-profit organizations. Here's what they're looking for:

✔ **Products that may assist them in implementing the nonprofit's mission:** The nonprofit needs financial resources to acquire goods it can distribute to its constituents. For example, an agency committed to reducing deforestation in developing nations may turn to your outdoor gear company because it manufactures camping stoves. Together you can design and market a clean-burning, affordable cook stove that the agency can then donate to the population it serves. Or maybe the local branch of Habitat for Humanity comes to you because you own a hardware shop; you can provide the nonprofit with thermal water heater wraps and compact fluorescent light bulbs.

✔ **People (from the part-time, hourly employee to the CEO) and services to assist them in implementing the nonprofit's mission:** Nonprofits often need manpower to make things happen; your organization has employees who can lend a hand. Consider incorporating a matching plan for employees who volunteer (perhaps one hour paid for every hour volunteered, up to a monthly cap). Or think about sharing nonprofit information with key investors to persuade them to donate their time and/or money. If your staff's already tapped out with volunteering, consider making your new nonprofit partnership a discussion item when you next meet with your key suppliers; they may want to be involved, too.

✔ **Industry expertise:** Nonprofits are often in search of people with industry-specific or technical know-how that applies to particular tasks they want to accomplish. Here's where you (or another representative of your business) can jump in. For example, a nonprofit board for an organization that develops affordable green housing by using low-income housing tax credits would gladly welcome the expertise of a mortgage banker or local developer.

✔ **Expanded networking capacity:** Nonprofits are always looking to build donor and volunteer databases, as well as spread their messages. Working with for-profit businesses helps them do both. Partnering is a particularly good way for nonprofits to gain access to new markets that they may not otherwise be able to penetrate, such as young professionals.

How the nonprofit helps you

At the same time you're providing resources to help further the nonprofit's mission, the nonprofit is also helping you. Your partner nonprofit's image, capacity to connect with your like-minded customers, and community connections will help your business

✔ Set ambitious and attainable goals to achieve a higher level of corporate social responsibility

✔ Find new ways of stimulating your own business capacity by tapping into creative thoughts about the nonprofit's mission

✔ Demonstrate how to do good, mission-driven work by providing an easy way to tap into marketing capacity that you probably wouldn't have tapped on your own

Additionally, partnering with a wisely selected, like-minded nonprofit organization can serve to strengthen your ties to the triple bottom line. Following are the main reasons that your company may find these nonprofit partnerships profitable on all three levels:

✔ **Capacity for free publicity (of sorts):** Sure the relationship may cost you money in terms of financial donations or lost profits from donated goods or services, but the extra, free publicity you'll receive from being tied to an organization that's tackling timely, relevant, and meaningful issues within the community is extremely beneficial. Because you're partnering to solve the issue at hand, your leadership will be spotlighted and your reputation enhanced — for far less than you'd spend on advertising.

Just consider what happens when a highly visible national environmental organization pairs with a consumer products conglomerate to get the word out about the latter's new line of green cleaning products. By mass e-mailing its large constituency, the nonprofit spreads the word of these new, environmentally sound cleaners in a way that would've cost the for-profit company tens of millions in advertising dollars.

✔ **New markets for your sustainable products or services:** Partnering with nonprofits creates additional opportunities for your company to network with other influential folks and identify new populations that may have an interest in your product or service due to your association with the nonprofit they support. Many times businesses find that their target market doesn't necessarily intersect with the specific market a particular nonprofit serves, so by partnering with the nonprofit, they gain access to a whole new realm of potential clients or customers.

When a local farm partners with an organization that provides community housing for seniors, for example, the farmer has a steady new stream of customers, meaning he or she can in turn put more money back into the local economy. At the same time, the seniors get to eat healthy, local food.

✔ **Improved customer loyalty due to a sense of community and shared ethics:** Community action is a powerful thing, and public sentiment in response to real and tangible change is a strong driver of consumer loyalty. This reciprocity between your business and the community-serving nonprofit revolves around a strong sense of mutual purpose, which customers can sense. Survey results strongly indicate that consumers favor socially responsible companies and hold back from supporting companies with potential ethical issues.

For example, as the owner of a fly shop, you can offer those who support your nonprofit partner (a bayou watershed education group) discounted rods with their nonprofit membership card, or a free fly when they commit to making a monthly electronic contribution to the nonprofit of $50 or more. Your new customers already feel a sense of camaraderie with your business due to a shared interest in healthy water, and you secure their loyalty further by offering them discounts that only like-minded people will receive.

✔ **Creative stimulation of ideas for new products or services:** Frequently collaborations with nonprofits inspire ideas for new projects or products that will diversify your revenue stream. How so? Well, pretend you're the entrepreneur for a small accessories boutique located next to the site of a proposed performing arts center. You approach your community cultural council to discuss collaborative efforts. The end result? An embroidered organic cotton tote that bears your logo next to the council's — a perfect marketing piece that arts supporters will carry as they go about their daily shopping chores. Now that's mobile advertising with a message!

Identifying Good Opportunities for Partnership

When searching for good nonprofit partnership opportunities, you want to look for thoughtful, relevant collaborations with established organizations that you believe in and that naturally complement your business. Don't just jump on the bandwagon of every nonprofit that comes a'knocking, because you might not get what you need out of the relationship. (See the preceding section for details of what you should get from a good partnership with the right nonprofit.)

Finding the best nonprofit to partner with is going to take some research on the part of your company's green team (for tips on building a green team, see Chapter 3). Your first priority is making sure your nonprofit affiliate meets your sustainability goals, so look for commonalities with potential nonprofit partners. You're engaged in a for-profit endeavor, and your potential partner exists to provide services for a target population; however, the tie-in between your two organizations should be seamless.

With that said, don't be afraid to be open to a wide range of organizations in your initial search for a nonprofit partner. Exploring the not-so-obvious opportunities can turn up some interesting bedfellows. These collaborations often broaden exposure, diversify and grow revenue streams, and develop new constituents for both parties — so long as your ideals are firmly rooted on the same page as your potential partner's.

Partnerships can develop and flourish around a shared need, such as assets (vehicles or specialized equipment), office space, or expertise. Before you get caught up in what *you* want from this relationship, look at the proposed partnership from the nonprofit's point of view. Doing so helps you anticipate possible conflicts or risk factors (like incongruent missions, differing scopes of influence, potential conflicts of interest, and any prior image problems either entity brings to the table) that may hinder the formation of a successful partnership.

Put simply, think about what you can contribute and who might need that (and vice versa) by asking these questions:

- ✔ What part of your mission are you currently not meeting as fully as you'd prefer?
- ✔ What areas of business do you want to focus on improving or expanding, and are there scale-up opportunities inherent in the potential partnership?
- ✔ What expertise or resources do you need but currently lack?
- ✔ What means of collaboration will best help achieve your objectives?

✔ Who are your customers, and what are they likely interested in?

✔ What customer or client base do you most want to build up, and does your potential partner help you in that capacity?

✔ What will increase your public exposure in a way that has lots of positive potential and very little negative risk?

Following are a few examples of some potential partnerships to help get you thinking:

✔ If you own a local pharmacy, a natural partnership fit is to work with a low-income children's healthcare organization because you both exist, in part or on the whole, to positively affect your community's healthfulness.

✔ If you manufacture or sell PCs, you may want to partner with an organization that's dedicated to finding answers to the mounting e-waste problem.

✔ If you run a chain of assisted living facilities, your best nonprofit partner may be a group that's working on Alzheimer's research.

What to do if an initial green team brainstorming session doesn't yield a standout collaborative prospect? Try going to `national.unitedway.org/myuw` to find your local United Way organization. It won't have an exhaustive list of nonprofits in your area, but its database is a solid starting point if you want to identify who's who in your community's nonprofit arena. Your local Chamber of Commerce or sustainable business council may also be able to give you an idea of nonprofits in your area by type of client served or mission focus. Additionally, many states and urban areas have nonprofit associations; find them by running a Web search with the name of your area or state and the keyword "nonprofit association" and see what pops up. Finally, if you're located in a larger area, check out your local newspapers and journals because they often spotlight local nonprofits.

Assessing the Candidates and Narrowing Your Options

After you've identified some potential nonprofit partners, you need to make an intelligent partnering choice by doing some background research on the candidates so that you can better assess their qualities and narrow down your options. First, you need to conduct a prescreen to ensure that the potential collaboration is even worth pursuing. Then you must evaluate the potential nonprofit partner's financial and operational health, as well as its image within the local community. Conducting this entire process, known as *due diligence,* is essential to choosing the right partner organization, and I walk you through each step in the following sections.

Prescreening before moving ahead

Before you dive into in-depth research surrounding a potential partnership and a corresponding series of meetings and discussions, you should conduct a prescreening review of your possible partner. Consider pulling a team together to sit down and go through the following list of questions. The ensuing discussion will help guide your decision to move ahead (or not!) with the more formalized assessment process that follows in the next sections on looking at your potential partner's financial and operational solidity.

- ✔ **How does *their* mission fit with *your* mission?** Your company's values must be congruent with those of your nonprofit affiliate. Additionally, the link between missions must be natural enough for people to make. Pet groomers supporting the Humane Society makes sense; pet groomers supporting disabled vets may be difficult for customers to grasp, and therefore to remember the connection.

- ✔ **How long has the organization been in the community?** You absolutely must be assured that the collaboration is with a strong, reputable, highly respected community group. Just because a potential partner is new doesn't mean it doesn't have these attributes; it just means there's more risk involved because of the organization's unproven record.

- ✔ **What type of reputation do the nonprofit's leaders have?** Check out the board's composition and investigate any other relationships the nonprofit may already have. Keep a keen eye out for any potentially controversial board members or executive directors. Nonprofit leaders who've been involved in high-profile litigation or been accused of inappropriate financial or ethical actions can harm your business image if you partner with their organization. Conversely, if the nonprofit has well-respected and well-known community members sitting on its board, that's a major boon to you should you choose to partner with the group.

- ✔ **What, specifically, is potentially synergistic about your collaboration?** Before moving forward with any partnership, you need to determine how it would be mutually beneficial. Do you envision engaging in public service projects together, giving money and/or time, or showcasing the nonprofit in your catalogues or storefronts?

A good prescreen usually results in up to five nonprofits that you feel comfortable moving through to the next stage.

Sizing up financial and operational health

After creating your shortlist of candidates via prescreening (described in the preceding section), your next step is to determine whether a potential non-profit partner is financially solvent and has a solid management team and a strong board. Review the organization's health by determining

- **Employee turnover percentage:** High employee turnover costs a company money and time and may be the result of a poor (or nonex-istent) human resource policy or inadequate management training. Low employee turnover almost always equates to satisfied, produc-tive employees and strong retention efforts. Ask the nonprofit's HR or accounting personnel for the organization's employee-retention stats.

   Be sure to look at the length of time the nonprofit's executive director (ED) has been in place, because employee turnover can be even more detrimental in that position. Lots of ED turnover may be indicative of tension between the ED and the board, or of a not-very-thorough execu-tive hiring process. On the other hand, don't assume that a long-time ED means all is well — sometimes that actually indicates stagnation within the organization. If the group has a long-time, widely respected ED, make sure to ask questions surrounding new visions and interests that the organization may be pursuing. And if you're not sure how long the ED has been in place, just ask.

- **Level of board involvement:** The board of directors is typically the driving force behind a nonprofit organization; it's also responsible for keeping the ED in check. High turnover of board members, low rates of meeting attendance, or lackadaisical financial and executive com-mittees generally shows a disinterested or dysfunctional board and a nonprofit that's neither highly effective nor closely managed. Promising signs include a vital subcommittee structure, good meeting attendance, annual retreats, and significant board giving.

   Gauge a potential partner's board member involvement by reviewing board minutes for attendance and membership composition. For exam-ple, is there a legal advisor? An accountant? A few professionals in the actual field of work? Identify the committee structure, looking specifi-cally for a Finance Committee and an Executive Committee that meet regularly (as evidenced by subcommittee minutes). You may also want to conduct an interview with a past board president to gather the unoffi-cial scoop on the level of board involvement.

✔ **Solvency as evidenced by financial statements:** A nonprofit's financial statements can tell you a lot. Increasing liabilities and decreasing revenue streams are red flags that you can easily spot on multiyear financial statements. Promising signs are manifested in desirable trends such as additional revenue sources, an increase in permanent endowment dollars, and stabilized expenses as a percentage of revenues. Ask your potential partner for three years of audited financial statements and search for these signs.

If this is your first go at a nonprofit partnership (and assuming you're a newbie on the green path), I heartily recommend that you put together an outline of what you want to cover in your due-diligence process. Using the outline gives you and your green team the added benefit of easily comparing nonprofits and making an objective decision as to which organization is the best partnership fit for you. Be sure to include the items in the preceding list, as well as any other factors that are important to you. Also, consider assigning a score to each of the preceding items to help you rank the candidates.

One of the easiest ways to do your background research on potential partners is to check out the local newspaper — pull *all* the press you can find about your various nonprofit candidates. Additionally, take a peek at the following Web sites; they're strong resources that can help you evaluate the financial and operational health of existing nonprofits.

✔ **www.guidestar.org:** Visit this Web site to gather an overview of a nonprofit's mission, verify a nonprofit's legitimacy, and view a scanned copy of the organization's recent 990 (a nonprofit tax return) to help understand the entity's financial position. The site offers three levels of service. The premium and select versions will cost you, but frankly, you should be able to glean all the info you need from the basic level of service, which is free.

✔ **www.charitynavigator.org:** This Web site shows evaluation results based on two criteria: how efficiently the nonprofit is using its financial resources today and to what extent it's growing programs and services over time.

Getting a feel for the community's response

A potential nonprofit partner's reputation within your local community is extremely important to the success of your partnership. Your chosen nonprofit partner's image should be harmonious with what you want to project.

Ask friends, family, and professional affiliates what they know about your individual nonprofit candidates and watch what sorts of responses you get when you mention prospective partners' names to others. If you get a vaguely disconcerting reaction from some folks, probe and ask why they have that opinion. If you observe a generally positive reaction, find out what people like or know about the organization. Also, take a look at your local newspaper and search the archives for stories (both positive and negative) to help you gauge the nonprofit's reputation within the community.

If no one has even heard of a particular nonprofit candidate, you may want to question how much capacity- and image-building that organization will be able to bring to the table.

Gauging community image is more an art than a science and is consequently very hard to qualify. However, by merging the hard research described in the preceding section with this more intangible information, you should see a pattern that will help shape your overall decision.

Choosing which candidates to proceed with

After sizing up your top candidates' financial and operational health, as well as the community's response to them, you should narrow your list of potential candidates down to no more than three organizations. Then, you need to compare them to each other to determine which partnership can bring the most benefit to you both.

Because one of the reasons for pursuing a partnership is to increase triple-bottom-line results, think about prioritizing which of the three areas — people, planet, or profit — is most critical to you. Each potential partner offers different opportunities for your company, so you need to have a clear idea of how those opportunities match up with your unique goals. For example, if you're working hard to build a reputation for social justice, Amnesty International's local chapter is arguably a better fit than a community land trust. In addition to weighing triple-bottom-line priorities, you should have a strong belief that your candidates have a true understanding of sustainable business development in general.

Meeting with the Nonprofit's Leadership

The face-to-face meeting is the next step after you've narrowed down your potential nonprofit partners to just a few candidates. This stage happens in two parts: a casual meeting where your respective boards and/or top-level management have their first "how do you do" moment with each other, and a meeting (either casual or formal) where you assess whether your prospective partner meets the social and environmental criteria you've outlined.

✔ **The meet and greet:** The goal of your first meeting is multipurpose: to banter, to get to know each other, to exchange business cards, and above all — *to get in touch with your basic gut feelings about the organization.* Make sure to share mission statements and specifics of your greening plans. Figure out where enhancing key stakeholder relationships comes in to play. Finally, identify organizational capacity and discern whether an innate connection exists among the people who are going to be involved.

Be sure to focus on the general vibes you get from this meeting. If you aren't feeling all warm and fuzzy about the partnership prospects, proceeding to the next stage probably isn't a good idea.

✔ **The sustainability values meeting:** This meeting is where you use the research you've already conducted (see the earlier section "Assessing the Candidates and Narrowing Your Options" if you haven't done this research) to gauge in person whether solid collaborative potential exists. By conducting this *social and environmental screen,* you and the nonprofit representative are identifying each other's organization's sustainability principles or values, accomplishments, collaborative ideas, and expectations in each area of the triple bottom line. Depending on your preference, these discussions can either focus on discrete processes or on mutual sustainability values and goals.

You're meeting with someone who's potentially going to help you move forward with your sustainability efforts. This person needs to talk the talk *and* prove he or she can walk the walk — and demonstrate a capacity to evaluate you through the same lens. Your contact should appear capable of growing *your* capacity as an ethically responsible organization, not just capable of taking whatever you're willing to offer.

What to bring with you

The sustainability values meeting requires a bit more preparation than is necessary when you're merely meeting and greeting a nonprofit candidate's leadership. Prior to this meeting, work up a set of talking points to express what value your company brings to the table. After all, you aren't the only one evaluating the partnership potential. A judicious board of directors and executive director will be looking at you just as critically to see what you and your business can offer to benefit the nonprofit's mission.

Be sure to bring hard evidence (press releases, media clippings, financial statements, business plan, and the like) along to back up any statements regarding your business's community reputation, financial health, or overall vision. This combination of strong talking points and good documentation exhibits your professionalism and allows your potential partner to ask the right questions of you.

If for some reason you didn't share your mission statement or the specifics of your greening plans during your first meeting, bring hard copies of these documents along and have talking points prepared to highlight the key concepts. If you've engaged in any sustainability planning or specific ecoinitiatives, now's the time to mention them.

What questions to consider

In order to make your final decision about which nonprofit to partner with, you need to pull together all the information you've gathered and ask yourself some key questions:

- ✔ Does the research you've conducted indicate financial and operational solidity?

- ✔ Do your management team and the nonprofit's leadership click and seem enthusiastic about shared goals?

- ✔ Do you care about the same constituents?

- ✔ Can this relationship take advantage of a deep sharing of expertise and resources?

- ✔ Can you generate a broad action plan of objectives you want to achieve together?

- ✔ Will partnering with this organization further your sustainability endeavors by enhancing capacity in that arena?

Solidifying the Partnership

Drafting effective partnering documentation can be an expensive, drawn-out process that involves attorneys and accountants. Some partnership-formation efforts, typically those involving small stakeholders, may find any sort of documentation too onerous. In that case, proceeding on a handshake is okay so long as both parties feel comfortable without written documentation.

But there is a middle ground — a straightforward way to indicate that you intend to pursue a common goal with your nonprofit (and vice versa) in the manner you both promised. This is called a Memorandum of Understanding (MOU). An *MOU* is a document that outlines partners' respective responsibilities — a type of old-fashioned gentlemen's agreement, if you will. It implies intent and isn't generally contractually binding.

Despite its fancy name, the MOU shouldn't be chock-full of legalese. Overly lawyered documents quickly lose meaning.

The outline that follows describes topics an MOU should cover (or what you should sketch out verbally if you're proceeding without written documentation):

- ✔ **What your missions are:** Briefly describe each organization's mission and state why you're entering into this mutually beneficial relationship. This language may be as simple as "We will enter this partnership to promote sustainable values in both our organizations as they pertain to enhancing animal welfare."

- ✔ **What both of you are trying to accomplish:** Be frank and open about the reason for your collaboration. If you're trying to expand your customer contacts by partnering with a nonprofit that has a green donor base, then say so. Identifying where your missions overlap is critical.

- ✔ **How you both plan to achieve your goals:** Setting goals is great, but good luck achieving them if you don't identify which partner is going to take the lead on which project. The language can be as simple as "I'll be the lead sponsor on your annual cruelty-free products event" or "We'll put our logos together on marketing materials to fundraise for your capital campaign for the new animal shelter." You may also want to provide a clear line of responsibility for who pays the expenses by including verbiage such as "Each party to this MOU is responsible for covering its own expenses in relation to actions contained within this MOU."

- ✔ **Who's going to be involved from both organizations:** If specific people from both organizations need to be charged with carrying out specific action plans, indicate that on the MOU. Also, if a particular project requires a larger team, identify who will be on that team. Be sure to document contact information for both organizations' representatives.

- ✔ **How decisions will be made:** Clarify the scope of responsibility of both side's representatives. For example, do you have full authority to make decisions on behalf of your organization, or do certain project ideas have to be run up the company president's flagpole? Be sure to specify how financial decisions will be made in particular. Set a dollar limit if necessary (by using language such as "No decisions that involve more than $1,000 can be made without additional line approval") and then state who manages that limit. For instance, if larger-ticket endeavors require approval from the board president or ED (for the nonprofit) and the financial director (for your company), spell that out in the MOU.

- ✔ **How often your boards will meet:** Specify any planned retreats, debriefings, and regularly scheduled joint board meetings. Also, plan to hold some type of formalized meeting at least semiannually.

- ✔ **How to jointly assess your progress in the future:** Identify upfront how you plan to determine whether the partnership is working. As in any new relationship, keep your goals flexible (especially if they're quantitative, such as increasing revenue from new green products). If your company states that "We hope to enhance our image as an organization concerned with animal rights," identify how you'll assess whether that's being achieved through your nonprofit partnership. For example, will you conduct focus groups or customer surveys? Either way, this assessment can be done at regular joint board meetings or at a separate time.

Sharing Your News

In order to give your new nonprofit partnership credibility and integrity, you need to make your company's entire value chain (including vendors, investors, and customers) aware of your initiative. You aren't trying to be like an anonymous donor; you, very publicly, want to celebrate your contribution to solving an identified societal problem with your partner.

Pepper the daily newspaper, local independent papers, community TV and radio spots, and nonprofit roundup forums with news about your collaboration. Use free media as much as possible and ask your nonprofit partner who it has ties to as well. You may be astounded at how local media strives to focus on the positive goings-on in the community — and how being part of that focus boosts both your image and your desire to do more to increase the exponential power of community involvement.

In order to avoid the perception of *greenwashing* (stating that your business is green without taking the actions necessary to back up that statement), and to leverage your partnership to the hilt, make the congruency between your two organizations' missions obvious to stakeholders. Saying "We're vested in the capital campaign for the new animal shelter because we're moving into a line of cruelty-free products" is a much more persuasive pitch than "We want to go green because of the compelling problems associated with climate change." You always sound more credible when there's an evident reason for your company to be involved in the issues and the work that the nonprofit engages in.

All the community goodwill that you generate must be sustained in order to have lasting effects on your customers, vendors, employees, and community members. Your partnering efforts are intended to not only influence these people but also to have a synergistic effect on your individual organizations' further work and community reputations. Tuning up furnaces for low-income day cares may not sound media worthy, but most community newspapers have a weekly nonprofit roundup that such a collaboration could be a great fit for. When your customers see your name in the paper, your logo in the day care's newsletter, and members of your management team working an early childhood education event (in a T-shirt that clearly indicates they represent your company, no less), the pieces of the puzzle start to fall together, forming a lasting impression.

Nurturing the Partnership and Monitoring Success

Your business and your nonprofit partner may come together in a honeymoon period where you're working diligently toward the same goals — only to find out that you diverge down the road on approach or implementation. As in any new venture, be aware that certain factors can threaten your partnership's success. Like all relationships, you need to assess your nonprofit partnership, either formally or informally, to determine whether the mutual benefits are accruing as anticipated. You also need to know how to recognize potential sources of conflict so you can resolve them early on.

Assessing the relationship

Complex quantitative models exist that can guide you through measuring a partnership's success, but each of them center on the answers to four keystone questions:

- ✔ **Are we meeting the goals we established collaboratively as outlined and on a timely basis?** Go back to the original targets and goals identified when the original agreement was drafted (see the earlier section "Solidifying the Partnership" for more on this process) and figure out specifically which have, and have not, been accomplished. Of the ones that haven't been accomplished, try to assess why not by asking whether the time frame was realistic and whether adequate resources were allocated.

- ✔ **Are the projects' results authentic and of high quality?** This assessment is qualitative by nature and requires you to clarify what kind of effect you're attempting to have, not *how much of it*. Probing questions that provoke conversation about how to identify exactly what it is both parties want to achieve are often required. For example, measuring the number of new hits on your Web site that's linked to your partner's site in no way indicates whether they originate from the demographic pool you're targeting. Instead, try to measure *where* the hits are coming from (for example, .edu indicates a university affiliation, and .org shows that there's a nonprofit connection).

- ✔ **Is there effective leadership in the project?** Because many business-nonprofit partnering opportunities rely upon a key relationship formed by representatives from both organizations, *their* relationship is paramount. Look at this team's project-leadership style. Is it multidimensional, flexible, and responsive to suggestions by affected parties? Are team members accessible by formal and informal communication channels? Are they creative and innovative? Do they invite feedback on the project's progress?

✔ **Are both parties contributing their fair share of resources (human, natural, and financial) toward the end goals?** Cost-benefit analysis is inherent in all partnerships. In your ongoing assessment, both parties should be able to single out what has been contributed on their respective ends. If you were to line out a scorecard, these lists should be roughly equivalent.

There's a reason you're in business for profit and your partner is pursuing social or environmental goals, but don't let that natural difference sway you. Redefine your mutual interests and leverage your successes to keep focused on building a good relationship.

Recognizing and resolving conflicts

Because all partnerships (and the people managing them) are unique, each dispute, of course, has its own particular nuances. The most common sources of potential dissension are

✔ **Feeling like you're giving more than you're getting:** Perhaps the non-profit begins asking for more and more without necessarily providing extra benefit on behalf of your company. Avoid this conflict through strong communication centered on analyzing costs and benefits on both parties' sides on a regular basis.

✔ **Disagreeing with implementation methods:** Although you outlined your common purposes and scope in your original partnership agreement, you may quickly find your implementation methods differing. To get your partnership back on track, be prepared to discuss what specifically you're having trouble with and how you'd accomplish the mutual goals differently. Listen to your partner's concerns and continue to come back to the reason that you partnered in the first place. Define what each of your roles and responsibilities are and outline any parameters that may help reel in the other party's actions.

✔ **Losing trust in your partner organization:** If missed deadlines, half-truths, or hidden agendas are creeping into the partnership, either you or the nonprofit may feel disrespected and become distrustful. A lack of trust erodes the foundation of a partnership quickly. Both parties must come together in open and honest dialogue to identify what the primary issues leading up to the lost trust entailed and how they can be alleviated in the future.

✔ **Experiencing unexpected negative outcomes:** If you worked on a project or event and, for whatever reason, experienced unexpected negative results, that can take away from the good work you've come together to do. Debrief immediately if a situation like this develops and identify why it happened, what perpetrated it, and how to avoid it in the future. Avoid pointing fingers and instead focus on how not to repeat the actions that resulted in the unwanted outcome.

If disputes and disagreements arise, employ the following tactics to resolve them:

✔ **Revisit your congruent mission and reasons for forming the partnership.** Nothing grounds you in your nonprofit partnership like remembering _why_ you came together. Discuss your accomplishments and define why they were successful, being as specific as possible.

✔ **Identify your short-term goals.** You may find that you now have new long-term goals or that the operating environment has changed. This realization may require reanalyzing immediate action plans to get you both refocused on what you need to do _right now_ to move ahead.

Collaborative efforts that further the nonprofit's mission and enhance your company's reputation must be sustained to accomplish both organizations' economic, social, and environmental goals.

Chapter 13

Greening Your Workforce and Your Human Resource Policies

*H*uman capital (a company's employees) and the systems surrounding it are the true cornerstones of building a sustainable business. Sure, you can argue that businesses are sustainable because of their operations and culture, but it's the employees who craft and execute those ecopolicies and create that green corporate culture. Without developing personnel and implementing sustainable strategies, it's rather difficult to go green successfully. That's why human resource (HR) practices are a key component of sustainable business development.

Training and educating employees, eliciting and developing their ideas, and using corporate social responsibility initiatives as a way to recruit top-notch talent are all core workforce-related functions. Yet many companies are slow to embrace the notion that sustainability strategy is deeply tied to the hiring, training, and retention of staff. Transitioning your existing HR practices or developing new ones that parallel your sustainability goals is essential for ecosuccess. This chapter can help you accomplish either task by highlighting the compensation-, recruitment-, training-, and policy-related initiatives that can affect your overall green business efforts.

Recognizing the Importance of Developing an Ecosavvy Workforce

The time has never been riper to tap into the talent that's searching for a green company to work for, and the signs are in the stats. For example, a Mortgage Lenders Network USA poll taken in 2007 shows that 72 percent of working women expressed a strong preference in working for green employers; 64 percent of men said the same. Other research shows that young professionals, in particular, want to make a difference in their chosen professions. A 2007 poll on green employment done by MonsterTRAK.com found that 92 percent of students and entry-level applicants preferred to work for a sustainable company and 80 percent of young professionals were interested in securing a job with a positive impact on the environment.

Consequently, using sustainability to build a positive employment brand in a tight recruiting market is a clever move. After all, the visionary and highly motivated entrepreneur-type prospects are naturally attracted to companies that pursue a socially and environmentally just agenda. (Flip to Chapter 3 to dive more fully into the mindset of a sustainability-oriented thinker.)

Having sustainably oriented employees offers several competitive advantages:

- **More inspired problem solving:** Employees who bring a sustainability lens to business decisions allow for a broader perspective that sparks innovative solutions to both common and newly emerging climate change–related business problems.

- **Increased desirability as an employer:** Intellectually knowing what sustainability is and practicing it in daily decision-making are two different animals. As you become known as a desirable green employer, you'll have your pick of the green talent pool — individuals who already understand sustainability and have practice in maximizing people, planet, and profit through business strategy. Bringing them onboard gives you a powerful market edge. Just look at Patagonia, a company that receives *thousands* of applicants for each posted job opening. The synergy that builds from green-minded employees working together in a business can be unbelievable.

- **Less stressed budget:** Many employees who are committed to sustainable careers are amenable to flexible compensation and benefits, often preferring alternative transportation, flex work schedules, and other low-cost benefits over hard dollar cost-of-living increases. These options can give you more bend in your budget.

- **Improved employee retention:** Many green companies these days boast low turnover rates compared to their nonsustainable counterparts. That's not just talk. In a green workplace survey conducted by the

Society for Human Resource Management (SHRM), 61 percent of respondents who worked for an environmentally conscientious company said they were "likely" or "very likely" to stay at the business because of those practices.

Understanding What Green HR Practices Entail

If your business offers sustainability training, actively recruits green thinkers for new openings, does a good job of aligning HR systems with the new sustainability agenda, and adequately communicates all of this, employees (both current and prospective) will warm to your company's ecoideals. As your workforce becomes cohesive in its efforts, you can bank on benefits to your *triple bottom line* (people, planet, and profit; see Chapter 1 for the scoop on this).

Employee motivation is affected by a wide variety of factors, including HR policies, corporate culture, development opportunities, management style, and, of course, other employees. To pack the biggest punch when greening your HR practices, be sure to address the following areas:

✓ **Training and motivation of current employees:** In order to set your green initiatives in motion, you need the help of the folks who implement them on a daily basis — your current staff. Spotting the green bug in existing employees wherever you can is important. As you cull them and build on their interest, the enthusiasm will gather momentum, build capacity, and effect scaled-up change.

✓ **Recruitment of like-minded folks:** A couple years ago, recruiting green-minded staffers would've hardly been worth a mention in print, because the list of institutions that turned out ecograduates may not have warranted a mention in *any* book. Recently, however, the halls of academia, from which your business is surely recruiting, have responded to the greening of the general marketplace in a particularly progressive and visionary way. Universities and colleges across North America are by and large engaged in significant greening efforts in core areas: curriculum; research and development; and development of operations, faculty, and staff. Other initiatives, such as carbon-reduction programs, sweatshop-free logo wear, and green dorms, have been led by student groups. Recruiting from these universities means bringing in young professionals who've been inundated with sustainable living and are already focused on basics like reducing waste, conserving water and energy, and creating a more equitable world.

✔ **Alignment of HR policies and practices with sustainability goals:**
Because recruiting and training sustainably minded employees are crucial activities for the success of your green goals, your basic HR policies should reflect an ecofocus. Wages are a powerful motivating factor in the world of business, so what better way to improve the odds of your greening effort's success than by connecting employees to green accomplishments through their paychecks? On the flip side, spouting your business's energy-efficiency efforts in the breakroom while planning a company picnic filled with nonrecyclable materials from vendors half a world away won't get you very far in the eyes of your staff.

Going Green with Current Employees

Filling newly created or freshly opened spots with employees who have a passion for green is great, but what about your existing staff?

When your employees come to work in the morning, they don't leave their value systems at the door. They bring them to the offices, assembly lines, sales meetings, research labs, and retail outlets that compose your business. Because sustainability is such an all-encompassing framework, for personal as well as commercial life, one of HR's jobs is to inundate personnel with ecothinking.

In this way, working for an organization that's committed to going green significantly impacts employees, who in turn find outside stimulus to bring back to the company, thereby contributing to a cycle of sustainability. The following sections show you how to jump-start that cycle within your company; the process includes a complex mix of training, communication, reward, and recognition.

Introducing sustainability and encouraging participation

Your task is to find out what people are interested in and move upon that, starting small but thinking big. Note that keeping your company's ecoagenda in front of staff day in and day out is a challenge. Instead of relying on department heads or divisional managers to keep the green ball rolling (unless you're lucky enough to have everyone onboard, of course), turn to the hiring folks to spearhead this endeavor.

Depending on their current knowledge of and interest in all things green, many existing employees may perceive widespread discussion of plans, policy shifts, and trendy training sessions focused on the latest green management technique as bothersome (at best) or a complete turnoff (at worst). How can you gauge where they're at before you dive in full-bore? Ask for their opinions!

Marry employee inquiry and a training plan with a little firsthand research in the form of a very simple sustainability interest survey, like the one shown in Figure 13-1. Ask your hiring folks to administer it and use the results to determine where your existing employees are at regarding sustainability.

Sustainability Interest Survey

☐ **Very concerned:** I am interested in participating in a discussion group over lunch twice per month aimed at envisioning how our company can increase its sustainability actions.

☐ **Moderately concerned:** I am interested in receiving information and research on how to integrate green thinking in my daily work life.

☐ **Mildly concerned:** I am interested in completing a sustainability survey to provide information on what I am willing to take action on now.

☐ **Too much on my plate right now:** I know that sustainability is important but am pressed for time. The thing I am most concerned with regarding how our company operates from an environmental and/or social standpoint is_____. If there's one thing I'd like to change it would be_____. Please e-mail me with follow-up information at_____.

Figure 13-1: A survey for gauging employee interest in sustainability efforts.

By reviewing the results of this survey, you can gather an idea, albeit informally, about what sustainability-related concerns people in your organization have. This is a rudimentary way to ferret out which employees have awareness and concern; it also gives you a chance to dial in on the most attention-worthy issues in your employees' eyes.

Beginning the discussions

The people handling HR procedures for your company can start informal education and communication by asking to facilitate a discussion on green business practices at various departmental meetings and functions. Their purpose? To make the case for sustainability as an emerging trend that each department should perhaps consider.

A great way to get the dialogue flowing in this setting is to start by providing employees with an essential informational article. I recommend using one of the following:

- ✔ "The NEXT Industrial Revolution" by William McDonough and Michael Braungart
- ✔ "A Road Map for Natural Capitalism" by Amory B. Lovins, L. Hunter Lovins, and Paul Hawken
- ✔ "A Deeper Look at the Four Systems Conditions" by Jill Rosenblum

Then, discuss how the article applies to your business. Be sure to bring in examples of best practices of companies already operating sustainably in your industry sector.

As you engage in discussions and follow up on the sustainability interest survey, always meet people where they are. Just because *you've* been eating, breathing, and living a green ethos doesn't mean everyone else has. Lots of people are just starting to become aware that some big changes are afoot. Transitioning them from awareness to behavior modification will take time.

Harnessing the enthusiasm of ecointrapreneurs

An *entrepreneur* is someone who's willing to take full financial risk to see a business prospect explored, developed, and grown. He or she is willing to be accountable for all aspects of the operation and thus enjoy the success (or lack thereof) associated with the outcome. A successful entrepreneur has the ability to organize existing financial, human, and natural resources in a way that adds value to the marketplace where it didn't exist previously.

Intrapreneur is a New Age term to describe entrepreneurs housed *inside* your company. Identifying them as socially or ecologically oriented (hence the *eco* prefix) puts yet another spin on the term. The typical *ecointrapreneur* isn't a zealot who forces his or her ideas down others' throats but a passionate person who leads by example, sowing the seeds of cultural shift in day-to-day work life. Ecointrapraneurs don't risk personal capital; instead, they expose themselves to risk by pursuing cutting-edge practices within your company.

Both ecointrapreneurs and ecoentrepreneurs have had the epiphany that business has the power to be the champion of change and is an integral part of a larger, sustainable society. But unlike their externally focused counteraprts, ecointrapreneurs aren't vested with authority per se; they effect change through their passion for sustainability.

As a leader in your business, your job is to seek out these individuals and capitalize on their enthusiasm as you roll out your sustainability plan. Make sure to elicit the best these folks have to give by

- ✔ Offering them the opportunity to organize cross-departmental teams for projects that have a visionary component
- ✔ Encouraging risk-taking and rewarding out-of-the-box thinking
- ✔ Showcasing their work in high-profile organizational events

If the people who aren't yet buying into the need to go green aren't immediately integral to moving ahead with your sustainability agenda, it may be best to work by example and let projects speak for themselves. Many times ideals change when people see how well sustainability initiatives actually work. You can create credibility by offering realistic expectations of the impact of projects and training efforts. Don't ever patronize or lecture though — that's a surefire turnoff!

Making implementation easy and enjoyable

One of the most widely touted changes in HR policies nowadays is the growth of telecommuting, also known as *e-work,* an arrangement whereby workers perform tasks for their employers via a telecommunication link. It's a highly popular phenomenon that will likely continue to increase in status as the costs of commuting to work in single-passenger vehicles (in both dollars and emissions) continues to rise. Telecommuting is especially good for jobs that involve computer design, online sales, and Web-based education and outreach. It's also beneficial for markets that rely on the Internet for digital databases, such as financial products.

For all of its benefits, telecommuting has a couple caveats: a lessened sense of team camaraderie and perhaps some upfront costs to provide employees with the tools they need to work from home. The shift in the office dynamic can be easily handled — schedule physical get-togethers so that a sense of team cohesiveness still exists. You can also try limiting telecommuting to one or two days per week rather than all five. Implementing even a minor telecommuting option can lead to significant savings.

Unless your business is a candidate for becoming a *virtual office* (a business without a physical location), some employees must commute to and from work. As part of your office's greening process, introducing ways to reduce fossil fuel emissions associated with this activity is a responsible and proactive maneuver. Some different strategies that may encourage staff to change their commuting habits include

- ✓ **Allowing flexible workweeks:** Flexible workweeks, particularly four ten-hour shifts, cut employee commuting expenses and carbon emissions by 20 percent. Often they reduce the overhead burden for the business as well.

- ✓ **Establishing a car-pool program:** Use the company e-newsletter or breakroom to get folks chatting about driving together, even a few days a week. Reward this behavior with recognition or small financial incentives (for ideas, see the following "Offering bonus incentives" section).

- ✓ **Offering free or discounted alternative transportation passes:** Look into the deals your local bus, passenger ferry, railway, or subway might be willing to offer your company.

- ✓ **Providing bike racks, showers, and a free helmet program:** This move encourages staff to cycle to work, which is healthy for them, the environment, and your budget.

- ✔ **Adding car sharing as an employee benefit:** Approximately 600 cities in the U.S. support shared-vehicle programs. Such programs give employees who commute via alternative transportation a means to accomplish errands during the workday without relying on their individual vehicles. Some programs even provide access to a vehicle after hours or for weekend outings.

- ✔ **Setting up Transportation Savings Accounts:** These accounts can be used to pay for employees to commute by mass transit or van pool. The limit that can be put away pretax (like an IRA) for transportation costs is $110 per month; this amount changes annually based on tax law. Employees get a tax-free transportation benefit, and employers receive a tax deduction for their contributions and associated payroll tax savings.

Following are a few other ways to encourage sustainable behavior that you may want to consider:

- ✔ **Feature socially responsible mutual fund families for retirement investment options.** Offer your employees the option of funding their 401(k) or SIMPLE by investing in some of the oldest and most-proven green fund families out there: Winslow, Calvert, PAX, or Dominici.

- ✔ **Offer unique community-oriented benefits.** These benefits could include

  - Promising employees a few paid hours per month to volunteer

  - Matching employee charitable contributions, within reasonable limits

  - Collectively choosing a social or environmental organization that's value-congruent with your company and then matching group donations

- ✔ **Promote sustainability competitions between departments with gift certificates to local businesses awarded to the winning group.** Try contests like logging the number of commutes per month not made in a single-person vehicle. If you have multiple sites, challenge employees to see who can reduce energy or solid waste by the biggest percentage.

Offering bonus incentives

Regardless of how your employees are compensated, there's always a way to incorporate sustainability into your compensation system by offering extra incentives. Innovation with rewards, cash and noncash pay, and benefits are musts, but designing these rewards, incentives, and recognition methods for employees who take on innovative sustainability efforts may require some out-of-the-box thinking. Consider HR-minded folks the creative leads when it comes to acknowledging employee performance, an ecowork ethic, and community participation.

Whether you add a component that ties attainment of specific sustainability initiatives as part of the review and reward system is highly dependent on your organization's sustainability goals. But no matter how lowly or lofty those goals may be, your HR-minded employees can craft a benefit package that rewards staff for changing behaviors.

Following are just some of the ways you can spice up your benefit package:

✓ **Set out a green suggestion box.** As you implement a green suggestion, return a portion of the savings that accrue from its results to the employee who provided the idea.

✓ **Celebrate employment anniversaries with ecofriendly gifts.** Rather than the useless bauble or yet another cake break, consider recognizing employee anniversaries with a gift certificate to the local natural food store or a free bus pass. New Belgium Brewing, for example, gives all employees a custom cruiser bike after one year of employment.

✓ **Reward the use of alternative transportation in employees' office commutes.** It may be helpful to structure this reward around an accrued point system. For example, Clif Bar awards points to employees for each commute where they walk, bike, or use alternative transportation. Employees can then redeem the green points for on-site massages, company merchandise, gift cards to local shops, or public transportation passes.

✓ **Restructure commissions.** If your objective is to promote green product sales, construct the commission structure so that sales reps get the most commission money from pushing your green goods.

✓ **Provide bonus pay.** Be willing to give employees extra money if they meet certain sustainable goals. Outline specific parameters for each department and allocate bonuses based upon attaining scores in each area. Or you can consider taking part of the savings you accrue from sustainable initiatives and giving that money to the workers who made it possible.

✓ **Offer financial incentives for employees who embrace energy-efficient cars.** Consider offering rebates to employees when they purchase a hybrid car, like Bank of America does, or give employees cash to put toward cars that get aggressive gas mileage, like Google does.

✓ **Create incentives for employees to change behaviors off the clock.** Any motivation you can provide employees to take green behaviors home with them is great. Consider ways to encourage them to personally recycle, downsize the family car, or increase home energy efficiency. Clif Bar, for example, gives employees up to $1,000 per year to help them add insulation, replace windows, or buy solar water heaters or Energy Star appliances for their homes.

Don't forget to reward the staff members who are involved in developing benchmarks and indicators surrounding sustainability accomplishments. (This brainstorming occurs during the sustainability-planning process, which I describe in Chapter 4.)

After you've determined which ecobenefits pack the biggest punch, market them aggressively. You can use all the classic employee messaging modes, such as newsletters, blurbs on the corporate Web site or blog, and old-fashioned posters in the breakroom.

Providing sustainability training

Training sessions, using both out-of-house and in-house resources, are a huge part of sustained outreach with employees about a company's green initiatives and overall ecoethic. When it comes to outside training opportunities, you'd have been hard-pressed five years ago to find a conference or webinar to attend if you or one of your employees were interested in sustainable development. Now you have to pick and choose wisely because in this new age of numerous green training opportunities around the globe, your company's financial resources are the constraint, not the availability of training.

Pretty soon your facilities manager may want to go to the U.S. Green Building Council's national conference in a major metropolitan city with 25,000 of her closest friends. Your marketing assistant may ask permission to attend a two-day workshop in Toronto to learn about sustainable branding with some of the biggest-name international leaders on green marketing. Or perhaps your controller is ready to formally use the Global Reporting Initiative's sustainability-reporting standards (which I delve into in Chapter 16) and wants to attend a seminar led by western European leaders who've been working with them for five years already. These are all great training opportunities, but most employers don't have the cash on hand to fund every single one that comes up.

Sooner or later you'll have to propose a *sustainability training package budget,* a fund pool that's been set aside for training employees about green initiatives in business. Approach this budget like you would any other educational budget proposal (meaning you still need to run it up the senior-management flagpole if that's standard procedure at your organization). Some companies

- ✔ Budget employee training as a percentage of gross payroll (and then a certain percentage of *that* number is used for sustainability training)

- ✔ Allocate different annual amounts based on job positions

- ✔ Ask for employees to request specific training and approve educational funds on a request-by-request basis

If your company can't afford to send employees here, there, and everywhere for training, rest assured that there are plenty of ways to educate them about sustainability in-house. Here are just a few ideas:

✔ **Bring in a consultant.** If your whole staff is eager to learn what's new in sustainability, you may want to consider bringing in an internal sustainable development expert. A recent Internet scan revealed an amazing 772,000 hits for green business consultants, so you can have your pick of who to hire. Often in-house training, particularly of a cross-functional nature, can provoke innovative green synergy between departments.

Because consultancy costs are totally dependent on location, scope, and your business's needs, addressing a specific cost-benefit analysis is difficult, but here's why brining a consultant onboard may be worthwhile:

- Consultants have often seen your specific challenges and opportunities in other arenas and can bring that experience to your table.

- They offer an objective view of which initiatives will pack the biggest punch and which can be put into the "mid- to long-term" category.

- Their insight may lead them to suggest new ideas or ways to massage existing initiatives to meet your individual green goals.

- Their enthusiasm for green business can be infectious. A good facilitator not only shares her knowledge but also her passion.

✔ **Organize a quarterly brown bag luncheon ecoseries.** Bring in general-interest speakers like a local contractor who works on green buildings, a recycling coordinator from your local university, and the town expert on alternative transportation, for example.

✔ **Set up a book nook in the cafeteria that focuses on sustainability.** Put out the Fair Trade Certified coffee or some relaxing teas and make it a welcoming place to read and browse. Make sure there's tons of natural daylighting and select reading materials that can be ingested in pieces so an employee can get some value from spending time there, even if it's only 20 minutes or so.

✔ **Subscribe to a popular industry-based sustainability journal and ensure it makes the rounds among staff.** Following are two journals to check out:

- *Sustainable Industries Journal,* www.sustainableindustries.com

- *Green Business Quarterly,* www.greenbusinessquarterly.com

✔ **Designate a go-to person for sustainability questions.** Employees need to know where to turn if they have green questions. If you don't have a Sustainability Director or VP of Environmental Management, you can still easily centralize responsibility for answering daily sustainability questions. One person, most likely someone in the office, should have access to answers about what can be recycled, green office supplies, who coordinates the company car share program, and how to use two-sided printing, for example.

Don't force anyone into this role. Instead, look for the opportunity to give an ecopassionate employee a shot at demonstrating his or her leadership ability.

Retention of visionary and progressive employees is enhanced when a firm is committed to sustainability. To keep the corporate sustainability commitment in front of newly hired employees, make sure your orientation sessions contain a significant green focus. Provide all new employees with a sustainability overview (possibly combined with education on the topic, depending on their familiarity with sustainability) and an idea of the tangible initiatives already in place. Be quick to point out references to green procedures and policies in your orientation package, which should include a mission and/or vision statement, a sustainability policy (if you're to that point yet), and an employee handbook. If you've established specific recycling policies, a green incentive package, or sustainability-oriented benefits, make sure to point those features out, too. And if you're really moving down the green path with a company-wide initiative like reducing greenhouse gases or creating products for the green marketplace, focus extensively on that in your orientation conversation.

Maintaining the green momentum with ongoing dialogue

Keeping an open dialogue with employees about your green business goals and initiatives is essential to avoid unnecessary conflict. Although few people are outright hostile to the general idea of sustainability, there are always those who are defiant of change in and of itself. The people handling HR for your business should reassure these individuals that company-wide sustainability efforts aren't about putting another to-do item on their lists. They should also ask questions as to *why* employees are skeptical and then actually listen to the answers. After all, in order to counter others' arguments, you have to understand where their thought processes are coming from.

All the great green programs in the world are meaningless unless you establish formal communication modes to share your sustainability progress. After you begin incorporating green business practices, be sure to continue communicating the positive tone and continued emphasis of green in your company. According to SHRM, two-thirds of U.S. companies with a written corporate social responsibility policy *regularly* communicate with employees about their efforts. Strive to include a discussion of your company's sustainability progress to date in traditional employee communication vehicles, like newsletters and blogs, as well as during events, training sessions, or meetings where top management is present. Based on what your goals are, powerful potential exists when the CEO announces that your company's carbon footprint has been reduced by 7 percent this year, or that the recycled content of your product has gone from 12 to 30 percent in the last two years.

You've probably already established formal and informal lines of communication with your employees. Now, to the best of your ability, add a green twist:

- ✔ **Write a "Going Green" column in the company newsletter** outlining goals and objectives, progress to date, fun green facts gleaned from a newsy green blog or journal, and any stats that show your company is really getting its green on. If you're tracking something like decreased kilowatt hours used per month or the number of employees using alternative transportation, that's the kind of data that can foot the bill here.

- ✔ **Post actual signage around your facility** such as "Notice our paper towels are now brown; that's because there's no harmful chlorine in them" in the breakroom or "This new paper feels a bit different because it's 80-percent recycled content" by the printer. Affix a green logo on all the signage to tie it together.

- ✔ **Have a link right from your Web site's home page** that outlines what your company's greening efforts are to date. Post the name of this month's green transportation award winner and show a spreadsheet of the company's energy usage (both before and after simple energy-saving ideas were implemented). These moves can help folks see that their parts in the greening efforts are paying off.

Education is also key to generating an ongoing dialogue about sustainability. When you come upon an interesting blog, e-zine, or article, pass it around, give people a couple days to look at it, and then ask them whether they've read it, all the while trying to generate further sustainability discussion. Of course, make sure nothing is too politicized or potentially offensive to folks who aren't sold on sustainability. Keep the readings simple and informational in nature.

Burnout risk is high if you feel compelled to get every single person onboard with the sustainability mission. That's simply unrealistic. Instead, continue to share research, model green behavior, and work with internal marketing staff to circulate informational and inspirational articles, columns, and other materials to employees on a regular basis.

Recruiting Ecosavvy Candidates

Increasingly, public tax dollars and private donations are infusing the United States' more than 4,100 colleges and universities with sustainability in the form of green curriculums, research, and events. As a result, graduates with degrees in climate change, sustainable business, green chemistry, and renewable energy will have a clear and direct impact on public policy, technology, and the market in general.

If you want to win these ecosavvy grads' attention for your company, now's the time to start actively scouting green prospects and identifying what you want them to be able to bring to your organization.

Actively pursuing a sustainability agenda and marketing your company accordingly offers you lots of opportunity to gain competitive advantage for the truly top-notch prospects. Just remember to be strategic not only with your image but also in identifying where these desirable candidates can be found.

If you're interested in finding sustainability-oriented employees, practice corporate social responsibility (CSR) in a transparent way. (*CSR* refers to pursuing commercial success while emphasizing your company's environmental and social contributions.) Make sure that your Web site and other research tools available for candidate access clearly outline your greening endeavors. Doing so gives your prospective employees a chance to develop questions and comments surrounding your business's social and ecological commitments. Clearly reflecting your sustainability agenda in your job descriptions and tailoring your interview questions to flesh out potential compatibility with your company's green goals are also part of the HR function of hiring top-notch green-minded employees.

Touting yourself as sustainable is great, but the candidates searching for green dream jobs can spot *greenwashing* (stating that your business is green without taking the actions necessary to back up that statement) a mile away. A spokesperson for SHRM's CSR and Sustainability Special Expertise panel credits prospective employees with doing thorough sustainability background checks.

Greening your job descriptions

Fleshing out specifics in a job description to match desirable sustainability attributes with a prospect's qualifications can be difficult. Often, embedding the necessary sustainability lingo in the job descriptions of senior management as an obvious requirement for positions like Sustainability Director or Chief Environmental Officer is the easiest approach.

But what if you're looking for a new product engineer or fiscal analyst and want the job description to reflect your green bend? Here's the lowdown on common sections of a job description and how to make them mirror your business's sustainability agenda:

- ✔ **Job title and chain of command:** This info helps prospects identify the nature of the position and who it reports to. It's not a section that will be impacted by your ecoemphasis (unless of course you have a Sustainability Department with a director who'll be overseeing green-related jobs).

- ✔ **Job purpose:** This section addresses *why* the job exists within the company and what makes it unique; it must contain a reference to sustainability. For example, if you want an engineer who designs with a green focus, you want to include the phrase "be leader of sustainable product design team."

- ✔ **Essential tasks or functions of the job:** This area covers the primary duties associated with the position and needs to highlight specific ecoaspects of the job. For example, if you want a fiscal analyst who employs sustainability metrics, or a product engineer who cuts waste and considers secondary market potential for byproducts, state those desires clearly in this section. Each description should be tightly written to reflect the position's specific green duties. For example, "monitor and conserve office energy" may be part of the Office Manager's job description. The position's compensation plan may then tie in a portion of compensation to quarterly energy reductions.

- ✔ **Job qualifications:** Here's where you specify the skills, abilities, education, and experience necessary for the position. A green job qualification section contains specific references to sustainability practices. You may want to cite familiarity with specific techniques, such as life cycle assessment for the fiscal analyst or *biomimicry* (design that emulates nature) for the engineer; I cover both of these approaches to product design in Chapter 7. However, because of the infancy of many of these fields, you may want to list them as *preferred* qualifications rather than *required* ones.

When you have the right sustainable job requirements and preferences crafted, you need to be able to explain them in your want ads. Refer to your company's commitment to sustainable development in your advertising and ask that all résumés contain evidence that the prospects have contributed to triple-bottom-line enhancement in prior positions. Use a prescreening instrument to determine which of the résumés received will get an interview and assign points to sustainable criteria, just like you would for any other skill set you're seeking.

Finding green prospects

If you want to secure visionary new recruits for your entry-level positions, go straight to the higher-education institutions that are pumping out students schooled in green theories and ideas. If you have a list of schools that you primarily recruit from already, search the schools' Web sites using "green" or "sustainable" as keywords. You can also try contacting the institutions' career-placement liaisons and asking about sustainability initiatives, curriculum efforts, or specific majors that prepare their graduates for the new green marketplace.

Actual degrees and departments in sustainable development are fairly new (and still mostly centered in MBA programs). That's why the best place to look for students who've had sustainability-specific classes is on www.aashe. org, a Web site operated by the Association for the Advancement of Sustainability in Higher Education (AASHE), a group of American and Canadian colleges and universities working to create a sustainable future.

Each year the group publishes a report outlining the state of sustainability at member institutions; the most recent edition is available at www.aashe.org. Scroll down the page until you see the Top Resources column on the right-hand side; then click the AASHE Digest 2007 link. After pulling up the file, turn to the index for news on the newest curriculum efforts at member institutions. You can also look for recruiting potential in specific areas, such as sustainable product design or renewable energy. The end of the curriculum chapter even features links to other reports that are helpful for recruiting specific employees, like individuals with green MBAs.

Many people conduct their job searches online these days, so if you want to catch the seasoned pros with a passion for sustainability, you need to post your positions where they're looking.

- ✔ **Green Dream Jobs:** This Web site, which claims to be the only sustainable business job service, seems to be the most comprehensive listing for ecopositions at socially responsible firms. Visit www.sustainable business.com/jobs to take a look.

- ✔ **GoodWork Canada:** This online job service, found at www.goodwork canada.ca, posts jobs that run the gamut. The organization prefers that you pay to post your positions on its site, but if your company just can't afford the extra expense (which isn't that much for small organizations), the good folks at GoodWork Canada let you post your openings anyway.

- ✔ **GreenBiz.com:** This Web site, located at jobs.greenbiz.com, features easy-to-see industry sectors.

Interviewing candidates and assessing their responses

How exactly can you determine whether your prospective candidates have a clue about sustainability? Just ask 'em. Structure your interview questions to encourage the candidates to showcase their knowledge in this area. Consider including the following questions in the interview:

✔ What sort of direct sustainability education and experiences have you had?

✔ Who is your biggest ecobusiness influence and why?

✔ What do you feel are the two biggest opportunities within this position to contribute to the triple bottom line?

I also recommend asking a question that specifically targets triple-bottom-line thinking in the area a particular candidate is applying for, such as, "How would you envision increasing sales by 12 percent next year while decreasing our company's carbon footprint by 5 percent?"

When it comes time to judge a candidate's answers, you should gauge how comfortable the candidate seems to be with sustainability-centered ideas based on his or her responses — regardless of whether every question was fully answered. Focus on assessing prospects' abilities to showcase that they've considered *how* their skill sets can contribute to a greener business environment.

Aligning HR Policies with Sustainability Goals

A business's human resources professionals play a crucial role in leading that organization's green movement. Being passionate isn't enough (although that certainly helps). HR pros have to turn passion into concrete action and real deliverables and make sure that all the business systems are aligned with the company's green culture. In addition to recruiting, training, evaluating, and compensating, topics covered earlier in this chapter, the following sections outline a couple additional matters for your hiring folks and human resources policymakers to consider.

Upholding fair wage standards

Setting and administering employee compensation often falls under HR policies, so whoever handles these tasks for your company should also be charged with ensuring employees receive a *living wage*. This is the calculated amount necessary to pay for housing, food, transportation, and healthcare in a specific locale. Living wage isn't the same as minimum wage, but it does vary by area. You can run a rough estimate for your area using the Living Wage calculator found at www.livingwage.geog.psu.edu.

Additionally, a solid green HR policy may include a reference to *wage differential,* which is how many multiples your highest-paid worker makes over your lowest-paid worker. In the U.S., this multiple can often be in the hundreds of times, whereas in Japan, for example, the average wage differential between a CEO and the lowest paid worker is eight times.

If your company is committed to limiting wage differentials to a certain multiple (such as 10 or 20 times), make sure to sing your own praises from on high. This is a fairly unique policy that plays to a cornerstone of triple-bottom-line theory: the integration of people, planet, and profit.

Tying compensation and benefits to green practices

A key HR duty is establishing wage ranges and rates for individual job positions, a process that's referred to as *compensation administration.* As you strive to implement sustainable business practices, consider adding a variable pay element to your compensation system by linking pay to ecoperformance. By including elements of sustainability in your compensation program, you can promote the behaviors you want to encourage in your employees.

Assuming you already have a good performance evaluation system in place, your next step is to make sure management and HR personnel agree on what percentage of the performance evaluation should be related to sustainability. This percentage should be large enough to be meaningful, but not overwhelming. A good starting point may be 10 percent. So, for example, if your employee-assessment system is based on points, about 10 percent of the total points would be based on sustainability performance under this model. For jobs specifically created to further sustainability goals (think Recycling Coordinator or Green Chemist), you don't need to have a specific green assessment allocation because all the position's tasks are sustainability-oriented.

Because of the wide variety of jobs that can incorporate some component of sustainability, there's no one formula for assessing green accomplishments. That's why it's important to have specific goals tied to specific incentives. *How* an employee achieves his or her sustainability goals is a matter of individual innovation, resource constraints, and corporate culture.

Try tying senior management's pay for performance compensation to meeting environmental and societal goals. Doing so sends a strong message that shifts priorities from short-term profits and daily share prices to long-term sustainability planning (which ultimately benefits your triple bottom line). Xcel Energy, a renewable energy company that's a member of the Dow Jones Sustainability North America Index, has 33 percent of its senior executives' incentive compensation rely on meeting environmental goals. These goals fluctuate, but they've included meeting yearly targets for reducing carbon dioxide emissions and developing innovative technologies. The goals are clearly outlined in the company's sustainability plan; each executive is then measured and compensated based on whether his or her department met those targets.

Greening the lingo on performance evaluations

Because performance evaluations are usually tied to accomplishing specific tasks outlined in job descriptions, be sure to update your job descriptions with references to specific green goals and tasks. See the earlier section, "Greening your job descriptions," for more info.

Always tread lightly when adding green performance criteria to the evaluations of current employees. A good way to handle reworking performance evaluations is to form a compensation team (which alleviates the perception that tying green achievements to compensation is a purely top-down mandate). Members of this compensation team should include someone who handles HR policies, a mid-level management representative, and various staff and line-level peers. You also need someone who understands the potential green aspects of different jobs. Ideally, you can harness internal expertise for this slot on the compensation team, but if no one jumps out at you, hire an external consultant (see the earlier "Providing sustainability training" section for more on hiring this outside help; then check out Chapter 3 for tips on how to find a sustainability consultant).

Make sure any new ecotasks or activities that are assigned to an existing position have a training budget attached to them. You can't go in and require people to perform new activities that have been written into job descriptions if they haven't been given the opportunity to learn how to do them. Phasing in new tasks over a particular time period may also be appropriate so employees' job descriptions don't appear to be altered overnight.

As always, communicate every step of the way. Members of the compensation team should be forthright and open about what their responsibilities are. They should also conduct in-depth interviews with employees to gather their opinions on existing job tasks and functions.

Ask employees to bring specific green ideas pertaining to their individual jobs to their performance evaluation meetings. Brainstorm together how these ideas can be incorporated into objectives for the upcoming year. Make it clear how much of next year's performance evaluation will be dependent on attaining these goals.

Setting an example with internal corporate events

As you consider ways to engage employees in sustainable thinking, set an example by making green front and center in your internal company events. When planning each internal corporate event, target reducing its associated waste output and energy usage, restricting its carbon footprint, and employing local food and fare as appropriate.

Include a short educational announcement that you're making every effort to green this summer's BBQ or quarterly seminar as part of the welcome to the event. Then cover what you've done in each of the target areas to work toward that goal. Be sure to have signs posted everywhere indicating what you've done to promote sustainability. Highlight the venue's sustainability features, such as new super-efficient lighting or the salvaged wood used to refloor the meeting area.

Limiting waste

Cutting down on the waste from internal corporate events is by far the most simple and visually effective way of showing employees how easy it is to decrease waste. Most events generate a tremendous amount of throwaway junk — styrofoam or plastic coffee cups, plates and utensils, plastic water bottles, office gunk, and other assorted landfill-bound items, most of which is completely unnecessary.

The educational impact comes from participants actively splitting their garbage into three well-labeled bins and seeing how little actually goes into the bound-for-the-landfill receptacle. Set up three bins, two mid-sized and one small. Line them with the new-on-the-market, sugar-spun garbage bags that dissolve completely and clearly label each bin to reflect what contents it should receive.

Here's what to put in the various bins:

✔ **Compost:** Place your compostable paper plates, napkins, cups, and utensils (called *bioplastics*), and all green garbage into one of the mid-sized cans. *Green garbage* is anything that's vegetable- or grain-based. This compost winds up at your local farm, community composting effort, or university-based composting project. To find out who takes compost in your area (often local folks pick up compost from events), try calling your local government cooperative office or your regional university's agricultural department. You can also check out the United States Composting Council's Web site at www.compostingcouncil.org for information on members and education.

To ensure everything in this bin is compostable, napkins and paper towels should be unbleached and made of 100-percent post-consumer waste. Check to see whether your bioplastic utensils (available online as well as in many local stores) are certified biodegradable by the International Organization for Standardization (ISO). If they are, they'll blend in with uneaten veggies and grains and be worm fodder in no time. Avoid placing meat products into your compost at all times.

✔ **Recycling:** Use the other mid-sized bin for recycling, preferably of aluminum cans. You may also need to provide glass or plastic recycling bins, but because you're providing all the products for the event, you can choose beverages housed in aluminum or drinks that can be poured into rice- or corn-based compostable cups.

✔ **Landfill-bound items:** Those few things that can't be composted or recycled belong in the small bin. Generally, this category consists of meat byproducts and anything people have brought with them to the event.

Next to the three bins, I usually set out a small cardboard receptacle labeled "recycled office paper" for handouts people don't want, or any other office paper waste. Because your handouts are all double-sided with 1/2-inch margins and available electronically anyway (see Chapter 6 if they aren't), there shouldn't be much content in here.

Decreasing an event's carbon footprint

Powering an event (and the transportation of attendees and speakers to and from it) is the primary carbon footprint generated by your average business event. To quickly estimate how many tons of emissions your internal event will generate, use The Climate Trust's Carbon Calculator for Events (found at www.climatetrust.org/content/calculators/Event_Calculator.pdf). The Climate Trust is a nonprofit organization that focuses on advocating for sound carbon offset policy and investing in stable offset projects. Don't worry about being pressured to purchase offsets by this organization.

After you have this number in hand, you can buy green tags from a regional provider to cut your reliance on nonrenewable energy to power the event. *Green tags,* a renewable-energy instrument that indicates investment in or purchase of a certain number of kilowatts of renewable energy, allow you to invest in regional renewable energy. Although they don't, in all areas, *directly* provide you with green power, they do provide capital for green power projects, thereby increasing the supply of renewable energy and contributing to downward price pressure for everyone. If this option doesn't appeal to you, you can always purchase carbon offsets for transportation-oriented carbon.

Depending on where your event is being held, you may have little to no control over the energy source used. However, if you do have the ability to supply your own energy source (say, by renting a biomass generator for a street dance you're sponsoring) or choose an energy-efficient venue (like booking a local meeting venue that gets its energy from solar panels for your annual stockholders' meeting), by all means go for it and loudly proclaim your renewable energy sourcing to anyone who'll listen.

Using local vendors for products and services

Set "100 percent local" as your goal for sourcing products and services necessary to put on your internal corporate event. You may not hit that target, but having it keeps everyone focused on looking for local options. One place to start looking is with the Business Alliance for Local Living Economies (BALLE). Visit www.livingeconomies.org to find the location of the chapter nearest you and turn to Chapter 11 for the full scoop on this organization.

You can also check to see whether local business alliances exist (particularly surrounding food). Be creative with your Internet searches and try plugging in the following terms in conjunction with your particular area:

- ✓ "Local food"
- ✓ "Green event planners"
- ✓ "Buy local"
- ✓ "Sustainable business alliance"

Part IV
Measuring and Reporting Results

The 5th Wave   By Rich Tennant

"Here's our environmental audit. The numbers are pretty impressive. By the way, you can eat the report after you're done."

In this part . . .

Like many other ventures in this world, green business is governed by standards. These standards are, however, still in the development stage and therefore need to be carefully applied. Adopting and applying standards can lend credibility to your greening efforts — so can applying for official certification as a sustainable company, as long as you're working with credible organizations. This part takes you through the different entities that set sustainability standards and provide company-wide green certifications.

On the other hand, all the great green progress in the world means little without a way to measure and communicate your results. If you spend time collecting data that tracks your progress toward achieving your various sustainability goals, you'll have an easier time pulling together an annual sustainability report to share with your employees, customers, and other stakeholders. That's why this part also introduces you to the process of conducting a formal assessment and compiling your measurements and commentary into an informative, easy-to-read sustainability report.

Chapter 14

Governing Bodies: Getting to Know the Standards and Certifications

Standards exist for pretty much everything in the commercial world: items you purchase, vendors you do business with, and transactions you conduct. It's probably no surprise, then, that standards are evolving to govern how green business is defined and conducted.

Certification shows compliance with established standards and is necessary because often assessing whether a company's green assertion is true is impossible. For example, it's great to rely on third-party certifiers to stamp "Certified Organic" on meat or "Fair Trade" on coffee beans and chocolate without having to delve further into the company's reputation.

This chapter introduces you to both green business standards and certifications, explains why and what you need to know about them, and tells you how you can use them as part of your sustainability plan, particularly when it comes to working with your suppliers.

The Basics on Standards and Certifications

When adopting standards and attaining certifications, what you're really doing is creating a set of governing principles that guide all of your sustainable business efforts, from selecting suppliers to establishing employee policies. Basically, you're laying out broad brush strokes to steer future ecoprojects across the board. Some companies refer to this set of guiding principles as a *corporate social responsibility policy,* a *sustainability policy,* or a *corporate consciousness policy.* Whatever the name, the theory's the same.

The overarching purpose of incorporating such standards into your sustainability plan is to achieve credibility in the eyes of your stakeholders. Doing so may not appear to mean a lot today, but it'll become more important as time rolls on and green business standards evolve to become the norm. The next few sections give you the rundown on what exactly standards and certifications are and what they mean for your business, who creates and manages them, and why they're beneficial to your sustainability plan.

What they are

Green business standards, sometimes known as *sustainability standards,* are essentially yardsticks developed by objective third parties against which you can measure your business's sustainability. They primarily have two common goals:

- ✔ Making sure a company is constantly striving to improve its business performance and acting in a way that sustains (and even rejuvenates) the environment and treats stakeholders with respect and dignity. In short, they encourage a business to embrace the *triple-bottom-line business model,* which considers people, planet, and profit. (You can find out more about the triple bottom line in Chapter 1.)

- ✔ Generating a common platform for understanding often overused terms such as *corporate social responsibility, sustainability,* and *green business practices.*

Standards are helpful for uniting efforts, maintaining focus, guiding managers, and crafting future expectations. When you're developing a sustainability plan (see Chapter 4 for more info on doing so) or a corporate social responsibility policy for your business, pointing stakeholders to a backbone of standards gives stability to your efforts internally and lends credibility externally.

Standards can also help your organization recognize various business challenges and possibilities. For example, ISO14004 (see the later sidebar on "Familiarizing yourself with common standards") identifies environmental risks and opportunities. It sets standards only for those elements that can be independently verified and strives to move a company forward with continuous improvement in environmental performance. If your company's efforts to meet this standard are effectively planned and executed, your overall environmental impact will be reduced over time.

Additionally, standards are grounded in organizations that provide wonderful networking opportunities. Adopting standards and collaborating with other like-kind organizations is a key component of developing a sound sustainability plan.

Of course, green business standards don't just involve setting forth a philosophy to follow. They also affect the day-to-day business operations of your company, as well as its overall *corporate culture of sustainability* (meaning the values, dictums, attitudes, and beliefs you and your employees espouse). Your company's image, as well as your operational policies and procedures, will be shaped by the standards that you choose to follow.

You may choose to adopt green business standards that

✔ Promote social responsibility regarding human and labor rights, organizational ethics, and your company's impact on biodiversity

✔ Enforce sustainability reporting standards (see Chapter 16 for more info on sustainability reporting)

✔ Regulate occupational health and safety management systems

✔ Encourage social accountability through the practice of collective bargaining, employee safety, and disciplinary practices

✔ Develop and provide guidance on administering an Environmental Management System

✔ Measure your company's impact on the community in which you operate

✔ Show loyalty to suppliers who engage in Fair Trade practices and environmental innovation and offer quality products at an ethical price

Green business standards aren't regulations. They're just guidelines. The sustainability police won't come knocking on your company's door if you don't comply with them. However, such standards do offer you a powerful vehicle to demonstrate your commitment to being green. They may also help you alleviate consumer concerns that you're just another company engaged in *greenwashing,* stating that your business is green without taking the actions necessary to back up that statement.

Aside from adopting the standards set forth by a governing body such as the United Nations Global Compact or the International Labour Organization, you can also become certified by any one of a number of bodies that specializes in making you "official." *Certification* indicates that your company has developed policies and procedures to manage the issues covered by the certification, including solid methods of documenting how you're ensuring compliance.

You should know that getting certified costs money. The number one consideration as to whether to pursue certification generally revolves around resources. But because certification shows your stakeholders that you're willing to walk the walk in your greening efforts, applying for certification shows you're putting your money where your mouth is.

As for whether you should pursue certification for your business, the decision is really up to you. I can tell you that many businesses and government agencies are writing new facility protocols to require that all new buildings comply with LEED standards, but are foregoing applying for the actual certification from the U.S. Green Building Council because of its cost. On the other hand, certification *does* allow you to display a stamp of approval that shows authentic third-party endorsement. Depending on your industry sector and customer base, this physical symbol of external approval may be important.

Where they come from

The standards that a green business may adopt didn't just drop out of the sky like a diver without a parachute. They were created by (and continue to be managed by) all kinds of organizations and certifying entities. Some of these groups working to establish frameworks and standards for business sustainability focus on the environmental aspect; others concentrate on social issues; and still others offer corporate social responsibility (CSR) outlines. (*CSR* refers to conducting business in a way that considers impact on stakeholders and the environment while maintaining commercial success.)

The following standard-setting groups can benefit your organization by helping you make persuasive arguments for sustainability (based on their frameworks and standards) to your upper management or board and by giving your greening efforts authenticity in the public eye:

- ✔ **Global Reporting Initiative (GRI):** Covered at great length in Chapter 16, the GRI provides standards for sustainability reporting.

- ✔ **International Labour Organization (ILO):** The ILO seeks to promote human and labor rights throughout the world through 22 conventions in areas such as worker safety, maternity protection, and indigenous rights. Its standards are used for setting the people piece of your CSR policy.

- ✔ **International Organization for Standardization (ISO):** The ISO is an independent, nongovernmental federation of national standards bodies. It establishes principles that respond to identified international needs and have global applicability. Technical committees made up of experts from the industry sector requesting the standard lead the efforts. International and regional organizations may ask to participate.

A proposed standard becomes an accepted ISO International Standard when two-thirds of the ISO national members that participated in its development reach a consensus. To date, the ISO has developed more than 17,000 International Standards, and more than 1,000 new standards are published every year.

✔ **Social Venture Network (SVN):** The SVN, created in 1987, has developed a written set of standards for conducting business in a responsible and ethical manner. The SVN Standards of Corporate Social Responsibility provide a comprehensive set of guidelines that can be used by a company looking to become more socially responsible. They offer principles, practices, and resources centered on nine topics: Ethics, Accountability, Governance, Financial Returns, Employment Practices, Business Relationships, Products and Services, Community Involvement, and Environmental Protection.

✔ **United Nations Global Compact:** First envisioned in 2000, the United Nations Global Compact is an affiliation of more than 3,300 companies, governments, and labor organizations that have adopted ten principles of CSR, making the compact the single largest voluntary CSR initiative in the world. If you have foreign partners or source materials outside of the U.S., this fact is particularly pertinent to your company. Businesses that follow the compact's principles (listed in the nearby sidebar) consider their impact on stakeholders and the environment, which makes them credible foreign partners for your continued sustainability efforts.

Just because a company participates in the United Nations Global Compact doesn't mean that it's *certified* as complying with the organization's principles. This fact is an important distinction, because a company that *complies* with principles isn't the same as one that's working toward compliance (that is, participating). On the other hand, a company's participation lets you know that it's engaged in policy dialogue surrounding CSR and that it belongs to a formal network.

As for where certifications come from, the entities that provide them (and by them I mean everything from overall green business certifications to certifications for sustainable products and facilities) are evolving rapidly. Why? Because as more companies tout themselves as green, the pressure to increase accountability for that statement is advancing. Some new certifying agencies are being born, and some older ones (such as Green America) are growing and developing in response to emerging green industry sectors.

States are starting to get into the certification mix too. California, for example, has published Green Business Standards that companies must meet if they want to receive official certification from the state as a truly green business. Check 'em out for yourself at www.greenbiz.ca.gov/BGStandards.html. I expect this trend to continue on a state-by-state basis.

Introducing the ten guiding principles of the United Nations Global Compact

With all the various green business standards out there, it helps to have a lay of the land regarding the overarching standards espoused by some of today's standard-setting bigwigs. Following is a rundown of the United Nations Global Compact's ten core principles, which participating companies adhere to:

- ✔ Support and protect internationally recognized human rights.

- ✔ Ensure participating companies aren't complicit in human rights abuses.

- ✔ Uphold the right to freedom of association and collective bargaining.

- ✔ Eliminate forced labor.

- ✔ Eliminate child labor.

- ✔ Eliminate discrimination in employment and occupation.

- ✔ Support a precautionary approach to environmental challenges.

- ✔ Initiate actions to promote environmental responsibility.

- ✔ Encourage the development and diffusion of environmentally friendly technologies.

- ✔ Develop anticorruption policies that target extortion and bribery.

With this breakdown, you can easily see which of these principles has applicability to your business or your suppliers and other value chain members. Use those principles to develop tangible actions. For expanded information on each of the ten principles, go to `www.unglobalcompact.org`.

Why they're beneficial to your sustainability efforts

At some point, you may decide that bringing individual projects and diverse efforts together under one umbrella in the form of standardization is important. Not only do you want to create some form of governing philosophy but you also want to be able to apply that philosophy to every aspect of your business operations. Why is that so beneficial you may ask? For a lot of reasons!

Adopting widely known and publicized standards and acquiring recognized certifications provide the following benefits to your company:

- ✔ Anyone from the outside looking in (from potential customers to the local news media) can see that sustainability is a priority for your company because you're dedicating time and resources to setting up and adhering to standards by which to run your business.

✔ You can better achieve triple-bottom-line results because more and more companies are only doing business with other certified companies. For example, many widely known chains are asking their suppliers to certify their products and/or companies in order to continue doing business with them.

✔ Your sustainability efforts receive added credibility because everyone in your organization can access the guidelines to determine where you're going, sustainably speaking.

✔ You can better guide employees when they pose the question, "Is this product, process, or decision that I'm about to make congruent with our sustainability mission?"

✔ Standards often ask hard questions or demand arduous preparations, like conducting energy audits and generating long lists of best practices, which often focus your green commitments into ecoactions.

Choosing Standards for Your Business

You can adopt green business standards in one of two ways: Use the standards set forth by a larger, international organization to build your own personal standards philosophy, or work with an accredited body to get officially certified in regards to your practices.

Developing your own set of standards isn't a task for the faint of heart. Do so only if you can't adapt existing frameworks to address your unique needs. Make sure to thoroughly peruse the Social Venture Network's standards before going it on your own. You can find them by visiting `www.cauxround table.org/resources.html`. Click the Guide to CSR and Business Ethics Codes link; on the next page, click the Social Venture Network Standards of Corporate Social Responsibility link.

The agencies described in the earlier "Where they come from" section have thrown lots of resources at standards development and gathered tons of expertise in order to create and publish their standards. Rather than re-create social or environmental standards to include in your sustainability plan, have your green team spend time looking at the standards that are most pertinent to your team's prioritized goals and determining which are the most relevant to your organization. You don't need to reinvent the wheel — just borrow someone else's tires!

As a small or mid-sized business, you may be surprised what you can pick up from the standards offered by organizations such as the United Nations Global Compact, the Social Venture Network, or the ISO. After all, many of the same principles apply whether your company employs 100 people or 100,000.

A bit of guidance for creating your own green business standards

If you're intent on going it alone and crafting your own green business standards, start by using the *cluster groups* (sustainability priority areas) you and your green team designated during the sustainability-planning process (see Chapter 4 for more on this topic) as a staging point. From there, use the Social Venture Network's strategy to identify the various dimensions of a standard.

1. Draft a brief value statement to support your cluster group.

2. Brainstorm as to what specific practices could be used to enhance your company's sustainability efforts in that cluster group.

3. Identify how you're going to assess how well those efforts are going.

Say, for example, that you want to adopt an anticorruption standard as a policy in your company. Because of your sustainability commitment to corporate governance, you feel it's important to have a set of persuasive talking points and rational arguments that will help your employees make good choices when dealing with decisions that cross into this area. Great! But how do you do that?

For starters, you can look up the United Nations Global Compact or Social Venture Network standard on this issue. Doing so gives you a brief value statement in the form of a principle that can broadly guide you in your next steps. In other words, it can help you practice what you preach so you can better develop a specific set of performance criteria to direct top management as to hiring and firing practices, corporate privacy, and the allocation of company funds. As part of pursuing the standard, you also want to address how it affects your employees in relation to topics of bribery, embezzlement, or extortion. Ultimately, your anticorruption standard can provide a measure of success (see Chapter 15 for more on metrics) on your company's path toward sustainability.

Even if you think things like corruption don't happen in small companies, providing guidance for your organization is invaluable. Cover any such issue with a standard.

Your challenge at this point is to identify whether any of the standards set forth by the governing organizations presented in this chapter are good guidelines to use for your benchmarks (see Chapter 4 for details on using benchmarks effectively).

Many of the green business standards being cooked up these days may seem applicable only to large, multinational corporations. With the exception of B Lab and Green America (which I describe in the later "Considering Certifications" section), most of the standard-setting bigwigs and third-party certifiers covered in this chapter impact mid- to large-sized corporations. But just because you manage a smaller company with 5 employees as opposed to 5,000 doesn't mean you can't run with the big dogs and adapt the same green business standards that they do.

Familiarizing yourself with common standards

Following are some examples of specific green business standards:

✔ **SA8000** is a global and auditable standard for decent working conditions; it's based on the ILO's Universal Declaration of Human Rights. More than 100 companies have adapted SA8000, which is administered by Social Accountability International. This standard provides specific criteria pertaining to labor laws, health and safety, freedom of association, discrimination, disciplinary practices, working hours, compensation, and management systems. The interesting fact about SA8000 is that it pertains not only to your company but also to all of your suppliers and subsuppliers.

✔ **ISO14000** is a series of standards that specifies what an Environmental Management System should look like. (All the ISO's standards, by the way, are further broken down into specific standards under the overarching standard.) ISO14000 has many parts, as shown in the following table. In order to comply with ISO14000, a program must be structured to truly minimize the environmental impact of a company's operations. If your company is interested in creating a program to accurately convey the environmental attribute of your product, for example, you'd be interested in ISO 14020–14025.

✔ **ISO26000** will be the first international standard to provide operable guidelines for social responsibility. The anticipated publication date of this standard is 2010. Because of the global visibility that the ISO has, the expectation is that lots of companies will move to this standard for assessing how they're doing with social policies and CSR reporting.

Specific ISO Standard	What Can This Guide Me in Doing?
ISO14001	Identifying which broad functional areas an EMS needs to have (the requirements).
ISO14004	Identifying environmental objectives and targets and illustrating how to develop and actually implement an EMS (the guidelines). Providing structure on how to integrate the EMS with other management systems.
ISO14020–14025	Identifying environmental communication, labeling, and declaration modes.
ISO14064	Identifying how to describe, measure, and offset greenhouse gas (GHG) emissions. Specifying how to validate your GHG declaration.

Considering Certifications

As you become more familiar with the standard-setting organizations, you may start wondering whether becoming certified by one or another accrediting body that can certify your entire business as green is best for you. Before moving forward with any such decision, you need to carefully consider the cost-benefit trade-off of pursuing certification.

For small to mid-sized businesses, certifying with either of the organizations described in the later "Reviewing two fairly new company-wide certifications" section is fairly low cost. What you get in return for that expense is a network of other companies to share information with and a way of showcasing your efforts to stakeholders.

Certification entities that are willing to certify your entire business as green without regard to your industry sector are popping out of the woodwork. (I found one that was willing to certify my business in just a few minutes!) This myriad of agencies may make it difficult for new green consumers, suppliers, and investors to know whether any certification you've received is from a valid agency. Such doubt can lessen the impact of your certification, negating any cost-benefits that came along with it. Answering a questionnaire about office recycling, carpooling, and computer sleep modes doesn't provide enough info to certify a company as green. Pay close attention to the different programs that claim to have the capacity to certify your business as green, and you'll find that very few are worth your time and effort.

To help you determine whether a particular certification-labeling scheme is authentic, visit `www.greenerchoices.org/eco-labels/eco-home.cfm`. This is a cool Web site that lets you plug in an ecolabel's name to see whether it's in the *Consumer Reports* database. If it is, you can pull up info and history on it.

Be mindful that reliable third-party certifications usually involve some sort of facility inspection and independent testing — consider these the auditing hoops you have to jump through. Authentic certifying bodies should also expect you to engage in follow-up assessments at regular intervals in order to keep your industry-specific certification intact.

Reviewing two fairly new company-wide certifications

The certifications you're considering at this point aren't product-related or industry-sector dependent. Instead, they apply holistically to your business's entire social and environmental realm. Certainly products and services are a key *part* of your social and environmental impact (see Chapter 10 for a listing of certifications available for individual products), but the certifications I present in the following sections apply to your company as a whole.

Becoming a B Corporation

If your company wants to be recognized for the green thread woven throughout it, and you want a way to showcase that you're not engaging in greenwashing, the B Corporation certification may be for you.

The *B Corporation certification* is a third-party certification for businesses that are truly committed to fundamentally changing the way they do business by embracing a sustainable model. It's managed by B Lab, a nonprofit organization formed in 2007 by three very successful entrepreneurs. B Lab works with companies that want to differentiate themselves from the pack because of an ingrained commitment to sustainability. Founding B Corporations include Seventh Generation, Method, Good Capital, and TBL Capital.

A company that's interested in becoming a B Corporation should have a business plan that reflects the desire to "create a public benefit" by virtue of its operations. Recertification is required every two years. To become a B Corporation, a company must

- ✔ Meet comprehensive social and environmental standards.

- ✔ Change its legal documents (such as articles of incorporation or partnership agreements) to reflect the fact that the company is committed to maximizing benefits for stakeholders (rather than just shareholders). The term *stakeholders* includes community members, employees, customers, suppliers, and the environment.

Here's how to apply for B Corporation certification:

1. **Register at the Web site, which is `www.bcorporation.net`.**

2. **Fill out a 60-minute survey to assess your current level of environmental and social performance.**

   If you score 80 out of 200 points, you may go on to the documentation template.

3. **Proceed through the documentation template in order to modify your legal documents to reflect your corporate commitment to greening.**

   The founders of B Lab feel strongly that amending your corporate or partnership documents to reflect your business's commitment to a wide array of stakeholders is necessary to reflect your sustainability pledge.

If your business's request for certification is approved, you receive the following:

✔ The ability to exhibit the B Corporation logo, as shown in Figure 14-1, in your marketing materials, on your packaging, and in your corporate facility

✔ Access to a network of like-minded businesses to help grow your company in a sustainable manner

Figure 14-1:
The B
Corporation
logo.

B Lab's rating system, which assesses whether you're meeting comprehensive social and environmental goals, uses measurements and standards found in the Global Reporting Initiative, Wiser Business (a project of the Natural Capital Institute), and the Social Venture Network. So although the B Corporation certification is a newcomer on the sustainability-certification scene (and so far the only one geared toward small businesses), it has highly credible roots.

Getting the Green America Seal of Approval

The *Green America Seal of Approval* is available to screened and approved members of the Green Business Network, a membership organization that aids companies with demonstrated commitment to corporate social responsibility. The Seal tells your stakeholders that your organization is leading its industry in social and environmental commitment and links consumers interested in stewardship with like-minded companies. Founded in 1982, Green America hosts green business conferences, makes ecomarketing reports available, and publishes the *National Green Pages,* a directory that links green producers and consumers (check it out at www.greenpages.org).

Before you can apply for the Seal, you must first join the Green Business Network. Go to www.greenamericatoday.org, hold your mouse over the Support Us link toward the top of the page, and click Join the Green Business Network. Fill in your information, pay a one-time screening fee of $95, and then budget in an annual membership fee (based on your annual revenues).

Seeking the Seal is your next step. Green America's board of directors appoints and supervises the screening team, which examines your company in order to answer the following questions. (*Note:* The screening committee often seeks third-party data to verify information provided by an applying company.)

✔ How familiar is your company with the social and environmental impact of your operations, products, and facilities?

✔ What level of commitment have you shown to mitigating negative impacts?

✔ What tangible actions has your company taken in relationship to this commitment?

One of the numerous benefits to receiving the Seal is that your company is then qualified to be listed in the *National Green Pages*. Another key benefit is that you get to include the widely recognized seal (shown in Figure 14-2) on your Web site, storefront, and tradeshow displays.

Figure 14-2:
The Green
America
Seal of
Approval.

Surveying your certification options by industry sector

Organizations are popping up all over the place for the purpose of certifying businesses that operate sustainably within specific industry sectors. On one hand, this situation is a good thing because greening a hotel requires meeting wholly different standards than operating a sustainable day care. But to your consumers who stay in hotels *and* take a child to day care, the myriad of certifying bodies may serve to confuse them. They may wonder why one umbrella organization can't be in charge of verifying the sustainability of all industry sectors.

Although not exhaustive by any means, Table 14-1 presents a list of the specific organizations that provide certifications for select industry sectors. (If you're more interested in the certifications available for specific products, make sure to check out Chapter 10.)

Table 14-1	Credible Groups that Certify by Industry Sector	
Industry Sector	*Certifying Body*	*Web Site*
Building & development	U.S. Green Building Council	www.usgbc.org
Carbon offsets	Green-e	www.green-e.org
Cleaning & custodial	Green Seal	www.greenseal.org
Electronics	Green Electronics Council	www.greenelectronicscouncil.org
Indoor building materials, furnishings, & finishings	Greenguard Environmental Institute	www.greenguard.org
Lodging	Green Seal	www.greenseal.org
Motorcoach	University of Vermont's Green Coach Certification	www.uvm.edu/tourismresearch/biodiesel.html
Organic foods	U.S. Department of Agriculture	www.usda.gov
Printing	EcoLogo	www.ecologo.org/en
Renewable energy	Green-e	www.green-e.org
Restaurants	Green Restaurant Association	www.dinegreen.com
Sustainable fisheries	Marine Stewardship Council	www.msc.org
Travel & tourism	Green Globe International, Inc.	www.greenglobeint.com
Vineyards	Low Input Viticulture & Enology, Inc.	www.liveinc.org
Wood & paper products	Forest Stewardship Council	www.fscus.org

Personalizing Standards for Your Business

When looking at various standards, use what's applicable to your individual business situation and scrap the rest. Keep an open mind and an eye on how to downsize the macro stuff to make it applicable to your company. For example, international human rights treaties may have no relevance for your roofing company in Chattanooga, Tennessee, but standards regarding workplace diversity or employee health and safety may have tons of significance and belong in your CSR policy or green mission statement. Although you may not be ready to implement a full-fledged Environmental Management System, info on the standard-setting bigwigs' Web sites may lead you to consider actions you might not have otherwise.

If your organization is interested in personalizing standards espoused by some of the standard-setting organizations presented earlier in this chapter, first determine the goal or objective you're trying to achieve per the standard, such as "Improve workplace diversity." Doing so helps you think about the issues you need to craft a good standard.

The International Organization for Standardization (ISO) offers a checklist of the four guiding principles inherent in setting a strong sustainability standard. Here's how you can make use of it:

- **Commitment and Policy:** Think about who will be accountable for upholding the standard and where the resources for meeting it will come from. For example, "The board of directors will analyze performance annually. The training budget necessary to develop workforce diversity will come from a 3.5 percent increase allocable to the HR department beginning next calendar year."

- **Planning:** Outline concrete interim objectives and corresponding methods of identifying the plan's impact. Something like "We seek to mirror the community from which we recruit in our management training program" is a great start, but you also want to craft specific ways to attract minorities with outreach and engagement efforts.

- **Implementation and Operation:** Consider what procedures are in place to achieve your targets and what documentation is required. Outlining interim measurements to see how you're doing is extremely important. Here's a good example: "At the end of each quarter, we hope to increase minority enrollment in our training programs by 6 percent, as shown by enrollment numbers."

✔ **Checking and Corrective Action:** Have a strong and systematic monitoring system in place to ensure that your programs and procedures are working. "If we haven't attained a 6-percent growth rate for minorities in our training program by the end of the first quarter, our outreach efforts will shift from using HR resources to marketing the program on the company intranet."

Applying Standards to Your Supply Chain

A green company is both accountable to its stakeholders and willing and motivated to extend that responsibility up and down its supply chain. *Greening the supply chain* refers to working with your suppliers, vendors, and logistics partners (distribution and warehousing) to ensure they're committed to sustainability practices. You absolutely must understand the environmental policies and processes of your suppliers, the conditions under which their workers labor, and their commitment level to greening their suppliers as you draft your sustainability plan.

Although you may not directly employ workers on a global scale, it's a fair bet that some of your suppliers do. If they operate in countries that have ratified the International Labour Organziation's (ILO) standards, they're bound by 'em. (For a quick look at which countries have ratified the ILO standards, go to www.ilo.org/ilolex/english/docs/declworld.htm.) The ILO's standards are compiled under the umbrella of four broad conventions that cover

✔ Freedom of association and collective bargaining

✔ Elimination of forced and compulsory labor

✔ Elimination of discrimination

✔ Abolition of child labor

When you're chatting with a supplier about its corporate greening efforts, inquire as to the following. Of course, if a supplier can provide you with green information about each of these topics, that demonstrates the company is willing to take action to match its ecoclaims — and that's exactly the kind of green supply partnership you want!

✔ **Its willingness to be innovative to help meet your unique needs for sustainable raw materials:** For example, you may want a finish for the cabinets in your woodworking business that's biobased and nontoxic. If your supplier is resistant to the idea of sourcing these kinds of products for you, it may be time to either look at some alternatives or present the business case for sustainability (which I share in Chapter 1) to get your current vendor onboard.

✔ **How it processes its manufacturing waste:** Minimizing waste streams throughout the supply chain is a primary goal of greening the supply chain. If your supplier's scrap becomes raw material for another supply chain, you're working with an efficient business that's on its way to becoming green.

✔ **What design processes and protocols it uses for proposing and crafting new products:** If it follows Cradle to Cradle protocol or assesses its product's life cycle to determine how to reduce usage of energy, natural resources, and water, you're dealing with a company that's on the right track. (Flip to Chapter 7 for more on these approaches to product design.)

✔ **The degree to which it engages in formal sustainability planning:** Does your supplier have a green team (see Chapter 3 for more on this essential element of the sustainability-planning process)? How about assessment instruments to chart ecoprogress and resources allocated to sustainability training? If your supplier has any of these things, that shows a commitment to sustainable corporate development.

✔ **The company's knowledge of and/or affiliation with any of the standard-setting or networking organizations:** Such organizations include the Global Reporting Initiative, Social Venture Network, Business for Social Responsibility, and the ILO. If a supplier has adopted an international organization's standards, that indicates the company has a powerful commitment to expanding its sustainability networking and knowledge. If the company has joined a sustainable business network, it's dedicated to learning about other companies' best practices and reaching out for education and connections in the green commercial world.

✔ **Its industry-specific certification status:** Is your supplier certified by one of the organizations listed in the earlier "Surveying your certification options by industry sector" section? If your supplier's industry isn't mentioned there, you can still find the certification potential within your supplier's specific industry by doing an Internet search for "green," "certification," and the type of industry.

Consider creating a preferred policy for suppliers working toward improved human and environmental practices. You may choose to quantify your supplier-assessment process by allocating points for formal environmental programs, active waste- and energy-reduction programs, certifications from reliable organizations, or work that they do with their own suppliers. You can even spark suppliers' interest in greening their own companies by offering to share sustainable educational resources. Let them know you'll do everything you can to help them get on the green bandwagon.

However you decide to proceed, make sure that members of your supply chain understand what your sustainability goals are and let them know how many points in your preferred policy are based on their diligence in helping you reach your targets (reduced energy, decreased packaging, or alternative components, for example).

Because greening your supply chain involves more than just your direct suppliers, be sure to ask whether your vendors use foreign manufacturers. Suppliers that aren't diligent about ensuring workplace standards are upheld throughout *their* supply chain can be negatively linked to your company, particularly if they suffer from adverse media exposure.

Some questions you may want to ask suppliers with foreign manufacturing partners include the following:

- ✔ **Are you affiliated with the United Nations Global Compact?** If they're participating in it, that's a good sign they're committed to social and environmental responsibility.

- ✔ **Do you have a written policy indicating compliance with applicable ILO conventions?** The ILO emphasizes helping people attain *decent work* (a phrase that addresses workers' aspirations for opportunity, income, workplace fairness, personal development, and gender equality). A written policy statement shows commitment to global sustainable development and reflects suppliers' understanding of the social aspect of the triple bottom line.

- ✔ **Does your purchasing policy favor suppliers that are compliant with SA8000 or ISO 14001 standards?** Suppliers that follow a sustainable business model are more advantageous for a number of reasons. In particular, those that have attained certification pose much less risk for your company because you can rest assured that they're socially and/or environmentally astute. If your suppliers have been certified under the SA800 standard in particular, you know they're maintaining reasonable evidence that companies throughout *their* supply chains are complying with the procedures as well.

Every situation is unique and many of your raw materials may not have multiple sources, but if you're truly committed to greening your business, you should share your vision and do all you can to engage not only your suppliers but also your suppliers' suppliers in your programs designed to green your value chain. The talking points you use to persuade your supply chain partners that sustainability is a compelling business model are the same ones you use to engage the top dogs at your company: enhanced revenue through new green consumers, reduced expenses through ecoefficiencies, decreased risk to volatile energy and raw material supplies, improved employee productivity, increased innovation, and enhanced access to capital markets. See Chapter 1 for the full scoop on each of these points.

If, despite all of your efforts, you find that some suppliers are resistant to embracing ecochange, you may need to consider how exposed you'll be in the future to sourcing materials and components from vendors that are ill-prepared for a carbon- and resource-constrained 21st century. When you're struggling to decide whether to stay in a particular supply chain partnership, ask yourself these questions:

- ✔ Is it worth it to continue to pursue a relationship that may lead my company to more risk down the road?
- ✔ Might my company's time be better spent developing supply chain relationships with like-minded vendors?

Many companies are performing environmental audits on their supply chain partners and outlining basic rules of green conduct to compare suppliers' actions against.

Chapter 15

Measuring Results and Tweaking Your Plan

. . . .

In This Chapter

▶ Recognizing the value of measuring your sustainability progress

▶ Discovering how to compile the data you need

▶ Looking critically at your results and adapting your sustainability plan (if necessary)

. . . .

Greening your business practices, like any commercial endeavor, is a fluid and dynamic process of setting goals, assessing success, modifying according to new information gleaned, and setting next year's goals. Assessing and communicating the results of your early sustainability projects is therefore critical — whether the news is of success or failure. Observation and informal conversations, in addition to statistical data, are the tools you need to measure the bigger green picture across all parts of your organization affected by your sustainability initiatives.

Quite frankly, there's very little you can't measure if you know how to appreciate the value of formal assessments and are happy using qualitative (as well as quantitative) data. You can pull all the data together and evaluate your current progress with an eye toward the future, so read on for the guidance you need to start making your sustainability plan even stronger.

Understanding the Function of Formal Assessments

You may be wondering why spending time assessing the results of your efforts is worthwhile. After all, if one of your goals is to reduce your company's waste output and you know that the number of metric tons your company puts out is smaller than when you started, why do you need to engage in a formal assessment process to showcase those results?

Well, the short answer is that you want to be able to track how well your company is performing in regard to the sustainability plan you created. The long answer is that you can use what you find out to do everything from rethinking your strategies and reaffirming your goals to cutting programs that don't work and putting more capital into ones that appear to be providing strong results. And although every business has its own unique identity and goals, the purpose of measuring is universal: to see where you've been and where you're going.

When you create your sustainability plan, you decide which key performance indicators (KPIs) you'll use to measure the success of your various initiatives. In the assessment phase, you simply gather data that applies to those KPIs, measure your current results, and compare your current standing to your preliminary results from the planning stage. (I explain all the fundamentals of the planning stage, including how to choose KPIs, in Chapter 4.)

This process is very similar to that of conducting employee performance evaluations, with new objectives evolving based on the addition of other targets and the knowledge gained from the previous year's efforts. I recommend conducting a full-fledged annual evaluation with interim (preferably quarterly) spot checks to give you a heads up about whether you're heading in the right direction with your current actions.

If you happen to be measuring something like the impact of your plant's wastewater on biodiversity, you probably aren't going to conduct a comprehensive analysis on a quarterly basis. Instead, you're better off taking a few random samples for water purity and holding off on the full assessment until the end of the fiscal year.

Regardless of when you choose to measure, your measurement process should focus on

- **Highlighting accomplishments:** This portion of the process is about digging into your data and finding a reason to smile. If you're spearheading your ecoefforts in a concerted way, I bet you'll find a ton of great reasons to pat yourself (and your employees) on the back when you review all that measurable data you've been accumulating. Accentuating your company's accomplishments is one great reason to measure your efforts.

- **Recognizing shortcomings:** There is, of course, always room for improvement, and looking at measurable data is a terrific way to identify the results your company can improve in the future. After all, if you can't come to terms with the actions that need improvement, you'll never be able to rack up more wins in the successes column. Sometimes your best accomplishments are the direct results of your failures. Again, taking a look at your sustainability plan can point you in the right direction.

Highlighting sustainability accomplishments within the current accounting system used in North America can be a challenge. Traditional measurements are remiss in culling out data that focuses on sustainability initiatives, and often budgeting and financial analysis ignore sustainability implications. Additionally, financial statements prepared using generally accepted accounting principles (or their derivatives) may misguide readers because of omissions that greatly influence green decision-making.

To fully report on your company's *triple-bottom-line performance* (meaning your impact on people, planet, and profit), you may want to compile a sustainability report. This document showcases how your business is doing in relation to its green goals by disclosing how those goals were established and what the key developments and trends over the past year looked like. See Chapter 16 for the full scoop on these reports.

Gathering Data

You can use measurements to chart your progress in virtually all priority areas of your sustainability plan, including employee training; customer satisfaction; waste, water, and energy reduction; supply chain greening; and community outreach. However, you must have something quantifiable in hand before you can measure it. That's precisely where data collection comes in.

Collect data using a systematic method and design process to ensure that the data is reliable. If you've created a sustainability plan, chances are you're already well on the way to accumulating baseline data. Now your task is to analyze the results from your various initiatives to see how you're coming on your goals. The next few sections help you break down data-collection responsibilities, ensure you have data you can work with, and measure your progress toward achieving your goals.

Assigning responsibilities for data collection

Theoretically, each specific sustainability initiative at your company is being implemented by a project team that formed during the planning process and is charged with meeting prioritized goals (see Chapter 4 for more on project teams). Each individual team is therefore responsible for collecting data related to its assigned initiative. Team members may in turn decide to appoint another logical assessment overseer. For example, if mitigating the effects of stormwater runoff is a priority area, the project team in charge of that initiative may have a hydrologist or facilities expert measure and assess runoff before and after the new swales are constructed.

Assigning accountability for these tasks depends on the expertise of individual project team members, the availability of consultants, and your company's resource constraints. Likewise, doling out specific data-collection assignments depends on what you're measuring.

If you want to measure something that's fairly easy for an accountant to handle (like charting electric bills on a spreadsheet), you have a couple choices. If a member of the accounting department is on your project team, then you're in luck! If not, you can always request that a member of your accounting staff work with the most logical project team candidate to help him or her develop the simple skills needed to read and chart the business's electric bills.

If your company is quite small and you don't have an accounting staff, perhaps your external CPA firm or bookkeeper can help you out. Just be sure to include any potential expense in your sustainability-budgeting process.

Some assignments, however, by their very nature need to be disbursed among a few folks. For example, gathering employee satisfaction surveys is most logically handled by having project team members administer the survey within their respective departments. One person from the team can then be delegated to compile all the data.

Lastly, some data collection is clearly beyond the scope of any in-house capacity. Unless you have an ecologist on your staff, identifying exactly how your local watershed's flora and fauna is going to be affected by adding scrubbers to your manufacturing facility is probably way out of your knowledge realm. Hiring an ecologist to help you identify which tests will most accurately depict and measure that impact is probably your only choice. Of course, you want to make sure that what you're measuring is an attainable proposition.

Acquiring data that's reliable and measurable

At this stage, you simply measure the same things you did before you implemented your sustainability initiatives, back when you did your baseline assessment of your key performance indicators (KPIs). Because your plan includes all sorts of KPIs and goals, you can measure everything from how much energy you saved in the company fleet by purchasing hybrids to how many trees you saved by converting to 100-percent post-consumer-waste paper products. These goals, which are set up to be measured over time, help keep your assertions that you're going green honest and credible.

When gathering data, use a wide variety of data sources, such as environmental and employee training records, purchasing records, financial reports, inventory/production reports, interviews, regulatory commentary, employee and customer satisfaction surveys, and so on. For quantitative data, the KPIs you decided on when creating your sustainability plan will show you directly where you need to pull the numbers from.

Sometimes, however, the data you need to collect isn't quantitative — rather, it's qualitative, which means you need to quantify the results as much as is feasible without skewing the data so that you can better measure and plot your progress. You usually have to go through this conversion with social goals because you're measuring opinions, not numerical data. So how do you gather the information and convert it to a format you can measure? Create informal surveys and interviews to gather human responses to existing programs and proposed solutions.

When attempting to gather data regarding stakeholder satisfaction with a certain program, frame your questions so that interviewees may scale their responses (a 5 means strongly agree, a 1 means strongly disagree, and so on), thereby allowing for some objective reporting on qualitative data. Be concise. For example, if you're gathering workers' thoughts on a proposed pay-for-performance plan, don't just ask people what they think. Instead, conduct a short survey of pointed and direct questions that will allow you to determine whether your compensation plan modifications accomplish what the employees hope they will.

For example, say your CPA firm has designed an online tax-interview process that replaces the need for your client to drive to the firm and physically meet with her accountant to hand over documents and discuss tax-planning issues. Your firm estimates this online procedure will reduce 100 tons of greenhouse gas emissions in the upcoming tax season. To assess clients' responses to this program, first ask questions about program specifics and then request clients rate their satisfaction with these elements on a scale of 1 to 5.

Whether you're using existing data (like how much you already drive the company car) or need to collect new data (like how much you've saved on energy bills since installing efficient light bulbs and programmable thermostats), remember that data integrity is essential for any report to be credible. Your data must be authentic and easy to read.

When possible, use a third party to ensure the data's integrity by involving outside objective documentation in your data compilation. For example, energy bills showing decreased kilowatt usage are based on verifiable third-party data (the energy provider's invoices). An informal supplier interview conducted by your purchasing agent isn't dependent on a third-party verifier. If, however, you ask your suppliers to be in a focus group facilitated by a coordinator, then your survey falls under the independent-verifier category.

Measuring progress based on the data you've gathered

Measuring your sustainability efforts in order to gauge your progress toward achieving your green goals is a process that involves many different players within your organization. Each department plays a part in your company's overall sustainability picture, especially the accounting or finance department. The accounting staff's function within a green business is one of the least defined or developed elements, but it's also one of the most important when it comes to measuring data.

Identifying the impact of sustainability initiatives on budget, as well as creating formal financial statements, is a critical job that lands squarely on your accounting staffers' shoulders. Their task is to design and test new measurement tools needed to assess environmental and social performance, in congruence with the project team overseeing a particular initiative.

Practices vary widely, depending on what specifically your company is measuring and what your current accounting information system looks like. However, there are some common first-step efforts in this area. Many companies engaged in sustainable development target energy-efficiency measures because of their immediate financial and environmental impact. Therefore, measuring electricity and gas usage (in both dollars of expense and kilowatts used per month) is important and fairly easy to chart.

After you have a handle on tracking the monthly numbers over time (your baseline and after six months of energy-conservation initiatives), you can start to play with *how* to present your data to show impact. Common choices include percentage change over current month of the prior year (comparing October to October, for example) or as a percentage of gross sales. You can also use this practice to follow trends for water and waste. As you begin to have a feel for the impact of your initiatives, you'll be better able to tighten future goals.

Regardless of how you choose to measure the data your project team has gathered, assess whether the initiative

✔ **Has a measurable sustainability impact:** This point is kind of a no-brainer. After all, you can't gauge the effects of a particular initiative on your triple bottom line if it doesn't have a measurable characteristic that you can tie to sustainability. As stakeholders begin to figure out what a green company is, your initiatives should help them see what the ramifications of going green are for your company's pocketbook, its ecological impact, and its influence on people. Not every initiative will touch on all three elements of the triple bottom line (people, planet, and profit), but when determining how to assess your initiatives, keep these elements in mind. For example, replacing the carpet in your office facility is all well and good, but you'll have difficulty tying that initiative to your sustainability efforts unless you can measure the improved health and efficiency of employees thanks to your new PVC-free carpet tiles.

✔ **Can be replicated:** The cost savings associated with crafting initiatives that can be used in multiple situations is what makes this consideration important. Initiatives that can be modified slightly and used in many different scenarios are more valuable to a company. The less time you have to spend reinventing the wheel the better so that you can devote more energy and focus to furthering your company's sustainability progress. For instance, evaluate whether that education program you designed to teach your suppliers about green practices can be used with your employees and community members as well. If so, this initiative is more desirable than one that has no applicability beyond its singular, targeted purpose.

✔ **Contains achievements that are easy to describe:** Part of compiling data and measuring your results involves looking at initiatives with a critical eye toward whether you can tout your company's ecosuccess in that arena to an audience of stakeholders that has a differing degree of knowledge about all things green. Determine whether the initiative in question has either obvious results or results that can be made more obvious to stakeholders by tying them to traditional business measurements or by using charts and other tools.

✔ **Has raised the social and environmental consciousness of the organization:** Successful initiatives need to yield tangible results and should contribute to cultural shift. Poor initiatives like esoteric production process changes that no one understands won't generate the buzz you want. On the other hand, successful initiatives often spawn water-cooler talk over time, which is where that qualitative data comes into play. If you're hearing more people talking about the triple-bottom-line benefits of recycling or using alternative transportation, then you know the initiative in question has stirred the green consciousness of your employee base.

Here's a comprehensive example: If one of your company's goals is to reduce stormwater runoff by 40 percent (so as to preserve groundwater quality in the region of your facility), you'd do the following:

✔ **Assess whether you met the goal.** To do this, you'd measure current stormwater runoff and compare it to the runoff you measured during your earlier baseline assessment, which was done before the installation of your new graywater system.

✔ **Gauge the triple-bottom-line impact of your progress.** In this case, you'd look at the reduced environmental degradation and the fact that your investment costs in the graywater system are being recaptured by decreased water costs and improved water quality that's better for people's health.

✔ **Determine whether you can replicate this same initiative elsewhere.** Evaluate whether you can apply this initiative to other facilities you own or whether you can share this data with your suppliers to build a case for their own conversions.

TECHNICAL STUFF

Social footprinting makes its debut

Many folks in the sustainable business world have long (and eagerly I might add) awaited the release of the *Social Footprint,* a measurement and reporting tool that appears destined to become as common as carbon footprinting within the next five years or so. And guess what. It's now available to help you quantify your business's social sustainability. In other words, it can help you determine your company's impact on society.

What the Ecological Footprint was to measuring organizational impact on natural capital, the Social Footprint is to measuring impact on *anthro capital,* defined as the basic facets that humans rely on to enhance their well-being.

A company that's committed to improving its social bottom line should target initiatives (developed as part of the sustainability-planning process described in Chapter 4) aimed at improving the following three facets of anthro capital:

✔ **Human capital:** This facet refers to all activities that affect personal health, skill, human rights, and so on. Essentially, it has to do with a company's direct contributions to its workers.

✔ **Social capital:** This facet refers to a company's impact on social networks like educational groups or child care co-ops. It's concerned with a company's direct

contribution to groups that are extraneous to your organization, such as nonprofits (see Chapter 12 for more on partnering up with nonprofits).

✔ **Constructed capital:** This facet refers to the material things people build, such as infrastructures and technologies, and the choices they make regarding whether to build and of what quality to build to (for instance, going whole-hog green or shooting for as cheap as you can make the project). Constructed capital impact favors a company that considers existing rail for distribution versus putting up a new distribution facility, for example.

The Social Footprint takes a quotients approach, which means that it defines a need for improved social capital. For example, say your textile firm has identified development and administration of an adult literacy project as its charitable giving target. The program requires $75,000 per year in funding (the denominator), and you're able to provide $50,000 for the project (the numerator).

In this example, the quotient approach returns a ratio of .67 ($^{50,000}/_{75,000}$). Anything less than 1.0 is unsustainable because there's a shortfall. Theoretically, this method can be used to quantify all areas of anthro capital to define minimum required needs and which activities are unsustainable.

Using Your Measurements to Make Strategic Plan Changes

After you've measured your company's progress toward various sustainability goals, what exactly do you *do* with all that info? Present your data (even if you just share the numbers with yourself at this point) so that you can take stock of what they mean to your organization. Doing so allows you to apply what you know about your sustainability efforts to tweaking vital components of your business operation, such as your budget, as well as your sustainability plan for the future.

Take into consideration how the numbers you came up with for each set of data (whether goal-related or otherwise) affect how your company is going to move forward with meeting its identified sustainability goals. That may mean revisiting your original goals in light of the success (or failure) of specific initiatives, resources needed, new impending regulations, competitive forces, market changes, or altered corporate priorities.

If a particular goal was attained, the project team whose initiative was responsible for the achievement should identify the next period's goals to continue on the sustainability course charted by your green team during the planning process.

If the goal wasn't met, can you figure out why not? Determining whether the initiative was off-target or whether the KPI used to measure it was inappropriate can be particularly trying. I recommend your project team start by gathering qualitative data (through interviews) as to how stakeholders and participants viewed the success of the initiative.

For example, if the recycling effort just never took off at your regional chain of nursing homes, the people to ask what worked and what didn't are the residents, staff members, and facilities workers at each of the homes. If the numbers you're charting show an unsuccessful program but the participants all feel that the initiative was of high quality, then you should turn to the KPI as the culprit. Maybe measuring reduced waste stream in terms of tonnage isn't indicative of success or failure because of new statutes requiring disposable bedding.

Assessing where an initiative has gone awry isn't a linear process by any means. The interaction of lots of variables (which some attribute to luck or good timing) can play into the success or failure of any business goal. Common mistakes with sustainability initiatives include setting overly ambitious goals. If progress looked promising but the big goal wasn't met, maybe a phased-in approach is most appropriate. Ask yourself whether the resources you needed to attain the goal were adequate. Did you have a hard time soliciting buy-in from folks who were essential to making the initiative work? Perhaps situations outside your control simply affected the attainability of the goal in a negative way.

Make sure to include any outside consultants who helped in the measurement process to get their opinion on whether the initiative has innate problems or whether the correct KPIs are being used. These experts can often guide your project team to consider facets they otherwise wouldn't have.

If you determine that an initiative has potential but that the KPI used to measure success is off-base, you should have some experience under your belt now that may help redirect you to another KPI. If that one is completely unrelated to the first, you may need to accumulate baseline data again. If the new KPI is in the same scope as the old (albeit unsuccessful) one, you may determine that a shortened time is necessary to accumulate baseline data (so perhaps you opt for charting employee turnover for three months rather than collecting employee satisfaction surveys for six months).

Maybe one of your prioritized goals is to eliminate all toxic raw material components from your product line. Say your elimination efforts come in at 60 percent rather than the full 100 percent you were hoping for. First, make sure that that goal wasn't overly ambitious to begin with. A 60-percent reduction is still significant, so analyze your data to determine whether the trend lines look like they're continuing down the path that will lead to more results in the future. Perhaps you find that although you've been diligently working with suppliers to meet this goal, one of your key suppliers is struggling to find a high-quality replacement for the toxic raw material it sells to you. Therefore, maybe progress isn't charted only by elimination percentage, but by the number of suppliers making efforts to find alternative materials. You may need to widen your parameters in order to reassess and modify your goals accordingly.

The road to measuring success doesn't come to a dead end after you collect data, measure your business's performance against it, and decide how you'll adjust your efforts for the future. Now you need to think about how to present your results and findings to the people they affect the most — namely key stakeholders, including shareholders, creditors, employees, suppliers, and customers. Chapter 16 guides you in creating reports that effectively inform your stakeholders of your efforts and engage them with your sustainability vision.

Chapter 16

Creating Sustainability Reports That Wow Stakeholders

. . . .

In This Chapter

▶ Understanding the function, form, and importance of sustainability reporting

▶ Gathering what you need to compile your report

▶ Pulling all of your data together into an easily accessible format

. . . .

Remember getting a report card in grade school? Running home to find your mom sitting at the kitchen table with that look on her face was always a nerve-racking experience, even if you were an A student. Although you sweated it a bit, those reports helped her see how you were progressing in school and whether you were making the right choices when it came to your studies. Now that you're all grown up and working on greening your business, you have the opportunity to self-report regarding your company's ecoprogress. You can use this reporting mechanism to provide a snapshot to yourself and your stakeholders showing exactly how you're doing in relation to attaining the goals of your overall sustainability plan. *Note:* Even if sustainability reporting is a ways off for your company, you should clearly define it as an objective at some point in the future.

The Basics of Sustainability Reporting

Before you jump right into the wonderful world of sustainability reporting, you first need to understand the concept of it. By finding out more about the what and why of this type of reporting, you can make stronger decisions when you sit down to create your business's account of its green performance.

Sustainability reporting helps make the correlation between your business's financial success and its environmental and social performance. A *sustainability report* is an objective document that details your *triple-bottom-line performance* (meaning your impact on people, planet, and profit; see Chapter 1 for more on the triple bottom line) over a fixed time period, usually a year. This report goes by different names, such as triple-bottom-line report, corporate citizenship report, and corporate social responsibility (CSR) report.

Thinking in a big picture sort of way, an effective sustainability report leaves readers with an understanding of what the plans for your company were in the year being covered and how well you did in achieving those goals. A good internal sustainability-reporting system measures and reports with due diligence and a constant eye toward improvement.

Most companies report on their CSR endeavors on an annual basis; some choose to offer biannual reports. When trying to determine when you should issue your sustainability report, why not coordinate with your financial reporting cycle?

The following sections delve into the topic of sustainability reporting in greater detail, including what reports usually include and why these documents are so valuable to your corporate greening efforts.

Understanding the functions of sustainability reports

Current traditional financial statements aren't designed to capture the information you need to assess your organization's sustainability performance, which is why sustainability reports are important if you want to showcase your efforts (and you should!).

A sustainability report gives your stakeholders a peek at your overall triple-bottom-line strategy and management approach to improving financial, social, and environmental performance so they can understand how you ascertain whether you're meeting your goals and whether trends are improving. Following are some of the myriad specific reasons stakeholders may use a sustainability report:

- **Benchmarking:** To see how your performance stacks up in comparison to existing external standards, codes, and initiatives.

- **Gauging sphere of influence:** To identify how deeply ingrained sustainability consciousness is in your company via its actions. Stakeholders want to get an idea whether all of your company's employees are striving to have a positive impact on society through your business and at what level your business is involved with external organizations that are committed to being a part of the paradigm shift toward greener businesses.

✔ **Judging comparability:** To seek information so they can compare your triple-bottom-line performance with that of similar companies. Stakeholders want to be able to assess you in comparison to other *like-kind companies,* meaning those that are the same size, target the same demographics, and/or belong to the same industry sector.

✔ **Assessing opportunities and risks:** To understand how you're positioned to take advantage of opportunities. Seemingly negative trends such as skyrocketing oil costs and climate change actually create business opportunity. Conversely, these same issues pose risks. In-tune-with-the-times stakeholders want to know how you're reducing your company's exposure to variables beyond your control.

Recognizing the value of reporting your progress

More than anything, sustainability reporting helps your investors and stakeholders track your sustainability efforts. Granted, investors are very concerned with what your past environmental and social performance looks like. But they're also super interested in how you might respond to future scenarios, such as wildly fluctuating fossil fuel prices or the limited availability of raw materials. This knowledge gives them an indication of your future ability to flourish in a very uncertain world and provides them with the basis they need to determine whether they want to enter into (or continue) a relationship with your business.

Providing sustainability reports to your stakeholders also enhances your corporate image as a transparent company that's dedicated to measuring and communicating its sustainability progress and maintaining a high level of CSR accountability. By creating a reporting system, you not only augment your sustainability work but also keep it in the forefront of your stakeholders' minds.

With recent research linking companies that perform socially and environmentally with those that perform well financially, expect to see your investors, creditors, suppliers, and the like asking for sustainability reports in the future. They want to know what's going on in your firm past the details available on your financial statements. After all, free markets flourish in great part due to investors' reliance on accurate and timely information, and a sustainability report is where they can get just that.

Lots of folks think sustainability reports are used only as external communication pieces. Nothing could be farther from the truth! The folks who benefit from sustainability reports the most are you and your employees. Many studies have shown that sustainability reporting yields significant internal benefits. Remember the old business adage "what gets measured gets managed"?

It's a spot-on comment when it comes to integrating sustainability reporting within your company. In the process of creating a report, you find that you're addressing not only *what's* getting measured but also *how* you're tackling improvement in that arena. You also begin tightening up your action plan to improve your company's sustainability performance.

Depending on where your employees' interests lie, a sustainability report can provoke stimulating ideas for them to become further involved with corporate sustainability initiatives. Areas in which an employee can jump right in with ideas and energy include

- Identifying ways to serve new and greener customers
- Expanding your product line to embrace more sustainable products or services
- Exploring ways that suppliers can be a part of ecoprogress
- Suggesting potential modifications to the area in which they operate
- Becoming engaged in small daily office behavior modifications that result in overall improved corporate environmental performance

Employee buy-in is part of Sustainability 101. Without it, you're destined to fail. But organizational communication can often be a challenging proposal at best — and downright nonexistent at worst. Because your sustainability report brings together the rich package of your core commitments, programs, initiatives, and objectives, all bound together by a clear overview of what you're succeeding at and what you're not, be sure to share this powerful tool with your employees.

Another great benefit of creating a sustainability report is the fact that you can use its content for other purposes, namely as a corporate marketing piece. As you spearhead the sustainability-reporting process, use what you discover about your business to spread the word to potential suppliers, investors, and customers.

Visualizing the big picture: An overview of the primary disclosures

As you go about preplanning, designing, writing, and publishing your sustainability report, you may want to obtain some direction from the guidelines promoted by the Global Reporting Initiative (GRI; a nonprofit organization that develops and disseminates sustainability-reporting standards globally). The GRI, based in Holland, is the internationally recognized patriarch of sustainability reporting.

Why traditional financial statements don't work for sustainability reporting

Financial statements crafted around generally accepted accounting principles (GAAP) have been the norm for reporting and assessing a company's performance for over a century. Yet these statements provide very little evaluative potential for the reader regarding a company's social and environmental performance. In fact, they can even mislead the uninformed reader.

Most shortcomings inherent in GAAP-based financial statements are due to the fact that natural capital or ecological services often aren't given any value. Consider some of these aberrations:

✔ The value of the services that a wetland provides, such as flood control, water purification, and biodiversity enhancement goes unrecorded as an asset on a traditional balance sheet. Instead, it's paved over with an asphalt parking lot (that's made up of petroleum and bitumen no less) to handle increased traffic to a new retail outlet. The loss never hits the income statement.

✔ Product costs for naturally harvested products are often grossly undervalued. For example, seafood product prices incorporate all the overhead associated with harvest, but they assign no cost to the raw material itself, skewing free market supply-and-demand forces. This fact has led to a dangerous global depletion of fisheries.

✔ Dumping toxic pesticides and petroleum-based fertilizers on agricultural land increases yield, which is reflected as an increase in sales on the income statement. What isn't reflected is a commensurate liability on the balance sheet showing future groundwater remediation costs or increased exposure to lawsuits due to ramifications on human health.

There's no right or wrong way to draft your sustainability report; the GRI simply offers guidance, inspiration, and structure for writing and designing such reports. Rather than mandates, this global organization provides the now universally accepted framework that can help get you started. You can modify this framework and use it as a basis for preparing something meaningful for either your family-owned vineyard or your small indie newspaper.

The most recent version of the GRI's sustainability-reporting framework, the *G3 Guidelines,* is designed to

✔ Outline principles for describing report content and ensuring information is credible

✔ Identify key performance indicators and other items of disclosure

✔ Provide guidance on specific technical topics

Although you have wide latitude when designing your report, the GRI suggests companies include the following bigger-picture disclosures in order to produce a strong sustainability report:

- ✔ **Corporate strategy and analysis:** Feature statements from the most senior executives in the business regarding the relevance and importance of sustainability to the organization. This analysis should cover trends, variables, risks, key achievements, and lessons learned. Major challenges and opportunities for the upcoming period should also be addressed.

- ✔ **Organizational profile:** Introduce your readers to the overall context in which you're operating. Include where you operate, what type of legal entity you are, and a quick overview of what you do. Also cover where your offices are located, what your core operational areas are, and what's happening with your research and development endeavors. Finally, consider whether you're embracing any guiding sustainability standards (see Chapter 14 for an overview of these).

- ✔ **Report parameters:** Provide readers with an overview as to how you're going to organize the topics you want to address. Let them know the scope of the information included, the reporting period, any changes in reporting style from the previous report, and the data-measurement techniques and models used. This disclosure should also feature a brief overview of the organization's management approach to each of the performance areas.

- ✔ **Governance, commitment, and engagements:** Inform readers how the organization is governed, who the highest sustainability-decision-maker is, and how stakeholders can provide recommendations. The sustainability principles you're adhering to and the networking bodies your company is a member of should be disclosed under this umbrella as well.

- ✔ **Categories of sustainable business along with key performance indicators (KPIs):** Address the following six categories:

  - Environmental

  - Human rights

  - Labor practices and decent work

  - Product responsibility

  - Governance

  - Economics

For each category, use KPIs to help stakeholders assess how well your organization is doing in meeting its social, ecological, and economic goals. Your KPIs can be either quantitative or qualitative (or both, if you prefer). Either way, they denote how you're going to measure the accomplishment of your goals in each area of the triple bottom line.

✔ **Management approach:** Provide your readers with an overview as to how you manage the sustainability topics you're addressing. Will KPIs be used to assess success? What training and awareness programs do you have surrounding the issue, and does your company have established policies regarding the category? How does your company develop programs, policies, and goals surrounding sustainability performance?

To access a handy two-page reference guide that walks you through the details of these disclosures, visit www.globalreporting.org. Hold your mouse over the Reporting Framework tab at the top of the page and click G3 Guidelines on the drop-down menu. On that page, click the More G3 Resources link and then click the G3 quick reference sheet link that follows the bulleted list.

Getting into the nitty-gritty details of report structure

Sustainability reports vary widely because every company presents its content in a way that makes sense for that particular business. Also, sometimes constraints — a lack of resources, data availability, and the like — may dictate how the actual document is laid out.

Regardless of the various factors in play, your sustainability report should highlight each element of the triple bottom line (people, planet, and profit). It should also include the following specific items:

✔ **A table of contents:** This overview of the document's setup is essential, especially for stakeholders who are new to sustainability reports. A reader should easily be able to find the primary disclosures described in the preceding section.

✔ **Commentary and overview from the board and/or top management:** This section is a direct report from the perspective of executive management and the board chair. It may contain a review of the company's sustainability vision and strategy. Just be sure to address accomplishments and challenges in each of the triple-bottom-line areas (social, environmental, and economic) from the company leaders' points of view.

✔ **An executive summary:** A condensed version of the whole report, an executive summary includes

• Major developments and trends

• A timeline of past events and future goals

• Identification of external variables impacting sustainable development (such as political movements or significant regulatory, market, or social reform)

✔ **A rundown of stakeholders:** Describe each of the parties affected by your sustainability efforts. Be sure to include commentary on your customers, employees, suppliers, shareholders, creditors, and community groups, as well as the organizations you're partnering with to achieve your goals.

✔ **A description of core developments and trends:** This portion of your sustainability report centers on the most crucial components of your sustainability progress. Identify key internal and external developments. If you've been tracking particular KPIs over time (such as number of customer complaints, percentage of staff attending multicultural training sessions, and so on), show them in an easy-to-read chart or line graph. Make sure to not only present data but to also comment on the ethical, commercial, and/or ecological aspects and implications of that data.

✔ **A comparison of benchmarks and targets:** Help readers see what indicators are being measured against and how you're setting your targets. For example, if the trade association for your industry sector releases customer satisfaction survey results, you can use this as a point of reference to discuss how well *your* company is meeting consumers' expectations. Voilà! You can now easily segue into a rundown of the sustainability goals you've established as they pertain to consumers' needs for the upcoming year.

The preceding isn't really an earth-shattering list, considering that it looks suspiciously like the early days when generally accepted accounting principles were being designed to guide the content and format of financial statements. But it's important to keep in mind as you set about identifying the who, what, when, where, and why to include in your sustainability report.

As for how many pages to take up with these nitty-gritty details, there's really no minimum or maximum number. Although the issues are often complex and interconnected, overanalyzing or exploring every facet of an issue is certain to confuse sustainability-reporting newbies, so you may want to operate under the theory that less is more.

Preparing to Write Your Report

All well-executed business endeavors require a planning stage, and sustainability reporting is no different. Start off by identifying who's going to be involved (green team members, accounting staff, marketing folks, product design engineers, and so on). If you've never been through the process before, then envisioning who all will have an impact on your report may be difficult. From an overview standpoint, try to think more holistically rather than narrowly as to who all may be required. Then check out the next few sections for further direction on setting a budget for the reporting process, taking advantage of reporting frameworks, and singling out core developments and trends to highlight in your report.

Creating a budget for the reporting process

Because you have a vested interest in producing a sustainability report year after year, you want to create a budget for the reporting process. A *sustainability-reporting budget* primarily includes employee time; in certain situations, it takes direct financial resources into account in the form of consultants to help you with data identification, procurement, and compilation.

You'll need to hire a consultant if you plan on measuring and reporting on greenhouse gas emissions by type, waste streams by category, water or soil analysis, materials testing, and the like. Basically, measuring anything that appears scientifically complex or unattainable with internal expertise may require the assistance of an outside consultant. Chapter 3 tells you what to look for in a qualified consultant and how to find one.

Compile a tracking sheet to log internal folks' time. Also, be sure to set up a mechanism within your accounting department so you can determine how much a sustainability report costs you to produce. You'll probably involve employees from many departments in its production, so think holistically here. Depending on your organization, you'll probably need to accumulate time logs from

- **Accounting staff:** These people typically coordinate everyone else's efforts. They compile information, fit it into the chosen report format, and keep everyone on track with their assigned tasks.

- **Operations and purchasing folks:** They help you gather data as to your facility's energy and water usage, waste streams, and purchasing policies. Because they work closely with suppliers, they can also highlight those vendors that may have human rights and/or child labor issues.

- **Human resource personnel:** These folks are helpful when compiling data related to training hours, discrimination lawsuits, workforce categorization, and benefits.

- **Marketing staff:** These creative minds can provide you with info on product labeling, compliance with marketing-communication laws, and voluntary industry standards. They may also serve as the central hub in your organization for conducting customer satisfaction surveys.

- **Information technology (IT) whizzes:** These invaluable individuals can help you establish a way for those working on the report to communicate and share documents electronically so everyone has access to the latest and greatest material.

Jot down what you think you'll need from each department in the way of hours, preferably on a monthly basis, and then track the actual hours spent. Of course, all you can do right now is guesstimate how much time you'll need from folks, but why not use what you know about the focus areas of your business to help you out? For example, if you're engaged in heavy life cycle assessment with your products (see Chapter 7 for more on this approach to product design), you know you'll need quite a bit of info from your product engineer.

After the first cycle, I promise you'll have a much better idea of how much time preparing your sustainability report is actually going to take. Additionally, your data-compilation infrastructure will be in place, so the needs for IT time, formatting time, and so on will be greatly reduced (as well as the corresponding financial costs).

Obtaining big-picture guidance from other businesses and reporting entities

Studying other businesses' reports is one way to find out more about what makes a successful sustainability report. For some sustainability-reporting inspiration, including ideas on how to present and format your info, check out *Spheres of Influence,* Seventh Generation's 2007 Corporate Consciousness Report. Just go to www.seventhgeneration.com, click the Corporate Responsibility link at the bottom of the page, and make your way to the report. For a look at a really professional and incredibly well-documented report, check out Co-operative Group's latest CSR report at www.co-operative. coop/en/corporate. Simply click the Sustainability link toward the top of the page to access the 2007/08 report.

Strangely enough, you may find out just as much from an inadequate report as a well-done one. Recognizing information gaps and insufficient reporting techniques helps you to chart your own course and avoid common mistakes.

After taking a look at reports for businesses comparable to your own, you'll start to see some trends in the reporting. All successful reports should have the following four governing attributes:

- ✔ **Materiality:** Is the information in your sustainability report really relevant to the environmental and social issues at hand? Some material information may not be available; your system should incorporate a way to reflect that. Ensure that the report is complete with regard to all sustainability-oriented areas.

- ✔ **Standardization:** Can an outsider look at your company's sustainability report and easily evaluate it against your competitor's? Is it possible to make a solid appraisal as to how you compare to each other? Standardization can be particularly challenging to achieve when data is aggregated to present different stores or distribution centers all within one snapshot.

✔ **Stakeholder inclusiveness:** Can the reader easily identify the stakeholders and see that his or her interests and questions have been reasonably addressed?

✔ **External verification:** Is there someone besides your company that says the information in this document is for real? Can you guarantee that the report gives a credible view of your company's sustainability profile?

The field of sustainability reporting is evolving rapidly. There are a plethora of different ways of looking at your firm's green journey and telling your story to others. Hence, being creative and visionary while simultaneously imparting useful information in a meaningful and user-friendly format is the name of the game.

Although not a mandatory report structure, many companies use the cornerstones of the Global Reporting Initiative's (GRI) sustainability-reporting principles in preparing their annual sustainability reports to help identify key issues and organize and present data. Why? Because the GRI does an excellent job providing an overview of what to report and how to report it. The cornerstones of the GRI's reporting principles and guidelines provide the following suggestions:

✔ **Showcase your accomplishments and identify your shortcomings.** You have to be prepared to bare all in this process. You may not want all of your stakeholders to know your actual carbon emissions have been going *up* on an annual basis, or that food waste in one of your employee cafeterias is around 16 percent. However, transparently identifying all of your business's risks and challenges (as well as its accomplishments and opportunities) is the foundation of a truly sustainable business.

Fill your readers in on what programs you have in process, how you're training employees or working with suppliers, where accountability lies in your firm, and what applicable certifications and regulations are out there.

✔ **Identify and address all stakeholders.** You must identify and categorize all possible stakeholders and show that company representatives have made an honest attempt to have open dialogue with all affected parties about their concerns and issues regarding the business's operations.

✔ **Keep it short, sweet, and relevant.** Throwing all the data you can at your readers is counter-productive. The information contained within your report should be couched within the context of improving sustainable performance. Tight correlations between what you're talking about and the company's triple-bottom-line performance keep stakeholders interested, whereas nebulous connections simply puzzle them.

✔ **Present results across the breadth of the value chain.** Exploring the full scope of impact up and down the value chain in order to convey your company's full sustainability footprint requires pulling it all together for a reader. Leaving big gaps out because you don't know what to report on or you haven't made any progress on an issue doesn't lend credibility to your report. For example, a recent report released by a big accounting firm shows that although 90 percent of firms mention climate change in their sustainability reports, only 20 percent of them mention it as one of their business risks. They focus only on climate change opportunities, which clearly doesn't paint a complete picture.

The GRI's full sustainability-reporting framework can be a bit overwhelming for small or mid-sized enterprises to use because it's primarily applicable to large organizations. That's why some companies are adopting trimmed-down versions of this extensive framework. Affectionately referred to as *GRI-Lite,* these versions embrace the idea of adapting comprehensive GRI standards to meet the needs of smaller organizations. GRI-Lite tones down to a less rigorous framework, but it's a great entry point for a small or mid-sized company that's new to sustainability reporting. The result more accurately reflects the unique challenges small companies face, as well as their progress toward meaningful change.

Although the GRI isn't a certifying agency, you can declare the level at which you applied GRI standards to your report. Essentially, you can tell your readers whether you're an advanced reporting entity, one that's just starting out, or one that has some experience (just not a ton). Simply self-declare which level (A, B, or C) your report complies with. (**Note:** You can only declare your report at an A+, B+ or C+ level if you've worked with a third party to verify the authenticity of your data.) Go to www.globalreporting.org/GRIReports/ApplicationLevels to see how to self-assess which level you're at and don't be upset if you have to declare at level C your first time out the gate. That's pretty common among sustainability-reporting newbies.

Whether you're working with the full GRI guidelines or the GRI-Lite version, the obvious tendency may be to cut and paste them into a spreadsheet and start down the list, checking off protocols as you go. However, doing so doesn't promote a systems-based vision for sustainability in your business. Use the checklist as a guide for the types of factors your company should consider and report on. Just don't make it into a glorified sustainability to-do list. If you stay in the traditional mode of ticking off items you've accomplished, you'll be locked into the old linear model of thinking. Although dotting i's and crossing t's is good, sustainability integration in your business will only be truly successful if you can transcend that approach. So use your reporting process to encourage collective thinking about big-picture stuff, like how your company can be regenerative, have positive impact on stakeholders, or develop employees' personal sustainable behavior. After all, you don't want to limit future goal-setting or brainstorming sessions with a checklist.

Ultimately, the reporting systems you design and implement should meet your stakeholders' identified needs (which you discover during the planning process described in Chapter 4). If you keep this fact in mind, you're guaranteed to ensure greater transparency, effective responsiveness to stakeholders, and improved overall organizational performance.

Identifying core developments and trends

You can't have an effective sustainability report without clearly defining the developments your company has made over the last year and mentioning trends you see in relation to your greening efforts. You want to first focus on the strides you've made that are most important to the success of your business. Some examples of developments you can list (as they relate to the triple bottom line, of course) are as follows:

- ✔ **People:** Present your progress toward your established social goals, such as enhanced customer reputation, examples of how you've helped improve human rights and labor standards, involvement in community initiatives, and the enhancement and diversification of your workforce.

- ✔ **Planet:** Outline ecological programs and policies that you're engaged in, such as greenhouse gas or energy audits, water-reduction efforts, and waste-minimization projects. Also, list your company's progress on specific targets, such as becoming a paperless office or transitioning 50 percent of employees to alternative transportation.

- ✔ **Profit:** Describe key financial strategies that you're pursuing, such as increasing revenues through expanded product lines, entry into new markets, enhanced profits, or earnings per share or debt reduction.

Make sure to be honest about trends, both positive and negative, so that your report's credibility is strong. For areas where targets haven't been achieved (for example, raw materials waste has decreased 10 percent when the prior year's goal was 18 percent), outline progress toward the goal and detail how efforts will be stepped up in the subsequent year to achieve it.

Putting Your Facts and Figures into a Presentable Format

The ability to critically reflect on the past year's performance and set aggressive but achievable targets for the next year should be woven throughout your sustainability report. Readers should easily see their concerns reflected, indicators established, and high-quality, meaningful data gathered to assess how well your business is progressing toward achieving each of its goals. Also, an ever-increasing level of sustainability consciousness should be reflected in ambitious targets for subsequent periods.

It may seem counterintuitive, but you want to consider adding some of the beginning elements of your report at the end of your compiling process. Parts such as the table of contents are hard to craft until you know the page location of each item. Likewise, the report from top management and the executive summary, see the earlier "Getting into the nitty-gritty details of report structure" section for more on these parts, may be easier to write after you know the big picture of your overall report.

The support of management is vital to creating a sound sustainability report, so keep top management apprised of your report-writing process. That way they won't be surprised when you ask them to craft an executive summary. If you're the top management at your organization, keep in mind that your report isn't complete without the addition of your bird's eye view from the big shot's chair.

In the spirit of sustainability, avoid printing and sending out your report in a paper format. Instead, make it available in a standard electronic format, such as .pdf, or make it accessible via popular word-processing software. If you want to be progressive, you can even prepare your sustainability report book-style by using Flash software. Some companies choose to publish their comprehensive reports online and include an executive summary, table of key ratios, and a management analysis of sustainability strategy in the form of a paper report accompanying their annual financial statements.

The following sections highlight how to compile a sustainability report that your stakeholders can readily understand.

Making the data easily accessible

When it comes to communicating your data and measurements to the decision-makers, advisors, and investors who help make your business hum, you have a myriad of options. You can present data in easy-to-read formats, such as bar charts or pie graphs, or in a tabular format that allows readers to see concrete numbers on an annual basis. Some reports include a simple key next to each major development area that shows whether the trend is increasing, staying static, or decreasing. If you use benchmarks (which I describe in Chapter 4), always be sure to cite their sources.

A sustainability report with easily accessible info

✔ **Shows trends in picture form with graphs or charts:** When presented over time, this information can be used to assess the success of particular programs or initiatives. For example, you may present a distribution graph to illustrate employees' degree of satisfaction with work life. What does this ratio look like over the last three years? Or, if you're just starting, provide the data for the current year and identify targets for improvement.

✔ **Compiles complex raw data into easy-to-read tables:** The goal of your sustainability report is to provide a readable and meaningful overview of your sustainability efforts and performance. Thus, more isn't better in this case. Particularly with energy, waste, and water calculations, showcase your results — not the volumes of data tracking factory waste or embedded fuel in raw materials. For all but the biggest die-hards, such info is a big yawn (at best) or a deal breaker (at worst).

✔ **Allows for easy comparison with other companies' sustainability reports:** If you can benchmark any aspects of your sustainability performance against those of other companies or standard-setting agencies, go for it! Showing how you're doing with minority recruitment is great, but establishing that you're beating statewide norms is potent.

Say you've charted data on recycled materials by type for the five preceding years. Offer your report's readers a glimpse of what's behind the numbers via commentary, but also present the actual data in tabular form (see Figure 16-1). If part of your sustainability plan is "Being zero waste by 2020" (which some progressive companies are in fact stating as a goal), make sure the graphical presentation addresses this goal.

Having one of these charts for one initiative in each of the cluster groups you selected during your sustainability-planning stage (see Chapter 4) is quite helpful. Note that not only does this table present recycling trends but it also addresses the fact that recycling progress is measured in comparison to traditional financial data (waste costs as a percentage of sales). Always think outside the box when presenting data.

As the saying goes, a picture's worth a thousand words. Instead of throwing a lot of statistics at your readers, show them how your metric tons of recyclables on an annual basis are doing with a visual overview. As you can see in Figure 16-2, a simple graphical representation helps folks understand the full impact of your recycling program.

TABULAR PRESENTATION OF RECYCLING PROGRAM'S IMPACT

Metric Tons Recycled Annually
Zion Graphic, Inc.

	2003	2004	2005	2006	2007
Cardboard post industrial recycled	64	85	107	247	380
Cardboard post consumer waste	225	342	580	696	766
Plastic post industrial recycled	62	82	91	102	155
Plastic post consumer waste	31	39	146	190	215
Paper post industrial recycled	600	655	708	722	808
Paper post consumer waste	2335	2580	3155	3344	3885
Total	**3317**	**3783**	**4787**	**5301**	**6209**
As % of waste stream	**26.3%**	**34%**	**48%**	**50%**	**46%**
Waste disposal costs as % of gross sales	**2.5%**	**2.3%**	**1.9%**	**1.4%**	**1.4%**

Figure 16-1: Charted data from recycling program assessment.

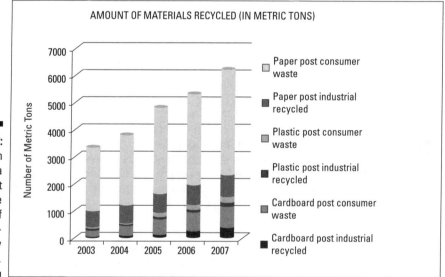

AMOUNT OF MATERIALS RECYCLED (IN METRIC TONS)

Figure 16-2: A graph offers a visual that shows the impact of your sustainability progress.

Just be careful not to go overboard with graphics. A few well-chosen images go a long way.

Anecdotal commentary personalizes data, so incorporate it where appropriate. Tell a story about how you were part of a group that developed an industrial park byproducts market and that's part of the reason your recycling numbers are looking so promising. Fill readers in on how many manufacturing companies have joined the byproducts consortium and the fact that the resulting recycling activity has generated eight new jobs within your community. (See the "Adding commentary to balance out shortcomings" section, later in this chapter, for more guidance on this topic.)

Helping stakeholders interpret the data

Members of your management team, as well as external stakeholders, need to be drawn into trends and analyses that show what you're trying to do and how well you're doing it. They need you to be to be simple, succinct, and easy to understand. Here are some tips to keep in mind:

- **Use internationally recognized measurements.** Obscure, industry-specific metrics aren't helpful. Instead, refer to easily recognizable units, such as tons of carbon dioxide emissions or number of employees impacted.

- **Present triple-bottom-line benefits whenever possible (maximizing people, planet, and profit simultaneously).** For example, say you've discovered that defect rates have decreased 4 percent since your facility-wide lighting retrofit intended to decrease carbon emissions. The increased productivity is the result of happier workers responding to more natural lighting, and the decreased rework costs will pay for the lighting in the next 18 months. A project oriented toward reduced energy costs has therefore yielded a triple-bottom-line winner and should be conveyed in your report.

- **Tie in social and environmental data to traditional financial trends.** Everyone is used to tracking gross sales. Take this traditional financial info a step further and show quarterly ecological ratios as a portion of that. For example, you can show carbon emissions as a percentage of gross sales. Couching the info this way is more meaningful than absolute data (tons of carbon emitted). It also gets folks familiar with reviewing environmentally oriented data and thinking about how that fits with traditional financial data.

- **Make sure the data are relevant to the goal.** If your goal is to minimize waste but you've just expanded your facility, reporting total waste isn't going to accurately reflect the results of your waste-reduction strategies because clearly with more employees, production, and/or square footage, your waste stream will likely increase. Instead, try presenting solid waste produced per square foot of commercial space. Plot it on a trend line so folks can get a visual of what's happening.

You don't have to incorporate sustainability metrics in your formal financial statements; you can always present them as a supplement to your financial statements. Formalizing your data is a great long-term goal, but don't get cowed by such magnanimous change. Instead, work on designing a page of key ratios that paints a picture about the triple-bottom-line issues your company is working on.

Adding commentary to balance out shortcomings

Your sustainability report can't be all moonlight and roses. Because businesses are run by human beings and sustainability is a journey, you're going to have hiccups along the way to achieving green greatness. Your investors and other stakeholders realize that and will appreciate your honesty when mentioning your company's sustainability shortcomings. Tell them the following:

✔ What limitations and challenges you faced

✔ What lessons you learned

✔ How you're reprioritizing to achieve your goals in the upcoming year

For example, perhaps you didn't hit your target of lower over-the-road shipping costs. Mention that, but then follow up by saying that you made great strides in that department and reduced those costs by 20 percent, partially due to incorporating rail in your shipping plan (which leads to reduced carbon emissions). The great part about owning up to your company's shortcomings is that you have the opportunity to create some new goals and targets for the next year.

Many companies fall short with supply chain efforts because of the need to secure buy-in and commitment from other companies' management teams. Address these issues by stressing systems and initiatives you're designing to achieve greater sustainability collaboration and lining out *how* you're helping your suppliers develop a culture of sustainability. For example, invite their employees to participate in a sustainability training you're sponsoring at your facility. As your employees mingle with your suppliers' employees and listen to the same presentation on greening your supply chain, they'll begin to establish a common ground and form a partnership geared toward attaining green goals.

Social goals are also often hard to meet because of a series of factors, including the complexity inherent in changing human values and behaviors and the difficulty in conducting multiple initiatives simultaneously. Continue to stress your new programs and talk about how many employees have joined the walk-at-lunch group or taken advantage of the dollar-for-dollar match to purchase a commuter bike. Keep conducting surveys so you can report in on new employee behaviors and, of course, log progress on the actual targets (such as reduced absenteeism and increased productivity).

Going the extra mile with a green audit or an assurance

As more publicly traded companies (over half the Standard & Poor's 500 so far) issue sustainability reports, stakeholder pressure for third-party report verification will grow. Standards will likely develop at a rapid pace, but for right now, companies are relatively on their own for ensuring the credibility of their sustainability reports. If pursuing third-party verification of your report is something you're interested in, you can either go for a green audit or an assurance.

The word *audit* strikes fear in the heart of anyone who pays taxes, but in the sustainability world, it's not anything to be afraid of. Audits involve a third party assessing the validity, reliability, and relevance of information that's being provided. The outcome of an audit is to express an opinion on the information as well as the internal controls in place in the company. The scope of a formal sustainability audit can vary, depending on what you feel your company needs to address. You can hire outside accountants to

✔ Ensure the integrity of data-collection processes and systems

✔ Address the quality and reliability of key performance indicators (KPIs)

✔ Conduct a full audit of your report to see whether it conforms to the Global Reporting Initiative's (GRI) standards, which are widely acknowledged as a comprehensive framework for sustainability reporting

Expect a formal sustainability audit to include a thorough review of the sustainability-reporting process, including an analysis of benchmarks, KPIs, and targets. When the audit is complete, you receive a letter outlining a series of recommendations, internal control improvement suggestions, and policies and procedures that you can institute to strengthen your company's sustainability effort in the upcoming year.

Because sustainability reporting is such a new field and isn't yet required in the U.S. and Canada, traditional auditors (found in accounting firms) have yet to significantly develop sustainability auditing services in North America. Realistically, however, most small or mid-sized companies aren't able to commit resources to a formal audit; therefore, they rely on informal approaches such as external stakeholder interviews to provide a sense of authenticity, called assurance, to their reports.

Assurance is a term used to express the result of an audit, but the two terms are used interchangeably to identify a third party's stamp of approval. *External assurance* is designed to complement the GRI's sustainability-reporting framework. It's an open-source standard that encourages input from all parties in its development. External assurance can also be expressed in the form of advisory panels made up of stakeholders (who can play an important role in the assurance process because they're third parties who are vested in the process and the credibility of the information).

Although financial statements have a formal engagement and assurance process, sustainability reporting requires the use of many kinds of professionals, such as scientists, sociologists, organizational behavioralists, and engineers. The qualifications for the different kinds of people involved in the external assurance of your sustainability report are highly dependent on your industry sector.

Interview stakeholders to solicit their responses in order to draft reports. Specifically, ask them whether all relevant issues are covered to their satisfaction and presented in a balanced, unbiased way. Publish highlights of the interviews. This is an informal yet authentic way of offering an independent assessment of your report's quality and can be very helpful in ensuring its credibility.

Only one of the Big Four CPA firms (Deloitte Touche Tohmatsu, KPMG, Pricewaterhouse Coopers, and Ernst & Young) offers assurance services for sustainability reports in the U.S.

For more info on Deloitte's assurance service for sustainability reports, go to the company's global Web site at www.deloitte.com/global. Hold your mouse over the Services tab toward the top of the page and click Enterprise Risk Services from the drop-down menu. Click the Corporate Responsibility and Sustainability link on the left-hand side and then click the Corporate Responsibility Assurance link found on the left-hand side of the new page.

AccountAbility, a UK-based standard-setting group, is one of the first organizations to publish formal assurance standards, known as the AA1000 Assurance Standard. CorporateRegister.com maintains an electronic directory of sustainability reports that have been tested against this standard; it's worth checking out to glean what you can from other folks' sustainability reports. More than 150 companies use or refer to the AA1000 Assurance Standard in their reporting, so you have plenty of opportunities for inspiration.

Part V
The Part of Tens

The 5th Wave   By Rich Tennant

"Certainly, I'm all for using biodegradable and organic materials, but does the public really want fake doggy poop that isn't plastic?"

In this part . . .

To pique your green interest, this part offers profiles of the visionaries, authors, CEOs, financiers, and entrepreneurs who make up my list of the (more than) ten socially responsible giants of the sustainable business world. And because you're bound to encounter myths about sustainability as you strive to move your company down a greener path, I also present you with a list of the ten most common myths about climate change, sustainability, and business — along with credible ways to refute these claims.

Chapter 17

More than Ten Green Business Visionaries and Their Success Stories

· ·

In This Chapter

▶ Recognizing the contributions of some of the most influential green business leaders

▶ Seeing how the written ideas of green thinkers have affected the green business movement

· ·

*A*ll great paradigm shifts throughout history have their heroes, and the Green Revolution is no different. Its heroes are the men and women with overarching visions for their businesses, fields of study, and society as a whole. These people understand the complexity and interdependencies of the challenges facing commerce today. Their mindset is such that they easily move past the traditional short-term, profit-driven mentality and envision how sustainability can create competitive advantage, new revenue streams, and innovative design capacity — all while recognizing the Earth's limits.

Most of these heroes were considered mavericks in their time, driving through green agendas before anyone really had a concept of what that meant. And yet, without exception, these people engendered fiercely loyal followers in their employees, colleagues, and stakeholders. In this chapter, I share (in alphabetical order) the stories of some of these early green giants. I hope that they may serve as inspiration for you, as they have for me, on your path to creating an economically, environmentally, and socially just business.

Ray Anderson, CEO, Interface, Inc.

In 1994, Canadian businessman Ray Anderson, CEO of Interface, Inc. (the world's largest commercial carpeting manufacturer), read Paul Hawken's *The Ecology of Commerce*. This book presents not only the historical scope of environmental destruction by industry but it also acknowledges the power of business to propel change and grow sustainably. Reading it brought about

Anderson's self-proclaimed epiphany, and from that point forward, he was driven to reduce the company's operational impact, create ecoinnovative products, and involve all the company's stakeholders in his efforts.

Anderson's guidance has since lead Interface to the forefront of meeting the sustainability challenge. A firm believer in industrial ecology and *closed-loop manufacturing* (zero-waste production methods based on the constant recycling of materials), Anderson has spearheaded a 33-percent reduction in Interface's organizational waste over the last decade. His strong commitment to eliminating petroleum from the company's product line has sparked a firestorm of creativity in recyclable materials, including the creation of Entropy — a carpet inspired by the asymmetrical patterns found in nature. Developed with help from Janine Benyus, an expert in biomimicry (described later in this chapter), this green product has become Interface's top-selling carpet line, representing about 40 percent of its overall carpet tile sales.

One of the basic precepts of natural capitalism (which I fully explain in Chapter 3) is to move toward a service and flow economy and away from a product-based economy (see Chapter 6 for more on these two economic models), and Interface is a front runner in implementing this idea. It leases commercial floor coverings (as opposed to making an outright sale) and installs carpet squares instead of laying huge quantities of carpet. This business model allows for replacing commercial carpeting tiles in heavy-traffic areas without having to pull up perfectly good carpet.

One thing's certain: With Interface's goal of complete sustainability by 2020, this company and its green leader are worth watching.

Joan Bavaria, CEO, Trillium Asset Management

A former *TIME Magazine* Hero for the Planet, Joan Bavaria (founder and CEO of Trillium Asset Management) is to socially responsible investing (SRI) what Sir Isaac Newton was to physics — minus the apple. Other people dabbled around the perimeter of ecofinancial markets, but no one created the alliances, energy, and fund families that went mainstream like Bavaria.

Bavaria's company is the United States' oldest independent SRI firm. Managing more than $1 billion in assets, Trillium has been instrumental in effecting corporate change through shareholder resolutions that target social and environmental improvements. It also donates 5 percent of its profits to philanthropic endeavors.

In addition to running the employee-owned Trillium, Bavaria founded two powerful nonprofit players in the SRI field:

- ✔ **Social Investment Forum:** This organization is a national association with more than 500 members (including foundations, financial advisors, and portfolio managers) that furthers research on and publication about SRI.

- ✔ **Coalition of Environmentally Responsible Economies:** CERES is the organization responsible for publishing the *CERES Principles,* a set of standards for corporate environmental management. Transnational companies (including General Motors and Bank of America) endorse these principles, which have served as the basis for many companies' desires to engage in sustainability reporting, transparency, and corporate social responsibility.

As Trillium continues to grow in asset base, its influence on the capital markets will grow commensurately. But even more profound than dollars of assets managed is the foundation that Trillium provided for the hundreds of firms and funds now dedicated to the green financial market. It'd be hard to imagine how far down the ecopath U.S. capital markets would be without Bavaria's visionary leadership.

Janine Benyus, Scientist and Author, Biomimicry

Janine Benyus, an avowed naturalist and a scientist by training, coined the term biomimicry in 1997. *Biomimicry* (from *bios* meaning life and *mimesi* meaning imitate) is now a widely used term in product design labs and international boardrooms alike. Benyus's book of the same name counsels engineers and designers to look to nature's nearly four billion years of experience for the answers to their most challenging design problems.

With clients like Nike, Hewlett Packard, and the British government, Benyus is widely sought after as both a speaker and a consultant to introduce product engineers to nature-inspired designs. (See Chapter 7 for a closer look at some of the amazing products inspired by Benyus's biomimicry.) In her spare time, Benyus founded The Biomimicry Institute, a nonprofit, open-source organization that links people from all corners of the globe who are working on sustainable technologies. She was honored as one of *TIME International's* Heroes of the Environment in 2007 — joining the ranks of past heroes Al Gore, Robert Redford, and Amory Lovins — for her innovative work in biomimicry.

Sir John Browne, Former CEO, British Petroleum

Oil drilling, refining, and chemical production are environmentally dangerous industries that are susceptible to ecoregulations and heavily peppered with climate change naysayers. But when Sir John Browne announced, one year after becoming CEO, that British Petroleum (BP) was leaving the American oil industry's lobby group because it acknowledged the reality of global climate change and intended to do something about it by setting greenhouse gas emission reduction targets, the industry took a giant green step forward.

In 2000, Browne spearheaded a $200 million rebranding campaign at BP, focusing future strategies around renewable energy development and changing the behemoth's name to Beyond Petroleum. Although BP isn't without its share of controversy, it has earned a "best of class" rating among socially responsible investment funds.

Browne has since stepped down from his role at BP, but he'll forever be known as a leading petrochemical executive who stopped questioning climate change science and started positioning his company for competitive advantage in solar, wind, and alternative fuels. With $250 billion in annual sales, the impact BP will have on revolutionizing energy at the global scale can only be imagined.

Yvon Chouinard, Founder, Patagonia, Inc.

In the 1960s, Yvon Chouinard turned a passion for rock climbing into a fledging company called Chouinard Equipment, which used its catalogue to stress the importance of *clean climbing* (leaving no scar on the rock). Chouinard understood early on that customer education was crucial to sustained behavioral change.

Patagonia — a company now known worldwide for its innovation, social and environmental friendliness, and the superb quality of its outdoor gear — evolved after the sale of Chouinard Equipment. As Chouinard traveled internationally to surf, fish, ice climb, and kayak, the rapidity with which environmental and native community destruction was occurring across the globe prompted him to analyze how Patagonia could reduce its impact.

During the 1990s, Chouinard led the company in aligning business practices with values by addressing how to mitigate the environmental harm it was causing. Patagonia's basic values, including the idea of striving to do no harm, emerged as a result. Patagonia has since developed core philosophies in product design, production, distribution, HR, finance, and management to guide business conduct in each area. One of the outcomes was that Patagonia became the first company to make catalogues from recycled paper.

Chouinard's enduring legend also includes cofounding 1% For The Planet, an affiliation of businesses that pledges to contribute at least one percent of annual revenues to grassroots environmental organizations. Building an amazingly profitable business that taxes itself and works diligently to operate in conjunction with nature and indigenous communities is quite an inspiration. Perhaps that's why Chouinard's brainchild receives 3,000 applications on average for just one job opening. Not bad results for a small climbing company that aspired to conduct business in a sustainable way, huh?

Paul Hawken, Author, The Ecology of Commerce

Paul Hawken, although influential in many arenas, has had the most impact on sustainable development as an author. His first book, *The Ecology of Commerce,* was not only used extensively in business schools but also widely touted as the authority on establishing environmental policy as it applies to commerce. It introduced the concept of *comprehensive outcome* — the idea that in order to truly gauge the impact of a business transaction, the decision-maker must analyze all affected parties by using systems-based thinking. This idea was a significant break with the simplistic notion that the driving goal of business is to maximize shareholder wealth, and it contributed significantly to the development of *full-cost accounting,* the practice of accumulating all costs (social, environmental, and economic) in the cost basis of a product. For example, anything made with petroleum would need to take into account the costs of climate change, groundwater remediation, and impact on biodiversity.

Natural Capitalism: Creating the Next Industrial Revolution, which he coauthored with Hunter Lovins and Amory Lovins, established consideration of the Earth's limits and carrying capacity as a key constraint in business decision-making. Hawken's 2007 book, *Blessed Unrest: How the Largest Movement in the World Came into Being and Why No One Saw It Coming,* identifies the union of the social and environmental movements as the most impactful social movement ever.

Aside from writing, Hawken travels and speaks widely on behalf of Wiser Earth, an organization he recently founded that connects the millions of organizations working on environmental and social issues. He has been a scholarly, guiding voice for many students, entrepreneurs, and businesspeople over the years, and he is widely considered one of the pivotal influences in the sustainability movement.

Jeffrey Hollender, President, Seventh Generation

Winner of the 2008 Fast Company/Monitor Group Social Capitalist Award for "using the tools of business to solve the world's most pressing problems," Jeffrey Hollender is President and Chief Inspired Protagonist of Seventh Generation. Commanding about 25 percent of the natural household products and cleaners' $150 million annual market, Seventh Generation has made inroads with such giants as Safeway, Wal-Mart, and Kroger. Hollender is also an author and founder of the Household Toxins Institute, which conducts research on the impact of household chemicals on human health.

Hollender's Burlington, Vermont–based company incorporates sustainability at every turn. Long before anyone mainstream thought of unbleached paper towels or natural dishwashing soap, Hollender and cofounder Alan Newman tallied sales of $1 million from their first year in business. The company has certainly had its ups and downs, but what sets Hollender and Seventh Generation apart is leadership's firm commitment to sustainability reporting and full transparency and its exceptional efforts to educate suppliers, consumers, and employees about the benefits of sustainable products and practices. Hollender has dared to enter his products into the mainstream market and has the market share and profits to show for it.

Jeffrey Immelt, CEO, General Electric

Chairman of the Board and CEO of General Electric (GE), Jeffrey Immelt is one of the founders of the U.S. Climate Action Partnership. In this alliance, he and his cohorts have pressured the federal government to control greenhouse gases through policy and regulation. Suffice it to say these actions haven't won him favor in some industry circles.

Undaunted, Immelt launched GE's *Ecoimagination* campaign, which famously declared that "Green is green" in May 2005. He has also actively led GE in pursuit of a sustainable agenda that embraces four measurable action items, all anticipated to occur between 2004 and 2010:

- ✔ Doubled investment in clean tech R&D between 2004 and 2010, peaking at $1.5 billion annually

- ✔ Increased introduction of products and services that exhibit marked environmental performance through the Ecoimagination line of products

- ✔ Significant reduction of greenhouse gas emissions through usage of products both in consumers' hands and in company facilities and operations

- ✔ Complete and total transparency to the public about how the campaign is quantitatively meeting its proclaimed goals

Not only has Immelt repositioned GE to be a leader in climate change solutions (including solar power, water-purification systems, and a plethora of energy-efficient jet and locomotive initiatives) but he has also inspired many other high-profile business leaders to manage in an environmentally and socially responsible way.

Amory Lovins, Coauthor, Natural Capitalism

Amory Lovins is that rare blend of visionary and realist — and one who has stayed true to the course he set out for himself more than 40 years ago. By the 1970s, he was already writing, talking, and testifying about the need for new North American energy policies. Combining an education in physics, ardent environmentalism, and a knack for business, Lovins created a buzz as a consultant for major international firms. Of the many books he has coauthored, *Natural Capitalism: Creating the Next Industrial Revolution* is arguably the most influential for its wide application as a sustainability framework for businesses of all shapes and sizes. (For more info on natural capitalism and how it's used as a working business framework, flip to Chapter 3.)

In the 1990s, Lovins cofounded the Rocky Mountain Institute (RMI), a not-for-profit energy consultancy firm. RMI's headquarters is located in a south-facing compound that's so energy efficient an adequate interior temperature is maintained from sunlight alone — even with Colorado's subzero winter temperatures. In fact, the building houses semitropical and tropical indoor plants!

Lovins continues to have a big impact on the world's largest corporations and governments by guiding such giants as Wal-Mart, Motorola, and the Australian and Canadian governments in their quests for sustainability.

William McDonough & Michael Braungart, Authors, Cradle to Cradle

When architect William McDonough and chemist Michael Braungart published their book, *Cradle to Cradle,* in 2002, the fact that their very basic premise hadn't been explored previously was simply astounding. The theory? That by emulating the natural world, all outputs should become inputs for another process, thereby completely eliminating the concept of waste.

According to this business model, green design concepts should be applied universally — whether you're consulting with a developer on the construction of a small subdivision or reconfiguring an auto manufacturer's production facility. Pollution and toxins are thus simply and completely eliminated, and any waste byproducts are deliberately introduced as raw materials for another process or product.

Guided by the idea that nothing goes to waste, McDonough and Braungart recommend that all design incorporate thoughtfulness about what happens to an item at the end of its useful life. They urge manufacturers to create products that can be easily disassembled so biological nutrients can return to the soil for natural decomposition. They also stress that *technical nutrients,* or noncompostable items, should be separated and used in an endless cycle of production. Using nature as a model for ecologically sound design has driven this team's work with Nike, Herman Miller, Ford, and Oberlin College, just to name a few of the well-known organizations they counsel.

Muhammad Yunus, Nobel Laureate and Founder, The Grameen Bank

Winner of the Nobel Peace Prize in 2006, Muhammad Yunus (also known as the Banker to the Poor) has been instrumental in fueling sustainable economic development in the Third World. He realized early on that lack of access to capital was a key impediment to eradicating poverty. For example, in his native Bangladesh, most of the rural poor could only source funds to start a small business from predatory street lenders. So Yunus decided to use his own money to grant the first microloans to basket weavers, giving birth to the Grameen Bank in the process.

Instead of following the western model of signing notes and offering collateral — a system that's irrelevant for many developing nations due to their high levels of poverty and illiteracy — the Grameen Bank model asks borrowers to have community members vouch for their character and offer a verbal commitment to repay the loan. Grameen Bank sports a repayment rate any commercial lender would be proud of, and it has lent out more than $7 billion and been profitable in all but three years since its inception in 1983. Today, the bank disburses 97 percent of its funds to women.

Not only has Yunus's Grameen Bank helped hundreds of thousands of people out of poverty and given them dignity to earn their own living but it has also provided a microfinance model that stresses cultural relevance, female empowerment, and community development — a model that's being replicated in more than 100 countries worldwide.

Chapter 18

Countering Ten Myths about Going Green

In This Chapter

▶ Capitalizing on the business case for sustainability

▶ Illustrating how even small changes can have a big impact

*N*o matter how far down the green path you may be, you're sure to encounter skepticism and maybe even scorn from colleagues, bosses, and business partners. Such negative reaction is usually fueled by concerns about cost and an increased workload.

Following are ten of the most common myths about greening a commercial endeavor. You may hear them on occasion, or your mind may even wander toward these thoughts when you're feeling less than inspired. Believe me, I know that some days it seems much easier to talk about all the reasons your business *can't* go green than to get moving and implement actions. However, I'm here to dispel these nasty rumors so you can move forward without a doubt that striving for sustainability is indeed worthwhile.

The Costs Outweigh the Profits

The idea that the costs of greening your business outweigh any potential profits is a very general argument that's actually part myth and part fact. Some projects, such as those designed to reduce waste production, energy usage, excessive materials use, or water usage, can actually *save* your company money. (These projects are referred to as the *low-hanging fruit* of green business practices.) The key is to focus on what can be done quickly and easily *now* — with low cost and big impact! (For a list of easy ways to green your daily office practices, consult Chapter 6.)

Other projects, specifically longer-range efforts, like installing a ground source heat pump, retrofitting all of your lighting ballasts, or even building a green facility, clearly have price tags associated with them. For these projects, make sure to convey the concept that as savings accrue from pick-ing the low-hanging fruit, the company will have seed capital to invest in other green projects that may require start-up funding. Emphasize the win-win nature of using short-term savings to fund long-term projects. After all, long-term triple-bottom-line benefits accrue from a portfolio of both short- and long-term projects.

Obviously, if you walk into your CEO's office with a blanket statement like, "Let's go green," you probably won't get the buy-in you want. Instead, try to convince him or her to look at an alternative business paradigm by talking the language. *Triple-bottom-line thinking* (giving equal consideration to people, planet, and profit) is a new model for many executives and managers. The way to work them into it is by starting with what they understand: the profit part of the equation. So get proficient with the business case outlined in Chapter 1 and relate these five compelling reasons as to why your boss should green your company:

✔ Increased revenues through the development of new products to meet evolving green consumers' needs

✔ Decreased expenses through the savings inherent in cutting water usage, waste output, and energy usage

✔ Increased access to business capital by tapping into the new pools of money aimed at funding green businesses

✔ Good positioning to meet future challenges, particularly those pertain-ing to energy volatility, so as to decrease future risk

✔ Happier and more productive employees working in a socially just and healthy environment

Going Green Requires Extensive Ecoknowledge

With words such as *eco, sustainable,* and *green* bombarding people day in and day out in the mass media, it's hard not to believe that going green means speaking an entirely different language and acquiring a vast, new knowledge base. However, the basic concepts of going green in the business world are rather easy to understand because they relate to subjects any business owner already knows all about: increasing revenues, decreasing expenses, meeting customers' needs, and establishing a game plan for the future.

When faced with this myth, respond with a series of irrefutable snippets that are easy to grasp, painless to remember, and simple to repeat. The following few sum up all you need to know about greening business practices in order to start convincing the naysayers:

✔ Green business is about focusing on the triple bottom line, which consists of people, planet, and profit, rather than looking solely at short-term profit. Thinking in these terms positions your company to cope with all the changes that are occurring in the business world.

✔ Reducing water usage, waste production, energy usage, and excessive materials use are all big parts of going green that save you money, both in the short and long term.

✔ Becoming sustainable is a journey, not a destination, so don't worry if you don't understand it all now. Your company will evolve as you make the transition.

Our Employees Are Too Busy to Implement Green Initiatives

The myth of employees who are too swamped to help green their companies isn't entirely far from the truth. If you take a snapshot of most companies now compared to ten years ago, you find that fewer people are doing more work for pay that hasn't kept pace with inflation. So what incentive is there for employees to participate in green team meetings or sort departmental recycling on top of their daily tasks? (Here's a hint: Preaching about how going green is the right thing to do isn't the answer!)

To mitigate employee resistance and incorporate greening efforts easily, make changes as simple as possible to implement, particularly in the introductory phase of greening your business. For example, if your recycling plan makes it easier to toss items in a recycling bin rather than throw them in the garbage, you'll have nearly full staff buy-in. Likewise, if you show employees how they can save $50 per week by carpooling, you'll pique their interest.

Avoid starting with projects or programs that add a ton of tasks to your staff members' to-do lists. On Day One, you must make change easy or you'll just be wasting everyone's time. As your employees' ecoconscious spirits awaken through small start-up initiatives, then you can play with ideas that require asking something of them.

My Business Is Too Small to Matter

I often hear businesspeople spout the myth that their companies are too small to effect powerful green change. Although I understand it's hard to imagine how setting $1/2$-inch margins to save office paper will have any impact on global issues such as social inequality and climate change, the truth is that any step toward sustainability (no matter how small) makes a difference. If all companies make small strides, the cumulative impact will be bigger than if they didn't start at all.

Many of the small beginner initiatives (like altering company printing practices to save paper or turning off lights in unused spaces) actually save companies money. Combine that savings with the lower expenses, higher profits, better job security, and superior positioning for the future that comes from greening a business, and even the smallest company can see how embracing sustainability can have an impact on both the environment and the corporate coffers.

Why Start Now? The Earth Is Already Doomed

It seems these days that lots of people have gone from a big collective yawn on the doom-and-gloom front to the "We're dust, why even bother?" state of mind. Although the changes in nature (described in Chapter 2) are worth being concerned about, staying focused on the positive is important. The exciting part of the story is how much opportunity exists for businesses to meet the challenges of the 21st century, craft solutions to some of the world's most pressing problems, and enjoy competitive advantages while doing so.

The next time you encounter some corporate honcho spouting off this myth, refer this person to the business case for sustainability (found in Chapter 1) so as to outline precisely how his or her business can cash in on the opportunities inherent in going green — starting today.

This Climate Change Thing Will Pass

The Intergovernmental Panel on Climate Change, made up of 160 scientists from all over the world, has been studying the issue of climate change for 20 years. Its increasingly solid conclusion? The planet is warming at a rate that most species can't adapt to, and there's a 90 percent likelihood that this warming is caused by human activities. However, some people you encounter will insist that human-accelerated climate change is just a passing phase. Chances are they'll have their own scientific evidence too because there are small-scale studies out there that show contrary results.

Unless you're a climatologist, forget debating the science. That's a no-win situation. Instead, focus on the fact that climate change, whether human accelerated or not, poses many challenges and opportunities for business moving forward. Speculating, even if just for a moment, as to what one's business will look like if the price of oil rises to $250 a barrel or if carbon emissions are capped is well worth any manager's time. Always redirect conversation about this myth toward scenario analysis and away from science.

Not to Worry — Technology Will Provide the Answers!

To assert that technology is the stand-alone answer to the tests facing business today (such as how to cope with climate change, peak oil, and trade deficits) is an easy out. Yes, investing in alternative transportation and fuels, sustainable agriculture, and green construction and building materials is essential to crafting a sustainable future. However, these technological investments aren't *instead of* conserving energy and water.

Technological advancements don't replace the need to reduce waste, use recycled materials, close the global equity gap, and treat foreign employees with dignity. All these different sustainability components work together. Minimizing your business's impact on nature's systems, via technology or not, is always important.

Our Shareholders Just Want Short-Term Results

Because of the commercial and cultural emphasis on immediate gratification, especially when it comes to short-term financial results, you may find people claiming that any initiatives requiring long-term thinking just won't fly with the company's shareholders. That's simply not true. Just invite a calculation of total returns over the lifetime of a green project versus its immediate impact.

If you point out that when current energy, carbon, or waste costs are factored in, there's a high likelihood of much bigger costs to deal with in the future, you'll have these folks' attention. (After all, whether your company succeeds or fails financially in the long run has an impact on them, too.) That societal need for immediate gratification will go right out the window — or at least to the back of people's minds for the time being.

The Whole Green Scene Is a Ploy by Whiny Ecoliberals

The false idea that the green movement is a stunt being pulled by left-wingers is a result of mass media's passion for segregating and categorizing the greater population to create controversy. After all, without controversy, there are no stories. The move toward greening business, however, can't truly be politicized with any credibility. How can increasing profits while lessening corporate impact on the Earth and contributing to community development possibly be political in nature?

Don't get caught up in this myth. Disarm any cynic who tries to defend it with a few choice facts that illustrate how sustainable businesses are outperforming their counterparts on the Dow Jones Sustainability North America Index, or how major multibillion-dollar corporations (think BP, Nike, Hewlett Packard, and GE) have fully embraced a green agenda to position their companies for the 21st century by being the first to enter and capture green niche markets.

 Above all, stay positive and focused on the reality of the business case for sustainability. Dispute is difficult if you stay out of the political arena and remain centered on business.

This Problem Isn't Ours to Solve

This myth belongs to a particular demographic group that questions why businesses should be forced to figure out their own sustainability strategies when government policies have been so remiss over the years in encouraging sustainable behavior. For example, it doesn't seem fair to many business owners why they should be left to absorb increased energy costs when government has passed on many opportunities to invest in alternatives.

This group thinks the nation's elected representatives need to lead the way in going green by enacting massive programs to encourage green building, sustainable product design, and research and development for renewable energy. It also believes the government should mandate prohibitive taxes on plastic bags, waste, and fossil fuel emissions.

In reality, the challenges and opportunities inherent in instituting green change on a nationwide scale are so great that it will take power, persuasion, policy, and behavior change on the part of everyone involved. To truly effect change that will enable a sustainable future, nonprofits; federal, state, and municipal governments; businesses; and individuals all need to contribute their resources and wisdom to that end. (To see how you and your business can start helping set policy that applies to the future of business overall, see Chapter 5.)

Index

• **C** •

• F •

• G •

• *H* •

• T •

USINESS, CAREERS & PERSONAL FINANCE

ounting For Dummies, 4th Edition*
-0-470-24600-9

okkeeping Workbook For Dummies†
-0-470-16983-4

mmodities For Dummies
-0-470-04928-0

ng Business in China For Dummies
-0-470-04929-7

E-Mail Marketing For Dummies
978-0-470-19087-6

Job Interviews For Dummies, 3rd Edition*†
978-0-470-17748-8

Personal Finance Workbook For Dummies*†
978-0-470-09933-9

Real Estate License Exams For Dummies
978-0-7645-7623-2

Six Sigma For Dummies
978-0-7645-6798-8

Small Business Kit For Dummies, 2nd Edition*†
978-0-7645-5984-6

Telephone Sales For Dummies
978-0-470-16836-3

USINESS PRODUCTIVITY & MICROSOFT OFFICE

ess 2007 For Dummies
-0-470-03649-5

el 2007 For Dummies
-0-470-03737-9

ice 2007 For Dummies
-0-470-00923-9

tlook 2007 For Dummies
-0-470-03830-7

PowerPoint 2007 For Dummies
978-0-470-04059-1

Project 2007 For Dummies
978-0-470-03651-8

QuickBooks 2008 For Dummies
978-0-470-18470-7

Quicken 2008 For Dummies
978-0-470-17473-9

Salesforce.com For Dummies, 2nd Edition
978-0-470-04893-1

Word 2007 For Dummies
978-0-470-03658-7

UCATION, HISTORY, REFERENCE & TEST PREPARATION

ican American History For Dummies
-0-7645-5469-8

ebra For Dummies
-0-7645-5325-7

ebra Workbook For Dummies
-0-7645-8467-1

History For Dummies
-0-470-09910-0

ASVAB For Dummies, 2nd Edition
978-0-470-10671-6

British Military History For Dummies
978-0-470-03213-8

Calculus For Dummies
978-0-7645-2498-1

Canadian History For Dummies, 2nd Edition
978-0-470-83656-9

Geometry Workbook For Dummies
978-0-471-79940-5

The SAT I For Dummies, 6th Edition
978-0-7645-7193-0

Series 7 Exam For Dummies
978-0-470-09932-2

World History For Dummies
978-0-7645-5242-7

OD, GARDEN, HOBBIES & HOME

dge For Dummies, 2nd Edition
-0-471-92426-5

n Collecting For Dummies, 2nd Edition
-0-470-22275-1

king Basics For Dummies, 3rd Edition
-0-7645-7206-7

Drawing For Dummies
978-0-7645-5476-6

Etiquette For Dummies, 2nd Edition
978-0-470-10672-3

Gardening Basics For Dummies*†
978-0-470-03749-2

Knitting Patterns For Dummies
978-0-470-04556-5

Living Gluten-Free For Dummies†
978-0-471-77383-2

Painting Do-It-Yourself For Dummies
978-0-470-17533-0

ALTH, SELF HELP, PARENTING & PETS

ger Management For Dummies
-0-470-03715-7

iety & Depression Workbook Dummies
-0-7645-9793-0

ting For Dummies, 2nd Edition
-0-7645-4149-0

g Training For Dummies, 2nd Edition
-0-7645-8418-3

Horseback Riding For Dummies
978-0-470-09719-9

Infertility For Dummies†
978-0-470-11518-3

Meditation For Dummies with CD-ROM, 2nd Edition
978-0-471-77774-8

Post-Traumatic Stress Disorder For Dummies
978-0-470-04922-8

Puppies For Dummies, 2nd Edition
978-0-470-03717-1

Thyroid For Dummies, 2nd Edition†
978-0-471-78755-6

Type 1 Diabetes For Dummies*†
978-0-470-17811-9

parate Canadian edition also available
parate U.K. edition also available

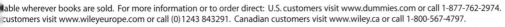

able wherever books are sold. For more information or to order direct: U.S. customers visit www.dummies.com or call 1-877-762-2974.
customers visit www.wileyeurope.com or call (0) 1243 843291. Canadian customers visit www.wiley.ca or call 1-800-567-4797.

WILEY

INTERNET & DIGITAL MEDIA

AdWords For Dummies
978-0-470-15252-2

Blogging For Dummies, 2nd Edition
978-0-470-23017-6

**Digital Photography All-in-One
Desk Reference For Dummies, 3rd Edition**
978-0-470-03743-0 ,

Digital Photography For Dummies, 5th Edition
978-0-7645-9802-9

**Digital SLR Cameras & Photography
For Dummies, 2nd Edition**
978-0-470-14927-0

**eBay Business All-in-One Desk Reference
For Dummies**
978-0-7645-8438-1

eBay For Dummies, 5th Edition*
978-0-470-04529-9

eBay Listings That Sell For Dummies
978-0-471-78912-3

Facebook For Dummies
978-0-470-26273-3

The Internet For Dummies, 11th Edition
978-0-470-12174-0

Investing Online For Dummies, 5th Edition
978-0-7645-8456-5

iPod & iTunes For Dummies, 5th Edit
978-0-470-17474-6

MySpace For Dummies
978-0-470-09529-4

Podcasting For Dummies
978-0-471-74898-4

**Search Engine Optimization
For Dummies, 2nd Edition**
978-0-471-97998-2

Second Life For Dummies
978-0-470-18025-9

**Starting an eBay Business For Dumm
3rd Edition†**
978-0-470-14924-9

GRAPHICS, DESIGN & WEB DEVELOPMENT

**Adobe Creative Suite 3 Design Premium
All-in-One Desk Reference For Dummies**
978-0-470-11724-8

**Adobe Web Suite CS3 All-in-One Desk
Reference For Dummies**
978-0-470-12099-6

AutoCAD 2008 For Dummies
978-0-470-11650-0

**Building a Web Site For Dummies,
3rd Edition**
978-0-470-14928-7

**Creating Web Pages All-in-One Desk
Reference For Dummies, 3rd Edition**
978-0-470-09629-1

**Creating Web Pages For Dummies,
8th Edition**
978-0-470-08030-6

Dreamweaver CS3 For Dummies
978-0-470-11490-2

Flash CS3 For Dummies
978-0-470-12100-9

Google SketchUp For Dummies
978-0-470-13744-4

InDesign CS3 For Dummies
978-0-470-11865-8

**Photoshop CS3 All-in-One
Desk Reference For Dummies**
978-0-470-11195-6

Photoshop CS3 For Dummies
978-0-470-11193-2

Photoshop Elements 5 For Dummie
978-0-470-09810-3

SolidWorks For Dummies
978-0-7645-9555-4

Visio 2007 For Dummies
978-0-470-08983-5

Web Design For Dummies, 2nd Edi
978-0-471-78117-2

Web Sites Do-It-Yourself For Dumm
978-0-470-16903-2

Web Stores Do-It-Yourself For Dumm
978-0-470-17443-2

LANGUAGES, RELIGION & SPIRITUALITY

Arabic For Dummies
978-0-471-77270-5

Chinese For Dummies, Audio Set
978-0-470-12766-7

French For Dummies
978-0-7645-5193-2

German For Dummies
978-0-7645-5195-6

Hebrew For Dummies
978-0-7645-5489-6

Ingles Para Dummies
978-0-7645-5427-8

Italian For Dummies, Audio Set
978-0-470-09586-7

Italian Verbs For Dummies
978-0-471-77389-4

Japanese For Dummies
978-0-7645-5429-2

Latin For Dummies
978-0-7645-5431-5

Portuguese For Dummies
978-0-471-78738-9

Russian For Dummies
978-0-471-78001-4

Spanish Phrases For Dummies
978-0-7645-7204-3

Spanish For Dummies
978-0-7645-5194-9

Spanish For Dummies, Audio Set
978-0-470-09585-0

The Bible For Dummies
978-0-7645-5296-0

Catholicism For Dummies
978-0-7645-5391-2

The Historical Jesus For Dummies
978-0-470-16785-4

Islam For Dummies
978-0-7645-5503-9

**Spirituality For Dummies,
2nd Edition**
978-0-470-19142-2

NETWORKING AND PROGRAMMING

ASP.NET 3.5 For Dummies
978-0-470-19592-5

C# 2008 For Dummies
978-0-470-19109-5

Hacking For Dummies, 2nd Edition
978-0-470-05235-8

Home Networking For Dummies, 4th Edition
978-0-470-11806-1

Java For Dummies, 4th Edition
978-0-470-08716-9

**Microsoft® SQL Server™ 2008 All-in-One
Desk Reference For Dummies**
978-0-470-17954-3

**Networking All-in-One Desk Reference
For Dummies, 2nd Edition**
978-0-7645-9939-2

**Networking For Dummies,
8th Edition**
978-0-470-05620-2

SharePoint 2007 For Dummies
978-0-470-09941-4

**Wireless Home Networking
For Dummies, 2nd Edition**
978-0-471-74940-0